Lineber[g]

Library

THE LOEB CLASSICAL LIBRARY

FOUNDED BY JAMES LOEB 1911

EDITED BY

JEFFREY HENDERSON

THE APOSTOLIC FATHERS

I

LCL 24

THE APOSTOLIC FATHERS

I CLEMENT · II CLEMENT
IGNATIUS · POLYCARP
DIDACHE

EDITED AND TRANSLATED BY

BART D. EHRMAN

HARVARD UNIVERSITY PRESS
CAMBRIDGE, MASSACHUSETTS
LONDON, ENGLAND
2003

5/0 M-W 6/4 21.50

Library of Congress Catalog Card Number 2002032744
CIP data available from the Library of Congress

.

ISBN 0-674-99607-0

CONTENTS

PREFACE

This new Greek-English edition of the Apostolic Fathers is to replace the original Loeb volumes produced by Kirsopp Lake. Lake was a superb scholar, and his two-volume Apostolic Fathers has been a *vade mecum* for scholars of Christian antiquity for over ninety years. Much of importance has happened during this period, however: advances in scholarship, manuscript discoveries, and changes in the English language. For this edition I have chosen not to revise Lake but to start afresh.

Because of the relatively sparse manuscript support for the texts of the Apostolic Fathers, modern Greek editions do not differ widely among themselves. For each of these works I have used a base text, modifying it to a greater or lesser extent, based on my evaluation of the textual evidence. For all of the books except the *Shepherd* of Hermas my base text has been Karl Bihlmeyer, *Die apostolischen Väter: Neubearbeitung der Funkschen Ausgabe*, 3rd ed., ed. W. Schneemelcher (Tübingen: Mohr-Siebeck, 1956); for the *Shepherd* I used Molly Whittaker, *Die apostolischen Väter:* vol. 1, *Der Hirt des Hermas* (GCS 48. 2nd ed. Berlin: Akademie Verlag, 1967). Both Bihlymeyer and Whittaker are now readily available in Andreas Lindemann and Henning Paulsen, *Die apostolischen Väter* (Tübingen: Mohr-Siebeck, 1992).

In keeping with the tenor of the Loeb series, I have restricted the Greek apparatus to textual variants that have a significant bearing on either the translation or our understanding of the transmission of the text. Because of the special problems they pose, I have not, in most instances, cited Patristic sources extensively. Thus, while the apparatus is more substantial than that found in the earlier Loeb volumes, it is not as full as serious scholars of Christian antiquity might like. More comprehensive apparatus may be found in the editions mentioned above.

The Apostolic Fathers are an unusual corpus, representing not the works of a single author (as in most Loeb volumes) but of eleven different authors, writing different kinds of works to different audiences in different times and places. In view of the nature of the material, the General Introduction will provide a basic overview of the corpus and the history of its collection, to be followed in the separate Introductions by fuller discussions of each of the texts and authors.

I have tried to make the translation both readable and closely tied to the Greek text. I have chosen not to remove the strong patriarchal biases of the texts, which form part of their historical interest and significance. And I have tried to reflect the occasional awkwardness of the texts, including, perhaps most noticeably, the striking anacolutha in the letters of Ignatius, which were evidently written in some haste.

Abbreviations for journals and biblical books are drawn from *The SBL Handbook of Style for Ancient Near Eastern, Biblical, and Early Christian Studies*, ed. Patrick H. Alexander et al. (Peabody, Mass.: Hendrickson, 1999).

PREFACE

I would like to acknowledge my gratitude to Margaretta Fulton, General Editor for the Humanities at Harvard University Press, for her encouragement and savvy guidance, and to Jeffrey Henderson, Professor of Classics and Dean of Arts and Sciences at Boston University and General Editor for the Loeb Classical Library, for his extraordinary willingness—eagerness even—to deal with issues, answer questions, and provide help at every stage.

I am indebted to a number of scholars who have assisted me in various aspects of the project. My colleagues at the University of North Carolina at Chapel Hill, William Race and Zlatko Plese, and my brother Radd K. Ehrman, in the Department of Classics at Kent State University, have generously provided advice on particularly thorny passages. Several colleagues in the field of early Christian studies have read parts of the translation and made useful suggestions, especially Ellen Aitken, Mark House, Phillip Long, Jeffrey MacDonald, Carolyn Osiek, Larry Swain, and Francis Weismann. Four scholars have been especially generous in reading my Introductions and making helpful comments: Andrew Jacobs of the University of California at Riverside; Clayton Jefford of the Meinard School of Theology; Carolyn Osiek of the Catholic Theological Union in Chicago; and, in a particular labor of love, my wife, Sarah Beckwith, in the English Department at Duke University. Finally, I am grateful to my graduate students in the Department of Religious Studies at the University of North Carolina at Chapel Hill, Stephanie Cobb (now on the faculty at Hofstra University), Carl Cosaert, and Pamela Mullins, for their assistance in my research. Above all I am indebted to my student Diane Wudel, now teaching at Wake Forest Divinity School, for her diligent and remarkably insightful help on every aspect of the project.

I have dedicated these volumes to Dr. Gerald Hawthorne, professor emeritus at Wheaton College, who many years ago taught me Greek and first introduced me to the texts of the Apostolic Fathers. Over the years Jerry has been a cherished mentor and a caring friend. As my teacher he always stressed, and himself embodied, the words of Ignatius of Antioch, ὅπου πλειὼν κόπος, πολὺ κέρδος (*Ign. Pol.* 1.2).

THE APOSTOLIC FATHERS

GENERAL INTRODUCTION

The Apostolic Fathers represent a disparate collection of early Christian writings whose authors were traditionally believed to have been followers or companions of the apostles of Jesus, and who were thought, then, to have produced their works soon after the books of the New Testament were completed. These historical judgments are no longer widely held, but the collection continues to serve a valuable purpose in providing the earliest noncanonical writings of authors who were forebears of what was to become, some centuries after their day, Christian orthodoxy. Even so, the utility and contents of the collection continue to be matters of debate among scholars of Christian antiquity.

The term "apostolic father" first occurs in the *Hogedos* of Anastasius, the seventh-century anti-monophysite abbot of St. Catherine's monastery on Mount Sinai,[1] who spoke of ὁ ἀποστολικὸς πατὴρ Διονύσιος ὁ Ἀρεο-

---

[1] Not, as R. M. Grant suggested, in Severus of Antioch (465–538 CE; "The Apostolic Fathers' First Thousand Years," *CH* 31 [1962] 421). See J. A. Fischer, "Die ältesten Ausgaben der Patres Apostolici: Ein Beitrag zu Begriff und Begrenzung der apostolischen Väter," *Historisches Jahrbuch* 94 (1974) 157–58. Fischer was mistaken, however, in attributing the *Hogedos* to an earlier Anastasius II of Antioch (599–609 CE); see now the critical edition

παγίτης. Somewhat ironically, the works of this Dionysius the Areopagite, allegedly the convert of the apostle Paul (Acts 17:34), have never been included in modern collections of the Apostolic Fathers: since the sixteenth century they have been recognized as forgeries of later times (possibly the early sixth century). In any event, neither Anastasius nor any other author prior to the seventeenth century referred to an entire corpus of writings (or authors) as the "Apostolic Fathers."

Collections of noncanonical proto-orthodox writings were made, of course, even in antiquity, long before the canon of the New Testament itself had reached its final form.[2] Already in the early second century, Polycarp of Smyrna wrote his letter to the Philippians to serve as a kind of cover letter for a collection of the writings of Ignatius, which Polycarp had himself assembled in response to a request from the Christians of Philippi (see Introduction to the Letter of Polycarp). This collection probably formed the basis for the manuscript tradition of Ignatius's letters that circulated, in expanded form, down through the Middle Ages (see Introduction to the Letters of Ignatius). Evidence of other collections of early Christian authors appears sporadically through the historical record: both the *Shepherd* of Hermas and the Epistle of Barnabas, for

of Karl-Heinz Uthemann, *Anastasia Sinaitae Viae Dux* (CSCG 8; Turnhout: Brepols and Leuven: University Press, 1981).

[2] The term "proto-orthodox" has come to be used to refer to the forebears of those Christians whose views were established as dominant (and thereby "orthodox") by the fourth century, as opposed to Christians with alternative theological views, who were eventually labeled, as a result, "heretical."

example, are included in the famous fourth-century biblical manuscript Codex Sinaiticus; and 1 and 2 Clement can be found in the slightly later Codex Alexandrinus. In these cases, however, the books were not reproduced as important *noncanonical* Christian works; on the contrary, the scribes of both codices evidently considered these writings to form part of the sacred Scriptures. Many of the oldest discussions of the Apostolic Fathers in fact involve just this issue, of whether one or another of their writings should be included in the canon.[3]

Like the books that were eventually canonized, the Apostolic Fathers were written and circulated as separate texts. Since they were not widely accepted into the canon, however, they continued to be copied and read, for the most part, not as a corpus of writings but individually. Some, of course, were more popular than others: the Epistle to Diognetus is never mentioned by any ancient source, whereas the *Shepherd* of Hermas was widely read and distributed in the early Christian centuries—more so even than several of the "general epistles" that came to be included in the Christian canon. There is some evidence, on the other hand, that several of the Apostolic Fathers were occasionally transmitted together, down through the Middle Ages. The Codex Hierosolymitanus, for example, written in 1056 and discovered by Philotheos Bryennios in 1873, includes the texts of 1 and 2 Clement, the Epistle of Barnabas, the *Didache*, and the long recension of Ignatius.

Despite such occasional collections, prior to the seventeenth century anyone interested in writings produced in

[3] See Grant, "The Apostolic Fathers' First Thousand Years," 421–29.

the generation after the books of the New Testament were completed would have been severely handicapped. On the one hand, few copies of these early-second century authors were available. Even more problematic, the most popular of the allegedly sub-apostolic writings were in fact, as now recognized, later forgeries, including Pseudo-Dionysius mentioned above, the long form of the letters of Ignatius (which included severely interpolated versions of the seven authentic Ignatian letters along with six other forgeries from the fourth century), and the entertaining fictional narratives concerning Clement of Rome (the Clementine *Homilies* and *Recognitions*).

An interest in the "church Fathers" did emerge in Western Europe among humanists of the Renaissance, many of whom saw in the golden age of patristics their own forebears: cultured scholars imbued with the classics of Western Civilization, concerned with deep religious and philosophical problems.[4] No wonder, then, that the humanists focused their attention on the writings of the "great" Fathers of the church such as Chrysostom, Ambrose, Augustine, Jerome, the Cappadocians, and the like, while showing virtually no interest in their comparatively "primitive" and "uncultured" predecessors, such as Ignatius of Antioch, Clement of Rome, Barnabas, and Hermas, who on no reckoning were cultured scholars or brilliant thinkers. When a "most ancient" church Father like

---

[4] See Irena Backus, *The Reception of the Church Fathers in the West: From the Carolingians to the Maurists* (Leiden: Brill, 1997), especially the articles of Jean-Louis Quantin, "The Fathers in 17th Century Roman Catholic Theology," 951–86, and "The Fathers in 17th Century Anglican Theology," 987–1008.

Irenaeus (who in fact wrote decades after most of the so-called Apostolic Fathers) was mentioned, it was usually in order to show the unrefined nature of his theology and to censure his aberrant doctrinal views, which failed to reflect the more mature and nuanced statements of later times.[5]

The Reformation provided some impetus for the study of Christian writings immediately after the New Testament period, but even then few scholars evinced an extensive interest in or knowledge of authors of the early second century, for reasons that, in hindsight, may seem obvious: for many Protestant thinkers, the notion of "sola scriptura" —that "scripture alone," not church tradition, should be authoritative—precluded the need to appeal to books immediately outside the canon, whereas most Catholic theologians were far more invested in the great theologians, councils, and creeds of later times.[6]

It was not until the seventeenth century that the terms of the discussion shifted dramatically, as all sides began to

---

5 Cf. Thomas More's reference to "the most ancient" church Fathers, whom he names as Augustine, Jerome, Ambrose, Cyprian, Chrysostom, Gregory, and Basil. See E. F. Rogers, *The Correspondence of Sir Thomas More* (Princeton: University Press, 1947) no. 60; and Stanley L. Greenslade, "The Authority of the Tradition of the Early Church in Early Anglican Thought," in Günther Gassmann and Vilmos Vajta, *Tradition im Luthertum und Anglikanismus* (Oecumenica; Strassburg: Centre d'Études Oecuménique, 1972) 9–33.

6 With several notable exceptions, such as Johannes Fischer, *Sacri sacerdotii defensio contra Lutherum*, available in an edition by Hermann Klein Schmeink (Corpus Catholicorum, 9; Münster, Aschendorff, 1925). See the discussion of Ralph Keen, "The Fa-

recognize the importance of the earliest noncanonical authors for establishing the antiquity of their own views, with Protestants (of various kinds) and Catholics taking their arguments beyond exegesis of the New Testament texts and the formulations of later church councils into the early years of the Christian movement.[7] This burgeoning interest in the earliest Fathers was intensified by significant manuscript discoveries, which provided a means of revising commonly received notions of Christian antiquity. Two of particular importance involved the writings of Clement of Rome and Ignatius.

In 1627, Cyril Lucar, Patriarch of Constantinople, presented the fifth-century biblical manuscript Codex Alexandrinus to Charles I of England. Six years later, the Royal Librarian, Patrick Young, published from this manuscript the text of 1 Clement, along with its fragmentary copy of 2 Clement. On internal grounds, the book was assigned to the end of the first century, and was believed to have been written by none other than Clement, bishop of Rome. This attribution (which is now open to question, although the dating appears to be correct) was then used to evaluate the other works relating to Clement, in particular the fictional accounts of his travels and homilies, which were eventually

thers in the Counter-Reformation," in Backus, *Reception of the Church Fathers*, vol. 2, 701–44. Later Fathers, of course, were often discussed: see Greenslade, "The Authority of the Tradition of the Early Church," and idem, *The English Reformers and the Fathers of the Church* (Oxford: Clarendon Press, 1960).

[7] On the importance of the shift away from scholasticism to "positive theology" for the study of the early Fathers, see Quantin, "The Fathers in 17th Century Roman Catholic Theology."

recognized as later forgeries. Yet more significantly, the text of 1 Clement was carried into the theological fray, as it could be cited in support of the later notion of "apostolic succession."

Of even greater importance were the debates over the writings of Ignatius, involving, among many others, two of the most famous British scholars of the period: James Ussher and (the young) John Milton.[8] When Anglican clerics such as Ussher claimed that Ignatius, writing soon after the apostles, demonstrates the primitive existence of the monepiscopacy, Puritans such as Milton responded that the Ignatian letters were forgeries from later times. It was Ussher himself who cut through this Gordian knot by first positing and then discovering (Latin) manuscript evidence that not all of the Ignatian corpus was forged, but only some of it (see Introduction to the Letters of Ignatius). Ussher's views, set forth in his monumental edition of Ignatius in 1644, were then confirmed by Isaac Voss's publication of a corresponding Greek text two years later. The debates continued for some time—they were not actually settled for two centuries, and have been reopened again today—but the significant point for the present discussion is that the attention of theologians and historians had now shifted significantly to the literary output of Christians writing soon after the period of the New Testament.

In some ways this shift culminated, and a new beginning was made, in 1672, with the first modern collection

[8] See the account in J. B. Lightfoot, *The Apostolic Fathers: Clement, Ignatius, and Polycarp*, 2nd. ed. Part 2, *Ignatius and Polycarp*, vol. 1 (Peabody, Mass.: Hendrickson, 1989; originally London: Macmillan, 1889) 237–46.

and publication of the writings of the Apostolic Fathers,[9] by the French patristic scholar J. Cotelier, in a work entitled *SS. Patrum qui temporibus apostolicis floruerunt: Barnabae, Clementis, Hermae, Ignatii, Polycarpi. Opera edita et inedita, vera et suppositicia. Unà cum Clementis, Ignatiis, Polycarpi Actis atque Martyriis.*[10] There has been some (rather pointless) discussion over whether Cotelier actually referred to these early authors as "Apostolic Fathers." He obviously did not do so in the title ("Holy Fathers who Flourished during the Apostolic Times"), but he does do so on two occasions in his Preface, where he refers to his "Apostolicorum Patrum collectio" (pp. vii and x).[11]

Cotelier's criterion for deciding which authors to include in his collection is in one sense unambiguous: these are authors who "apostolorum partim comites exstitere,

---

[9] Although this Greek-Latin edition was preceded by an English translation of three of the Fathers, Ignatius, Polycarp, and Barnabas, by Thomas Elborowe: *The Famous epistles of Saint Polycarp and Saint Ignatius, disciples to the holy Evangelist and Apostle Saint John: with the epistle of St. Barnabas and some remarks upon their lives and deaths / translated according to the best copies out of the original Greek into English* (London: William Grantham, 1668).

[10] Copies of this first edition are extremely rare; soon after printing, and prior to distribution, most were destroyed by a fire at the College of Montaigu.

[11] The first to use the term (or its close approximation) in the title of a collection was William Wake, in his 1693 English edition, *The Genuine Epistles of the Apostolical Fathers, S. Barnabas, S. Clement, S. Ignatius, S. Polycarp, The Shepherd of Hermas, and the Martyrdoms of St. Ignatius and St. Polycarp* (London), as pointed out by H. J. de Jonge, "On the Origin of the Term 'Apostolic Fathers,'" *JTS* n.s. 29 (1978) 503–05.

8

partim discipuli" (who were either companions or disciples of the apostles; by "apostles" Cotelier meant the earthly disciples of Jesus and the apostle Paul). On the other hand, he included numerous writings that were not actually written by these early Christian writers, but were only loosely connected with them, as he himself avers. Just in his section on Clement of Rome, for example, he includes not only 1 and 2 Clement, both of which he accepts as authentic, but also the *Apostolic Constitutions*, the *Apostolic Canons*, the Pseudo-Clementine *Recognitions* and *Homilies*, the pseudonymous letter from Peter to James introducing the *Homilies*, the pseudonymous letter of James in reply, the Greek Epitome of the Homilies, the later *Martyrdom* of Clement, and a report attributed to Ephraem of Cherson describing a miracle that allegedly occurred on the day commemorating the date of Clement's death. This collection, in other words, was not made on strictly historical grounds; just about everything from antiquity relating to Clement was included.

A second edition of Cotelier was produced by Jean LeClerc in 1698, who provided the same texts evidently on the same grounds, but with such an enlarged apparatus of commentary and scholarly discussion (reproduced from the writings of other patristic scholars) that Cotelier's own perspectives virtually disappeared from view in the mass of new material.[12]

A distinctive set of criteria for inclusion was advanced by the Lutheran theologian Thomas Ittig in his 1699 work,

---

[12] See especially, Dominique Bertrand, "Jean-Baptiste Cotelier et les pères apostoliques?" in *Les Pères de l'église au XVIIe siècle*, ed. E. Bury and B. Meunier (Paris: Cerf, 1993) 175–89.

"Bibliotheca Patrum Apostolicorum Graeco-Latina."[13] In this collection, Ittig chose not to include all the non-canonical authors who could be plausibly considered contemporaries of the apostles, but only those who stood in what he considered to be the apostolic tradition—that is, who approximated the "spirit" and views found in the writings of the New Testament.[14] On these grounds, Ittig deemed that neither the Epistle of Barnabas nor the *Shepherd* of Hermas was worthy of inclusion, even though, as he conceded, they fit within the appropriate chronological framework. His edition contained, then, 1 and 2 Clement, the seven authentic letters and Martyrdom of Ignatius, and the Letter and Martyrdom of Polycarp.

The debate over what to include among the writings of the Apostolic Fathers has continued down to the present day.[15] The matter became complicated with the addition of other authors to the corpus: the Epistle to Diognetus and the fragments of the early second-century authors Papias and Quadratus, for example, were included in the edition by A. Galandi in 1765; the *Didache* has been generally admitted since its discovery and publication by Bryennios in 1883.[16]

---

[13] Contrary to the claim of some scholars, this is not the first modern edition to entitle the collection "The Apostolic Fathers." See n. 11.

[14] See esp. Fischer, "Die ältesten Ausgaben," 178.

[15] See Matthias Günther, *Einleitung in die apostolischen Väter* (ARGU 4; Frankfurt: Peter Lang, 1997) 7.

[16] For a convenient chart listing the works included in important collections of the Apostolic Fathers since Cotelier, see Günther, *Einleitung,* 7.

In view of the complications, some scholars have urged that the idea of the corpus should be abandoned altogether, and with some good arguments.[17] The collection, as we have seen, is a modern fabrication. Some of the books were clearly not written near the time of, let alone by companions of, the apostles (e.g., 2 Clement and the Epistle to Diognetus), whereas other books that are not included in the collection probably *do* go back to at least the first part of the second century (e.g., the Gospels of Thomas and Peter, which have never been included in the corpus). Moreover, some of the books have been included because of false ascriptions (e.g., Barnabas and 2 Clement). Unlike other sensible groupings such as the "apologists," these books do not share the same genre: a good number of them are letters (1 Clement, Polycarp, seven of Ignatius), but there is also a tractate (Barnabas), a church manual (the *Didache*), a homily (2 Clement), a martyrology (Martyrdom of Polycarp), a kind of apocalypse (the *Shepherd*), and an apology (Epistle to Diognetus; so also the fragment of Quadratus). Nor do these books cohere in terms of social and theological outlook: the *Shepherd* of Hermas and 1 Clement, for example, represent radically different views of church structure and the relationship of Christians to Roman rule.[18]

Against the view that the collection should be abandoned, however, are a number of compelling consider-

[17] See G. Jouassard, "Le Groupement des pères dits apostoliques," *MScRel* 14 (1957) 129–34.

[18] See James S. Jeffers, *Conflict at Rome: Social Order and Hierarchy in Early Christianity* (Minneapolis: Fortress Press, 1991).

ations. Most striking is the circumstance that many of the same arguments could be mounted against the canon of the New Testament itself: it too consists of documents that were written over an extended period of time, some of them anonymous (the Gospels) or falsely attributed (2 Peter was probably not written by Peter nor, as widely thought in antiquity, Revelation by John the son of Zebedee); they represent a variety of genres (gospels, acts, epistles, an apocalypse), and embody a wide range of social and theological outlook. And this canon too is a "fabricated" collection: its authors did not produce their books in order to form a "New Testament."

Other scholars argue that the Apostolic Fathers should include only those writers who can actually be placed near the time of the apostles and for whom plausible arguments can be made that they both knew and stood in continuity with Jesus' own apostles—for example, Clement, Ignatius, and Polycarp.[19] This view, however, creates other problems, as it depends on historical judgments that are subject to dispute (was 1 Clement written by Clement of Rome? Did Ignatius actually know Peter or Paul? Was Polycarp a disciple of John? etc.). Were these strict criteria to be followed, there might be no collection left.

Probably the most widely accepted view, then, is that the Apostolic Fathers should be recognized precisely as a rather arbitrary collection of writings made for the sake of convenience and based on (modern) tradition. The most generous view would admit into the collection the eleven authors who have been widely taken to belong in it, and so would include 1 and 2 Clement, Ignatius (the seven

19 Cf. the editions of Lightfoot and Fischer.

authentic letters), Polycarp's letter to the Philippians, the Martyrdom of Polycarp, the *Didache*, Barnabas, the Epistle to Diognetus, the *Shepherd* of Hermas, and the fragments of Papias and Quadratus (preserved for us in Eusebius). These do indeed cover a range of genres, dates, and perspectives. But most of them were written in the first half of the second century (1 Clement a bit earlier; 2 Clement, the Martyrdom of Polycarp, and the Epistle to Diognetus, probably, a bit later); and most of them embody in one way or another views that later came to be embraced by the winners in the struggles to establish Christian orthodoxy by the fourth century. In other words, these are "Apostolic Fathers" because they were written and read by Christians who advocated views roughly similar to those embraced by the Christians of later times who collected the twenty-seven books of the New Testament into a canon and developed the creedal statements that eventually came to be construed as orthodoxy. As a result, this collection can be seen as comparable to other, similarly arbitrary collections of second- and third-century Christian writings, including those of the apologists (among which, for example, the Epistle to Diognetus and Quadratus are normally not included), the heresiologists (which normally do not include Gnostic writings that polemicize against what *they* understood to be "heresy"), and the Nag Hammadi Library (a collection of principally, but not exclusively, Gnostic texts, discovered in 1945).

The Apostolic Fathers, then, is not an authoritative collection of books, but a convenient one, which, in conjunction with these other collections, can enlighten us concerning the character of early Christianity, its external appeal and inner dynamics, its rich and significant diver-

———— "The Study of the Early Fathers in Modern Times." In R. M. Grant, *After the New Testament*. Philadelphia: Fortress, 1967; 3–19.

Greenslade, S. L. *The English Reformers and the Fathers of the Church*. Oxford: Clarendon Press, 1960.

———— "Patristic Tradition in Anglican Thought 1660–1900." In G. Gassmann and V. Vajta eds. *Tradition im Luthertum und Anglikanismus. Oecumenica*, 1971/2, Gutersloh, 1972; 9–33.

Günther, Matthias. *Einleitung in die apostolischen Väter*. Frankfurt: Peter Lang, 1997.

Jefford, Clayton. *Reading the Apostolic Fathers*. Peabody, Mass.: Hendrickson, 1996.

Jonge, Henk J de. "On the Origin of the Term 'Apostolic Fathers.'" *JTS* n.s. 29 (1978) 503–05.

Jouassard, G. "Le groupement des Pères dits apostoliques." *MScRel* 14 (1957) 129–34.

Schoedel, William R. "The Apostolic Fathers." In *The New Testament and Its Modern Interpreters*, eds. Eldon J. Epp and George W. MacRae. Philadelphia: Fortress; Atlanta: Scholars, 1989; 457–98.

Tugwell, Simon. *The Apostolic Fathers*. Harrisburg, Penn.: Morehouse, 1989.

FIRST LETTER OF CLEMENT
TO THE CORINTHIANS

INTRODUCTION

The "First Letter of Clement" is a misnomer, as no other letter from the author survives: "Second Clement," which is not a letter, comes from a different hand (see Introduction to Second Clement). Moreover, the present letter does not claim to be written by Clement, who, in fact, is never mentioned in its text.

Overview of the Letter

The letter is addressed by the church of Rome to the church of Corinth, and is written in order to deal with problems that had arisen there. Although allusions to the situation are found already in chapter 1, its full nature is not made clear until nearly two-thirds of the way into the letter (esp. chs. 42–44, 47). The church in Corinth had experienced a turnover in leadership, which the author of the letter considered a heinous grab for power by a group of jealous upstarts, who had deposed the ruling group of presbyters and assumed control of the church for themselves. The letter is a strong "request . . . for peace and harmony" (63:2), which upbraids the Corinthian church for its disunity, convicts members of the guilty party of the error of their ways, and urges them to return the deposed presbyters to their positions of authority.

It is a very long letter for such a direct purpose, and some critics (Wrede, Knopf) have claimed that its rambling and digressive character indicate that the author forgot his original reason for writing it until near the end. Others (e.g., Lona, Bowe) have found more intricate and subtle organizing principles in the letter, and have argued that rather than simply deal with the immediate issue head-on, the author has chosen to employ standard rhetorical ploys and extensive illustrations in order to make his larger points, that the church of God is to be harmonious and unified, that peace in the church is more important than personal advancement to places of leadership, and that the envy and jealousy that have led to the ecclesiastical coup need to be rooted out.

Scholars have occasionally wrangled, somewhat needlessly, over whether the rhetorical strategies of the letter are better situated in a Jewish or a Hellenistic milieu (Sanders, Beyschlag). To be sure, the letter's interest in and commitment to the Jewish Bible is obvious: from beginning to end the author establishes his views by citing the authority of the Septuagint, the Greek translation of the Jewish Scriptures, used by Hellenistic Jews and Christians alike. Examples of both exemplary and dishonorable behavior are drawn from narratives of the Old Testament from Cain and Abel onwards, including Abraham, Lot, Lot's wife, Moses, Rahab, David, Daniel, and so on. And biblical injunctions, commandments, and prophecies, cited at length throughout the epistle, are among its most obvious and striking features.

At the same time, the letter as a whole, along with its constituent parts, shows clear familiarity with Hellenistic rhetorical forms. In particular, the letter functions as a kind of "homonoia (= harmony) speech," a rhetorical form common among Greek and Roman orators for urging peace and harmony in a city-state experiencing internal strife and disruption. To some extent, then, the church is here conceptualized as a political entity, which needs to function as a harmonious unit in order to fulfil its divinely appointed mission and so do the will of the God who created it.

The notion of "order" is thus of paramount importance to the author, who not only cites Old Testament precedents to make his case (e.g., the orderly sacrifices and liturgical functions assigned to priests and Levites in Scripture, ch. 40) but also mounts a wide range of arguments to show that God is a God of harmony and order, not of factions and strife. He appeals, for example, to nature as revelatory of God's orderly handiwork: the sun, moon, and stars were created to function together without disrupting each other's work, the seasons succeed one another in orderly sequence, the oceans and their tides follow divine strictures on their scope and power (ch. 20). Moreover, those who disrupt God's harmonious order will face punishment, if not in this age then after the resurrection, which is sure to occur, as God himself reveals through both mundane and extraordinary facts of nature—from the sequence of night and day (the night dies, the day arises) to the death and rebirth of the phoenix in a regular 500-year cycle (chs. 24–25).

The church of Corinth, then, characterized by shameful faction, schism, and disunity is urged to restore harmony by reinstating its presbyters, submitting to their authority, and seeking peace through brotherly love, apart from all envy, jealousy, and strife.

20

INTRODUCTION

Author

Even though the letter claims to be written by the "church . . . residing in Rome," it has from early times been attributed to Clement, a leader of the Roman church near the end of the first century. In his celebrated church history, Eusebius sets forth the tradition, earlier found in the writings of the third-century church Father Origen, that this Clement was the companion of the apostle Paul mentioned in Philippians 4:3 (*Eccl. Hist.* 3.4.15; see Origen *Comm. Jn.* 6.36). Some of the early traditions claim that Clement was the second bishop of Rome, ordained by Peter himself (Tertullian, *Prescription* 32); more commonly it was thought that he was the third, following Linus and Anacletus (thus Irenaeus in *Agst. Heresies* 3.3.1 and Eusebius *Eccl. Hist.* 3.4.21). The first reference to any Roman Christian named Clement is by a near contemporary, Hermas, author of the *Shepherd* (see Introduction to the *Shepherd* of Hermas), who is instructed to send two copies of a book to Rome, one of them for "Clement" who was then to distribute it to churches in other locations, "for that is his commission" (*Shepherd* 8.2). This Clement, then, appears to have had an official role in the church, at least in Hermas's time (first part of the second century), as some kind of secretary in charge of foreign correspondence.

As early as the middle of the second century it was claimed by Dionysius of Corinth that Clement had written this epistle to the Corinthians, which, he indicated, continued to be read in his own day during regular church gatherings (ca. 170 CE; also claimed, about the same time, by Hegessipus). This tradition is followed, then, by Eusebius (*Eccl. Hist.* 4.23) and down through the ages; it is evi-

have raised serious questions. What is clear is that since the letter is mentioned by Dionysius of Corinth and Hegessipus somewhat before 170 CE on the one hand, and since it refers to the martyrdoms of Peter and Paul, usually placed in the reign of Nero, ca. 64, on the other hand, it must have been written sometime between these two dates. The traditional date of 95–96 is based on the indication of Eusebius that it was written near the end of the reign of Domitian (emperor from 81–96). Support for the dating was found in the ancient view, also advanced by Eusebius, that during his final years Domitian instigated a persecution of Christians in Rome. This context of persecution was used to explain the opening of the letter, which speaks of the "sudden and repeated misfortunes and setbacks we have experienced"—which were taken to refer to the arrest and prosecution of Christians during a Domitianic reign of terror.

This view of the historical context is now by and large rejected. There is nothing in the epistle that suggests it was written in the context of persecution: the "misfortunes and setbacks" could just as easily have been internal struggles within the church. Moreover, there is no solid evidence from the period itself of a persecution of Christians under Domitian.

Even so, a date near the end of Domitian's reign is altogether plausible. The epistle could not have been written much later: it indicates that the deaths of Peter and Paul took place "within our own generation" (ch. 5) and assumes that there are still living leaders of the Christian churches who had been appointed by the apostles of Jesus, that is, sometime no later than early in the second half of the first century (chs. 42, 44). Moreover, there is no indication that the hierarchical structures later so important to proto-orthodox Christians—in which there was a solitary bishop over a group of presbyters and deacons—was yet in place.

Some scholars have gone so far as to claim that the letter may well have been written much earlier than traditionally supposed, possibly prior to 70 (see Welborn). But the letter calls the Corinthian church "ancient" (ch. 47), which seems somewhat inappropriate if it were only twenty-five or thirty years old; it assumes that some churches are headed by leaders twice removed from Jesus' apostles (appointees of those ordained by the apostles, ch. 46); and it suggests that the bearers of the letter from Rome have been faithful members of the church "from youth to old age," which must make them older than their mid-40s (ch. 63). For these reasons, it appears best to assume a date sometime near the end of the first century, possibly, as traditionally thought, in the mid 90s during the reign of Domitian.

Historical Significance

If this dating is correct, then 1 Clement was produced at about the same time as or even before some of the writings of the New Testament (e.g., 2 Peter and Revelation). It is, at any rate, the oldest Christian writing outside of the New Testament. This makes aspects of the letter highly significant for historians interested in the development of the Christian church in the earliest period. The following are just three of the important issues.

(1) The use of Scripture. Even though the author of the book gives no indication that he is Jewish, he is thoroughly

conversant with the Jewish Scriptures, as these were known in the Greek translation known today as the Septuagint, and he is committed to their authority (see Hagner). This is significant because some later Christians—even Christians in Rome (e.g., the "heretic" Marcion and his followers)—rejected the Old Testament altogether, whereas others (e.g., the Gnostic Valentinus and, in a different way, Barnabas) believed that it needed to be interpreted allegorically, and yet others (e.g., Polycarp) valued its teachings but did not really know them (see *Pol. Phil.* 12.1).

At the same time, it is clear that this author (a) does not yet have anything like a canon of "New Testament" Scriptures, and yet (b) is beginning to ascribe authority to the words of Jesus and the writings of his apostles (see Hagner). He quotes Jesus' words on several occasions (see chs. 13 and 46), evidently as he knows them from oral traditions rather than written Gospels, since the quotations do not match any of our surviving texts. In addition he refers explicitly to Paul's first letter to the Corinthians (ch. 47) and alludes on numerous occasions to other writings that later came to form part of the New Testament canon (for example, Hebrews; see ch. 36). That is to say, we can see here the very beginnings of the process in which Christian authorities (Jesus and his apostles) are assigned authority comparable to that of the Jewish Scriptures, the beginnings, in other words, of the formation of the Christian canon.

In this connection, it is worth noting that some Christians in later centuries regarded 1 Clement itself as scriptural. It is quoted as such by Clement of Alexandria at the end of the second century, and it is included as part of the New Testament, along with 2 Clement, in one of our surviving Greek manuscripts, the famous fifth-century Codex Alexandrinus, as well as in one of our Coptic witnesses and in our solitary Syriac manuscript.

(2) *The influence of the Roman Church.* Eventually, of course, Rome became the dominant center of the Christian church in the West. The letter of 1 Clement is the first surviving instance in which this church attempts to extend its influence over another Christian community. To be sure, there is no indication of the hierarchical structure and efficient organization that would become characteristic of the church in Rome: no single bishop, let alone a pope, for example, at the top of a rigid ecclesiastical structure. Nor does the author or the church he represents stake out any theological claim to personal authority. Instead the letter uses rhetorical techniques, scriptural precedents, and reasoned arguments to establish its position. On the other hand, the letter does have a direct and clearcut purpose: the Christians of Rome are insisting that the Christians in Corinth reinstate their deposed presbyters as a way of overcoming the factionalism of the community. And there is no indication that they were asked to intervene in the affair. As the church in Rome became larger, better structured, and more powerful, interactions with other communities and interventions of a comparable sort became increasingly common.

(3) *The proto-orthodox claim to apostolic succession.* Within a century or so of the writing of 1 Clement, proto-orthodox Christians had become accustomed to opposing "aberrant" forms of Christianity by arguing that the bishops of the leading sees could trace their lineage back through their personal predecessors to the apostles themselves, who had appointed them. This argument from "ap-

27

ostolic succession" (which was used by representatives of "heretical" sects as well) is not found yet in full form in 1 Clement; as we have seen, there was not yet even a solitary bishop over the church in Rome or Corinth. But a more ancient form of the argument is used already in this letter to convince the Corinthian usurpers and their followers to renounce their positions (chs. 42, 44). According to the author, Christ appointed the apostles who appointed the leaders of the churches, who then hand picked their successors. Since the (deposed) presbyters of Corinth stood in the lineage of leaders chosen by the apostles, to oppose them meant to set oneself against the handpicked successors of the apostles, who had been chosen by Christ, who had been sent from God. The author is quick to add that these Corinthian presbyters had ministered to the church "blamelessly and with humility, gently and unselfishly." And so, on the grounds of both their apostolic lineage and their good service, they were to be reinstated in office.

Textual Tradition and Editions

1 Clement was known and appreciated in parts of the Christian church for several centuries. According to Dionysius of Corinth, it was read during services of the church in Corinth in the mid-second century—possibly as a text of Scripture, much like Paul's letters to the Corinthians. And it was cited, sometimes as Scripture, by such eminent church Fathers as Clement of Alexandria, Origen, Eusebius, Didymus the Blind, and Jerome. It was eventually included among the books of the New Testament in several of our surviving manuscripts.

But the letter was not widely circulated throughout the Middle Ages. In one of history's ironies, Clement of Rome himself was well known, as he became an important figure of Christian legend through a series of tales about his traveling adventures, preaching activities, and interactions with the apostle Peter (the Clementine *Homilies* and *Recognitions*; both probably from the fourth century, based on a now-lost work of the third). These became popular even as the letter of 1 Clement itself became less widely copied and read.

The text of the letter was for the most part lost to Christian scholars and readers until the early seventeenth century, when Cyril Lucar, Patriarch of Constantinople, offered the Codex Alexandrinus to King James I of England. In 1627, after James's death, the manuscript was brought to England and presented to Charles I. Soon thereafter, the Royal Librarian and patristics scholar Patrick Young used the manuscript to publish the *editio princeps* of 1 and 2 Clement (1633).

This manuscript is lacking the final page of 1 Clement (57.7–63.4); a full photographic edition was published by the British Museum under the direction of E. Maunde Thompson (1879–83); a reduced facsimile by F. G. Kenyon followed in 1909.

Another Greek witness—the Codex Hierosolymitanus (sometimes called Constantinopolitanus), more famous for its preservation of the previously unknown *Didache* (see Introduction to the *Didache*)—was discovered by Philotheos Bryennios in the Library of the Most Holy Sepulchre in Constantinople in 1873. Bryennios published the text of 1 and 2 Clement two years later. Complete photographs of its text of 1 and 2 Clement are provided by Lightfoot (vol. 1.1; 425ff).

Along with the occasional patristic citations—especially those of Clement of Alexandria (*Stromateis* 4.105–09)—these two manuscripts are our sole witnesses to the Greek text. Where the manuscripts differ, Codex Alexandrinus usually, but not always, presents a superior form of the text. Textual decisions, however, need to be made on a case-by-case basis, in view of support of the patristic evidence and the witness of the Latin, Syriac, and Coptic versions discovered at the end of the nineteenth century and beginning of the twentieth.

Manuscripts and Abbreviations

Greek

A   Alexandrinus (5th c.; lacks 57.7–63.4)

H   Hierosolymitanus (1056 CE)

Versions

L   Latin: an 11th c. ms, edited by G. Morin (possibly representing a second- or third-century translation)

S   Syriac: a ms of the New Testament dated 1169 CE, with 1 and 2 Clement located after the Catholic epistles, edited by R. L. Bensly (possibly representing an eighth-century translation)

C   a 4th c. Coptic ms in Berlin, edited by C. Schmidt (omits 34.6–42.2)

C¹   a highly fragmentary 5th c. (?) Coptic ms from Strasbourg, which also contains portions of the epistle of James and the Gospel of John, edited by F. Rösch (1–26.2)

SELECT BIBLIOGRAPHY

Beyschlag, Karlmann. *Clemens Romanus und der Früh-katholizismus*. BHTh 35. Tübingen: Mohr-Siebeck, 1966.

Bowe, Barbara Ellen. *A Church in Crisis: Ecclesiology and Paraenesis in Clement of Rome*. Minneapolis: Fortress Press, 1988.

Brunner, Gerbert. *Die theologische Mitte des ersten Klemensbriefs*. FTS 11. Frankfurt am Main: Knecht, 1972.

Grant, Robert M., and H. H. Graham. *First and Second Clement*. Vol. 2 of *The Apostolic Fathers: A New Translation and Commentary*, ed. Robert M. Grant. Camden, N.J.: Thomas Nelson, 1965.

Hagner, Donald A. *The Use of the Old and New Testaments in Clement of Rome*. NovTSup 34. Leiden: Brill, 1973.

Henne, Philippe. *La Christologie chez Clément de Rome et dans le Pasteur d'Hermas*. Freibourg, Switzerland: Éditions universitaires, 1992.

Jaubert, Annie. *Clément de Rome, Épître aux Corinthiens*. SC 167. Paris: Cerf, 1971; corrected ed., 2000.

Jeffers, James S. *Conflict at Rome: Social Order and Hierarchy in Early Christianity*. Minneapolis: Fortress Press, 1991.

Kennett, R. H., and R. L. Bensly, *The Epistles of S. Clement to the Corinthians in Syriac. Edited from the manuscript with notes by the late R. L. Bensly*. Cambridge: University Press, 1899.

Kenyon, F. G. *The Codex Alexandrinus (Royal ms. 1 D v-viii) in Reduced Photographic Facsimile*. London: British Museum, 1909.

Knopf, Rudolf. *Die apostolischen Väter. Die Lehre der zwölf Apostel, Die zwei Clemensbriefe.* Vol. 1. HNTSup. Tübingen: Mohr-Siebeck, 1920.

Lampe, Peter. *Die Stadtrömischen Christen in den ersten beiden Jahrhunderten: Untersuchungen zur Sozialgeschichte.* Tübingen: Mohr-Siebeck, 1987.

Lightfoot, Joseph Barber. The Apostolic Fathers: Clement, Ignatius, and Polycarp. Part I: Clement. 2 vols. London: Macmillan, 1889; reprinted Peabody, Mass.: Hendrickson, 1989.

Lindemann, Andreas. *Die Clemensbriefe.* Tübingen: Mohr-Siebeck, 1992.

Lona, Horacio E. *Der erste Clemensbrief.* Göttingen: Vandenhoeck and Ruprecht, 1998.

Mees, Michael. "Das Christusbild des ersten Klemensbriefes." *ETL* 66 (1990) 297–318.

Morin, G. *Sancti Clementis Romani ad Corinthos epistulae versio latina antiquissima. Anecdota Maredsolana* II. Maredsous, Belgium, 1894.

Rösch, Friedrich, ed. *Bruchstücke des ersten Clemensbriefes: Nach dem achmimischen Papyrus der Strasburger Universitäts- und Landesbibliothek.* Strasbourg: Schlesier and Schweikhardt, 1910.

Sanders, Louis. *L'Hellenisme de saint Clément de Rome et la Paulinisme.* Studia Hellenistica 2. Leuven: Bibliotheca Universitatis Lovanii, 1943.

Schmidt, C. *Der erste Clemensbrief in altkoptischer Übersetzung.* TU 32,1. Leipzig: J. C. Hinrichs, 1908.

Thompson, E. Maunde. *Facsimile of the Codex Alexandrinus.* London: British Museum, 1879–83.

van Unnik, W. C. "Is 1 Clement 20 Purely Stoic?" *VC* 4 (1950) 181–89.

Welborn, Lawrence L. "On the Date of First Clement."
   BR 29 (1984) 35–54.
Wrede, W. *Untersuchungen zum ersten Klemensbriefe.*
   Göttingen: Vandenhoeck and Ruprecht, 1891.

ΚΛΗΜΕΝΤΟΣ ΠΡΟΣ ΚΟΡΙΝΘΙΟΥΣ Α΄[1]

Ἡ ἐκκλησία τοῦ θεοῦ ἡ παροικοῦσα Ῥώμην τῇ ἐκκλησίᾳ τοῦ θεοῦ τῇ παροικούσῃ Κόρινθον, κλητοῖς, ἡγιασμένοις ἐν θελήματι θεοῦ διὰ τοῦ κυρίου ἡμῶν Ἰησοῦ Χριστοῦ. χάρις ὑμῖν καὶ εἰρήνη ἀπὸ παντοκράτορος θεοῦ διὰ Ἰησοῦ Χριστοῦ πληθυνθείη.

1

Διὰ τὰς αἰφνιδίους καὶ ἐπαλλήλους γενομένας ἡμῖν συμφορὰς καὶ περιπτώσεις[2] βράδιον νομίζομεν ἐπιστροφὴν πεποιῆσθαι περὶ τῶν ἐπιζητουμένων παρ' ὑμῖν πραγμάτων, ἀγαπητοί, τῆς τε ἀλλοτρίας καὶ ξένης τοῖς ἐκλεκτοῖς τοῦ θεοῦ, μιαρᾶς καὶ ἀνοσίου στάσεως, ἣν ὀλίγα πρόσωπα προπετῆ καὶ αὐθάδη ὑπάρχοντα εἰς τοσοῦτον ἀπονοίας ἐξέκαυσαν, ὥστε τὸ σεμνὸν καὶ περιβόητον καὶ πᾶσιν ἀνθρώποις ἀξιαγάπητον ὄνομα ὑμῶν μεγάλως βλασφημηθῆναι.

---

[1] ΚΛ. Π. Κορ. Α΄ Η: . . . Σ ΚΟΡΙΝΘΙΟΥΣ Α: *Incipit Epistola Clementis ad Corinthios* L: *Epistula catholica Clementis*

slandered. 2. For who has ever visited you and not approved your highly virtuous and stable faith? And not been astonished by your temperate and gentle piety in Christ? And not proclaimed the magnificent character of your hospitality? And not uttered a blessing for your perfect and unwavering knowledge? 3. For you used to act impartially in all that you did, and you walked according to the ordinances of God, submitting yourselves to your leaders and rendering all due honor to those who were older [Or: presbyters] among you. You instructed your young people to think moderate and respectful thoughts. You directed women to accomplish all things with a blameless, respectful, and pure conscience, dutifully loving their husbands. And you taught them to run their households respectfully, living under the rule of submission, practicing discretion in every way.

2

And all of you used to be humble in mind, not arrogant in the least, being submissive rather than forcing submission, giving more gladly than receiving,[1] being satisfied with the provisions supplied by Christ. You heeded his words, carefully storing them up in your inner selves. And his sufferings were present before your eyes. 2. For this reason a deep and rich peace was given to all, along with an insatiable desire for doing good; and a full outpouring of the Holy

[1] Acts 20:35.

---

4 καὶ σεμνῇ A H: om. L S C
5 Χριστοῦ H L S C (C¹): θ̅υ̅ A

ἔκχυσις ἐπὶ πάντας ἐγίνετο· 3. μεστοί τε ὁσίας βου-
λῆς, ἐν ἀγαθῇ προθυμίᾳ μετ᾿ εὐσεβοῦς πεποιθήσεως
ἐξετείνετε τὰς χεῖρας ὑμῶν πρὸς τὸν παντοκράτορα
θεόν, ἱκετεύοντες αὐτὸν ἵλεων γενέσθαι, εἴ τι ἄκοντες
ἡμάρτετε. 4. ἀγὼν ἦν ὑμῖν ἡμέρας τε καὶ νυκτὸς ὑπὲρ
πάσης τῆς ἀδελφότητος, εἰς τὸ σῴζεσθαι μετὰ δέους[6]
καὶ συνειδήσεως[7] τὸν ἀριθμὸν τῶν ἐκλεκτῶν αὐτοῦ.
5. εἰλικρινεῖς καὶ ἀκέραιοι ἦτε καὶ ἀμνησίκακοι εἰς
ἀλλήλους. 6. πᾶσα στάσις καὶ πᾶν σχίσμα βδε-
λυκτὸν ἦν ὑμῖν. ἐπὶ τοῖς παραπτώμασιν τῶν πλησίον
ἐπενθεῖτε· τὰ ὑστερήματα αὐτῶν ἴδια ἐκρίνετε.
7. ἀμεταμέλητοι ἦτε ἐπὶ πάσῃ ἀγαθοποιΐᾳ, ἕτοιμοι εἰς
πᾶν ἔργον ἀγαθόν. 8. τῇ παναρέτῳ καὶ σεβασμίῳ
πολιτείᾳ κεκοσμημένοι πάντα ἐν τῷ φόβῳ αὐτοῦ ἐπε-
τελεῖτε· τὰ προστάγματα καὶ τὰ δικαιώματα τοῦ
κυρίου ἐπὶ τὰ πλάτη τῆς καρδίας ὑμῶν ἐγέγραπτο.

3

Πᾶσα δόξα καὶ πλατυσμὸς ἐδόθη ὑμῖν, καὶ ἐπετε-
λέσθη τὸ γεγραμμένον· ἔφαγεν καὶ ἔπιεν καὶ ἐπλα-
τύνθη καὶ ἐπαχύνθη καὶ ἀπελάκτισεν ὁ ἠγαπημένος.
2. ἐκ τούτου ζῆλος καὶ φθόνος, ἔρις καὶ στάσις,
διωγμὸς καὶ ἀκαταστασία, πόλεμος καὶ αἰχμαλωσία.
3. οὕτως ἐπηγέρθησαν οἱ ἄτιμοι ἐπὶ τοὺς ἐντίμους, οἱ

[6] μετὰ δέους H: μετ᾿ ἐλέους A L S C C[1]
[7] συνειδήσεως A H S: add ἀγαθῆς L C C[1]

Spirit came upon everyone. 3. And being filled with his holy will, you used to stretch out your hands to the all-powerful God, zealous for the good, with pious confidence, begging him to be gracious if you inadvertently committed any sin. 4. Day and night you struggled on behalf of the entire brotherhood, that the total number of his chosen ones might be saved, with mortal fear and self-awareness *[Or: conscientiously]*. 5. You were sincere and innocent and bore no grudges against one another. 6. Every faction and schism was loathsome to you. You used to grieve over the unlawful acts of your neighbors and considered their shortcomings your own. 7. You had no regrets when doing good; you were prepared for every good deed.[2] 8. You were adorned with a highly virtuous and honorable way of life, and you accomplished all things in reverential awe of him. The commandments and righteous demands of the Lord were inscribed upon the tablets of your heart.[3]

3

All glory and enlargement was given to you, and that which was written was fulfilled: "My loved one ate and drank and became large and grew fat and kicked out with his heels."[4] 2. From this came jealousy and envy, strife and faction, persecution and disorderliness, war and captivity. 3. And so the dishonorable rose up against the honorable, the dis-

[2] Titus 3:1.
[3] Prov 7:3.
[4] Deut 32:15.

ἄδοξοι ἐπὶ τοὺς ἐνδόξους, οἱ ἄφρονες ἐπὶ τοὺς φρονίμους, οἱ νέοι ἐπὶ τοὺς πρεσβυτέρους. 4. διὰ τοῦτο
πόρρω ἄπεστιν ἡ δικαιοσύνη καὶ εἰρήνη, ἐν τῷ ἀπο-
λιπεῖν ἕκαστον τὸν φόβον τοῦ θεοῦ καὶ ἐν τῇ πίστει
αὐτοῦ ἀμβλυωπῆσαι, μηδὲ ἐν τοῖς νομίμοις τῶν προσ-
ταγμάτων αὐτοῦ πορεύεσθαι μηδὲ πολιτεύεσθαι κατὰ
τὸ καθῆκον τῷ Χριστῷ, ἀλλὰ ἕκαστον βαδίζειν κατὰ
τὰς ἐπιθυμίας τῆς καρδίας αὐτοῦ τῆς πονηρᾶς, ζῆλον
ἄδικον καὶ ἀσεβῆ ἀνειληφότας, δι' οὗ καὶ θάνατος
εἰσῆλθεν εἰς τὸν κόσμον.

4

Γέγραπται γὰρ οὕτως· καὶ ἐγένετο μεθ' ἡμέρας,
ἤνεγκεν Κάϊν ἀπὸ τῶν καρπῶν τῆς γῆς θυσίαν τῷ
θεῷ,[8] καὶ Ἄβελ ἤνεγκεν καὶ αὐτὸς ἀπὸ τῶν πρωτο-
τόκων τῶν προβάτων καὶ ἀπὸ τῶν στεάτων αὐτῶν. 2. καὶ
ἐπεῖδεν ὁ θεὸς ἐπὶ Ἄβελ καὶ ἐπὶ τοῖς δώροις αὐτοῦ, ἐπὶ
δὲ Κάϊν καὶ ἐπὶ ταῖς θυσίαις αὐτοῦ οὐ προσέσχεν. 3. καὶ
ἐλυπήθη Κάϊν λίαν, καὶ συνέπεσεν τὸ πρόσωπον
αὐτοῦ. 4. καὶ εἶπεν ὁ θεὸς πρὸς Κάϊν· ἱνατί περίλυπος
ἐγένου, καὶ ἱνατί συνέπεσεν τὸ πρόσωπόν σου; οὐκ,
ἐὰν ὀρθῶς προσενέγκῃς, ὀρθῶς δὲ μὴ διέλῃς, ἥμαρ-
τες; 5. ἡσύχασον· πρὸς σὲ ἡ ἀποστροφὴ αὐτοῦ, καὶ σὺ
ἄρξεις αὐτοῦ. 6. καὶ εἶπεν Κάϊν πρὸς Ἄβελ τὸν
ἀδελφὸν αὐτοῦ· διέλθωμεν εἰς τὸ πεδίον. καὶ ἐγένετο
ἐν τῷ εἶναι αὐτοὺς ἐν τῷ πεδίῳ ἀνέστη Κάϊν ἐπὶ Ἄβελ
τὸν ἀδελφὸν αὐτοῦ καὶ ἀπέκτεινεν αὐτόν. 7. ὁρᾶτε,

reputable against the reputable, the senseless against the sensible, the young against the old *[Or: the presbyters]*.[5] 4. For this reason, righteousness and peace are far removed,[6] since each has abandoned the reverential awe of God and become dim-sighted in faith, failing to proceed in the ordinances of his commandments and not living according to what is appropriate in Christ. Instead, each one walks according to the desires of his evil heart, which have aroused unrighteous and impious jealousy—through which also death entered the world.[7]

4

For so it is written, "It came about that after some days, Cain brought an offering to God from the fruits of the earth; and for his part, Abel brought from the first born of the sheep and their fat. 2. And God looked favorably upon Abel and his gifts but paid no regard to Cain and his offerings. 3. And Cain was extremely upset and became downcast. 4. And God said to Cain, 'Why have you become so upset and downcast? If you brought the proper sacrifice but did not exercise proper discernment, have you not sinned?[8] 5. Be calm. He will return to you and you will rule over him.' 6. And Cain said to his brother Abel, 'Let us go into the field.' And it came about that when they were in the field, Cain rose up against his brother Abel and mur-

---

[5] Isa 3:5.   [6] Isa 59:14.

[7] Wis 2:24.

[8] The Greek is obscure, as is the Hebrew on which it is based.

---

[8] θεῷ A S C C[1]: κυρίῳ H L

ἀδελφοί, ζῆλος καὶ φθόνος ἀδελφοκτονίαν κατειρ-
γάσατο. 8. διὰ ζῆλος ὁ πατὴρ ἡμῶν Ἰακὼβ ἀπέδρα
ἀπὸ προσώπου Ἠσαῦ τοῦ ἀδελφοῦ αὐτοῦ. 9. ζῆλος
ἐποίησεν Ἰωσὴφ μέχρι θανάτου διωχθῆναι καὶ μέχρι
δουλείας εἰσελθεῖν. 10. ζῆλος φυγεῖν ἠνάγκασεν
Μωϋσῆν ἀπὸ προσώπου Φαραὼ βασιλέως Αἰγύπτου
ἐν τῷ ἀκοῦσαι αὐτὸν ἀπὸ τοῦ ὁμοφύλου· τίς σε
κατέστησεν κριτὴν ἢ[9] δικαστὴν ἐφ' ἡμῶν; μὴ ἀνελεῖν
μέ σὺ θέλεις, ὃν τρόπον ἀνεῖλες ἐχθὲς τὸν Αἰγύπτιον;
11. διὰ ζῆλος Ἀαρὼν καὶ Μαριὰμ ἔξω τῆς παρεμ-
βολῆς ηὐλίσθησαν. 12. ζῆλος Δαθὰν καὶ Ἀβειρὼν
ζῶντας κατήγαγεν εἰς ᾅδου διὰ τὸ στασιάσαι αὐτοὺς
πρὸς τὸν θεράποντα τοῦ θεοῦ Μωϋσῆν. 13. διὰ ζῆλος
Δαυὶδ φθόνον ἔσχεν οὐ μόνον ὑπὸ τῶν ἀλλοφύλων,
ἀλλὰ καὶ ὑπὸ Σαοὺλ βασιλέως Ἰσραὴλ ἐδιώχθη.

5

Ἀλλ' ἵνα τῶν ἀρχαίων ὑποδειγμάτων παυσώμεθα,
ἔλθωμεν ἐπὶ τοὺς ἔγγιστα γενομένους ἀθλητάς·
λάβωμεν τῆς γενεᾶς ἡμῶν τὰ γενναῖα ὑποδείγματα.
2. διὰ ζῆλον καὶ φθόνον οἱ μέγιστοι καὶ δικαιότατοι
στῦλοι ἐδιώχθησαν καὶ ἕως θανάτου ἤθλησαν.
3. λάβωμεν πρὸ ὀφθαλμῶν ἡμῶν τοὺς ἀγαθοὺς
ἀποστόλους· 4. Πέτρον, ὃς διὰ ζῆλον ἄδικον οὐχ ἕνα
οὐδὲ δύο, ἀλλὰ πλείονας ὑπήνεγκεν πόνους καὶ οὕτω

---

[9] κριτὴν ἢ A: ἄρχοντα ἢ L: ἄρχοντα καί H S C (C[1])

dered him."[9] 7. You see, brothers, jealousy and envy brought about the murder of a brother. 8. Because of jealousy our father Jacob fled from the presence of Esau, his brother.[10] 9. Jealousy caused Joseph to be persecuted to the point of death and to enter into slavery.[11] 10. Jealousy forced Moses to flee from the presence of Pharoah, king of Egypt, when he heard from his fellow countryman, "Who made you an arbitrator or judge over us? Do you want to kill me, as you killed the Egyptian yesterday?"[12] 11. Because of jealousy Aaron and Miriam had to stay outside the camp.[13] 12. Jealousy brought Dathan and Abiram down into Hades while still alive because they created a faction against the servant of God, Moses.[14] 13. Because of jealousy not only did David incur envy from foreigners, but he was even persecuted by Saul, the king of Israel.[15]

5

But to stop giving ancient examples, let us come to those who became athletic contenders in quite recent times. We should consider the noble examples of our own generation. 2. Because of jealousy and envy the greatest and most upright pillars were persecuted, and they struggled in the contest even to death. 3. We should set before our eyes the good apostles. 4. There is Peter, who because of unjust jealousy bore up under hardships not just once or twice, but many times; and having thus borne his witness he went

[9] Gen 4:3–8.   [10] Gen 27:41ff.
[11] Gen 37.   [12] Exod 2:14.
[13] Num 12.   [14] Num 16:13.
[15] 1 Sam 18ff.

43

μαρτυρήσας ἐπορεύθη εἰς τὸν ὀφειλόμενον τόπον τῆς
δόξης. 5. διὰ ζῆλον καὶ ἔριν Παῦλος ὑπομονῆς βραβεῖον ἔδειξεν· 6. ἑπτάκις δεσμὰ φορέσας, φυγαδευ-
θείς, λιθασθείς, κῆρυξ γενόμενος ἔν τε τῇ ἀνατολῇ καὶ
ἐν τῇ δύσει, τὸ γενναῖον τῆς πίστεως αὐτοῦ κλέος
ἔλαβεν. 7. δικαιοσύνην[10] διδάξας ὅλον τὸν κόσμον,
καὶ ἐπὶ τὸ τέρμα τῆς δύσεως ἐλθὼν καὶ μαρτυρήσας
ἐπὶ τῶν ἡγουμένων, οὕτως ἀπηλλάγη τοῦ κόσμου καὶ
εἰς τὸν ἅγιον τόπον ἀνελήμφθη,[11] ὑπομονῆς γενόμενος
μέγιστος ὑπογραμμός.

6

Τούτοις τοῖς ἀνδράσιν ὁσίως πολιτευσαμένοις συν-
ηθροίσθη πολὺ πλῆθος ἐκλεκτῶν, οἵτινες πολλας
αἰκίας καὶ βασάνους διὰ ζῆλος παθόντες ὑπόδειγμα
κάλλιστον ἐγένοντο ἐν ἡμῖν. 2. διὰ ζῆλος διωχθεῖσαι
γυναῖκες Δαναΐδες καὶ Δίρκαι,[12] αἰκίσματα δεινὰ καὶ

---

[10] κλ. ἔλαβεν δικαιοσύνης H S
[11] ἀνελήμφθη C C[1] L S: ἐπορεύθη A H
[12] Δαναΐδες καὶ Δίρκαι (δεὶρ καὶ H) A H L S C (C[1] lacking):
νεανίδες παιδίσκαι cj. Wordsworth

---

16 The author's meaning is unclear. Some scholars have suggested that he is referring to Christian women martyred under
Nero, who was known for his creatively brutal excesses; see Sue-
tonius, Nero 11, 12. If so, women executed as Dircae may have
been dragged to death in the arena, bound to the horns of a bull,

to the place of glory that he deserved. 5. Because of jealousy and strife Paul pointed the way to the prize for endurance. 6. Seven times he bore chains; he was sent into exile and stoned; he served as a herald in both the East and the West; and he received the noble reputation for his faith. 7. He taught righteousness to the whole world, and came to the limits of the West, bearing his witness before the rulers. And so he was set free from this world and transported up to the holy place, having become the greatest example of endurance.

6

To these men who have conducted themselves in such a holy way there has been added a great multitude of the elect, who have set a superb example among us by the numerous torments and tortures they suffered because of jealousy. 2. Women were persecuted as Danaids and Dircae[16] and suffered terrifying and profane torments be-

like Dirce of Greek myth. The reference to the Danaids is more puzzling. Some scholars have seen it as an allusion to the legend that the daughters of Danaus were taken by men against their will—i.e., that the Christian women were publicly raped before being put to death. Others have thought that it refers to the punishment of Danaus's daughters in the afterlife, where they were compelled perpetually to fill leaking vessels—i.e. that the Christian women were subject to pointless and seemingly endless torments prior to their deaths. In either event, the text is so difficult that several emendations have been suggested to eliminate the reference to "Danaids and Dircae" altogether, the most popular of which is given in the Greek apparatus: "persecuted as women, maidens, and slave girls."

ἀνόσια παθοῦσαι, ἐπὶ τὸν τῆς πίστεως βέβαιον δρό-
μον κατήντησαν καὶ ἔλαβον γέρας γενναῖον αἱ ἀσθενεῖς τῷ σώματι. 3. ζῆλος ἀπηλλοτρίωσεν γαμετὰς
ἀνδρῶν καὶ ἠλλοίωσεν τὸ ῥηθὲν ὑπὸ τοῦ πατρὸς ἡμῶν
Ἀδάμ· τοῦτο νῦν ὀστοῦν ἐκ τῶν ὀστέων μου καὶ σὰρξ
ἐκ τῆς σαρκός μου. 4. ζῆλος καὶ ἔρις πόλεις μεγάλας
κατέστρεψεν καὶ ἔθνη μεγάλα ἐξερίζωσεν.

7

Ταῦτα, ἀγαπητοί, οὐ μόνον ὑμᾶς νουθετοῦντες ἐπι-
στέλλομεν, ἀλλὰ καὶ ἑαυτοὺς ὑπομιμνήσκοντες· ἐν
γὰρ τῷ αὐτῷ ἐσμὲν σκάμματι, καὶ ὁ αὐτὸς ἡμῖν ἀγὼν
ἐπίκειται. 2. διὸ ἀπολίπωμεν τὰς κενὰς καὶ ματαίας
φροντίδας, καὶ ἔλθωμεν ἐπὶ τὸν εὐκλεῆ καὶ σεμνὸν τῆς
παραδόσεως ἡμῶν κανόνα, 3. καὶ ἴδωμεν, τί καλὸν καὶ
τί τερπνὸν καὶ τί προσδεκτὸν ἐνώπιον τοῦ ποιήσαντος
ἡμᾶς. 4. ἀτενίσωμεν εἰς τὸ αἷμα τοῦ Χριστοῦ καὶ
γνῶμεν, ὡς ἔστιν τίμιον τῷ πατρὶ αὐτοῦ,[13] ὅτι διὰ τὴν
ἡμετέραν σωτηρίαν ἐκχυθὲν παντὶ τῷ κόσμῳ μετανοίας χάριν ὑπήνεγκεν. 5. διέλθωμεν εἰς τὰς γενεὰς
πάσας καὶ καταμάθωμεν, ὅτι ἐν γενεᾷ καὶ γενεᾷ
μετανοίας τόπον ἔδωκεν ὁ δεσπότης τοῖς βουλομένοις
ἐπιστραφῆναι ἐπ᾽ αὐτόν. 6. Νῶε ἐκήρυξεν μετάνοιαν,
καὶ οἱ ὑπακούσαντες ἐσώθησαν. 7. Ἰωνᾶς Νινευΐταις
καταστροφὴν ἐκήρυξεν· οἱ δὲ μετανοήσαντες ἐπὶ τοῖς
ἁμαρτήμασιν αὐτῶν ἐξιλάσαντο τὸν θεὸν ἱκετεύσαν-

cause of jealousy. But they confidently completed the race of faith, and though weak in body, they received a noble reward. 3. Jealousy estranged wives from their husbands and nullified what was spoken by our father Adam, "This now is bone from my bones and flesh from my flesh."[17] 4. Jealousy and strife overturned great cities and uprooted great nations.

7

We are writing these things, loved ones, not only to admonish you but also to remind ourselves. For we are in the same arena and the same contest is set before us. 2. For this reason we should leave behind empty and frivolous thoughts and come to the famous and venerable rule of our tradition. 3. We should realize what is good and pleasing and acceptable before the one who made us. 4. We should gaze intently on the blood of Christ and realize how precious it is to his Father; for when it was poured out for our salvation, it brought the gracious gift of repentance to the entire world. 5. Let us review all the generations and learn that from one generation to the next the Master has provided an opportunity for repentance to those wanting to return to him. 6. Noah proclaimed repentance, and those who heeded were saved from danger.[18] 7. Jonah proclaimed an impending disaster to the Ninevites; and those who repented of their sins appeased God through their

---

[17] Gen 2:23.   [18] Gen 7.

---

[13] τῷ πατρὶ αὐτοῦ L S C C¹: τῷ θῷ [καὶ πατρ]ι αὐτοῦ A: τῷ π. αὐτοῦ τῷ θεῷ H

τες καὶ ἔλαβον σωτηρίαν, καίπερ ἀλλότριοι τοῦ θεοῦ
ὄντες.

8

Οἱ λειτουργοὶ τῆς χάριτος τοῦ θεοῦ διὰ πνεύματος
ἁγίου περὶ μετανοίας ἐλάλησαν· 2. καὶ αὐτὸς δὲ ὁ
δεσπότης τῶν ἁπάντων περὶ μετανοίας ἐλάλησεν μετὰ
ὅρκου· ζῶ γὰρ ἐγώ, λέγει κύριος, οὐ βούλομαι τὸν
θάνατον τοῦ ἁμαρτωλοῦ ὡς τὴν μετάνοιαν, προστιθεὶς
καὶ γνώμην ἀγαθήν· 3. μετανοήσατε, οἶκος Ἰσραήλ,
ἀπὸ τῆς ἀνομίας ὑμῶν· εἶπον τοῖς υἱοῖς τοῦ λαοῦ μου·
ἐὰν ὦσιν αἱ ἁμαρτίαι ὑμῶν ἀπὸ τῆς γῆς ἕως τοῦ
οὐρανοῦ καὶ ἐὰν ὦσιν πυρρότεραι κόκκου καὶ
μελανώτεραι σάκκου, καὶ ἐπιστραφῆτε πρὸς μὲ ἐξ
ὅλης τῆς καρδίας[14] καὶ εἴπητε Πάτερ, ἐπακούσομαι
ὑμῶν ὡς λαοῦ ἁγίου. 4. καὶ ἐν ἑτέρῳ τόπῳ λέγει οὕτως·
λούσασθε καὶ καθαροὶ γένεσθε, ἀφέλεσθε τὰς
πονηρίας ἀπὸ τῶν ψυχῶν ὑμῶν ἀπέναντι τῶν ὀφθαλμῶν μου· παύσασθε ἀπὸ τῶν πονηριῶν ὑμῶν, μάθετε
καλὸν ποιεῖν, ἐκζητήσατε κρίσιν, ῥύσασθε ἀδικούμε-
νον, κρίνατε ὀρφανῷ καὶ δικαιώσατε χήρᾳ· καὶ δεῦτε
καὶ διελεγχθῶμεν, λέγει κύριος· καὶ ἐὰν ὦσιν αἱ ἁμαρτίαι ὑμῶν ὡς φοινικοῦν, ὡς χιόνα λευκανῶ· ἐὰν δὲ
ὦσιν ὡς κόκκινον, ὡς ἔριον λευκανῶ· καὶ ἐὰν θέλητε
καὶ εἰσακούσητέ μου, τὰ ἀγαθὰ τῆς γῆς φάγεσθε· ἐὰν
δὲ μὴ θέλητε μηδὲ εἰσακούσητέ μου, μάχαιρα ὑμᾶς
κατέδεται· τὸ γὰρ στόμα κυρίου ἐλάλησεν ταῦτα.

fervent pleas and received salvation, even though they had been estranged from God.[19]

8

Those who administered the gracious gift of God spoke through the Holy Spirit about repentance. 2. And the Master of all things himself spoke about repentance with an oath: "For as I live, says the Lord, I do not want the sinner to die but to repent."[20] And to this he added a good pronouncement: 3. "Repent from your lawlessness, house of Israel. Say to the children of my people, 'If your sins extend from the earth to the sky and are redder than scarlet and blacker than sackcloth, but you return to me with your whole heart and say, "Father," I will listen to you as to a holy people.'"[21] 4. And in another place he speaks as follows: "Wash and become clean; remove from yourselves the evils that are before my eyes; put an end to your evil deeds; learn to do good; pursue justice, rescue those who are treated unjustly, render a decision for the orphan and do what is right for the widow. And come, let us reason together, says the Lord. Even if your sins are like crimson, I will make them white as snow; and if they are like scarlet, I will make them white as wool. If you are willing and obey me, you will eat the good things of the earth; but if you are not willing and do not obey me, a sword will devour you. For the mouth of the Lord has spoken these things."[22]

[19] Jonah 3.   [20] Cf. Ezek 33:11.
[21] Possibly drawn from Ezek 33.   [22] Isa 1:16–20.

---

[14] καρδίας A C C[1] Clem Al: ψυχῆς H L S

5. πάντας οὖν τοὺς ἀγαπητοὺς αὐτοῦ βουλόμενος μετανοίας μετασχεῖν ἐστήριξεν τῷ παντοκρατορικῷ βουλήματι αὐτοῦ.

9

Διὸ ὑπακούσωμεν τῇ μεγαλοπρεπεῖ καὶ ἐνδόξῳ βουλήσει αὐτοῦ, καὶ ἱκέται γενόμενοι τοῦ ἐλέους καὶ τῆς χρηστότητος αὐτοῦ προσπέσωμεν καὶ ἐπιστρέψωμεν ἐπὶ τοὺς οἰκτιρμοὺς αὐτοῦ, ἀπολιπόντες τὴν ματαιοπονίαν τήν τε ἔριν καὶ τὸ εἰς θάνατον ἄγον ζῆλος. 2. ἀτενίσωμεν εἰς τοὺς τελείως λειτουργήσαντας τῇ μεγαλοπρεπεῖ δόξῃ αὐτοῦ. 3. λάβωμεν Ἐνώχ, ὃς ἐν ὑπακοῇ δίκαιος εὑρεθεὶς μετετέθη, καὶ οὐχ εὑρέθη αὐτοῦ θάνατος. 4. Νῶε πιστὸς εὑρεθεὶς διὰ τῆς λειτουργίας αὐτοῦ παλιγγενεσίαν κόσμῳ ἐκήρυξεν, καὶ διέσωσεν δι᾽ αὐτοῦ ὁ δεσπότης τὰ εἰσελθόντα ἐν ὁμονοίᾳ ζῷα εἰς τὴν κιβωτόν.

10

Ἀβραάμ, ὁ φίλος προσαγορευθείς, πιστὸς εὑρέθη ἐν τῷ αὐτὸν ὑπήκοον γενέσθαι τοῖς ῥήμασιν τοῦ θεοῦ. 2. οὗτος δι᾽ ὑπακοῆς ἐξῆλθεν ἐκ τῆς γῆς αὐτοῦ καὶ ἐκ τῆς συγγενείας αὐτοῦ καὶ ἐκ τοῦ οἴκου τοῦ πατρὸς αὐτοῦ, ὅπως γῆν ὀλίγην καὶ συγγένειαν ἀσθενῆ καὶ οἶκον μικρὸν καταλιπὼν κληρονομήσῃ τὰς ἐπαγγελίας τοῦ θεοῦ. λέγει γὰρ αὐτῷ· 3. ἄπελθε ἐκ τῆς γῆς

5. Because he wanted all his loved ones to have a share in repentance, he set it in place by his all-powerful will.

9

For this reason we should obey his magnificent and glorious will and, as petitioners of his mercy and kindness, fall down before him and turn to his compassionate ways, leaving behind our pointless toil and strife and the jealousy that leads to death. 2. We should gaze intently on those who have perfectly served his magnificent glory. 3. We should consider Enoch, who was transported to another place because he was found to be righteous in his obedience; and his death was never found.[23] 4. Noah, who was found to be faithful through his service, proclaimed a new beginning to the world; and through him the Master saved the living creatures that entered the ark in harmony.[24]

10

Abraham, who was called "The Friend,"[25] was found to be faithful when he became obedient to God's words. 2. In obedience he left his land, his family, and his father's house, so that by abandoning a paltry land, an insignificant family, and a small house he might inherit the promises of God. For God said to him, 3. "Depart from your land, your

23 Gen 5:24; Heb 11:5.
24 Gen 6:8; Heb 11:7.
25 Cf. Isa 41:8; Jas 2:23.

σου καὶ ἐκ τῆς συγγενείας σου καὶ ἐκ τοῦ οἴκου τοῦ
πατρός σου εἰς τὴν γῆν, ἣν ἄν σοι δείξω· καὶ ποιήσω
σε εἰς ἔθνος μέγα καὶ εὐλογήσω σε καὶ μεγαλυνῶ τὸ
ὄνομά σου, καὶ ἔσῃ εὐλογημένος· καὶ εὐλογήσω τοὺς
εὐλογοῦν τάς σε καὶ καταράσομαι τοὺς καταρωμένους
σε, καὶ εὐλογηθήσονται ἔν σοι πᾶσαι αἱ φυλαὶ τῆς
γῆς. 4. καὶ πάλιν ἐν τῷ διαχωρισθῆναι αὐτὸν ἀπὸ Λὼτ
εἶπεν αὐτῷ ὁ θεός· Ἀναβλέψας τοῖς ὀφθαλμοῖς σου
ἴδε ἀπὸ τοῦ τόπου, οὗ νῦν σὺ εἶ, πρὸς βορρᾶν καὶ
λίβα καὶ ἀνατολὰς καὶ θάλασσαν, ὅτι πᾶσαν τὴν γῆν,
ἣν σὺ ὁρᾷς, σοὶ δώσω αὐτὴν καὶ τῷ σπέρματί σου ἕως
αἰῶνος. 5. καὶ ποιήσω τὸ σπέρμα σου ὡς τὴν ἄμμον
τῆς γῆς· εἰ δύναταί τις ἐξαριθμῆσαι τὴν ἄμμον τῆς
γῆς, καὶ τὸ σπέρμα σου ἐξαριθμηθήσεται. 6. καὶ
πάλιν λέγει· ἐξήγαγεν ὁ θεὸς τὸν Ἀβραὰμ καὶ εἶπεν
αὐτῷ· ἀνάβλεψον εἰς τὸν οὐρανὸν καὶ ἀρίθμησον τοὺς
ἀστέρας, εἰ δυνήσῃ ἐξαριθμῆσαι αὐτούς· οὕτως ἔσται
τὸ σπέρμα σου. ἐπίστευσεν δὲ Ἀβραὰμ τῷ θεῷ, καὶ
ἐλογίσθη αὐτῷ εἰς δικαιοσύνην. 7. διὰ πίστιν καὶ
φιλοξενίαν ἐδόθη αὐτῷ υἱὸς ἐν γήρᾳ, καὶ δι᾽ ὑπακοῆς
προσήνεγκεν αὐτὸν θυσίαν τῷ θεῷ πρὸς ἓν τῶν ὀρέων
ὧν[15] ἔδειξεν αὐτῷ.

11

Διὰ φιλοξενίαν καὶ εὐσέβειαν Λὼτ ἐσώθη ἐκ Σοδό-
μων, τῆς περιχώρου πάσης κριθείσης διὰ πυρὸς καὶ
θείου, πρόδηλον ποιήσας ὁ δεσπότης, ὅτι τοὺς ἐλπί-

family, and your father's house to the land I will show you. And I will form you into a great nation and I will bless you and make your name great; and you will be blessed. And I will bless those who bless you and curse those who curse you, and all the tribes of the earth will be blessed in you."[26] 4. And again when Abraham separated from Lot, God said to him, "Lift up your eyes and look out from where you are now to the north, south, east, and west; for I will give all the land that you see to you and your offspring forever. 5. And I will make your offspring like the sand of the earth. If anyone is able to count the sand of the earth, your offspring will also be counted."[27] 6. Again it says, "God led Abraham out and said to him, 'Look up into the sky and count the stars, if you are able to number them. So will your offspring be.' And Abraham trusted God, and it was accounted to him as righteousness."[28] 7. Because of his faith and hospitality, a son was given to him in his old age; and in obedience he offered him up as a sacrifice to God on one of the mountains that he showed him.[29]

11

Because of his hospitality and piety, Lot was saved out of Sodom when all the surrounding countryside was judged by fire and brimstone.[30] The Master thus made it clear that

26 Gen 12:1–3. 27 Gen 13:14–16.
28 Gen 15:5–6; Rom 4:3.
29 Gen 18:21; Gen 22; Heb 11:17.
30 The following account is drawn from Gen 19.

---

15 ἐν τῶν ὀρέων ὧν A H S C: τὸ ὄρος ὃ L

ζοντας ἐπ᾽ αὐτὸν οὐκ ἐγκαταλείπει, τοὺς δὲ ἑτερο-
κλινεῖς ὑπάρχοντας εἰς κόλασιν καὶ αἰκισμὸν τίθησιν.
2. συνεξελθούσης γὰρ αὐτῷ τῆς γυναικὸς ἑτερογνώ-
μονος ὑπαρχούσης καὶ οὐκ ἐν ὁμονοίᾳ, εἰς τοῦτο[16]
σημεῖον ἐτέθη, ὥστε γενέσθαι αὐτὴν στήλην ἁλὸς ἕως
τῆς ἡμέρας ταύτης, εἰς τὸ γνωστὸν εἶναι πᾶσιν, ὅτι οἱ
δίψυχοι καὶ οἱ διστάζοντες περὶ τῆς τοῦ θεοῦ δυ-
νάμεως εἰς κρίμα καὶ εἰς σημείωσιν πάσαις ταῖς
γενεαῖς γίνονται.

12

Διὰ πίστιν καὶ φιλοξενίαν ἐσώθη Ῥαὰβ ἡ[17] πόρνη.
2. ἐκπεμφθέντων γὰρ ὑπὸ Ἰησοῦ τοῦ τοῦ Ναυὴ κατα-
σκόπων εἰς τὴν Ἰεριχώ, ἔγνω ὁ βασιλεὺς τῆς γῆς ὅτι
ἥκασιν κατασκοπεῦσαι τὴν χώραν αὐτῶν, καὶ ἐξέπεμ-
ψεν ἄνδρας τοὺς συλλημψομένους αὐτούς, ὅπως συλ-
λημφθέντες θανατωθῶσιν. 3. ἡ οὖν φιλόξενος Ῥαὰβ
εἰσδεξαμένη αὐτοὺς ἔκρυψεν εἰς τὸ ὑπερῷον ὑπὸ τὴν
λινοκαλάμην. 4. ἐπισταθέντων δὲ τῶν παρὰ τοῦ βασιλέως καὶ λεγόντων· πρὸς σὲ εἰσῆλθον οἱ κατάσκοποι
τῆς γῆς ἡμῶν· ἐξάγαγε αὐτούς, ὁ γὰρ βασιλεὺς οὕτως
κελεύει, ἥδε[18] ἀπεκρίθη· εἰσῆλθον μὲν οἱ ἄνδρες, οὓς
ζητεῖτε, πρὸς μέ, ἀλλ᾽ εὐθέως ἀπῆλθον καὶ πορεύονται
τῇ ὁδῷ, ὑποδεικνύουσα αὐτοῖς ἐναλλάξ. 5. καὶ εἶπεν
πρὸς τοὺς ἄνδρας· γινώσκουσα γινώσκω ἐγὼ ὅτι

[16] τοῦτο A S: om. H C

he does not abandon those who hope in him, but hands over to punishment and torment those who turn away. 2. Lot's wife was made a sign of this: for when she left with him but then changed her mind and fell out of harmony, she was turned into a pillar of salt until this day—so that everyone may know that those who are of two minds and who doubt the power of God enter into judgment and become a visible sign for all generations.

12

Because of her faith and hospitality Rahab the prostitute was saved from danger.[31] 2. For when reconnaissance scouts had been sent into Jericho by Joshua, the son of Nun, the king of the land discovered that they had come to scout out their country and sent men to arrest them, so that once detained they could be executed. 3. And so, the hospitable Rahab brought them inside and hid them in the upper room under a pile of thatching straw *[Or: fine linen; or: flax]*. 4. When the king's men arrived and said "Those who are scouting out our land came into your house; bring them out, for so the king has ordered," she replied, "The men you are seeking did come in to see me, but they left right away and are going on down the road." And she pointed them in the wrong direction. 5. And she said to the men, "I know full well that the Lord God is handing this

---

[31] The following account is drawn from Joshua 2. Cf. Heb 11:31; Jas 2:25.

---

17 ἡ A Clem Al: add ἐπιλεγομένη H L S C C¹
18 ἥδε L: ἡ δὲ H S C (A dub.)

κύριος ὁ θεὸς παραδίδωσιν ὑμῖν τὴν γῆν ταύτην· ὁ
γὰρ φόβος καὶ ὁ τρόμος ὑμῶν ἐπέπεσεν τοῖς
κατοικοῦσιν αὐτήν. ὡς ἐὰν οὖν γένηται λαβεῖν αὐτὴν
ὑμᾶς, διασώσατέ με καὶ τὸν οἶκον τοῦ πατρός μου.
6. καὶ εἶπαν αὐτῇ· ἔσται οὕτως, ὡς ἐλάλησας ἡμῖν. ὡς
ἐὰν οὖν γνῷς παραγινομένους ἡμᾶς, συνάξεις πάντας
τοὺς σοὺς ὑπὸ τὸ στέγος σου, καὶ διασωθήσονται·
ὅσοι γὰρ ἐὰν εὑρεθῶσιν ἔξω τῆς οἰκίας, ἀπολοῦνται.
7. καὶ προσέθεντο αὐτῇ δοῦναι σημεῖον, ὅπως ἐκ-
κρεμάσῃ ἐκ τοῦ οἴκου αὐτῆς κόκκινον, πρόδηλον
ποιοῦντες ὅτι διὰ τοῦ αἵματος τοῦ κυρίου[19] λύτρωσις
ἔσται πᾶσιν τοῖς πιστεύουσιν καὶ ἐλπίζουσιν ἐπὶ τὸν
θεόν. 8. ὁρᾶτε, ἀγαπητοί, ὅτι οὐ μόνον πίστις, ἀλλὰ
καὶ προφητεία ἐν τῇ γυναικὶ γέγονεν.

13

Ταπεινοφρονήσωμεν οὖν, ἀδελφοί, ἀποθέμενοι πᾶσαν
ἀλαζονείαν καὶ τῦφος καὶ ἀφροσύνην καὶ ὀργάς, καὶ
ποιήσωμεν τὸ γεγραμμένον· λέγει γὰρ τὸ πνεῦμα τὸ
ἅγιον· μὴ καυχάσθω ὁ σοφὸς ἐν τῇ σοφίᾳ αὐτοῦ μηδὲ
ὁ ἰσχυρὸς ἐν τῇ ἰσχύϊ αὐτοῦ μηδὲ ὁ πλούσιος ἐν τῷ
πλούτῳ αὐτοῦ, ἀλλ᾽ ὁ καυχώμενος ἐν κυρίῳ καυχάσθω, τοῦ ἐκζητεῖν αὐτὸν καὶ ποιεῖν κρίμα καὶ δι-
καιοσύνην· μάλιστα μεμνημένοι τῶν λόγων τοῦ
κυρίου Ἰησοῦ, οὓς ἐλάλησεν διδάσκων ἐπιείκειαν καὶ
μακροθυμίαν· 2. οὕτως γὰρ εἶπεν· ἐλεᾶτε, ἵνα ἐλεη-
θῆτε· ἀφίετε, ἵνα ἀφεθῇ ὑμῖν· ὡς ποιεῖτε, οὕτω ποιη-

land over to you, for fear and trembling has seized its in-
habitants because of you. When you take the land, save me
and my father's household." 6. They said to her, "It will be
just as you have spoken to us. So, when you know that we
are approaching, gather all your family under your roof
and they will be saved. For whoever is found outside the
house will perish." 7. And they proceeded to give her a sign
[Or: in addition they told her to give a sign], that she
should hang a piece of scarlet from her house—making it
clear that it is through the blood of the Lord that redemp-
tion will come to all who believe and hope in God. 8. You
see, loved ones, not only was faith found in the woman, but
prophecy as well.

13

And so we should be humble-minded, brothers, laying
aside all arrogance, conceit, foolishness, and forms of anger; and we should act in accordance with what is written.
For the Holy Spirit says, "The one who is wise should not
boast about his wisdom, nor the one who is strong about his
strength, nor the one who is wealthy about his wealth; instead, the one who boasts should boast about the Lord,
seeking after him and doing what is just and right."[32] We
should especially remember the words the Lord Jesus
spoke when teaching about gentleness and patience.
2. For he said: "Show mercy, that you may be shown mercy;
forgive, that it may be forgiven you. As you do, so it will be

[32] Jer 9:23–24; 1 Cor 1:31; 2 Cor 10:17.

---

[19] κυρίου A H L (C¹): Χριστοῦ S C

θήσεται ὑμῖν· ὡς δίδοτε, οὕτως δοθήσεται ὑμῖν· ὡς
κρίνετε, οὕτως κριθήσεσθε· ὡς χρηστεύεσθε, οὕτως
χρηστευθήσεται ὑμῖν· ᾧ μέτρῳ μετρεῖτε, ἐν αὐτῷ[20]
μετρηθήσεται ὑμῖν. 3. ταύτῃ τῇ ἐντολῇ καὶ τοῖς
παραγγέλμασιν τούτοις στηρίξωμεν ἑαυτοὺς εἰς τὸ
πορεύεσθαι ὑπηκόους ὄντας τοῖς ἁγιοπρεπέσι λόγοις
αὐτοῦ, ταπεινοφρονοῦντες· φησὶν γὰρ ὁ ἅγιος λόγος·
4. ἐπὶ τίνα ἐπιβλέψω, ἀλλ᾽ ἢ ἐπὶ τὸν πραῢν καὶ
ἡσύχιον καὶ τρέμοντά μου τὰ λόγια;[21]

14

Δίκαιον οὖν καὶ ὅσιον, ἄνδρες ἀδελφοί, ὑπηκόους
ἡμᾶς μᾶλλον γενέσθαι τῷ θεῷ ἢ τοῖς ἐν ἀλαζονείᾳ καὶ
ἀκαταστασίᾳ μυσεροῦ ζήλους ἀρχηγοῖς ἐξακολου-
θεῖν. 2. βλάβην γὰρ οὐ τὴν τυχοῦσαν, μᾶλλον δὲ
κίνδυνον ὑποίσομεν μέγαν, ἐὰν ῥιψοκινδύνως ἐπιδῶμεν ἑαυτοὺς τοῖς θελήμασιν τῶν ἀνθρώπων, οἵτινες
ἐξακοντίζουσιν εἰς ἔριν[22] καὶ στάσεις, εἰς τὸ ἀπαλλο-
τριῶσαι ἡμᾶς τοῦ καλῶς ἔχοντος. 3. χρηστευσώμεθα
ἑαυτοῖς κατὰ τὴν εὐσπλαγχνίαν καὶ γλυκύτητα τοῦ
ποιήσαντος ἡμᾶς. 4. γέγραπται γάρ· χρηστοὶ ἔσονται
οἰκήτορες γῆς, ἄκακοι δὲ ὑπολειφθήσονται ἐπ᾽ αὐτῆς·
οἱ δὲ παρανομοῦντες ἐξολεθρευθήσονται ἀπ᾽ αὐτῆς.
5. καὶ πάλιν λέγει· εἶδον ἀσεβῆ[23] ὑπερυψούμενον καὶ
ἐπαιρόμενον ὡς τὰς κέδρους τοῦ Λιβάνου· καὶ παρ-

---

[20] ἐν αὐτῷ (αυτη A): οὕτω H

done to you; as you give, so it will be given to you; as you judge, so you will be judged; as you show kindness, so will kindness be shown to you; the amount you dispense will be the amount you receive."[33] 3. Let us strengthen one another in this commandment and these demands, so that we may forge ahead, obedient to his words (which are well-suited for holiness) and humble-minded. For the holy word says, 4. "Upon whom will I look, but upon the one who is meek and mild and who trembles at my sayings?"[34]

14

And so it is right and holy for us to obey God, brothers, rather than follow those who instigate a foul jealousy with arrogance and disorderliness. 2. For we will subject ourselves not to some ordinary harm, but to real danger, if we rashly hand ourselves over to the desires of those who rush headlong into strife and faction and so estrange us from what is good for us. 3. We should treat one another kindly, according to the compassion and sweet character of the one who made us. 4. For it is written, "Those who are kind will inhabit the land, and the innocent will be left upon it; but those who break the law will be destroyed from it."[35] 5. And again it says, "I saw one who was impious greatly exalted and raised high as the cedars of Lebanon. Then I

33 Matt 5:7; 6:14–15; 7:1–2, 12; Luke 6:31, 36–38.
34 Isa 66:2.   35 Prov 2:21–22; Ps 37:9, 38.

---

21 τὰ λόγια A: τοὺς λόγους H
22 ἔριν A C (C¹): ἔρεις L S: αἱρέσεις H
23 ἀσεβῆ (A): τὸν ἀσεβῆ H C C¹ Clem Al

ἦλθον καὶ ἰδού, οὐκ ἦν, καὶ ἐξεζήτησα τὸν τόπον
αὐτοῦ, καὶ οὐχ εὗρον.²⁴ φύλασσε ἀκακίαν καὶ ἴδε
εὐθύτητα, ὅτι ἐστὶν ἐγκατάλειμμα ἀνθρώπῳ εἰρηνικῷ.

15

Τοίνυν κολληθῶμεν τοῖς μετ᾽ εὐσεβείας εἰρηνεύουσιν,
καὶ μὴ τοῖς μεθ᾽ ὑποκρίσεως βουλομένοις εἰρήνην.
2. λέγει γάρ που· οὗτος ὁ λαὸς τοῖς χείλεσίν²⁵ με τιμᾷ,
ἡ δὲ καρδία αὐτῶν πόρρω ἄπεστιν²⁶ ἀπ᾽ ἐμοῦ. 3. καὶ
πάλιν· τῷ στόματι αὐτῶν εὐλογοῦσαν, τῇ δὲ καρδίᾳ
αὐτῶν κατηρῶντο. 4. καὶ πάλιν λέγει· ἠγάπησαν
αὐτὸν τῷ στόματι αὐτῶν καὶ τῇ γλώσσῃ αὐτῶν
ἐψεύσαντο αὐτόν, ἡ δὲ καρδία αὐτῶν οὐκ εὐθεῖα μετ᾽
αὐτοῦ, οὐδὲ ἐπιστώθησαν ἐν τῇ διαθήκῃ αὐτοῦ. 5. διὰ
τοῦτο ἄλαλα γενηθήτω τὰ χείλη τὰ δόλια τὰ
λαλοῦντα κατὰ τοῦ δικαίου ἀνομίαν. καὶ πάλιν· ἐξ-
ολεθρεύσαι κύριος πάντα τὰ χείλη τὰ δόλια,²⁷ γλῶσσαν μεγαλορήμονα, τοὺς εἰπόντας· τὴν γλῶσσαν
ἡμῶν μεγαλυνοῦμεν, τὰ χείλη ἡμῶν παρ᾽ ἡμῖν ἐστιν·
τίς ἡμῶν κύριός ἐστιν; 6. ἀπὸ τῆς ταλαιπωρίας τῶν
πτωχῶν καὶ τοῦ στεναγμοῦ τῶν πενήτων νῦν ἀναστήσομαι, λέγει κύριος· θήσομαι ἐν σωτηρίῳ,²⁸
7. παρρησιάσομαι ἐν αὐτῷ.

²⁴ τὸν τόπον—εὗρον A H C C¹: αὐτὸν καὶ οὐχ εὑρέθη ὁ
τόπος αὐτοῦ L S Clem Al
²⁵ τοῖς χείλεσιν A L S C Clem Al: τῷ στόματι H

passed by and look! He was no more. And I searched for his place, but did not find it. Protect what is innocent and focus on what is upright, because the one who lives in peace will have a posterity."[36]

15

Therefore we should cling to those who keep the peace with piety, not those who wish for peace out of hypocrisy. 2. For it says somewhere, "This people honors me with their lips, but their heart is far removed from me."[37] 3. And again: "They blessed with their mouth but cursed in their heart."[38] 4. And again it says, "They loved him with their mouth and with their tongue they lied against him; but their heart was not right with him, nor did they prove faithful to his covenant."[39] 5. "For this reason let the deceitful lips that speak a lawless word against the righteous one be silenced."[40] And again, "May the Lord destroy all deceitful lips, the boastful tongue, and those who say, 'We will exalt our tongue; our lips are under our control. Who is lord over us?' 6. Now, says the Lord, I will rise up because of the humility of the poor and the groaning of the needy. I will establish him in salvation, 7. and deal boldly with him."[41]

36 Ps 37:35–37.
37 Isa 29:13; Mark 7:6; Matt 15:8.
38 Ps 62:4.   39 Ps 78:36–37.
40 Ps 31:18.   41 Ps 12:4–6.

26 ἄπεστιν A Clem Al: ἀπέχει H
27 τὰ λαλοῦντα—τὰ δόλια S: om. A H L C C¹ Clem Al
28 ἐν σωτηρίῳ L Clem Al: ἐν σωτηρίᾳ A: om. H

16

Ταπεινοφρονούντων γάρ ἐστιν ὁ Χριστός, οὐκ ἐπαι-
ρομένων ἐπὶ τὸ ποίμνιον αὐτοῦ. 2. τὸ σκῆπτρον τῆς
μεγαλωσύνης τοῦ θεοῦ, ὁ κύριος Ἰησοῦς Χριστός, οὐκ
ἦλθεν ἐν κόμπῳ ἀλαζονείας οὐδὲ ὑπερηφανίας, καίπερ
δυνάμενος, ἀλλὰ ταπεινοφρονῶν, καθὼς τὸ πνεῦμα τὸ
ἅγιον περὶ αὐτοῦ ἐλάλησεν· φησὶν γάρ· 3. Κύριε, τίς
ἐπίστευσεν τῇ ἀκοῇ ἡμῶν; καὶ ὁ βραχίων κυρίου τίνι
ἀπεκαλύφθη; ἀνηγγείλαμεν ἐναντίον αὐτοῦ, ὡς παι-
δίον, ὡς ῥίζα ἐν γῇ διψώσῃ· οὐκ ἔστιν εἶδος αὐτῷ οὐδὲ
δόξα, καὶ εἴδομεν αὐτόν, καὶ οὐκ εἶχεν εἶδος οὐδὲ
κάλλος, ἀλλὰ τὸ εἶδος αὐτοῦ ἄτιμον, ἐκλεῖπον παρὰ
τὸ εἶδος τῶν ἀνθρώπων· ἄνθρωπος ἐν πληγῇ ὢν καὶ
πόνῳ καὶ εἰδὼς φέρειν μαλακίαν, ὅτι ἀπέστραπται τὸ
πρόσωπον αὐτοῦ, ἠτιμάσθη καὶ οὐκ ἐλογίσθη. 4. οὗτος τὰς ἁμαρτίας ἡμῶν φέρει καὶ περὶ ἡμῶν ὀδυνᾶται,
καὶ ἡμεῖς ἐλογισάμεθα αὐτὸν εἶναι ἐν πόνῳ καὶ ἐν
πληγῇ καὶ ἐν κακώσει. 5. αὐτὸς δὲ ἐτραυματίσθη διὰ
τὰς ἁμαρτίας[29] ἡμῶν καὶ μεμαλάκισται διὰ τὰς ἀνομίας ἡμῶν· παιδεία εἰρήνης ἡμῶν ἐπ᾽ αὐτόν· τῷ μώ-
λωπι αὐτοῦ ἡμεῖς ἰάθημεν. 6. πάντες ὡς πρόβατα
ἐπλανήθημεν, ἄνθρωπος τῇ ὁδῷ αὐτοῦ ἐπλανήθη.
7. καὶ κύριος παρέδωκεν αὐτὸν ὑπὲρ τῶν ἁμαρτιῶν
ἡμῶν, καὶ αὐτὸς διὰ τὸ κεκακῶσθαι οὐκ ἀνοίγει τὸ
στόμα. ὡς πρόβατον ἐπὶ σφαγὴν ἤχθη, καὶ ὡς ἀμνὸς

---

[29] ἁμαρτίας . . . ἀνομίας A L: ~ H S C C[1]

16

For Christ belongs to those who are humble-minded, not to those who vaunt themselves over his flock. 2. The scepter of God's majesty, the Lord Jesus Christ, did not come with an ostentatious show of arrogance or haughtiness— even though he could have done so—but with a humble mind, just as the Holy Spirit spoke concerning him. For he says, 3. "Lord, who believed our report? And to whom was the arm of the Lord revealed? We made our announcement before him: he was like a child, like a root in a dry land. He had no striking form or glorious presence. We saw him, and he had no striking form or beauty; but his form was dishonorable, inferior to the form of others. He experienced trauma and toil; he knew what it meant to bear weakness. For his face was turned aside; he was dishonored and given no regard. 4. This one bears our sins and for our sake experiences pain. And we regarded him as having borne toil, trauma, and oppression. 5. But he was wounded because of our sins and weakened because of our lawless acts. The punishment that brought us peace came upon him. By his bruising we were healed. 6. We have all wandered astray like sheep; each has wandered on his own path. 7. The Lord handed him over for our sins, but he did not open his mouth because of his mistreatment. He was led like a sheep going to slaughter; and like a lamb, silent

ἐναντίον τοῦ κείραντος ἄφωνος, οὕτως οὐκ ἀνοίγει τὸ
στόμα αὐτοῦ. ἐν τῇ ταπεινώσει ἡ κρίσις αὐτοῦ ἤρθη.
8. τὴν γενεὰν αὐτοῦ τίς διηγήσεται; ὅτι αἴρεται ἀπὸ
τῆς γῆς ἡ ζωὴ αὐτοῦ. 9. ἀπὸ τῶν ἀνομιῶν τοῦ λαοῦ
μου ἥκει εἰς θάνατον. 10. καὶ δώσω τοὺς πονηροὺς
ἀντὶ τῆς ταφῆς αὐτοῦ καὶ τοὺς πλουσίους ἀντὶ τοῦ
θανάτου αὐτοῦ· ὅτι ἀνομίαν οὐκ ἐποίησεν, οὐδὲ εὑρέθη
δόλος ἐν τῷ στόματι αὐτοῦ. καὶ κύριος βούλεται
καθαρίσαι αὐτὸν τῆς πληγῆς. 11. ἐὰν δῶτε περὶ ἁμαρτίας, ἡ ψυχὴ ὑμῶν ὄψεται σπέρμα μακρόβιον. 12. καὶ
κύριος βούλεται ἀφελεῖν ἀπὸ τοῦ πόνου τῆς ψυχῆς
αὐτοῦ, δεῖξαι αὐτῷ φῶς καὶ πλάσαι τῇ συνέσει, δικαι-
ῶσαι δίκαιον εὖ δουλεύοντα πολλοῖς· καὶ τὰς ἁμαρτίας αὐτῶν αὐτὸς ἀνοίσει. 13. διὰ τοῦτο αὐτὸς κληρο-
νομήσει πολλοὺς καὶ τῶν ἰσχυρῶν μεριεῖ σκῦλα, ἀνθ'
ὧν παρεδόθη εἰς θάνατον ἡ ψυχὴ αὐτοῦ, καὶ ἐν τοῖς
ἀνόμοις ἐλογίσθη. 14. καὶ αὐτὸς ἁμαρτίας πολλῶν
ἀνήνεγκεν καὶ διὰ τὰς ἁμαρτίας αὐτῶν παρεδόθη.
15. καὶ πάλιν αὐτός φησιν· ἐγὼ δέ εἰμι σκώληξ καὶ
οὐκ ἄνθρωπος, ὄνειδος ἀνθρώπων καὶ ἐξουθένημα
λαοῦ. 16. πάντες οἱ θεωροῦντές με ἐξεμυκτήρισάν με,
ἐλάλησαν ἐν χείλεσιν, ἐκίνησαν κεφαλήν· ἤλπισεν
ἐπὶ κύριον, ῥυσάσθω αὐτόν, σωσάτω αὐτόν, ὅτι θέλει
αὐτόν. 17. ὁρᾶτε, ἄνδρες ἀγαπητοί, τίς ὁ ὑπογραμμὸς
ὁ δεδομένος ἡμῖν· εἰ γὰρ ὁ κύριος οὕτως ἐταπεινο-
φρόνησεν, τί ποιήσωμεν ἡμεῖς οἱ ὑπὸ τὸν ζυγὸν τῆς
χάριτος αὐτοῦ δι' αὐτοῦ ἐλθόντες;

before the one who shears it, so he did not open his mouth. Justice was denied him in his humiliation. 8. Who will describe his generation? For his life is removed from the earth. 9. Because of the lawless acts of my people, he has entered the realm of death. 10. And I will exchange those who are evil for his burial and those who are wealthy for his death; for he broke no law, nor was any deceit found in his mouth. And the Lord wants to cleanse him of his wound. 11. If you give an offering for sin, your soul will see offspring who live long. 12. And the Lord wants to remove the burden from his soul, to reveal a light to him and to mold him with understanding, to give justice to the one who is just, who serves many people well. And he himself will bear their sins. 13. For this reason he will inherit many and will divide the spoils of the strong; for his soul was handed over to death and he was counted among the lawless. 14. He bore the sins of many and was handed over because of their sins."[42] 15. And again he himself says, "I am a worm, not a human, reproached by others and despised by the people. 16. Everyone who sees me has mocked me; they spoke with their lips and shook their heads, 'He hoped in the Lord; let the Lord rescue him. Let him save him, since he desires him.'"[43] 17. You see, beloved men, the example that he has given us. For if the Lord was humble-minded in this way, what shall we ourselves do, who through him have assumed the yoke of his gracious favor?

[42] Isa 53:1–12.
[43] Ps 22:6–8.

17

Μιμηταὶ γενώμεθα κἀκείνων, οἵτινες ἐν δέρμασιν αἰ-
γείοις καὶ μηλωταῖς περιεπάτησαν κηρύσσοντες τὴν
ἔλευσιν τοῦ Χριστοῦ· λέγομεν δὲ Ἡλίαν καὶ Ἐλισαιέ,
ἔτι δὲ καὶ Ἰεζεκιήλ, τοὺς προφήτας· πρὸς τούτοις
καὶ τοὺς μεμαρτυρημένους. 2. ἐμαρτυρήθη μεγάλως
Ἀβραὰμ καὶ φίλος προσηγορεύθη τοῦ θεοῦ, καὶ λέγει
ἀτενίζων εἰς τὴν δόξαν τοῦ θεοῦ ταπεινοφρονῶν· ἐγὼ
δέ εἰμι γῆ καὶ σποδός. 3. ἔτι δὲ καὶ περὶ Ἰὼβ οὕτως
γέγραπται· Ἰὼβ δὲ ἦν δίκαιος καὶ ἄμεμπτος, ἀληθινός, θεοσεβής, ἀπεχόμενος ἀπὸ παντὸς κακοῦ.
4. ἀλλ᾽ αὐτὸς ἑαυτοῦ κατηγορεῖ λέγων· οὐδεὶς καθαρὸς
ἀπὸ ῥύπου, οὐδ᾽ ἂν μιᾶς ἡμέρας ἡ ζωὴ αὐτοῦ.
5. Μωϋσῆς πιστὸς ἐν ὅλῳ τῷ οἴκῳ αὐτοῦ ἐκλήθη, καὶ
διὰ τῆς ὑπηρεσίας αὐτοῦ ἔκρινεν ὁ θεὸς Αἴγυπτον διὰ
τῶν μαστίγων καὶ τῶν αἰκισμάτων αὐτῶν· ἀλλὰ
κἀκεῖνος δοξασθεὶς μεγάλως οὐκ ἐμεγαλορημόνησεν,
ἀλλ᾽ εἶπεν ἐκ[30] τῆς βάτου χρηματισμοῦ αὐτῷ διδο-
μένου· τίς εἰμι ἐγώ, ὅτι με πέμπεις; ἐγὼ δέ εἰμι
ἰσχνόφωνος καὶ βραδύγλωσσος. 6. καὶ πάλιν λέγει·
ἐγὼ δέ εἰμι ἀτμὶς ἀπὸ κύθρας.

[30] ἐκ L C¹ Clem Al: ἐπὶ H S C

17

We should become imitators also of those who went about in the skins of goats and sheep,[44] proclaiming the coming of Christ. We mean Elijah and Elisha, and also Ezekiel, the prophets; and in addition to these, those who had a good reputation. 2. Abraham was given a great reputation and was called "Friend of God." While he gazed intently upon the glory of God with a humble mind, he said, "I am just dust and ashes."[45] 3. Also concerning Job it is written: "But Job was upright and blameless, truthful, one who revered God and was far removed from all evil."[46] 4. But he accused himself, saying, "No one is clean from filth, even if his life lasts for single day."[47] 5. Moses was called faithful in his entire house,[48] and through his service God judged Egypt through their plagues and torments; but even though he was greatly exalted, he did not boast aloud. Instead, when the revelation was given to him from the bush, he said, "Who am I that you send me? For I am feeble in speech and slow in tongue."[49] 6. And again he said, "I am just steam from a pot."[50]

[44] Heb 11:37.
[45] Gen 18:27.
[46] Job 1:1.
[47] Job 14:4–5 (LXX).
[48] Num 12:7; Heb 3:2.
[49] Exod 3:11; 4:10.
[50] Source unknown.

18

Τί δὲ εἴπωμεν ἐπὶ τῷ μεμαρτυρημένῳ Δαυίδ; πρὸς ὃν
εἶπεν ὁ θεός· εὗρον ἄνδρα κατὰ τὴν καρδίαν μου,
Δαυὶδ τὸν τοῦ Ἰεσσαί· ἐν ἐλέει αἰωνίῳ ἔχρισα αὐτόν.
2. ἀλλὰ καὶ αὐτὸς λέγει πρὸς τὸν θεόν· ἐλέησόν με, ὁ
θεός, κατὰ τὸ μέγα ἔλεός σου, καὶ κατὰ τὸ πλῆθος τῶν
οἰκτιρμῶν σου ἐξάλειψον τὸ ἀνόμημά μου. 3.[31] ἐπὶ
πλεῖον πλῦνόν με ἀπὸ τῆς ἀνομίας μου καὶ ἀπὸ τῆς
ἁμαρτίας μου καθάρισόν με· ὅτι τὴν ἀνομίαν μου ἐγὼ
γινώσκω, καὶ ἡ ἁμαρτία μου ἐνώπιόν μου ἐστὶν δια-
παντός. 4. σοὶ μόνῳ ἥμαρτον καὶ τὸ πονηρὸν ἐνώπιόν
σου ἐποίησα, ὅπως ἂν δικαιωθῇς ἐν τοῖς λόγοις σου
καὶ νικήσῃς ἐν τῷ κρίνεσθαί σε. 5. ἰδοὺ γὰρ ἐν
ἀνομίαις συνελήμφθην, καὶ ἐν ἁμαρτίαις ἐκίσσησέν
με ἡ μήτηρ μου. 6. ἰδοὺ γὰρ ἀλήθειαν ἠγάπησας· τὰ
ἄδηλα καὶ τὰ κρύφια τῆς σοφίας σου ἐδήλωσάς μοι.
7. ῥαντιεῖς με ὑσσώπῳ, καὶ καθαρισθήσομαι· πλυνεῖς
με, καὶ ὑπὲρ χιόνα λευκανθήσομαι. 8. ἀκουτιεῖς με
ἀγαλλίασιν καὶ εὐφροσύνην, ἀγαλλιάσονται ὀστᾶ
τεταπεινωμένα. 9. ἀπόστρεψον τὸ πρόσωπόν σου ἀπὸ
τῶν ἁμαρτιῶν μου, καὶ πάσας τὰς ἀνομίας μου
ἐξάλειψον. 10. καρδίαν καθαρὰν κτίσον ἐν ἐμοί, ὁ
θεός, καὶ πνεῦμα εὐθὲς ἐγκαίνισον ἐν τοῖς ἐγκάτοις
μου. 11. μὴ ἀπορίψῃς με ἀπὸ τοῦ προσώπου σου, καὶ
τὸ πνεῦμα τὸ ἅγιόν σου μὴ ἀντανέλῃς ἀπ᾽ ἐμοῦ.
12. ἀπόδος μοι τὴν ἀγαλλίασιν τοῦ σωτηρίου σου, καὶ
πνεύματι ἡγεμονικῷ στήρισόν με. 13. διδάξω ἀνόμους

20

The heavens, which move about under his management, are peacefully subject to him. 2. Day and night complete the racecourse laid out by him, without impeding one another in the least. 3. Sun and moon and the chorus of stars roll along the tracks that have been appointed to them, in harmony, never crossing their lines, in accordance with the arrangement he has made. 4. By his will and in the proper seasons, the fertile earth brings forth its rich abundance of nourishment for humans, beasts, and all living things that dwell on it, without dissenting or altering any of the decrees he has set forth. 5. Both the inscrutable regions of the abysses and the indescribable realms of the depths are constrained by the same commands. 6. The basin of the boundless sea, established by his workmanship to hold the waters collected, does not cross its restraining barriers, but acts just as he ordered. 7. For he said, "You shall come this far, and your waves shall crash down within you."[54] 8. The ocean, boundless to humans, and the worlds beyond it are governed by the same decrees of the Master. 9. The seasons—spring, summer, fall, and winter—succeed one another in peace. 10. The forces [Or: stations] of the winds complete their service in their own proper season, without faltering. And the eternal fountains, created for enjoyment and health, provide their life-giving breasts to humans

[54] Job 38:11.

---

35 κλίματα cj. Wotton: κρίματα A H L S C

ποις μαζούς· τά τε ἐλάχιστα τῶν ζῴων τὰς συν-
ελεύσεις αὐτῶν ἐν ὁμονοίᾳ καὶ εἰρήνῃ ποιοῦνται.
11. ταῦτα πάντα ὁ μέγας δημιουργὸς καὶ δεσπότης
τῶν ἁπάντων ἐν εἰρήνῃ καὶ ὁμονοίᾳ προσέταξεν εἶναι,
εὐεργετῶν τὰ πάντα, ὑπερεκπερισσῶς δὲ ἡμᾶς τοὺς
προσπεφευγότας τοῖς οἰκτιρμοῖς αὐτοῦ διὰ τοῦ κυρίου
ἡμῶν Ἰησοῦ Χριστοῦ, 12. ᾧ ἡ δόξα καὶ ἡ μεγαλωσύνη εἰς τοὺς αἰῶνας τῶν αἰώνων. ἀμήν.

21

Ὁρᾶτε, ἀγαπητοί, μὴ αἱ εὐεργεσίαι αὐτοῦ αἱ πολλαὶ
γένωνται εἰς κρίμα πᾶσιν ἡμῖν,[36] ἐὰν μὴ ἀξίως αὐτοῦ
πολιτευόμενοι τὰ καλὰ καὶ εὐάρεστα ἐνώπιον αὐτοῦ
ποιῶμεν μεθ᾽ ὁμονοίας. 2. λέγει γάρ που· πνεῦμα
κυρίου λύχνος ἐρευνῶν τὰ ταμιεῖα τῆς γαστρός.
3. ἴδωμεν, πῶς ἐγγύς ἐστιν, καὶ ὅτι οὐδὲν λέληθεν
αὐτὸν τῶν ἐννοιῶν ἡμῶν οὐδὲ τῶν διαλογισμῶν ὧν
ποιούμεθα. 4. δίκαιον οὖν ἐστὶν μὴ λειποτακτεῖν ἡμᾶς
ἀπὸ τοῦ θελήματος αὐτοῦ. 5. μᾶλλον ἀνθρώποις
ἄφροσι καὶ ἀνοήτοις καὶ ἐπαιρομένοις καὶ ἐγκαυχω-
μένοις ἐν ἀλαζονείᾳ τοῦ λόγου αὐτῶν προσκόψωμεν ἢ
τῷ θεῷ. 6. τὸν κύριον Ἰησοῦν Χριστόν, οὗ τὸ αἷμα
ὑπὲρ ἡμῶν ἐδόθη, ἐντραπῶμεν, τοὺς προηγουμένους
ἡμῶν αἰδεσθῶμεν, τοὺς πρεσβυτέρους[37] τιμήσωμεν,
τοὺς νέους παιδεύσωμεν τὴν παιδείαν τοῦ φόβου τοῦ
θεοῦ, τὰς γυναῖκας ἡμῶν ἐπὶ τὸ ἀγαθὸν διορθωσώ-
μεθα. 7. τὸ ἀξιαγάπητον τῆς ἁγνείας ἦθος ἐνδει-

without ceasing. The most insignificant living creatures associate with one another *[Or: have sexual intercourse]* in harmony and peace. 11. The great Creator and Master of all appointed all these things to be in peace and harmony, bringing great benefits to all things, but most especially to us, who flee to his compassion through our Lord Jesus Christ. 12. To him be the glory and the majesty forever and ever. Amen.

21

Loved ones, you should take care that his many acts of kindness do not lead to judgment against all of us. For this will happen if we fail to conduct ourselves worthily of him and to do the things that are good and pleasing before him, in harmony. 2. For somewhere it says, "The Spirit of the Lord is a lamp that searches out the recesses deep within us."[55] 3. We should realize how near he is, and that none of our thoughts or the disputes we have had is hidden from him. 4. And so it is right for us not to desert from his will. 5. It is better for us to offend foolish, senseless, and presumptuous people who boast in the arrogance of their own talk than to offend God. 6. We should revere the Lord Jesus Christ, whose blood was given for us; we should respect our leaders; we should honor the elderly *[Or: the presbyters]*; we should discipline our youth in the reverential fear of God; we should set our wives along the straight path that leads to the good. 7. Let them display a character

[55] Prov 20:27.

---

[36] πᾶσιν ἡμῖν A: σὺν ἡμῖν H: ἡμῖν L S C C1
[37] πρεσβυτέρους H L S C C1 Clem Al: add ἡμῶν A

ξάσθωσαν, τὸ ἀκέραιον τῆς πραΰτητος αὐτῶν βούλημα ἀποδειξάτωσαν, τὸ ἐπιεικὲς τῆς γλώσσης αὐτῶν
διὰ τῆς φωνῆς[38] φανερὸν ποιησάτωσαν, τὴν ἀγάπην
αὐτῶν μὴ κατὰ προσκλίσεις, ἀλλὰ πᾶσιν τοῖς φοβου-
μένοις τὸν θεὸν ὁσίως ἴσην παρεχέτωσαν. 8. τὰ τέκνα
ἡμῶν τῆς ἐν Χριστῷ παιδείας μεταλαμβανέτωσαν·
μαθέτωσαν, τί ταπεινοφροσύνη παρὰ θεῷ ἰσχύει, τί
ἀγάπη ἁγνὴ παρὰ θεῷ δύναται, πῶς ὁ φόβος αὐτοῦ
καλὸς καὶ μέγας καὶ σῴζων πάντας τοὺς ἐν αὐτῷ
ὁσίως ἀναστρεφομένους ἐν καθαρᾷ διανοίᾳ.[39] 9. ἐρευ-
νητὴς γάρ ἐστιν ἐννοιῶν καὶ ἐνθυμήσεων· οὗ ἡ πνοὴ
αὐτοῦ ἐν ἡμῖν ἐστίν, καὶ ὅταν θέλῃ, ἀνελεῖ[40] αὐτήν.

22

Ταῦτα δὲ πάντα βεβαιοῖ ἡ ἐν Χριστῷ πίστις· καὶ γὰρ
αὐτὸς διὰ τοῦ πνεύματος τοῦ ἁγίου οὕτως προσκαλεῖται ἡμᾶς· δεῦτε, τέκνα, ἀκούσατέ μου, φόβον κυρίου
διδάξω ὑμᾶς. 2.[41] τίς ἐστιν ἄνθρωπος ὁ θέλων ζωήν,
ἀγαπῶν ἡμέρας ἰδεῖν ἀγαθάς; 3. παῦσον τὴν γλῶσ-
σάν σου ἀπὸ κακοῦ καὶ χείλη σου τοῦ μὴ λαλῆσαι
δόλον. 4. ἔκκλινον ἀπὸ κακοῦ καὶ ποίησον ἀγαθόν.
5. ζήτησον εἰρήνην καὶ δίωξον αὐτήν. 6. ὀφθαλμοὶ
κυρίου ἐπὶ δικαίους, καὶ ὦτα αὐτοῦ πρὸς δέησιν αὐ-
τῶν· πρόσωπον δὲ κυρίου ἐπὶ ποιοῦντας κακά, τοῦ
ἐξολεθρεῦσαι ἐκ γῆς τὸ μνημόσυνον αὐτῶν. 7. ἐκέκρα-

---

38 φωνῆς A: σιγῆς H L S C

of purity, worthy of love; let them exhibit the innocent will of their meekness; let them manifest the gentleness of their tongues through how they speak; let them show their love not with partiality, but equally to all those who stand in reverential awe of God in a holy way. 8. Let our children partake of the discipline that is in Christ. Let them learn the strength of humility before God and the power of pure love before God. Let them learn how the reverential awe of him is beautiful and great, and how it saves all those who conduct themselves in it *[Or: in him]* in a holy way, with a clear understanding. 9. For he is the one who explores our understandings and desires. His breath is in us, and when he wishes, he will remove it.

22

The faith that is in Christ guarantees all these things. For he himself calls to us through the Holy Spirit: "Come, children, and hear me; I will teach you the reverential awe of the Lord. 2. Who is the person who wants to live and yearns to see good days? 3. Stop your tongue from speaking evil and your lips from spouting deceit. 4. Move away from evil and do what is good. 5. Seek after peace and pursue it. 6. The eyes of the Lord are upon the upright, and his ears attend to their prayer. But the face of the Lord is against those who do evil and destroys any recollection of them from the face of the earth. 7. The one who is upright has

---

39 διανοίᾳ A H S: καρδίᾳ Clem Al L (C C¹?)
40 ἀνελεῖ A L C Clem Al: ἀναιρεῖ H S
41 vv. 2–7 om. H

ξεν ὁ δίκαιος, καὶ ὁ κύριος εἰσήκουσεν αὐτοῦ καὶ ἐκ
πασῶν τῶν θλίψεων αὐτοῦ ἐρύσατο αὐτόν.[42] 8. πολλαὶ[43] αἱ μάστιγες τοῦ ἁμαρτωλοῦ, τοὺς δὲ ἐλπίζοντας[44] ἐπὶ κύριον ἔλεος κυκλώσει.

23

Ὁ οἰκτίρμων κατὰ πάντα καὶ εὐεργετικὸς πατὴρ ἔχει
σπλάγχνα ἐπὶ τοὺς φοβουμένους αὐτόν· ἠπίως τε καὶ
προσηνῶς τὰς χάριτας αὐτοῦ ἀποδιδοῖ τοῖς προσερ-
χομένοις αὐτῷ ἁπλῇ διανοίᾳ. 2. διὸ μὴ διψυχῶμεν,
μηδὲ ἰνδαλλέσθω ἡ ψυχὴ ἡμῶν ἐπὶ ταῖς ὑπερβαλλού-
σαις καὶ ἐνδόξοις δωρεαῖς αὐτοῦ. 3. πόρρω γενέσθω
ἀφ᾽ ἡμῶν ἡ γραφὴ αὕτη, ὅπου λέγει· ταλαίπωροί εἰσιν
οἱ δίψυχοι, οἱ διστάζοντες τῇ ψυχῇ, οἱ λέγοντες· ταῦτα
ἠκούσαμεν καὶ ἐπὶ τῶν πατέρων ἡμῶν, καὶ ἰδού,
γεγηράκαμεν, καὶ οὐδὲν ἡμῖν τούτων συνβέβηκεν.
4. ὦ ἀνόητοι, συμβάλετε ἑαυτοὺς ξύλῳ· λάβετε ἄμπε-
λον· πρῶτον μὲν φυλλοροεῖ, εἶτα βλαστὸς γίνεται,
εἶτα φύλλον, εἶτα ἄνθος, καὶ μετὰ ταῦτα ὄμφαξ, εἶτα
σταφυλὴ παρεστηκυῖα. ὁρᾶτε, ὅτι ἐν καιρῷ ὀλίγῳ εἰς
πέπειρον καταντᾷ ὁ καρπὸς τοῦ ξύλου. 5. ἐπ᾽ ἀληθείας
ταχὺ καὶ ἐξαίφνης τελειωθήσεται τὸ βούλημα αὐτοῦ,
συνεπιμαρτυρούσης καὶ τῆς γραφῆς, ὅτι· ταχὺ ἥξει

---

42 αὐτόν A L C C[1]: add πολλαὶ αἱ θλίψεις τοῦ δικαίου, καὶ
ἐκ πασῶν αὐτῶν ῥύσεται αὐτὸν ὁ κύριος S
43 πολλαὶ A L C C[1]: εἶτα· πολλαὶ H: καὶ πάλιν· πολλαὶ S

called out, and the Lord has heard him and delivered him from all his afflictions."[56] 8. "Many are the plagues of the sinner, but mercy will surround those who hope in the Lord."[57]

23

The beneficent father, compassionate in every way, has pity on those who stand in awe of him; gently and kindly does he bestow his gracious gifts on those who approach him with a pure resolve. 2. And so, we should not be of two minds, nor should we entertain wild notions about his superior and glorious gifts. 3. May this Scripture be far removed from us that says: "How miserable are those who are of two minds, who doubt in their soul, who say, 'We have heard these things from the time of our parents, and look! We have grown old, and none of these things has happened to us.' 4. You fools! Compare yourselves to a tree. Take a vine: first it sheds its leaves, then a bud appears, then a leaf, then a flower, and after these an unripe grape, and then an entire bunch fully grown."[58] You see that the fruit of the tree becomes ripe in just a short time. 5. In truth, his plan will come to completion quickly and suddenly, as even the Scripture testifies, when it says, "He will

---

56 Ps 34:11–17, 19.
57 Ps 32:10.
58 Source unknown. Cf. 2 Clem 11:2–3.

---

44 τοὺς δὲ ἐλπίζοντας A L Clem Al: τὸν δὲ ἐλπίζοντα H S C

καὶ οὐ χρονιεῖ, καὶ· ἐξαίφνης ἥξει ὁ κύριος εἰς τὸν
ναὸν αὐτοῦ, καὶ ὁ ἅγιος, ὃν ὑμεῖς προσδοκᾶτε.

24

Κατανοήσωμεν, ἀγαπητοί, πῶς ὁ δεσπότης ἐπι-
δείκνυται διηνεκῶς ἡμῖν τὴν μέλλουσαν ἀνάστασιν
ἔσεσθαι, ἧς τὴν ἀπαρχὴν ἐποιήσατο τὸν κύριον
Ἰησοῦν Χριστὸν[45] ἐκ νεκρῶν ἀναστήσας. 2. ἴδωμεν,
ἀγαπητοί, τὴν κατὰ καιρὸν γινομένην ἀνάστασιν.
3. ἡμέρα καὶ νὺξ ἀνάστασιν ἡμῖν δηλοῦσιν· κοιμᾶται
ἡ νύξ, ἀνίσταται ἡ ἡμέρα· ἡ ἡμέρα ἄπεισιν, νὺξ
ἐπέρχεται. 4. λάβωμεν τοὺς καρπούς· ὁ σπόρος πῶς
καὶ τίνα τρόπον γίνεται; 5. ἐξῆλθεν ὁ σπείρων καὶ
ἔβαλεν εἰς τὴν γῆν ἕκαστον τῶν σπερμάτων, ἅτινα
πεσόντα εἰς τὴν γῆν ξηρὰ καὶ γυμνὰ διαλύεται· εἶτ᾽ ἐκ
τῆς διαλύσεως ἡ μεγαλειότης τῆς προνοίας τοῦ
δεσπότου ἀνίστησιν αὐτά, καὶ ἐκ τοῦ ἑνὸς πλείονα
αὔξει καὶ ἐκφέρει καρπόν.

25

Ἴδωμεν τὸ παράδοξον σημεῖον τὸ γινόμενον ἐν τοῖς
ἀνατολικοῖς τόποις, τουτέστιν τοῖς περὶ τὴν Ἀραβίαν.
2. ὄρνεον γάρ ἐστιν, ὃ προσονομάζεται φοῖνιξ· τοῦτο
μονογενὲς ὑπάρχον ζῇ ἔτη πεντακόσια, γενόμενόν τε

45 Χριστὸν A S L C: om. H C[1]

come quickly and not delay. And suddenly the Lord will come to his temple—he who is holy, the one you await."[59]

24

We should consider, loved ones, how the Master continuously shows us the future resurrection that is about to occur, of which he made the Lord Jesus Christ the first fruit by raising him from the dead.[60] 2. We should look, loved ones, at the resurrection that happens time after time. 3. Day and night reveal to us a resurrection: the night sleeps and the day arises; the day departs and the night arrives. 4. We should consider the crops: how, and in what way, does the sowing occur? 5. The sower goes out and casts each of the seeds onto the soil.[61] Because they are dry and barren they decay when they fall onto the soil. But then the magnificent forethought of the Master raises them up out of their decay, and from the one seed grow more, and so bring forth the crop.

25

Let us consider the incredible sign that occurs in the eastern climes, that is, in the regions near Arabia. 2. For there is a bird called the Phoenix. This unique creature lives five

[59] Cf. Isa 13:22 (LXX); Mal 3:1.
[60] 1 Cor 15:20.
[61] Mark 4:3; cf. 1 Cor 15:36ff.

ἤδη πρὸς ἀπόλυσιν τοῦ ἀποθανεῖν αὐτό, σηκὸν ἑαυτῷ
ποιεῖ ἐκ λιβάνου καὶ σμύρνης καὶ τῶν λοιπῶν ἀρωμάτων, εἰς ὃν πληρωθέντος τοῦ χρόνου[46] εἰσέρχεται
καὶ τελευτᾷ. 3. σηπομένης δὲ τῆς σαρκὸς σκώληξ τις
γεννᾶται, ὃς ἐκ τῆς ἰκμάδος τοῦ τετελευτηκότος ζῴου
ἀνατρεφόμενος πτεροφυεῖ· εἶτα γενναῖος γενόμενος
αἴρει τὸν σηκὸν ἐκεῖνον, ὅπου τὰ ὀστᾶ τοῦ προ-
γεγονότος ἐστίν, καὶ ταῦτα βαστάζων διανύει ἀπὸ τῆς
Ἀραβικῆς χώρας ἕως τῆς Αἰγύπτου εἰς τὴν λεγομένην
Ἡλιούπολιν. 4. καὶ ἡμέρας, βλεπόντων πάντων, ἐπιπτὰς[47] ἐπὶ τὸν τοῦ ἡλίου βωμὸν τίθησιν αὐτὰ καὶ
οὕτως εἰς τοὐπίσω ἀφορμᾷ. 5. οἱ οὖν ἱερεῖς ἐπισκέ-
πτονται τὰς ἀναγραφὰς τῶν χρόνων καὶ εὑρίσκουσιν
αὐτὸν πεντακοσιοστοῦ ἔτους πεπληρωμένου ἐληλυθέναι.

26

Μέγα καὶ θαυμαστὸν οὖν νομίζομεν εἶναι, εἰ ὁ δημιουργὸς τῶν ἁπάντων ἀνάστασιν ποιήσεται τῶν
ὁσίως αὐτῷ δουλευσάντων ἐν πεποιθήσει πίστεως
ἀγαθῆς, ὅπου καὶ δι᾽ ὀρνέου δείκνυσιν ἡμῖν τὸ μεγαλεῖον τῆς ἐπαγγελίας αὐτοῦ; 2. λέγει γάρ που· καὶ
ἐξαναστήσεις με, καὶ ἐξομολογήσομαί σοι, καί·
ἐκοιμήθην καὶ ὕπνωσα, ἐξηγέρθην,[48] ὅτι σὺ μετ᾽ ἐμοῦ
εἶ. 3. καὶ πάλιν Ἰὼβ λέγει· καὶ ἀναστήσεις τὴν σάρκα
μου ταύτην τὴν ἀναντλήσασαν ταῦτα πάντα.

hundred years. And when at last it approaches its dissolution through death, it makes a tomb for itself out of frankincense, myrrh, and other spices. Then, when the time has been fulfilled, it enters into the tomb and dies. 3. But when its flesh rots, a worm is born. And nourished by the secretions of the dead creature, it sprouts wings. Then when it becomes strong, it takes the tomb containing the bones of its predecessor and bears these from Arabia to Egypt, to the city called Heliopolis. 4. In the daytime, while all are watching, it flies onto the altar of the sun and deposits these things, and so hastens back. 5. Then the priests examine the records of the times and discover that it has come after five hundred years have elapsed.

26

Do we then think that it is so great and marvelous that the Creator of all things will raise everyone who has served him in a holy way with the confidence of good faith, when he shows us the magnificence of his promise even through a bird? 2. For it says somewhere, "You will raise me up and I will praise you,"[62] and, "I lay down and slept, and I arose, because you are with me."[63] 3. And again, Job says, "You will raise this flesh of mine, which has endured all these things."[64]

---

[62] Ps 28:7.   [63] Ps 3:5.   [64] Job 19:26.

---

[46] χρόνου A H C C¹: add τοῦ βίου L S
[47] ἐπιπτὰς A H C C¹: om. H
[48] ἐξηγέρθην A H S L: ἐξεγερθήσομαι C C¹

27

Ταύτῃ οὖν τῇ ἐλπίδι προσδεδέσθωσαν[49] αἱ ψυχαὶ
ἡμῶν τῷ πιστῷ ἐν ταῖς ἐπαγγελίαις καὶ τῷ δικαίῳ ἐν
τοῖς κρίμασιν. 2. ὁ παραγγείλας μὴ ψεύδεσθαι, πολλῷ
μᾶλλον αὐτὸς οὐ ψεύσεται; οὐδὲν γὰρ ἀδύνατον παρὰ
τῷ θεῷ εἰ μὴ τὸ ψεύσασθαι. 3. ἀναζωπυρησάτω οὖν ἡ
πίστις αὐτοῦ ἐν ἡμῖν, καὶ νοήσωμεν, ὅτι πάντα ἐγγὺς
αὐτῷ ἐστίν. 4. ἐν λόγῳ τῆς μεγαλωσύνης αὐτοῦ
συνεστήσατο τὰ πάντα, καὶ ἐν λόγῳ δύναται αὐτὰ
καταστρέψαι. 5. τίς ἐρεῖ αὐτῷ· τί ἐποίησας; ἢ τίς
ἀντιστήσεται τῷ κράτει τῆς ἰσχύος αὐτοῦ; ὅτε θέλει
καὶ ὡς θέλει, ποιήσει πάντα, καὶ οὐδὲν μὴ παρέλθῃ
τῶν δεδογματισμένων ὑπ᾽ αὐτοῦ. 6. πάντα ἐνώπιον
αὐτοῦ εἰσίν, καὶ οὐδὲν λέληθεν τὴν βουλὴν αὐτοῦ, 7. εἰ
οἱ οὐρανοὶ διηγοῦνται δόξαν θεοῦ, ποίησιν δὲ χειρῶν
αὐτοῦ ἀναγγέλλει τὸ στερέωμα· ἡ ἡμέρα τῇ ἡμέρᾳ
ἐρεύγεται ῥῆμα, καὶ νὺξ νυκτὶ ἀναγγέλλει γνῶσιν· καὶ
οὐκ εἰσὶν λόγοι οὐδὲ λαλιαί, ὧν οὐχὶ[50] ἀκούονται αἱ
φωναὶ αὐτῶν.

28

Πάντων οὖν βλεπομένων καὶ ἀκουομένων, φοβηθῶμεν
αὐτὸν καὶ ἀπολίπωμεν φαύλων ἔργων μιαρᾶς ἐπιθυμίας, ἵνα τῷ ἐλέει αὐτοῦ σκεπασθῶμεν ἀπὸ τῶν

49 προσδεχέσθωσαν Η   50 ἡ ἡμέρα—οὐχί· καὶ Η

27

Let our souls, therefore, be bound by this hope to the one who is faithful in his promises and upright in his judgments. 2. The one who commanded us not to lie, how much more will he not lie? For nothing is impossible for God, except lying. 3. Let his faithfulness *[Or: faith in him]* be rekindled within us and let us realize that all things are near to him. 4. By the word of his majesty he has established all things, and by his word he is able to destroy them. 5. "Who will say to him, 'What are you doing?' Or who will oppose his mighty power?"[65] He will do all things when he wishes and as he wishes, and nothing decreed by him will pass away. 6. Everything is before him, and nothing escapes his will. 7. "For the heavens declare the glory of God and the firmament proclaims the work of his hands. One day utters a word to another, and one night proclaims knowledge to the next. And there are no words or speeches whose voices are not heard."[66]

28

Since everything is seen and heard, we should stand in awe of him, leaving behind depraved desires for evil works, that by his mercy we may be protected from the judgments

---

[65] Wis 12:12.
[66] Ps 19:1–3.

30

Ἁγία[52] οὖν μερὶς ὑπάρχοντες ποιήσωμεν τὰ τοῦ ἁγιασμοῦ πάντα, φεύγοντες καταλαλιάς, μιαράς τε καὶ ἀνάγνους συμπλοκάς, μέθας τε καὶ νεωτερισμοὺς καὶ βδελυκτὰς ἐπιθυμίας, μυσερὰν τε[53] μοιχείαν καὶ[54] βδελυκτὴν ὑπερηφανίαν. 2. θεὸς γάρ, φησίν, ὑπερηφάνοις ἀντιτάσσεται, ταπεινοῖς δὲ δίδωσιν χάριν. 3. κολληθῶμεν οὖν ἐκείνοις, οἷς ἡ χάρις ἀπὸ τοῦ θεοῦ δέδοται· ἐνδυσώμεθα τὴν ὁμόνοιαν ταπεινοφρονοῦντες, ἐγκρατευόμενοι, ἀπὸ παντὸς ψιθυρισμοῦ καὶ καταλαλιᾶς πόρρω ἑαυτοὺς ποιοῦντες, ἔργοις δικαιούμενοι καὶ μὴ λόγοις. 4. λέγει γάρ· ὁ τὰ πολλὰ λέγων καὶ ἀντακούσεται· ἢ ὁ εὔλαλος οἴεται εἶναι δίκαιος; 5. εὐλογημένος γεννητὸς γυναικὸς ὀλιγόβιος. μὴ πολὺς ἐν ῥήμασιν γίνου. 6. ὁ ἔπαινος ἡμῶν ἔστω ἐν θεῷ καὶ μὴ ἐξ αὐτῶν· αὐτεπαινετοὺς γὰρ μισεῖ ὁ θεός. 7. ἡ μαρτυρία τῆς ἀγαθῆς[55] πράξεως ἡμῶν διδόσθω ὑπ᾽ ἄλλων, καθὼς ἐδόθη τοῖς πατράσιν ἡμῶν τοῖς δικαίοις. 8. θράσος καὶ αὐθάδεια καὶ τόλμα τοῖς κατηραμένοις ὑπὸ τοῦ θεοῦ· ἐπιείκεια καὶ ταπεινοφροσύνη καὶ πραΰτης παρὰ τοῖς ηὐλογημένοις ὑπὸ τοῦ θεοῦ.

52 ἁγία L S: ἄγια H: ἁγίου A: ἁγίων C
53 τε H L S: om. A
54 καὶ H L S C: om. A
55 ἀγαθῆς: om. H

30

Since then we are a holy portion, we should do everything that pertains to holiness, fleeing slander and vile and impure sexual embraces, drunken revelries, rebellions and loathsome passions, foul adultery and loathsome haughtiness. 2. "For God," it says, "opposes the haughty but gives grace to the humble."[70] 3. We should, therefore, cling to those who have been bestowed with God's gracious gift; we should be clothed with harmony, being humble in mind, showing self-restraint, distancing ourselves from all gossip and slander, acquiring an upright character through deeds, not just words. 4. For it says, "The one who speaks many things must also listen in return. Or does someone who is eloquent think he is right? 5. Blessed is one born of a woman but who lives a short life. Do not be profuse in your words."[71] 6. Let our praise be with God and not from ourselves. For God hates those who praise themselves. 7. Let the testimony of our good behavior be given by others, just as it was given to our ancestors who were upright. 8. Audacity, insolence, and effrontery belong to those who are cursed by God; gentleness, humility, and meekness to those blessed by God.

[70] Prov 3:34; Jas 4:6; 1 Pet 5:5.
[71] Job 11:2–3 (LXX).

31

Κολληθῶμεν οὖν τῇ εὐλογίᾳ αὐτοῦ καὶ ἴδωμεν, τίνες
αἱ ὁδοὶ τῆς εὐλογίας. ἀνατυλίξωμεν τὰ ἀπ᾽ ἀρχῆς
γενόμενα. 2. τίνος χάριν ηὐλογήθη ὁ πατὴρ ἡμῶν
Ἀβραάμ; οὐχὶ δικαιοσύνην καὶ ἀλήθειαν διὰ πίστεως[56] ποιήσας; 3. Ἰσαὰκ μετὰ πεποιθήσεως γινώσκων τὸ μέλλον ἡδέως προσήγετο θυσία. 4. Ἰακὼβ
μετὰ ταπεινοφροσύνης ἐξεχώρησεν τῆς γῆς αὐτοῦ δι᾽
ἀδελφὸν καὶ ἐπορεύθη πρὸς Λαβὰν καὶ ἐδούλευσεν,
καὶ ἐδόθη αὐτῷ τὸ δωδεκάσκηπτρον τοῦ Ἰσραήλ.

32

Ὁ ἐάν τις καθ᾽ ἓν ἕκαστον εἰλικρινῶς κατανοήσῃ,
ἐπιγνώσεται μεγαλεῖα τῶν ὑπ᾽ αὐτοῦ δεδομένων δωρεῶν. 2. ἐξ αὐτοῦ[57] γὰρ ἱερεῖς καὶ λευῖται πάντες οἱ
λειτουργοῦντες τῷ θυσιαστηρίῳ τοῦ θεοῦ· ἐξ αὐτοῦ ὁ
κύριος Ἰησοῦς τὸ κατὰ σάρκα· ἐξ αὐτοῦ βασιλεῖς καὶ
ἄρχοντες καὶ ἡγούμενοι κατὰ τὸν Ἰούδαν· τὰ δὲ λοιπὰ
σκῆπτρα αὐτοῦ οὐκ ἐν μικρᾷ δόξῃ[58] ὑπάρχουσιν, ὡς
ἐπαγγειλαμένου τοῦ θεοῦ, ὅτι ἔσται τὸ σπέρμα σου
ὡς οἱ ἀστέρες τοῦ οὐρανοῦ. 3. πάντες οὖν ἐδοξάσθη-
σαν καὶ ἐμεγαλύνθησαν οὐ δι᾽ αὐτῶν ἢ τῶν ἔργων
αὐτῶν ἢ τῆς δικαιοπραγίας ἧς κατειργάσαντο, ἀλλὰ
διὰ τοῦ θελήματος αὐτοῦ. 4. καὶ ἡμεῖς οὖν, διὰ θελή-

56 διὰ πίστεως: om. H

31

And so we should cling to his blessing and discern the paths that lead to it. We should unravel in our minds what has taken place from the beginning. 2. Why was our father Abraham blessed? Was it not because he did what was righteous and true through faith?[72] 3. Isaac gladly allowed himself to be brought forward as a sacrifice, confident in the knowledge of what was about to happen.[73] 4. Jacob departed with humility from his land on account of his brother and went to Laban to serve as a slave; and the twelve scepters of Israel were given to him.[74]

32

Whoever will honestly consider each of these matters will recognize the greatness of the gifts given by God. 2. For from Jacob came the priests and all the Levites who minister at the altar of God. From him came the Lord Jesus according to the flesh. From him came the kings, rulers, and leaders in the line of Judah. And his other scepters enjoyed no small glory either, since God had promised, "Your offspring will be like the stars of heaven."[75] 3. All of these, therefore, were glorified and exalted not through themselves or their deeds or the upright actions they did, but through his own will. 4. So too we who have been called

[72] Gen 15:6.   [73] Gen 22.
[74] Gen 28ff.   [75] Cf. Gen 15:5; 22:17; 26:4.

---

[57] αὐτοῦ L S C: αὐτῶν A H
[58] δόξῃ: τάξει H

ματος αὐτοῦ ἐν Χριστῷ Ἰησοῦ κληθέντες, οὐ δι᾽
ἑαυτῶν δικαιούμεθα—οὐδὲ διὰ τῆς ἡμετέρας σοφίας ἢ
συνέσεως ἢ εὐσεβείας ἢ ἔργων ὧν κατειργασάμεθα ἐν
ὁσιότητι καρδίας—ἀλλὰ διὰ τῆς πίστεως, δι᾽ ἧς πάντας τοὺς ἀπ᾽ αἰῶνος ὁ παντοκράτωρ θεὸς ἐδικαίωσεν·
ᾧ ἔστω ἡ δόξα εἰς τοὺς αἰῶνας τῶν αἰώνων. ἀμήν.

33

Τί οὖν ποιήσωμεν, ἀδελφοί; ἀργήσωμεν ἀπὸ τῆς ἀγα-
θοποιΐας καὶ ἐγκαταλίπωμεν τὴν ἀγάπην; μηθαμῶς
τοῦτο ἐάσαι ὁ δεσπότης ἐφ᾽ ἡμῖν γε γενηθῆναι, ἀλλὰ
σπεύσωμεν μετὰ ἐκτενείας καὶ προθυμίας πᾶν ἔργον
ἀγαθὸν ἐπιτελεῖν. 2. αὐτὸς γὰρ ὁ δημιουργὸς καὶ
δεσπότης τῶν ἁπάντων ἐπὶ τοῖς ἔργοις αὐτοῦ ἀγαλ-
λιᾶται. 3. τῷ γὰρ παμμεγεθεστάτῳ αὐτοῦ κράτει
οὐρανοὺς ἐστήρισεν καὶ τῇ ἀκαταλήπτῳ αὐτοῦ συνέσει διεκόσμησεν αὐτούς· γῆν τε διεχώρισεν ἀπὸ τοῦ
περιέχοντος αὐτὴν ὕδατος καὶ ἥδρασεν ἐπὶ τὸν ἀσφα-
λῆ τοῦ ἰδίου βουλήματος θεμέλιον· τά τε ἐν αὐτῇ ζῷα
φοιτῶντα τῇ ἑαυτοῦ διατάξει ἐκέλευσεν εἶναι· θάλασσαν καὶ τὰ ἐν αὐτῇ ζῷα προετοιμάσας⁵⁹ ἐνέκλεισεν τῇ
ἑαυτοῦ δυνάμει. 4. ἐπὶ πᾶσι τὸ ἐξοχώτατον καὶ παμ-
μέγεθες κατὰ διάνοιαν,⁶⁰ ἄνθρωπον, ταῖς ἱεραῖς καὶ
ἀμώμοις χερσὶν ἔπλασεν, τῆς ἑαυτοῦ εἰκόνος χαρακτῆρα. 5. οὕτως γάρ φησιν ὁ θεός· ποιήσωμεν ἄνθρωπον κατ᾽ εἰκόνα καὶ καθ᾽ ὁμοίωσιν ἡμετέραν. καὶ
ἐποίησεν ὁ θεὸς τὸν ἄνθρωπον, ἄρσεν καὶ θῆλυ ἐποίη-

through his will in Christ Jesus are made upright not through ourselves—through our own wisdom or understanding or piety or the deeds we have done with a devout heart—but through faith, through which the all-powerful God has made all these people upright, from the beginning of the ages. To him be the glory forever and ever. Amen.

33

What then shall we do, brothers? Shall we grow idle and not do what is good? Shall we abandon our acts of love? May the Master never let this happen to us! Instead, we should hasten with fervor and zeal to complete every good work. 2. For the Creator and Master of all things rejoices in his works. 3. For he established the heavens by his all-superior power, and by his incomprehensible understanding he set them in order. And he separated the earth from the water that surrounded it, and established it upon the firm foundation of his own will. By his own decree he commanded the living creatures that roam about on it to come into being. Having prepared in advance the sea and all the living beings in it, he then enclosed them by his own power. 4. And with his holy and perfect hands he formed the one who was preeminent and superior in intelligence to all, the human, stamped with his own image. 5. For as God says, "Let us make a human according to our own image and likeness. And God made the human; male and

---

59 προετοιμάσας H L S C: προδημι[ουργή]σας A
60 κατὰ διάνοιαν A H: om. L S C

σεν αὐτούς. 6. ταῦτα οὖν πάντα τελειώσας ἐπήνεσεν
αὐτὰ καὶ ηὐλόγησεν καὶ εἶπεν· αὐξάνεσθε καὶ πλη-
θύνεσθε. 7. ἴδωμεν, ὅτι ἐν ἔργοις ἀγαθοῖς πάντες
ἐκοσμήθησαν οἱ δίκαιοι, καὶ αὐτὸς δὲ ὁ κύριος ἔργοις
ἀγαθοῖς ἑαυτὸν κοσμήσας ἐχάρη. 8. ἔχοντες οὖν τοῦτον τὸν ὑπογραμμὸν ἀόκνως προσέλθωμεν τῷ θελήματι αὐτοῦ· ἐξ ὅλης τῆς ἰσχύος ἡμῶν ἐργασώμεθα
ἔργον δικαιοσύνης.

34

Ὁ ἀγαθὸς ἐργάτης μετὰ παρρησίας λαμβάνει τὸν
ἄρτον τοῦ ἔργου αὐτοῦ, ὁ νωθρὸς καὶ παρειμένος οὐκ
ἀντοφθαλμεῖ τῷ ἐργοπαρέκτῃ αὐτοῦ. 2. δέον οὖν ἐστὶν
προθύμους ἡμᾶς εἶναι εἰς ἀγαθοποιΐαν· ἐξ αὐτοῦ γάρ
ἐστιν τὰ πάντα. 3. προλέγει γὰρ ἡμῖν· ἰδοὺ ὁ κύριος,
καὶ ὁ μισθὸς αὐτοῦ πρὸ προσώπου αὐτοῦ, ἀποδοῦναι
ἑκάστῳ κατὰ τὸ ἔργον αὐτοῦ. 4. προτρέπεται οὖν ἡμᾶς
πιστεύοντας[61] ἐξ ὅλης τῆς καρδίας ἐπ᾽ αὐτῷ, μὴ
ἀργοὺς μηδὲ παρειμένους εἶναι ἐπὶ πᾶν ἔργον ἀγαθόν.
5. τὸ καύχημα ἡμῶν καὶ ἡ παρρησία ἔστω ἐν αὐτῷ·
ὑποτασσώμεθα τῷ θελήματι αὐτοῦ· κατανοήσωμεν τὸ
πᾶν πλῆθος τῶν ἀγγέλων αὐτοῦ, πῶς τῷ θελήματι
αὐτοῦ λειτουργοῦσιν παρεστῶτες. 6.[62] λέγει γὰρ ἡ
γραφή· μύριαι μυριάδες παρειστήκεισαν αὐτῷ, καὶ
χίλιαι χιλιάδες ἐλειτούργουν αὐτῷ, καὶ ἐκέκραγον·
ἅγιος, ἅγιος, ἅγιος κύριος σαβαώθ, πλήρης πᾶσα ἡ

female he made them."[76] 6. When he had finished all these things, he praised and blessed them, and said "Increase and become numerous."[77] 7. We should realize that all those who are upright have been adorned with good works, and even the Lord himself, when he adorned himself with good works, rejoiced. 8. With such a model before us, we should come to do his will without delay; with all our strength we should engage in righteous work.

34

The good worker receives bread for his toil with forthright confidence; the one who is lazy and slovenly does not look his employer in the eye. 2. And so we must be eager to do what is good. For all things come from him. 3. For he tells us in advance, "Behold the Lord! And the wage he offers is before him, to bestow on each according to his work."[78] 4. Thus he urges us who believe in him with our entire heart not to be idle or slovenly in every good work. 5. Our boast and forthright confidence should be in him. We should be submissive to his will. We should consider how the entire multitude of his angels stands beside him, administering his will. 6. For the Scripture says, "Myriads upon myriads stood before him, and thousands upon thousands were ministering to him; and they cried out, 'Holy, holy, holy, Lord Sabaoth, all of creation is full of his

76 Gen 1:26–27.   77 Gen 1:28.
78 Cf. Rev 22:12; Isa 40:10.

---

61 πιστεύοντας: om. A
62 c. 34.6–42.2 om. C

κτίσις[63] τῆς δόξης αὐτοῦ. 7. καὶ ἡμεῖς οὖν ἐν ὁμονοίᾳ
ἐπὶ τὸ αὐτὸ συναχθέντες τῇ συνειδήσει, ὡς ἐξ ἑνὸς
στόματος βοήσωμεν πρὸς αὐτὸν ἐκτενῶς εἰς τὸ
μετόχους ἡμᾶς γενέσθαι τῶν μεγάλων καὶ ἐνδόξων
ἐπαγγελιῶν αὐτοῦ. 8. λέγει γάρ· ὀφθαλμὸς[64] οὐκ εἶδεν
καὶ οὖς οὐκ ἤκουσεν καὶ ἐπὶ καρδίαν ἀνθρώπου οὐκ
ἀνέβη, ὅσα ἡτοίμασεν κύριος[65] τοῖς ὑπομένουσιν[66]
αὐτόν.

35

Ὡς μακάρια καὶ θαυμαστὰ τὰ δῶρα τοῦ θεοῦ, ἀγαπη-
τοί· 2. ζωὴ ἐν ἀθανασίᾳ, λαμπρότης ἐν δικαιοσύνῃ,
ἀλήθεια ἐν παρρησίᾳ, πίστις ἐν πεποιθήσει, ἐγ-
κράτεια ἐν ἁγιασμῷ· καὶ ταῦτα ὑπέπιπτεν πάντα ὑπὸ
τὴν διάνοιαν ἡμῶν. 3. τίνα οὖν ἄρα ἐστὶν τὰ ἑτοι-
μαζόμενα τοῖς ὑπομένουσιν; ὁ δημιουργὸς καὶ πατὴρ
τῶν αἰώνων ὁ πανάγιος αὐτὸς γινώσκει τὴν ποσότητα
καὶ τὴν καλλονὴν αὐτῶν. 4. ἡμεῖς οὖν ἀγωνισώμεθα
εὑρεθῆναι ἐν τῷ ἀριθμῷ τῶν ὑπομενόντων,[67] ὅπως
μεταλάβωμεν τῶν ἐπηγγελμένων δωρεῶν. 5. πῶς δὲ
ἔσται τοῦτο, ἀγαπητοί; ἐὰν ἐστηριγμένη ᾖ ἡ διάνοια
ἡμῶν πιστῶς[68] πρὸς τὸν θεόν, ἐὰν ἐκζητῶμεν τὰ εὐάρεστα καὶ εὐπρόσδεκτα αὐτῷ, ἐὰν ἐπιτελέσωμεν τὰ
ἀνήκοντα τῇ ἀμώμῳ βουλήσει αὐτοῦ καὶ ἀκολου-
θήσωμεν τῇ ὁδῷ τῆς ἀληθείας, ἀπορρίψαντες ἀφ᾽
ἑαυτῶν πᾶσαν ἀδικίαν καὶ ἀνομίαν,[69] πλεονεξίαν,
ἔρεις, κακοηθείας τε καὶ δόλους, ψιθυρισμούς τε καὶ

glory.'"[79] 7. So too we should gather together in harmony, conscientiously, as we fervently cry out to him with one voice, that we may have a share in his great and glorious promises. 8. For he says, "No eye has seen nor ear heard, nor has it entered into the human heart, what the Lord has prepared for those who await him."[80]

35

Loved ones, how blessed and marvelous are the gifts of God: 2. life in immortality, splendor in righteousness, truth in boldness, faith in confidence, self-restraint in holiness; and all these things are subject to our understanding. 3. What therefore has been prepared for those who wait? The Maker and Father of the ages, the All Holy One, he himself knows both their magnitude and their beauty. 4. We should therefore strive to be counted among those who wait, so that we may receive the gifts he has promised. 5. But how will this be, loved ones? When our understanding is faithfully fixed on God, when we seek after what is pleasing and acceptable to him, when we accomplish what accords with his perfect will and follow in the path of truth, casting from ourselves all injustice and lawlessness, greed, strife, malice and deceit, gossip and slander, hatred of

---

[79] Dan 7:10; Isa 6:3.   [80] 1 Cor 2:9.

---

[63] κτίσις: γῆ H   [64] ὀφθαλμὸς A: ἃ ὀφθ. H L S Clem Al
[65] κύριος H L S: om. A
[66] ὑπομένουσιν A L: ἀγαπῶσιν H S   [67] ὑπομενόντων
H L S: add αυτον A   [68] πιστῶς H L: πίστεως A: διὰ πίστεως S   [69] ἀνομίαν A: πονηρίαν H L S

καταλαλιάς, θεοστυγίαν, ὑπερηφανίαν τε καὶ ἀλαζονείαν, κενοδοξίαν τε καὶ ἀφιλοξενίαν. 6. ταῦτα γὰρ οἱ
πράσσοντες στυγητοὶ τῷ θεῷ ὑπάρχουσιν· οὐ μόνον
δὲ οἱ πράσσοντες αὐτά, ἀλλὰ καὶ οἱ συνευδοκοῦντες
αὐτοῖς. 7. λέγει γὰρ ἡ γραφή· τῷ δὲ ἁμαρτωλῷ εἶπεν ὁ
θεός· ἱνατί σὺ διηγῇ τὰ δικαιώματά μου, καὶ ἀνα-
λαμβάνεις τὴν διαθήκην μου ἐπὶ στόματός σου; 8.[70]
σὺ δὲ ἐμίσησας παιδείαν καὶ ἐξέβαλες τοὺς λόγους
μου εἰς τὰ ὀπίσω. εἰ ἐθεώρεις κλέπτην, συνέτρεχες
αὐτῷ, καὶ μετὰ μοιχῶν τὴν μερίδα σου ἐτίθεις. τὸ
στόμα σου ἐπλεόνασεν κακίαν, καὶ ἡ γλῶσσά σου
περιέπλεκεν δολιότητα. καθήμενος κατὰ τοῦ ἀδελφοῦ
σου κατελάλεις, καὶ κατὰ τοῦ υἱοῦ τῆς μητρός σου
ἐτίθεις σκάνδαλον. 9. ταῦτα ἐποίησας, καὶ ἐσίγησα·
ὑπέλαβες, ἄνομε, ὅτι ἔσομαί σοι ὅμοιος. 10. ἐλέγξω
σε καὶ παραστήσω σε κατὰ πρόσωπόν σου. 11. σύνετε
δὴ ταῦτα, οἱ ἐπιλανθανόμενοι τοῦ θεοῦ, μήποτε ἁρ-
πάσῃ ὡς λέων, καὶ μὴ ᾖ ὁ ῥυόμενος. 12. θυσία
αἰνέσεως δοξάσει με, καὶ ἐκεῖ ὁδός, ἣν δείξω αὐτῷ τὸ
σωτήριον τοῦ θεοῦ.

36

Αὕτη ἡ ὁδός, ἀγαπητοί, ἐν ᾗ εὕρομεν τὸ σωτήριον
ἡμῶν, Ἰησοῦν Χριστόν, τὸν ἀρχιερέα τῶν προσφορῶν
ἡμῶν, τὸν προστάτην καὶ βοηθὸν τῆς ἀσθενείας
ἡμῶν. 2. διὰ τούτου ἀτενίζομεν εἰς τὰ ὕψη τῶν
οὐρανῶν, διὰ τούτου ἐνοπτριζόμεθα τὴν ἄμωμον καὶ

God, haughtiness and arrogance, vanity and inhospitality. 6. For those who do these things are hateful to God—and not only those who do them, but also those who approve of them. 7. For the Scripture says, "God says to the sinner, 'Why do you declare my righteous deeds and receive my covenant in your mouth? 8. For you despised discipline and tossed my words aside. When you saw a robber, you ran along with him; and you joined forces with adulterers. Your mouth multiplied evil and your tongue wove threads of deceit. You sat and spoke slanders against your brother and caused the son of your mother to stumble. 9. You did these things and I was silent. You have supposed, oh lawless one, that I will be like you. 10. I will convict you and set you up against your own face. 11. So, understand these things, you who forget about God—lest like a lion he seize you, and there be no one to deliver you. 12. A sacrifice of praise will glorify me; there is the path I will show him as the salvation of God.'"[81]

36

This is the path, loved ones, in which we have found our salvation—Jesus Christ, the high priest of our offerings, the benefactor who helps us in our weaknesses.[82] 2. Through this one we gaze into the heights of the heavens; through this one we see the reflection of his perfect

[81] Ps 50:16–23.
[82] Cf. Heb 3:1; 2:18.

---

[70] vv. 8–11 om. H

ὑπερτάτην ὄψιν αὐτοῦ, διὰ τούτου ἠνεῴχθησαν ἡμῶν
οἱ ὀφθαλμοὶ τῆς καρδίας, διὰ τούτου ἡ ἀσύνετος καὶ
ἐσκοτωμένη διάνοια ἡμῶν ἀναθάλλει εἰς τὸ[71] φῶς, διὰ
τούτου ἠθέλησεν ὁ δεσπότης τῆς ἀθανάτου γνώσεως
ἡμᾶς γεύσασθαι, ὃς ὢν ἀπαύγασμα τῆς μεγαλωσύνης αὐτοῦ, τοσούτῳ μείζων ἐστὶν ἀγγέλων, ὅσῳ
διαφορώτερον ὄνομα κεκληρονόμηκεν. 3. γέγραπται
γὰρ οὕτως· ὁ ποιῶν τοὺς ἀγγέλους αὐτοῦ πνεύματα
καὶ τοὺς λειτουργοὺς αὐτοῦ πυρὸς φλόγα. 4. ἐπὶ δὲ τῷ
υἱῷ αὐτοῦ οὕτως εἶπεν ὁ δεσπότης· υἱός μου εἶ σύ, ἐγὼ
σήμερον γεγέννηκά σε· αἴτησαι παρ᾽ ἐμοῦ, καὶ δώσω
σοι ἔθνη τὴν κληρονομίαν σου καὶ τὴν κατάσχεσίν
σου τὰ πέρατα τῆς γῆς. 5. καὶ πάλιν λέγει πρὸς
αὐτόν· κάθου ἐκ δεξιῶν μου, ἕως ἂν θῶ τοὺς ἐχθρούς
σου ὑποπόδιον τῶν ποδῶν σου. 6. τίνες οὖν οἱ ἐχθροί;
οἱ φαῦλοι καὶ ἀντιτασσόμενοι τῷ θελήματι αὐτοῦ.

37

Στρατευσώμεθα οὖν, ἄνδρες ἀδελφοί, μετὰ πάσης
ἐκτενείας ἐν τοῖς ἀμώμοις προστάγμασιν αὐτοῦ.
2. κατανοήσωμεν τοὺς στρατευομένους τοῖς ἡγουμένοις ἡμῶν, πῶς εὐτάκτως, πῶς ἐκτικῶς,[72] πῶς
ὑποτεταγμένως ἐπιτελοῦσιν τὰ διατασσόμενα. 3. οὐ
πάντες εἰσὶν ἔπαρχοι οὐδὲ χιλίαρχοι οὐδὲ ἑκατόνταρ-
χοι οὐδὲ πεντηκόνταρχοι οὐδὲ τὸ καθεξῆς, ἀλλ᾽
ἕκαστος ἐν τῷ ἰδίῳ τάγματι τὰ ἐπιτασσόμενα ὑπὸ τοῦ
βασιλέως καὶ τῶν ἡγουμένων ἐπιτελεῖ. 4. οἱ μεγάλοι

and superior countenance; through this one the eyes of our hearts have been opened; through this one our foolish and darkened understanding springs up into the light; through this one the Master has wished us to taste the knowledge of immortality. He is the radiance of his magnificence, as superior to the angels as he has inherited a more excellent name.[83] 3. For so it is written, "The one who makes his angels spirits and his ministers a tongue of fire."[84] 4. But the Master says this about his Son: "You are my Son, today I have given you birth. Ask from me, and I will give you the nations as your inheritance, and the ends of the earth as your possession."[85] 5. And again he says to him, "Sit at my right hand, until I make your enemies a footstool for your feet."[86] 6. Who then are the enemies? Those who are evil and oppose his will.

37

And so, brothers, with all eagerness let us do battle as soldiers under his blameless commands. 2. Consider those who soldier under our own leaders, how they accomplish what is demanded of them with such order, habit, and submission. 3. For not all are commanders-in-chief or commanders over a thousand troops, or a hundred, or fifty, and so on. But each one, according to his own rank, accomplishes what is ordered by the king and the leaders.

---

[83] Cf. Heb. 1:3, 4.   [84] Heb 1:7; Ps 104:4.
[85] Ps 2:7–8; Heb 1:5.   [86] Ps 110:1; Heb 1:13.

---

[71] τὸ L S Clem Al: add θαυμαστὸν H: add θαυμαστὸν αὐτοῦ A   [72] ἐκτικῶς H: εἰκτικῶς A: *leniter* S: om. L

δίχα τῶν μικρῶν οὐ δύνανται εἶναι οὔτε οἱ μικροὶ δίχα
τῶν μεγάλων· σύγκρασίς τίς ἐστιν ἐν πᾶσιν, καὶ ἐν
τούτοις χρῆσις. 5. λάβωμεν τὸ σῶμα ἡμῶν· ἡ κεφαλὴ
δίχα τῶν ποδῶν οὐδέν ἐστιν, οὕτως οὐδὲ οἱ πόδες δίχα
τῆς κεφαλῆς· τὰ δὲ ἐλάχιστα μέλη τοῦ σώματος ἡμῶν
ἀναγκαῖα καὶ εὔχρηστά εἰσιν ὅλῳ τῷ σώματι· ἀλλὰ
πάντα συνπνεῖ καὶ ὑποταγῇ μιᾷ χρῆται εἰς τὸ
σώζεσθαι ὅλον τὸ σῶμα.

38

Σωζέσθω οὖν ἡμῶν ὅλον τὸ σῶμα ἐν Χριστῷ Ἰησοῦ,[73]
καὶ ὑποτασσέσθω ἕκαστος τῷ πλησίον αὐτοῦ, καθὼς
ἐτέθη ἐν τῷ χαρίσματι αὐτοῦ. 2. ὁ ἰσχυρὸς τημελείτω[74] τὸν ἀσθενῆ, ὁ δὲ ἀσθενὴς ἐντρεπέσθω τὸν
ἰσχυρόν· ὁ πλούσιος ἐπιχορηγείτω τῷ πτωχῷ, ὁ δὲ
πτωχὸς εὐχαριστείτω τῷ θεῷ, ὅτι ἔδωκεν αὐτῷ, δι' οὗ
ἀναπληρωθῇ αὐτοῦ τὸ ὑστέρημα· ὁ σοφὸς ἐν-
δεικνύσθω τὴν σοφίαν αὐτοῦ μὴ ἐν λόγοις, ἀλλ' ἐν
ἔργοις ἀγαθοῖς· ὁ ταπεινοφρονῶν μὴ ἑαυτῷ μαρτυ-
ρείτω, ἀλλ' ἐάτω ὑφ' ἑτέρου ἑαυτὸν μαρτυρεῖσθαι· ὁ
ἁγνὸς ἐν τῇ σαρκὶ μὴ ἀλαζονευέσθω, γινώσκων, ὅτι
ἕτερός ἐστιν ὁ ἐπιχορηγῶν αὐτῷ τὴν ἐγκράτειαν.
3. ἀναλογισώμεθα οὖν, ἀδελφοί, ἐκ ποίας ὕλης
ἐγενήθημεν, ποῖοι καὶ τίνες εἰσήλθαμεν εἰς τὸν
κόσμον, ἐκ ποίου τάφου καὶ σκότους ὁ πλάσας ἡμᾶς

[73] Ἰησοῦ A L: om. H S

4. Those who are great cannot survive without the lowly nor the lowly without the great. There is a certain commixture in all things, and this proves to be useful for them. 5. Take our own body. The head is nothing without the feet, just as the feet are nothing without the head. And our body's most insignificant parts are necessary and useful for the whole. But all parts work together in subjection to a single order, to keep the whole body healthy *[Or: safe]*.[87]

38

And so, let our whole body be healthy *[Or: be saved]* in Christ Jesus, and let each person be subject to his neighbor, in accordance with the gracious gift he has received. 2. Let the one who is strong take care of the weak; and let the weak show due respect to the strong. Let the wealthy provide what is needed to the poor, and let the poor offer thanks to God, since he has given him someone to supply his need. Let the one who is wise show forth wisdom not through words but through good deeds. Let the one who is humble not testify to himself but permit another to testify on his behalf. Let the one who is pure in the flesh not act arrogantly, knowing that another has provided him with his self-restraint. 3. Let us carefully consider, brothers, the material from which we have been made, and who and what sort of people we were when we entered into the world; and let us consider from what kind of tomb and

[87] 1 Cor 12:21.

74 τημελείτω H L S: μητμμελειτω A

καὶ δημιουργήσας εἰσήγαγεν εἰς τὸν κόσμον αὐτοῦ, προετοιμάσας τὰς εὐεργεσίας αὐτοῦ, πρὶν ἡμᾶς γεννηθῆναι. 4. ταῦτα οὖν πάντα ἐξ αὐτοῦ, ἔχοντες ὀφείλομεν κατὰ πάντα εὐχαριστεῖν αὐτῷ· ᾧ ἡ δόξα εἰς τοὺς αἰῶνας τῶν αἰώνων. ἀμήν.

39

Ἄφρονες καὶ ἀσύνετοι καὶ μωροὶ καὶ ἀπαίδευτοι χλευάζουσιν ἡμᾶς καὶ μυκτηρίζουσιν, ἑαυτοὺς βουλόμενοι ἐπαίρεσθαι ταῖς διανοίαις αὐτῶν. 2. τί γὰρ δύναται θνητός; ἢ τίς ἰσχὺς γηγενοῦς; 3. γέγραπται γάρ· οὐκ ἦν μορφὴ πρὸ ὀφθαλμῶν μου, ἀλλ' ἢ αὔραν καὶ φωνὴν ἤκουον· 4. τί γάρ; μὴ καθαρὸς ἔσται βροτὸς ἔναντι κυρίου; ἢ ἀπὸ τῶν ἔργων αὐτοῦ ἄμεμπτος ἀνήρ, εἰ κατὰ παίδων αὐτοῦ οὐ πιστεύει, κατὰ δὲ ἀγγέλων αὐτοῦ σκολιόν τι ἐπενόησεν; 5. οὐρανὸς δὲ οὐ καθαρὸς ἐνώπιον αὐτοῦ· ἔα δέ, οἱ κατοικοῦντες οἰκίας πηλίνας, ἐξ ὧν καὶ αὐτοὶ ἐκ τοῦ αὐτοῦ πηλοῦ ἐσμέν. ἔπαισεν αὐτοὺς σητὸς τρόπον, καὶ ἀπὸ πρωΐθεν ἕως ἑσπέρας οὐκ ἔτι εἰσίν· παρὰ τὸ μὴ δύνασθαι αὐτοὺς ἑαυτοῖς βοηθῆσαι ἀπώλοντο. 6. ἐνεφύσησεν αὐτοῖς, καὶ ἐτελεύτησαν παρὰ τὸ μὴ ἔχειν αὐτοὺς σοφίαν. 7. ἐπικάλεσαι δέ, εἴ τίς σοι ὑπακούσεται, ἢ εἴ τινα ἁγίων ἀγγέλων ὄψῃ· καὶ γὰρ ἄφρονα ἀναιρεῖ ὀργή, πεπλανημένον δὲ θανατοῖ ζῆλος. 8. ἐγὼ δὲ ἑώρακα ἄφρονας ῥίζας βάλοντας, ἀλλ' εὐθέως ἐβρώθη αὐτῶν ἡ δίαιτα. 9. πόρρω γένοιν-

darkness we were led into the world by the one who fashioned and made us, after he prepared his kindly acts in advance, even before we were born. 4. Since we have all these things from him, we ought to thank him in every way. To him be the glory forever and ever. Amen.

39

Those who are ignorant, unlearned, foolish, and uneducated mock and ridicule us, wishing to vaunt themselves in their own thoughts. 2. But what can a mortal accomplish? Or what power belongs to the one born of earth? 3. For it is written, "There was no form before my eyes, but I heard a puff of air and the sound of a voice. 4. What then? Can a mortal be pure before the Lord? Or can a man be blameless in what he does, when he does not trust his own servants and detects something crooked in his own messengers? 5. Not even heaven is pure before him. But see! We who inhabit clay houses are ourselves made from the same clay. He smashed them like a moth, and from dawn to dusk they are no more. They perished, unable to come to their own assistance. 6. He breathed upon them and they died for want of wisdom. 7. But call out; see if anyone listens or if you observe any of the holy angels. For wrath destroys the ignorant and zeal kills the one who has been deceived. 8. I have seen the ignorant casting forth their roots, but their sustenance was immediately consumed.

το οἱ υἱοὶ αὐτῶν ἀπὸ σωτηρίας· κολαβρισθείησαν ἐπὶ
θύραις ἡσσόνων, καὶ οὐκ ἔσται ὁ ἐξαιρούμενος. ἃ γὰρ
ἐκείνοις ἡτοίμασται, δίκαιοι ἔδονται· αὐτοὶ δὲ ἐκ
κακῶν οὐκ ἐξαίρετοι ἔσονται.

40

Προδήλων οὖν ἡμῖν ὄντων τούτων, καὶ ἐγκεκυφότες
εἰς τὰ βάθη τῆς θείας γνώσεως, πάντα τάξει ποιεῖν
ὀφείλομεν, ὅσα ὁ δεσπότης ἐπιτελεῖν ἐκέλευσεν κατὰ
καιροὺς τεταγμένους· 2. τάς τε προσφορὰς καὶ λειτουργίας ἐπιτελεῖσθαι, καὶ[75] οὐκ εἰκῇ ἢ ἀτάκτως
ἐκέλευσεν γίνεσθαι, ἀλλ᾽ ὡρισμένοις καιροῖς καὶ
ὥραις· 3. ποῦ τε καὶ διὰ τίνων ἐπιτελεῖσθαι θέλει,
αὐτὸς ὥρισεν τῇ ὑπερτάτῃ αὐτοῦ βουλήσει, ἵν᾽ ὁσίως
πάντα γινόμενα ἐν εὐδοκήσει εὐπρόσδεκτα εἴη τῷ
θελήματι αὐτοῦ. 4. οἱ οὖν τοῖς προστεταγμένοις καιροῖς ποιοῦντες τὰς προσφορὰς αὐτῶν εὐπρόσδεκτοί τε
καὶ μακάριοι· τοῖς γὰρ νομίμοις τοῦ δεσπότου ἀκο-
λουθοῦντες οὐ διαμαρτάνουσιν. 5. τῷ γὰρ ἀρχιερεῖ
ἴδιαι λειτουργίαι δεδομέναι εἰσί, καὶ τοῖς ἱερεῦσιν
ἴδιος ὁ τόπος προστέτακται, καὶ λευΐταις ἴδιαι δια-
κονίαι ἐπίκεινται· ὁ λαϊκὸς ἄνθρωπος τοῖς λαϊκοῖς
προστάγμασιν δέδεται.[76]

[75] ἐπιτελεῖσθαι καὶ A H: om. L S
[76] δέδεται A: δέδοται H L S

9. May their children be far removed from safety; may they be derided before the doors of their inferiors, with no one there to deliver them. For the food prepared for them will be devoured by the upright, and they will not be delivered from those who are evil."[88]

40

Since these matters have been clarified for us in advance and we have gazed into the depths of divine knowledge, we should do everything the Master has commanded us to perform in an orderly way and at appointed times. 2. He commanded that the sacrificial offerings and liturgical rites be performed not in a random or haphazard way, but according to set times and hours. 3. In his superior plan he set forth both where and through whom he wished them to be performed, so that everything done in a holy way and according to his good pleasure might be acceptable to his will. 4. Thus, those who make their sacrificial offerings at the arranged times are acceptable and blessed. And since they follow the ordinances of the Master, they commit no sin. 5. For special liturgical rites have been assigned to the high priest, and a special place has been designated for the regular priests, and special ministries are established for the Levites. The lay person is assigned to matters enjoined on the laity.

[88] Job 4:16–18; 15:15; 4:19–5:5.

41

Ἕκαστος ἡμῶν, ἀδελφοί, ἐν τῷ ἰδίῳ τάγματι εὐαρεστείτω⁷⁷ τῷ θεῷ ἐν ἀγαθῇ συνειδήσει ὑπάρχων, μὴ παρεκβαίνων τὸν ὡρισμένον τῆς λειτουργίας αὐτοῦ κανόνα, ἐν σεμνότητι. 2. οὐ πανταχοῦ, ἀδελφοί, προσφέρονται θυσίαι ἐνδελεχισμοῦ ἢ εὐχῶν ἢ περὶ ἁμαρτίας καὶ πλημμελείας, ἀλλ' ἢ ἐν Ἰερουσαλὴμ μόνῃ· κἀκεῖ δὲ οὐκ ἐν παντὶ τόπῳ προσφέρεται, ἀλλ' ἔμπροσθεν τοῦ ναοῦ πρὸς τὸ θυσιαστήριον, μωμοσκοπηθὲν τὸ προσφερόμενον διὰ τοῦ ἀρχιερέως καὶ τῶν προειρημένων λειτουργῶν. 3. οἱ οὖν παρὰ τὸ καθῆκον τῆς βουλήσεως αὐτοῦ ποιοῦντές τι θάνατον τὸ πρόστιμον ἔχουσιν. 4. ὁρᾶτε, ἀδελφοί· ὅσῳ πλείονος κατηξιώθημεν γνώσεως, τοσούτῳ μᾶλλον ὑποκείμεθα κινδύνῳ.

42

Οἱ ἀπόστολοι ἡμῖν εὐηγγελίσθησαν ἀπὸ τοῦ κυρίου Ἰησοῦ Χριστοῦ, Ἰησοῦς ὁ Χριστὸς ἀπὸ τοῦ θεοῦ ἐξεπέμφθη. 2. ὁ Χριστὸς οὖν ἀπὸ τοῦ θεοῦ καὶ οἱ ἀπόστολοι ἀπὸ τοῦ Χριστοῦ· ἐγένοντο οὖν ἀμφότερα εὐτάκτως ἐκ θελήματος θεοῦ. 3. παραγγελίας οὖν λαβόντες καὶ πληροφορηθέντες διὰ τῆς ἀναστάσεως τοῦ κυρίου ἡμῶν Ἰησοῦ Χριστοῦ καὶ πιστωθέντες ἐν τῷ λόγῳ τοῦ θεοῦ, μετὰ πληροφορίας πνεύματος ἁγίου ἐξῆλθον εὐαγγελιζόμενοι, τὴν βασιλείαν τοῦ θεοῦ μέλ-

41

Brothers, let each of us be pleasing to God by keeping to our special assignments with a good conscience, not violating the established rule of his ministry, acting in reverence. 2. The sacrifices made daily, or for vows, or for sin and transgression are not offered everywhere, brothers, but in Jerusalem alone; and even there a sacrifice is not made in just any place, but before the sanctuary on the altar, after the sacrificial animal has been inspected for blemishes by both the high priest and the ministers mentioned earlier. 3. Thus, those who do anything contrary to his plan bear the penalty of death. 4. You see, brothers, the more knowledge we have been deemed worthy to receive, the more we are subject to danger.

42

The apostles were given the gospel for us by the Lord Jesus Christ, and Jesus Christ was sent forth from God. 2. Thus Christ came from God and the apostles from Christ. Both things happened, then, in an orderly way according to the will of God. 3. When, therefore, the apostles received his commands and were fully convinced through the resurrection of our Lord Jesus Christ and persuaded by the word of God, they went forth proclaiming the good news that the Kingdom of God was about to come, brimming with con-

---

77 εὐαρεστείτω H L S: εὐχαριστείτω A

3. καὶ κλείσας τὴν σκηνὴν ἐσφράγισεν τὰς κλεῖδας ὡσαύτως καὶ τὰς ῥάβδους,[79] 4. καὶ εἶπεν αὐτοῖς· ἄνδρες ἀδελφοί, ἧς ἂν φυλῆς ἡ ῥάβδος βλαστήσῃ, ταύτην ἐκλέλεκται ὁ θεὸς εἰς τὸ ἱερατεύειν καὶ λειτουργεῖν αὐτῷ. 5. πρωΐας δὲ γενομένης συνεκάλεσεν πάντα τὸν Ἰσραήλ, τὰς ἑξακοσίας χιλιάδας τῶν ἀνδρῶν, καὶ ἐπεδείξατο τοῖς φυλάρχοις τὰς σφραγῖδας. καὶ ἤνοιξεν τὴν σκηνὴν τοῦ μαρτυρίου καὶ προεῖλεν τὰς ῥάβδους· καὶ εὑρέθη ἡ ῥάβδος Ἀαρὼν οὐ μόνον βεβλαστηκυῖα, ἀλλὰ καὶ καρπὸν ἔχουσα. 6. τί δοκεῖτε, ἀγαπητοί; οὐ προῄδει Μωϋσῆς τοῦτο μέλλειν ἔσεσθαι; μάλιστα ᾔδει· ἀλλ᾽ ἵνα μὴ ἀκαταστασία γένηται ἐν τῷ Ἰσραήλ, οὕτως ἐποίησεν, εἰς τὸ δοξασθῆναι τὸ ὄνομα τοῦ ἀληθινοῦ καὶ μόνου·[80] ᾧ ἡ δόξα εἰς τοὺς αἰῶνας τῶν αἰώνων. ἀμήν.

44

Καὶ οἱ ἀπόστολοι ἡμῶν ἔγνωσαν διὰ τοῦ κυρίου ἡμῶν Ἰησοῦ Χριστοῦ, ὅτι ἔρις ἔσται ἐπὶ[81] τοῦ ὀνόματος τῆς ἐπισκοπῆς. 2. διὰ ταύτην οὖν τὴν αἰτίαν πρόγνωσιν εἰληφότες τελείαν κατέστησαν τοὺς προειρημένους καὶ μεταξὺ ἐπινομίδα ἔδωκαν,[82] ὅπως, ἐὰν[83] κοιμηθῶσιν, διαδέξωνται ἕτεροι δεδοκιμασμένοι ἄνδρες τὴν λειτουργίαν αὐτῶν. 3. τοὺς οὖν κατασταθέντας ὑπ᾽

[79] ῥάβδους A H L C: θύρας S
[80] μόνου L: add θεοῦ S C: add κυρίου H: def. A C[1]

3. He shut the Tent and sealed the keys just as he had
done with the rods. 4. He said to them, "Brothers, the tribe
whose rod will blossom has been chosen by God to serve
as his priests and ministers." 5. When early morning came
he called together all Israel, some six hundred thousand
men, and showed the tribal leaders the seals. He opened
the Tent of Testimony and brought out the rods. And the
rod of Aaron was found not only to have blossomed, but
even to be bearing fruit. 6. What do you think, loved ones?
That Moses did not know in advance this would happen?
Of course he knew. But he did this so that there might be
no disorderliness in Israel, that the name of the one who is
true and unique might be glorified. To him be the glory
forever and ever. Amen.

44

So too our apostles knew through our Lord Jesus Christ
that strife would arise over the office of the bishop. 2. For
this reason, since they understood perfectly well in advance what would happen, they appointed those we have
already mentioned; and afterwards they added a codicil,[92]
to the effect that if these should die, other approved men
should succeed them in their ministry. 3. Thus we do not

92 Translating the emendation by Hort, which makes sense in
context and in light of the variant readings.

---

81 ἐπὶ A: περὶ H L C (S)
82 ἐπινομίδα ἔδωκεν cj. Hort: ἐπινομὴν ἐδώκασιν A (L):
ἐπιδομὴν ἔδωκαν H: ἐπὶ δοκιμὴν (or -μῃ) ἔδωκαν (S)
83 ἐὰν A L: add τινες H S C

ἐκείνων ἢ μεταξὺ ὑφ' ἑτέρων ἐλλογίμων ἀνδρῶν συν-
ευδοκησάσης τῆς ἐκκλησίας πάσης, καὶ λειτουργήσαντας ἀμέμπτως τῷ ποιμνίῳ τοῦ Χριστοῦ μετὰ
ταπεινοφροσύνης, ἡσύχως καὶ ἀβαναύσως, μεμαρτυρημένους τε πολλοῖς χρόνοις ὑπὸ πάντων, τούτους οὐ
δικαίως νομίζομεν ἀποβάλλεσθαι τῆς λειτουργίας.
4. ἁμαρτία γὰρ οὐ μικρὰ ἡμῖν ἔσται, ἐὰν τοὺς ἀμέμπτως καὶ ὁσίως προσενεγκόντας τὰ δῶρα τῆς ἐπισκοπῆς ἀποβάλωμεν. 5. μακάριοι οἱ προοδοιπορή-
σαντες πρεσβύτεροι, οἵτινες ἔγκαρπον καὶ τελείαν
ἔσχον τὴν ἀνάλυσιν· οὐ γὰρ εὐλαβοῦνται, μή τις
αὐτοὺς μεταστήσῃ ἀπὸ τοῦ ἱδρυμένου αὐτοῖς τόπου.
6. ὁρῶμεν γάρ, ὅτι ἐνίους ὑμεῖς μετηγάγετε καλῶς
πολιτευομένους ἐκ τῆς ἀμέμπτως αὐτοῖς τετιμημένης
λειτουργίας.

45

Φιλόνεικοι ἔστε, ἀδελφοί, καὶ ζηλωταὶ περὶ τῶν ἀνηκόντων εἰς σωτηρίαν. 2. ἐγκεκύφατε εἰς τὰς ἱερὰς
γραφάς, τὰς ἀληθεῖς, τὰς διὰ τοῦ πνεύματος τοῦ
ἁγίου. 3. ἐπίστασθε, ὅτι οὐδὲν ἄδικον οὐδὲ παραπε-
ποιημένον γέγραπται ἐν αὐταῖς. οὐχ εὑρήσετε δικαίους ἀποβεβλημένους ἀπὸ ὁσίων ἀνδρῶν. 4. ἐδιώχθησαν δίκαιοι, ἀλλ' ἀπὸ ἀνόμων· ἐφυλακίσθησαν, ἀλλ'
ὑπὸ ἀνοσίων· ἐλιθάσθησαν ὑπὸ παρανόμων· ἀπεκτάν-
θησαν ἀπὸ τῶν μιαρὸν καὶ ἄδικον ζῆλον ἀνειληφότων.
5. ταῦτα πάσχοντες εὐκλεῶς ἤνεγκαν. 6. τί γὰρ

think it right to remove from the ministry those who were appointed by them or, afterwards, by other reputable men, with the entire church giving its approval. For they have ministered over the flock of Christ blamelessly and with humility, gently and unselfishly, receiving a good witness by all, many times over. 4. Indeed we commit no little sin if we remove from the bishop's office those who offer the gifts in a blameless and holy way. 5. How fortunate are the presbyters who passed on before, who enjoyed a fruitful and perfect departure from this life. For they have no fear that someone will remove them from the place established for them. 6. But we see that you have deposed some from the ministry held blamelessly in honor among them, even though they had been conducting themselves well.

45

You should strive hard, brothers, and be zealous *[Or: You are contentious, brothers, and envious]* in matters that pertain to salvation! 2. You have gazed into the holy and true Scriptures that were given through the Holy Spirit. 3. You realize that there is nothing unjust or counterfeit written in them. There you will not find the upright cast out by men who were holy. 4. The upright were persecuted, but by the lawless. They were imprisoned, but by the unholy. They were stoned by those who transgressed the law and killed by those who embraced vile and unjust envy. 5. And they bore up gloriously while suffering these things. 6. For

εἴπωμεν,[84] ἀδελφοί; Δανιὴλ ὑπὸ τῶν φοβουμένων τὸν
θεὸν ἐβλήθη εἰς λάκκον λεόντων; 7. ἢ Ἀνανίας καὶ
Ἀζαρίας καὶ Μισαὴλ ὑπὸ τῶν θρησκευόντων τὴν
μεγαλοπρεπῆ καὶ ἔνδοξον θρησκείαν τοῦ ὑψίστου
κατείρχθησαν εἰς κάμινον πυρός; μηθαμῶς τοῦτο
γένοιτο. τίνες οὖν οἱ ταῦτα δράσαντες; οἱ στυγητοὶ καὶ
πάσης κακίας πλήρεις εἰς τοσοῦτο ἐξήρισαν θυμοῦ,
ὥστε τοὺς ἐν ὁσίᾳ καὶ ἀμώμῳ προθέσει δουλεύοντας
τῷ θεῷ εἰς αἰκίαν περιβαλεῖν, μὴ εἰδότες, ὅτι ὁ
ὕψιστος ὑπέρμαχος καὶ ὑπερασπιστής ἐστιν τῶν ἐν
καθαρᾷ συνειδήσει λατρευόντων τῷ παναρέτῳ ὀνόματι αὐτοῦ· ᾧ ἡ δόξα εἰς τοὺς αἰῶνας τῶν αἰώνων.
ἀμήν. 8. οἱ δὲ ὑπομένοντες ἐν πεποιθήσει δόξαν καὶ
τιμὴν ἐκληρονόμησαν, ἐπήρθησάν τε καὶ ἔγγραφοι
ἐγένοντο ἀπὸ τοῦ θεοῦ ἐν τῷ μνημοσύνῳ αὐτῶν[85] εἰς
τοὺς αἰῶνας τῶν αἰώνων. ἀμήν.

46

Τοιούτοις οὖν ὑποδείγμασιν κολληθῆναι καὶ ἡμᾶς δεῖ,
ἀδελφοί. 2. γέγραπται γάρ· κολλᾶσθε τοῖς ἁγίοις, ὅτι
οἱ κολλώμενοι αὐτοῖς ἁγιασθήσονται. 3. καὶ πάλιν ἐν
ἑτέρῳ τόπῳ λέγει· μετὰ ἀνδρὸς ἀθώου ἀθῷος ἔσῃ καὶ
μετὰ ἐκλεκτοῦ ἐκλεκτὸς ἔσῃ, καὶ μετὰ στρεβλοῦ
διαστρέψεις. 4. κολληθῶμεν οὖν τοῖς ἀθῴοις καὶ

---

[84] εἴπωμεν cj. Junius: εἴπομεν A: εἴποιμεν H (C?): *dicam* S:
dicimus L

what shall we say, brothers? Was Daniel cast into the lions' den by those who feared God?[93] 7. Or were Ananias, Azarias, and Misael shut up in the fiery furnace by those who participated in the magnificent and glorious worship of the Most High?[94] This could never be! Who then did these things? Those who were hateful and full of every evil were roused to such a pitch of anger that they tortured those who served God with holy and blameless resolve. But they did not know that the Most High is the champion and protector of those who minister to his all-virtuous name with a pure conscience. To him be the glory forever and ever. Amen. 8. But those who endured in confidence inherited glory and honor; and they were exalted and inscribed by God in their own memorial forever and ever. Amen.

46

And so, we too must cling to these examples, brothers. 2. For it is written, "Cling to those who are holy; for those who cling to them will themselves be made holy."[95] 3. And again in another place it says, "With an innocent man, you too will be innocent and with one who is chosen, you will be chosen. But with one who is corrupt, you will cause corruption."[96] 4. Therefore we should cling to those who are

[93] Dan 6:16.
[94] Dan 3:19ff.
[95] Source unknown.
[96] Ps 18:25–26.

---

[85] αὐτῶν A: αὐτοῦ H S C

ἀνδρὶ δεδοκιμασμένῳ παρ᾽ αὐτοῖς. 5. νυνὶ δὲ κατα-
νοήσατε, τίνες ὑμᾶς διέστρεψαν καὶ τὸ σεμνὸν τῆς
περιβοήτου φιλαδελφίας ὑμῶν ἐμείωσαν. 6. αἰσχρά,
ἀγαπητοί, καὶ λίαν αἰσχρὰ καὶ ἀνάξια τῆς ἐν Χριστῷ
ἀγωγῆς[87] ἀκούεσθαι, τὴν βεβαιοτάτην καὶ ἀρχαίαν
Κορινθίων ἐκκλησίαν δι᾽ ἓν ἢ δύο πρόσωπα στασιά-
ζειν πρὸς τοὺς πρεσβυτέρους. 7. καὶ αὕτη ἡ ἀκοὴ οὐ
μόνον εἰς ἡμᾶς ἐχώρησεν, ἀλλὰ καὶ εἰς τοὺς ἑτεροκ-
λινεῖς ὑπάρχοντας ἀφ᾽ ἡμῶν, ὥστε καὶ βλασφημίας
ἐπιφέρεσθαι τῷ ὀνόματι κυρίου διὰ τὴν ὑμετέραν
ἀφροσύνην, ἑαυτοῖς δὲ κίνδυνον ἐπεξεργάζεσθαι.

48

Ἐξάρωμεν οὖν τοῦτο ἐν τάχει καὶ προσπέσωμεν τῷ
δεσπότῃ καὶ κλαύσωμεν ἱκετεύοντες αὐτόν, ὅπως
ἵλεως γενόμενος ἐπικαταλλαγῇ ἡμῖν καὶ ἐπὶ τὴν σεμ-
νὴν τῆς φιλαδελφίας ἡμῶν ἁγνὴν ἀγωγὴν ἀποκατα-
στήσῃ ἡμᾶς. 2. πύλη γὰρ δικαιοσύνης ἀνεῳγυῖα εἰς
ζωὴν αὕτη, καθὼς γέγραπται· ἀνοίξατέ μοι πύλας
δικαιοσύνης· εἰσελθὼν ἐν αὐταῖς ἐξομολογήσομαι[88]
τῷ κυρίῳ. 3. αὕτη ἡ πύλη τοῦ κυρίου· δίκαιοι εἰσ-
ελεύσονται ἐν αὐτῇ. 4. πολλῶν οὖν πυλῶν ἀνεῳγυιῶν
ἡ ἐν δικαιοσύνῃ αὕτη ἐστὶν ἡ ἐν Χριστῷ, ἐν ᾗ

[87] ἀγωγῆς: ἀγάπης H
[88] ἐξομολογήσομαι H L: -ήσωμαι A S C Clem Al

approved by them. 5. But now consider who has corrupted you and diminished the respect you had because of your esteemed love of others. 6. It is shameful, loved ones, exceedingly shameful and unworthy of your conduct in Christ, that the most secure and ancient church of the Corinthians is reported to have created a faction against its presbyters, at the instigation of one or two persons. 7. And this report has reached not only us but even those who stand opposed to us, so that blasphemies have been uttered against the Lord's name because of your foolishness; and you are exposing yourselves to danger.

48

And so let us dispose of this problem quickly and fall down before the Master and weep, begging him to be merciful and to be reconciled to us, and to restore us to our respected and holy conduct, seen in our love of others. 2. For this is a gate of righteousness that opens up onto life, just as it is written, "Open up for me gates of righteousness; when I enter through them I will give praises to the Lord. 3. This is the gate of the Lord, and the upright will enter through it."[100] 4. Although many gates open, this is the one that leads to righteousness—the one that is in Christ. All those

[100] Ps 118:19–20.

μακάριοι πάντες οἱ εἰσελθόντες καὶ κατευθύνοντες τὴν
πορείαν αὐτῶν ἐν ὁσιότητι καὶ δικαιοσύνῃ, ἀταράχως
πάντα ἐπιτελοῦντες. 5. ἤτω τις πιστός, ἤτω δυνατὸς
γνῶσιν ἐξειπεῖν, ἤτω σοφὸς ἐν διακρίσει λόγων, ἤτω
ἁγνὸς ἐν ἔργοις· 6. τοσούτῳ γὰρ μᾶλλον ταπεινο-
φρονεῖν ὀφείλει, ὅσῳ δοκεῖ μᾶλλον μείζων εἶναι, καὶ
ζητεῖν τὸ κοινωφελὲς πᾶσιν, καὶ μὴ τὸ ἑαυτοῦ.

49

Ὁ ἔχων ἀγάπην ἐν Χριστῷ ποιησάτω τὰ τοῦ Χριστοῦ
παραγγέλματα. 2. τὸν δεσμὸν τῆς ἀγάπης τοῦ θεοῦ
τίς δύναται ἐξηγήσασθαι; 3. τὸ μεγαλεῖον τῆς καλ-
λονῆς αὐτοῦ τίς ἀρκετὸς ἐξειπεῖν; 4. τὸ ὕψος, εἰς ὃ
ἀνάγει ἡ ἀγάπη, ἀνεκδιήγητόν ἐστιν. 5. ἀγάπη κολλᾷ
ἡμᾶς τῷ θεῷ, ἀγάπη καλύπτει πλῆθος ἁμαρτιῶν,
ἀγάπη πάντα ἀνέχεται, πάντα μακροθυμεῖ· οὐδὲν
βάναυσον ἐν ἀγάπῃ, οὐδὲν ὑπερήφανον· ἀγάπη
σχίσμα οὐκ ἔχει, ἀγάπη οὐ στασιάζει, ἀγάπη πάντα
ποιεῖ ἐν ὁμονοίᾳ· ἐν τῇ ἀγάπῃ ἐτελειώθησαν πάντες οἱ
ἐκλεκτοὶ τοῦ θεοῦ, δίχα ἀγάπης οὐδὲν εὐάρεστόν ἐστιν
τῷ θεῷ. 6. ἐν ἀγάπῃ προσελάβετο ἡμᾶς ὁ δεσπότης·
διὰ τὴν ἀγάπην, ἣν ἔσχεν πρὸς ἡμᾶς, τὸ αἷμα αὐτοῦ
ἔδωκεν ὑπὲρ ἡμῶν Ἰησοῦς Χριστὸς ὁ κύριος ἡμῶν ἐν
θελήματι θεοῦ, καὶ τὴν σάρκα ὑπὲρ τῆς σαρκὸς ἡμῶν
καὶ τὴν ψυχὴν ὑπὲρ τῶν ψυχῶν ἡμῶν.

who enter it are most fortunate; they make their path straight in holiness and righteousness, accomplishing all things without disorder. 5. Let a person be faithful, let him be able to speak forth knowledge, let him be wise in his discernment of words, let him be pure in deeds. 6. For the more he appears to be great, the more he should be humble, striving for the good of all, not just of himself.

49

The one who experiences love in Christ should do what Christ commanded. 2. Who can explain the bond of God's love? 3. Who is able to recount the greatness of its beauty? 4. The height to which love leads is beyond description. 5. Love binds us to God; love hides a multitude of sins;[101] love bears all things and endures all things. There is nothing vulgar in love, nothing haughty. Love has no schism, love creates no faction, love does all things in harmony. Everyone chosen by God has been perfected in love; apart from love nothing is pleasing to God.[102] 6. The Master has received us in love. Because of the love he had for us, our Lord Jesus Christ gave his blood for us, by God's will—his flesh for our flesh, his soul for our souls.

[101] 1 Pet 4:8.
[102] Cf. 1 Cor 13:4–7.

50

Ὁρᾶτε, ἀγαπητοί, πῶς μέγα καὶ θαυμαστόν ἐστιν ἡ ἀγάπη, καὶ τῆς τελειότητος αὐτῆς οὐκ ἔστιν ἐξήγησις. 2. τίς ἱκανὸς ἐν αὐτῇ εὑρεθῆναι, εἰ μὴ οὓς ἂν καταξιώσῃ[89] ὁ θεός; δεώμεθα οὖν καὶ αἰτώμεθα ἀπὸ τοῦ ἐλέους αὐτοῦ, ἵνα ἐν ἀγάπῃ εὑρεθῶμεν δίχα προσκλίσεως ἀνθρωπίνης, ἄμωμοι. 3. αἱ γενεαὶ πᾶσαι ἀπὸ Ἀδὰμ ἕως τῆσδε[90] ἡμέρας παρῆλθον, ἀλλ' οἱ ἐν ἀγάπῃ τελειωθέντες κατὰ τὴν τοῦ θεοῦ χάριν ἔχουσιν χῶρον εὐσεβῶν, οἳ φανερωθήσονται ἐν τῇ ἐπισκοπῇ τῆς βασιλείας τοῦ Χριστοῦ.[91] 4. γέγραπται γάρ· εἰσέλθετε εἰς τὰ ταμεῖα μικρὸν ὅσον ὅσον, ἕως οὗ παρέλθῃ ἡ ὀργὴ καὶ ὁ θυμός μου, καὶ μνησθήσομαι ἡμέρας ἀγαθῆς, καὶ ἀναστήσω ὑμᾶς ἐκ τῶν θηκῶν ὑμῶν. 5. μακάριοί ἐσμεν,[92] ἀγαπητοί, εἰ τὰ προστάγματα τοῦ θεοῦ ἐποιοῦμεν ἐν ὁμονοίᾳ ἀγάπης, εἰς τὸ ἀφεθῆναι ἡμῖν δι' ἀγάπης τὰς ἁμαρτίας. 6. γέγραπται γάρ· μακάριοι, ὧν ἀφέθησαν αἱ ἀνομίαι καὶ ὧν ἐπεκαλύφθησαν αἱ ἁμαρτίαι· μακάριος ἀνήρ, οὗ οὐ μὴ λογίσηται κύριος ἁμαρτίαν, οὐδέ ἐστιν ἐν τῷ στόματι αὐτοῦ δόλος. 7. οὗτος ὁ μακαρισμὸς ἐγένετο ἐπὶ τοὺς ἐκλελεγμένους ὑπὸ τοῦ θεοῦ διὰ Ἰησοῦ Χριστοῦ τοῦ κυρίου ἡμῶν, ᾧ ἡ δόξα εἰς τοὺς αἰῶνας τῶν αἰώνων. ἀμήν.

[89] καταξιώσῃ: καταδιώξῃ H
[90] τῆσδε: add τῆς H
[91] Χριστοῦ A (?) L C Clem Al: θεοῦ H S

50

You see, loved ones, how great and amazing love is; there can be no exposition of its perfection. 2. Who is adequate to be found in it, except those whom God has made worthy? And so we should implore and plead for his mercy, that we may be found in his love, removed from any human partisanship, blameless. 3. All the generations from Adam till today have passed away, but those perfected in love through the gracious gift of God have a place among the godly. And they will be revealed when the kingdom of Christ appears. 4. For it is written, "Come into the inner rooms for just a short while, until my anger and wrath pass by; and I will remember a good day and raise you up from your tombs."[103] 5. We are blessed, loved ones, when we keep God's commandments in the harmony of love, that our sins may be forgiven us through love. 6. For it is written, "Blessed are those whose lawless acts are forgiven and whose sins have been covered over. Blessed is the man whose sin the Lord does not take into account and in whose mouth is found no deceit."[104] 7. This blessing comes to those who have been chosen by God through our Lord Jesus Christ. To him be the glory forever and ever. Amen.

[103] Isa 26:20; Ezek 37:12.
[104] Ps 32:1–2; Rom 4:7–9.

[92] ἐσμεν A L: ἦμεν H S C

52

Ἀπροσδεής, ἀδελφοί, ὁ δεσπότης ὑπάρχει τῶν ἀπάν-
των· οὐδὲν οὐδενὸς χρῄζει εἰ μὴ τὸ ἐξομολογεῖσθαι
αὐτῷ. 2. φησὶν γὰρ ὁ ἐκλεκτὸς Δαυίδ· ἐξομολογήσομαι τῷ κυρίῳ, καὶ ἀρέσει αὐτῷ ὑπὲρ μόσχον νέον
κέρατα ἐκφέροντα καὶ ὁπλάς· ἰδέτωσαν πτωχοὶ καὶ
εὐφρανθήτωσαν. 3. καὶ πάλιν λέγει· θῦσον τῷ θεῷ
θυσίαν αἰνέσεως καὶ ἀπόδος τῷ ὑψίστῳ τὰς εὐχάς
σου· καὶ ἐπικάλεσαί με ἐν ἡμέρᾳ θλίψεώς σου, καὶ
ἐξελοῦμαί σε, καὶ δοξάσεις με. 4. θυσία γὰρ τῷ θεῷ
πνεῦμα συντετριμμένον.

53

Ἐπίστασθε γὰρ καὶ καλῶς ἐπίστασθε τὰς ἱερὰς γραφάς, ἀγαπητοί, καὶ ἐγκεκύφατε εἰς τὰ λόγια τοῦ θεοῦ.
πρὸς ἀνάμνησιν οὖν ταῦτα γράφομεν. 2. Μωϋσέως
γὰρ ἀναβάντος εἰς τὸ ὄρος καὶ ποιήσαντος τεσσεράκοντα ἡμέρας καὶ τεσσεράκοντα νύκτας ἐν
νηστείᾳ καὶ ταπεινώσει, εἶπεν πρὸς αὐτὸν ὁ θεός·
Μωϋσῆ, Μωϋσῆ,[95] κατάβηθι τὸ τάχος ἐντεῦθεν, ὅτι
ἠνόμησεν ὁ λαός σου, οὓς ἐξήγαγες ἐκ γῆς Αἰγύπτου·
παρέβησαν ταχὺ ἐκ τῆς ὁδοῦ ἧς ἐνετείλω αὐτοῖς,
ἐποίησαν ἑαυτοῖς χωνεύματα. 3. καὶ εἶπεν κύριος πρὸς
αὐτόν· λελάληκα πρὸς σὲ ἅπαξ καὶ δὶς λέγων· ἑώρακα
τὸν λαὸν τοῦτον, καὶ ἰδού ἐστιν σκληροτράχηλος·
ἔασόν με ἐξολεθρεῦσαι αὐτούς, καὶ ἐξαλείψω τὸ ὄνομα

52

The Master is in need of nothing, brothers, and craves nothing from anyone, but to be praised. 2. For the chosen one, David, says: "I will praise the Lord and it will please him more than a young calf bearing horns and hooves. Let those who are poor see this and rejoice."[107] 3. And again he says, "Give to God a sacrifice of your praise and render to the Most High your prayers. And call upon me in the day of your affliction, and I will rescue you; and you will give glory to me."[108] 4. "For a crushed spirit is a sacrifice to God."[109]

53

For you know the sacred Scriptures, loved ones—and know them quite well—and you have gazed into the sayings of God. And so we write these things simply as a reminder. 2. For after Moses went up onto the mountain and spent forty days and nights in fasting and humility,[110] God said to him, "Moses, Moses, go down from here at once: your people, whom you brought out of the land of Egypt, have broken the Law. They have departed quickly from the path you commanded them to take and have cast metal idols for themselves." 3. And the Lord said to him, "I have spoken with you once and again: I have seen this people and know they are stiff-necked. Let me destroy them and

---

[107] Ps 69:30–32.   [108] Ps 50:14–15.

[109] Ps 51:17.   [110] The following account is drawn from Exod 32:7–10, 31–32 and Deut 9:12–14.

---

95 Μωϋσῆ, Μωϋσῆ A: Μωσῆ, Μωσῆ H: om. L S C

αὐτῶν ὑποκάτωθεν τοῦ οὐρανοῦ, καὶ ποιήσω σε εἰς
ἔθνος μέγα καὶ θαυμαστὸν καὶ πολὺ μᾶλλον ἢ τοῦτο.
4. καὶ εἶπεν Μωϋσῆς· μηθαμῶς, κύριε· ἄφες τὴν
ἁμαρτίαν τῷ λαῷ τούτῳ, ἢ κἀμὲ ἐξάλειψον ἐκ βίβλου
ζώντων. 5. ὦ μεγάλης ἀγάπης, ὦ τελειότητος
ἀνυπερβλήτου· παρρησιάζεται θεράπων πρὸς κύριον,
αἰτεῖται ἄφεσιν τῷ πλήθει, ἢ καὶ ἑαυτὸν ἐξαλειφθῆναι
μετ᾽ αὐτῶν ἀξιοῖ.

54

Τίς οὖν ἐν ὑμῖν γενναῖος, τίς εὔσπλαγχνος, τίς πεπλη-
ροφορημένος ἀγάπης; 2. εἰπάτω· εἰ δι᾽ ἐμὲ στάσις καὶ
ἔρις καὶ σχίσματα, ἐκχωρῶ, ἄπειμι, οὗ ἐὰν βούλησθε,
καὶ ποιῶ τὰ προστασσόμενα ὑπὸ τοῦ πλήθους· μόνον
τὸ ποίμνιον τοῦ Χριστοῦ εἰρηνευέτω μετὰ τῶν καθ-
εσταμένων πρεσβυτέρων. 3. τοῦτο ὁ ποιήσας ἑαυτῷ
μέγα κλέος ἐν Χριστῷ περιποιήσεται, καὶ πᾶς τόπος
δέξεται αὐτόν. τοῦ γὰρ κυρίου ἡ γῆ καὶ τὸ πλήρωμα
αὐτῆς. 4. ταῦτα οἱ πολιτευόμενοι τὴν ἀμεταμέλητον
πολιτείαν τοῦ θεοῦ ἐποίησαν καὶ ποιήσουσιν.

55

Ἵνα δὲ καὶ ὑποδείγματα⁹⁶ ἐθνῶν ἐνέγκωμεν· πολλοὶ
βασιλεῖς καὶ ἡγούμενοι, λοιμικοῦ τινος ἐνστάντος

---

96 ὑποδείγματα A L: ὑπόδειγμα S C: ὑπομνήματα H

I will blot their name out from beneath the sky; and I will make you into a great and spectacular nation, much greater than this one." 4. And Moses said, "May it never be Lord! Forgive the sin of this people—or blot me also out from the book of the living." 5. O great love! O incomparable perfection! The servant speaks boldly to the Lord, and asks for the multitude to be forgiven—or pleads for himself to be blotted out with them.

54

Who, therefore, among you is noble? Or compassionate? Or filled with love? 2. Let that one say, "If I am the cause of faction, strife, and schisms, I will depart; I will go wherever you wish and do what is commanded by the congregation. Only allow the flock of Christ to be at peace with the presbyters who have been appointed." 3. The one who does this will have made himself eminent in Christ and will be welcomed everywhere. "For the earth, and all that is in it, belongs to the Lord."[111] 4. Those who have performed their civic duty to God, without regrets, have done these things and will continue to do them.

55

But we should bring in examples from the Gentiles as well. Many kings and rulers, after receiving instruction from an

111 Ps 24:1.

καιροῦ χρησμοδοτηθέντες παρέδωκαν ἑαυτοὺς εἰς
θάνατον, ἵνα ῥύσωνται διὰ τοῦ ἑαυτῶν αἵματος τοὺς
πολίτας· πολλοὶ ἐξεχώρησαν ἰδίων πόλεων, ἵνα μὴ
στασιάζωσιν ἐπὶ πλεῖον. 2. ἐπιστάμεθα πολλοὺς ἐν
ἡμῖν παραδεδωκότας ἑαυτοὺς εἰς δεσμά, ὅπως ἑτέρους
λυτρώσονται· πολλοὶ ἑαυτοὺς παρέδωκαν εἰς δουλεί-
αν, καὶ λαβόντες τὰς τιμὰς αὐτῶν ἑτέρους ἐψώμισαν.
3. πολλαὶ γυναῖκες ἐνδυναμωθεῖσαι διὰ τῆς χάριτος
τοῦ θεοῦ ἐπετελέσαντο πολλὰ ἀνδρεῖα. 4. Ἰουδὶθ ἡ
μακαρία, ἐν συγκλεισμῷ οὔσης τῆς πόλεως, ᾐτήσατο
παρὰ τῶν πρεσβυτέρων ἐαθῆναι αὐτὴν ἐξελθεῖν εἰς
τὴν παρεμβολὴν τῶν ἀλλοφύλων. 5. παραδοῦσα οὖν
ἑαυτὴν τῷ κινδύνῳ ἐξῆλθεν δι᾽ ἀγάπην τῆς πατρίδος
καὶ τοῦ λαοῦ τοῦ ὄντος ἐν συγκλεισμῷ, καὶ παρέδωκεν
κύριος Ὀλοφέρνην ἐν χειρὶ θηλείας. 6. οὐχ ἧττον[97]
καὶ ἡ τελεία κατὰ πίστιν Ἐσθὴρ κινδύνῳ ἑαυτὴν
παρέβαλεν, ἵνα τὸ δωδεκάφυλον τοῦ Ἰσραὴλ μέλλον
ἀπολέσθαι ῥύσηται· διὰ γὰρ τῆς νηστείας καὶ τῆς
ταπεινώσεως αὐτῆς ἠξίωσεν τὸν παντεπόπτην δεσπό-
την, θεὸν τῶν αἰώνων· ὃς ἰδὼν τὸ ταπεινὸν τῆς ψυχῆς
αὐτῆς ἐρύσατο τὸν λαόν, ὧν χάριν ἐκινδύνευσεν.

56

Καὶ ἡμεῖς οὖν ἐντύχωμεν περὶ τῶν ἔν τινι παρα-
πτώματι ὑπαρχόντων, ὅπως δοθῇ αὐτοῖς ἐπιείκεια καὶ

[97] ἧττον H L S C: ἥττονι (ηττονει) A

oracle, have handed themselves over to death during the time of plague, in order to deliver their fellow citizens by shedding their own blood. Many left their own cities to avoid creating more factions. 2. Among ourselves, we know many who put themselves in prison in order to ransom others; many placed themselves in slavery and fed others with the purchase price they received. 3. Many women were empowered by the gracious gift of God to perform numerous "manly" deeds. 4. The blessed Judith, when her city lay under siege, asked the elders for permission to go out to the foreigners' camp.[112] 5. And so she handed herself over to danger, going out because she loved her homeland and the people under siege. And the Lord handed Holofernes over to the hand of a female. 6. No less did Esther, a woman perfect in faith, put herself in danger to rescue the twelve tribes of Israel who were about to perish.[113] For through her fasting and humility she petitioned the all-seeing Master, the God of eternity, who saw the humbleness of her soul and rescued the people for whom she put herself in danger.

56

And so we should pray for those caught up in any unlawful act, that gentleness and humility may be given them, so

[112] The account is drawn from Judith 8ff.
[113] The account is drawn from Esther 7; 4:16.

ταπεινοφροσύνη εἰς τὸ εἶξαι αὐτοὺς μὴ ἡμῖν, ἀλλὰ τῷ
θελήματι τοῦ θεοῦ· οὕτως γὰρ ἔσται αὐτοῖς ἔγκαρπος
καὶ τελεία ἡ πρὸς τὸν θεὸν καὶ τοὺς ἁγίους μετ᾽
οἰκτιρμῶν μνεία. 2. ἀναλάβωμεν παιδείαν, ἐφ᾽ ᾗ οὐδεὶς ὀφείλει ἀγανακτεῖν, ἀγαπητοί. ἡ νουθέτησις, ἣν
ποιούμεθα εἰς ἀλλήλους, καλή ἐστιν καὶ ὑπεράγαν
ὠφέλιμος· κολλᾷ γὰρ ἡμᾶς τῷ θελήματι τοῦ θεοῦ.
3. οὕτως γὰρ φησιν ὁ ἅγιος λόγος· παιδεύων ἐπαί-
δευσέν με ὁ κύριος, καὶ τῷ θανάτῳ οὐ παρέδωκέν με.
4. ὃν γὰρ ἀγαπᾷ κύριος, παιδεύει, μαστιγοῖ δὲ πάντα
υἱόν, ὃν παραδέχεται. 5. παιδεύσει με γάρ, φησίν,
δίκαιος ἐν ἐλέει καὶ ἐλέγξει με· ἔλαιον δὲ ἁμαρτωλῶν[98]
μὴ λιπανάτω τὴν κεφαλήν μου. 6. καὶ πάλιν λέγει·
μακάριος ἄνθρωπος, ὃν ἤλεγξεν ὁ κύριος· νουθέτημα
δὲ παντοκράτορος μὴ ἀπαναίνου· αὐτὸς γὰρ ἀλγεῖν
ποιεῖ, καὶ πάλιν ἀποκαθίστησιν· 7. ἔπαισεν, καὶ αἱ
χεῖρες αὐτοῦ ἰάσαντο. 8. ἑξάκις ἐξ ἀναγκῶν ἐξελεῖταί
σε, ἐν δὲ τῷ ἑβδόμῳ οὐχ ἅψεταί σου κακόν. 9. ἐν λιμῷ
ῥύσεταί σε ἐκ θανάτου, ἐν πολέμῳ δὲ ἐκ χειρὸς σιδή-
ρου λύσει σε· 10. καὶ ἀπὸ μάστιγος γλώσσης σε
κρύψει, καὶ οὐ μὴ φοβηθήσῃ κακῶν ἐπερχομένων.
11. ἀδίκων καὶ ἀνόμων καταγελάσῃ, ἀπὸ δὲ θηρίων
ἀγρίων οὐ μὴ φοβηθῇς· 12. θῆρες γὰρ ἄγριοι εἰρη-
νεύσουσίν σοι. 13. εἶτα γνώσῃ, ὅτι εἰρηνεύσει σου ὁ
οἶκος, ἡ δὲ δίαιτα τῆς σκηνῆς σου οὐ μὴ ἁμάρτῃ.
14. γνώσῃ δέ, ὅτι πολὺ τὸ σπέρμα σου, τὰ δὲ τέκνα
σου ὥσπερ τὸ παμβότανον τοῦ ἀγροῦ. 15. ἐλεύσῃ δὲ
ἐν τάφῳ ὥσπερ σῖτος ὥριμος κατὰ καιρὸν θεριζόμε-

that they may yield themselves not to us but to the will of God. For so the compassionate remembrance of them by God and the saints will be fruitful and perfect. 2. We should welcome discipline, loved ones; no one should be irritated by it. It is good and supremely useful to rebuke one another, for this binds us to the will of God. 3. For thus says the holy word: "The Lord disciplined me harshly but did not hand me over to death. 4. For the Lord disciplines the one he loves and whips every son he receives."[114] 5. "For the one who is upright will discipline me in his mercy," it says, "and he will set me straight. But may the oil of sinners not anoint my head."[115] 6. And again it says, "How fortunate is the one whom the Lord sets straight. Do not spurn the rebuke of the All-powerful. For he causes pain and again brings relief. 7. He strikes and his hands provide healing. 8. Six times he will rescue you from anguish and the seventh time evil will not touch you. 9. During time of famine he will rescue you from death, and in time of war he will free you from the hand that wields the sword. 10. He will hide you from the scourge of the tongue and you will not be afraid when evils draw near. 11. You will mock those who are unjust and lawless; you will not fear the wild beasts. 12. For wild beasts will be at peace with you. 13. Then you will know that your household will be at peace, and the tent you inhabit will never fail. 14. And you will know that your descendants will be numerous, your children like all the plants of the field. 15. And you will enter the grave like ripened grain harvested at the proper

114 Prov 3:12; cf. Heb 12:6.   115 Ps 141:5.

98 ἁμαρτωλῶν A: ἁμαρτωλοῦ H L S C

νος, ἢ ὥσπερ θημωνιὰ ἅλωνος καθ᾽ ὥραν συγκο-
μισθεῖσα. 16. βλέπετε, ἀγαπητοί, πόσος ὑπερα-
σπισμός ἐστιν τοῖς παιδευομένοις ὑπὸ τοῦ δεσπότου·
πατὴρ γὰρ ἀγαθὸς ὢν παιδεύει εἰς τὸ ἐλεηθῆναι ἡμᾶς
διὰ τῆς ὁσίας παιδείας αὐτοῦ.

57

Ὑμεῖς οὖν οἱ τὴν καταβολὴν τῆς στάσεως ποιήσαντες
ὑποτάγητε τοῖς πρεσβυτέροις καὶ παιδεύθητε εἰς
μετάνοιαν, κάμψαντες τὰ γόνατα τῆς καρδίας ὑμῶν.
2. μάθετε ὑποτάσσεσθαι, ἀποθέμενοι τὴν ἀλαζόνα καὶ
ὑπερήφανον τῆς γλώσσης ὑμῶν αὐθάδειαν· ἄμεινον
γάρ ἐστιν ὑμῖν, ἐν τῷ ποιμνίῳ τοῦ Χριστοῦ μικροὺς
καὶ ἐλλογίμους εὑρεθῆναι, ἢ καθ᾽ ὑπεροχὴν δοκοῦντας
ἐκριφῆναι ἐκ τῆς ἐλπίδος αὐτοῦ. 3. οὕτως γὰρ λέγει ἡ
πανάρετος σοφία· ἰδού, προήσομαι ὑμῖν ἐμῆς πνοῆς
ῥῆσιν, διδάξω δὲ ὑμᾶς τὸν ἐμὸν λόγον. 4. ἐπειδὴ
ἐκάλουν καὶ οὐχ ὑπηκούσατε, καὶ ἐξέτεινον λόγους καὶ
οὐ προσείχετε· ἀλλὰ ἀκύρους ἐποιεῖτε τὰς ἐμὰς βου-
λάς, τοῖς δὲ ἐμοῖς ἐλέγχοις ἠπειθήσατε· τοιγαροῦν
κἀγὼ τῇ ὑμετέρᾳ ἀπωλείᾳ ἐπιγελάσομαι, καταχαροῦ-
μαι δὲ ἡνίκα ἂν ἔρχηται ὑμῖν ὄλεθρος καὶ ὡς ἂν
ἀφίκηται ὑμῖν ἄφνω θόρυβος, ἡ δὲ καταστροφὴ ὁμοία
καταιγίδι παρῇ, ἢ ὅταν ἔρχηται ὑμῖν θλῖψις⁹⁹ καὶ
πολιορκία. 5. ἔσται γάρ, ὅταν ἐπικαλέσησθέ με, ἐγὼ
δὲ οὐκ εἰσακούσομαι ὑμῶν· ζητήσουσίν με κακοί, καὶ
οὐχ εὑρήσουσιν. ἐμίσησαν γὰρ σοφίαν, τὸν δὲ φόβον

time, or like a heap of sheaves on the threshing floor, gathered together at the right hour."[116] 16. You see, loved ones, what a great protection there is for those who are disciplined by the Master. For since he is a good father, he disciplines us, that through his holy discipline we may receive mercy.

57

Thus you who laid the foundation of the faction should be subject to the presbyters and accept the discipline that leads to repentance, falling prostrate in your heart. 2. Learn to be submissive; lay aside the arrogant and haughty insolence of your tongue. For it is better for you to be considered insignificant but reputable in the flock of Christ than to appear prominent while sundered from his hope. 3. For thus says his all-virtuous Wisdom: "Look, I will utter a saying to you with my breath and teach you my word. 4. For I was calling and you did not listen, and I was sending forth my words and you paid no attention. But you repudiated my advice and disobeyed when I reproached you. For this reason I too will mock when you are annihilated and rejoice when destruction comes upon you and turmoil suddenly appears among you, when catastrophe arrives like a tempest, or when adversity and distress come upon you. 5. For then when you call on me, I will not listen to you. Those who are evil will seek me out but not find me. For they hated wisdom and chose not to accept the rever-

116 Job 5:17–26.

---

99 θλῖψις A L S C: add καὶ στενοχωρία H

τοῦ κυρίου οὐ προείλαντο, οὐδὲ ἤθελον ἐμαῖς προσέχειν βουλαῖς, ἐμυκτήριζον δὲ ἐμοὺς ἐλέγχους. 6. τοιγαροῦν ἔδονται τῆς ἑαυτῶν ὁδοῦ τοὺς καρποὺς καὶ τῆς
ἑαυτῶν ἀσεβείας πλησθήσονται.[100] 7. ἀνθ’ ὧν γὰρ
ἠδίκουν νηπίους φονευθήσονται, καὶ ἐξετασμὸς ἀσε-
βεῖς ὀλεῖ· ὁ δὲ ἐμοῦ ἀκούων κατασκηνώσει ἐπ’ ἐλπίδι
πεποιθὼς καὶ ἡσυχάσει ἀφόβως ἀπὸ παντὸς κακοῦ.

58

Ὑπακούσωμεν οὖν τῷ παναγίῳ καὶ ἐνδόξῳ ὀνόματι
αὐτοῦ φυγόντες τὰς προειρημένας διὰ τῆς σοφίας τοῖς
ἀπειθοῦσιν ἀπειλάς, ἵνα κατασκηνώσωμεν πεποιθότες
ἐπὶ τὸ ὁσιώτατον τῆς μεγαλωσύνης αὐτοῦ ὄνομα.
2. δέξασθε τὴν συμβουλὴν ἡμῶν, καὶ ἔσται ἀμετα-
μέλητα ὑμῖν. ζῇ γὰρ ὁ θεὸς καὶ ζῇ ὁ κύριος Ἰησοῦς
Χριστὸς καὶ τὸ πνεῦμα τὸ ἅγιον, ἥ τε πίστις καὶ ἡ
ἐλπὶς τῶν ἐκλεκτῶν, ὅτι ὁ ποιήσας ἐν ταπεινοφροσύνῃ
μετ’ ἐκτενοῦς ἐπιεικείας ἀμεταμελήτως τὰ ὑπὸ τοῦ
θεοῦ δεδομένα δικαιώματα καὶ προστάγματα, οὗτος
ἐντεταγμένος καὶ ἐλλόγιμος ἔσται εἰς τὸν ἀριθμὸν[101]
τῶν σῳζομένων διὰ Ἰησοῦ Χριστοῦ, δι’ οὗ ἐστιν αὐτῷ
ἡ δόξα εἰς τοὺς αἰῶνας τῶν αἰώνων. ἀμήν.

[100] πλησθήσονται: after πλησθησον to the beginning of
c. 64 A is lacking
[101] τὸν ἀριθμὸν H S: add τῶν ἐθνῶν L C

ential awe of the Lord. Nor did they wish to accept my advice, but they mocked when I rebuked them. 6. For this reason they will consume the fruits of their own path and be filled with their own impious deeds. 7. For since they treated the young with injustice, they will be murdered, and an inquiry will destroy those who are impious. But the one who hears me will dwell in hope with all confidence; he will be at rest, fearing no evil."[117]

58

For this reason we should be obedient to his most holy and glorious name, fleeing the dangers foretold by Wisdom, which threaten the disobedient. In this way we will dwell with confidence in the most holy name of his magnificence. 2. Take our advice and you will have no regrets. For as God, the Lord Jesus Christ, and the Holy Spirit all live—as do *[Or: who are]* the faith and hope of those who are chosen—the one who does the righteous demands and commandments given by God with humility and fervent gentleness, and without regret, will be included and held in esteem among the number of those who will be saved through Jesus Christ. Through whom be glory to him forever and ever. Amen.

[117] Prov 1:23–33.

59

Ἐὰν δέ τινες ἀπειθήσωσιν τοῖς ὑπ᾽ αὐτοῦ δι᾽ ἡμῶν
εἰρημένοις, γινωσκέτωσαν, ὅτι παραπτώσει καὶ κινδύνῳ οὐ μικρῷ ἑαυτοὺς ἐνδήσουσιν.[102] 2. ἡμεῖς δὲ
ἀθῷοι ἐσόμεθα ἀπὸ ταύτης τῆς ἁμαρτίας καὶ αἰτη-
σόμεθα ἐκτενῆ τὴν δέησιν καὶ ἱκεσίαν ποιούμενοι,
ὅπως τὸν ἀριθμὸν τὸν κατηριθμημένον τῶν ἐκλεκτῶν
αὐτοῦ ἐν ὅλῳ τῷ κόσμῳ διαφυλάξῃ ἄθραυστον ὁ
δημιουργὸς τῶν ἁπάντων διὰ τοῦ ἠγαπημένου παιδὸς
αὐτοῦ Ἰησοῦ Χριστοῦ,[103] δι᾽ οὗ ἐκάλεσεν ἡμᾶς ἀπὸ
σκότους εἰς φῶς, ἀπὸ ἀγνωσίας εἰς ἐπίγνωσιν δόξης
ὀνόματος αὐτοῦ. 3. Δὸς ὑμῖν, Κύριε,[104] ἐλπίζειν ἐπὶ τὸ
ἀρχέγονον πάσης κτίσεως ὄνομά σου, ἀνοίξας τοὺς
ὀφθαλμοὺς τῆς καρδίας ἡμῶν εἰς τὸ γινώσκειν σε τὸν
μόνον ὕψιστον ἐν ὑψίστοις, ἅγιον ἐν ἁγίοις ἀναπαυ-
όμενον· τὸν ταπεινοῦντα ὕβριν ὑπερηφάνων, τὸν
διαλύοντα λογισμοὺς ἐθνῶν, τὸν ποιοῦντα ταπεινοὺς
εἰς ὕψος καὶ τοὺς ὑψηλοὺς ταπεινοῦντα, τὸν πλουτί-
ζοντα καὶ πτωχίζοντα, τὸν ἀποκτείνοντα[105] καὶ ζῆν
ποιοῦντα, μόνον εὐεργέτην[106] πνευμάτων καὶ θεὸν
πάσης σαρκός· τὸν ἐπιβλέποντα ἐν τοῖς ἀβύσσοις,
τὸν ἐπόπτην ἀνθρωπίνων ἔργων, τὸν τῶν κινδυνευ-
όντων βοηθόν, τὸν τῶν ἀπηλπισμένων σωτῆρα, τὸν
παντὸς πνεύματος κτίστην καὶ ἐπίσκοπον· τὸν πληθύ-

[102] ἐνδήσουσιν H S C: ἐνδώσουσιν (tradent) L
[103] Χριστοῦ H: add τοῦ κυρίου ἡμῶν L S C
[104] Δὸς ὑμῖν Κύριε cj. Lightfoot: om. H C L S

59

But if some disobey the words he has spoken through us, they should realize that they entangle themselves in transgression and no little danger. 2. But we ourselves will be innocent of this sin, and we will ask with a fervent prayer and petition that the Creator of all safeguard the number of those counted among his elect throughout the entire world, through his beloved child Jesus Christ, through whom he called us out of darkness into light, from ignorance into the knowledge of his glorious name. 3. Grant us, O Lord,[118] that we may hope in your name, the ultimate source of all creation. Open the eyes of our heart, that we may recognize you as the one alone who is the highest among the highest, the holy one who rests among the holy, the one who humbles the insolence of the proud, who destroys the reasonings of the nations, who exalts the humble to the heights and humiliates the exalted, the one who enriches and impoverishes, who kills and brings to life, the sole benefactor of spirits and the God of all flesh, the one who peers into the places of the abyss, who observes the works of humans and helps those in danger, the savior of those who have abandoned hope, the creator and overseer of every spirit, the one who multiplies the nations upon

118 Translating the emendation proposed by Lightfoot, which restores three words to indicate that the prayer of the following chapters begins here.

---

105 ἀποκτείνοντα H C: add καὶ σώζοντα L S
106 εὐεργέτην H: εὑρετὴν L S: κτίστην C

νοντα ἔθνη ἐπὶ γῆς καὶ ἐκ πάντων ἐκλεξάμενον τοὺς
ἀγαπῶντάς σε διὰ Ἰησοῦ Χριστοῦ τοῦ ἠγαπημένου
παιδός σου, δι᾽ οὗ ἡμᾶς ἐπαίδευσας, ἡγίασας, ἐτίμη-
σας. 4. ἀξιοῦμέν σε, δέσποτα, βοηθὸν γενέσθαι καὶ
ἀντιλήπτορα ἡμῶν. τοὺς ἐν θλίψει ἡμῶν σῶσον, τοὺς
ταπεινοὺς ἐλέησον,[107] τοὺς πεπτωκότας ἔγειρον, τοῖς
δεομένοις ἐπιφάνηθι, τοὺς ἀσθενεῖς ἴασαι, τοὺς πλα-
νωμένους τοῦ λαοῦ σου ἐπίστρεψον· χόρτασον τοὺς
πεινῶντας, λύτρωσαι τοὺς δεσμίους ἡμῶν, ἐξανάστη-
σον τοὺς ἀσθενοῦντας, παρακάλεσον τοὺς ὀλιγοψυ-
χοῦντας· γνώτωσάν σε[108] ἅπαντα τὰ ἔθνη, ὅτι σὺ εἶ ὁ
θεὸς μόνος καὶ Ἰησοῦς Χριστὸς ὁ παῖς σου καὶ ἡμεῖς
λαός σου καὶ πρόβατα τῆς νομῆς σου.

60

Σὺ γὰρ τὴν ἀέναον τοῦ κόσμου σύστασιν διὰ τῶν
ἐνεργουμένων ἐφανεροποίησας· σύ, κύριε, τὴν οἰκουμένην ἔκτισας, ὁ πιστὸς ἐν πάσαις ταῖς γενεαῖς,
δίκαιος ἐν τοῖς κρίμασιν, θαυμαστὸς ἐν ἰσχύϊ καὶ
μεγαλοπρεπείᾳ, ὁ σοφὸς ἐν τῷ κτίζειν καὶ συνετὸς ἐν
τῷ τὰ γενόμενα ἑδράσαι, ὁ ἀγαθὸς ἐν τοῖς ὁρωμένοις
καὶ χρηστὸς[109] ἐν τοῖς πεποιθόσιν ἐπὶ σέ. ἐλεῆμον καὶ
οἰκτίρμον, ἄφες ἡμῖν τὰς ἀνομίας ἡμῶν καὶ τὰς ἀδικίας καὶ τὰ παραπτώματα καὶ πλημμελείας. 2. μὴ
λογίσῃ πᾶσαν ἁμαρτίαν δούλων σου καὶ παιδισκῶν,
ἀλλὰ καθάρισον ἡμᾶς τὸν καθαρισμὸν τῆς σῆς ἀληθείας, καὶ κατεύθυνον τὰ διαβήματα ἡμῶν ἐν ὁσιότητι

the earth and who from them all has chosen those who love you through Jesus Christ, your beloved child, through whom you have disciplined, sanctified, and honored us. 4. We ask you, O Master, to be our helper and defender. Save those of us who are in affliction, show mercy to those who are humble, raise those who have fallen, show yourself to those who are in need, heal those who are sick, set straight those among your people who are going astray. Feed the hungry, ransom our prisoners, raise up the weak, encourage the despondent. Let all the nations know you, that you alone are God, that Jesus Christ is your child, and that we are your people and the sheep of your pasture.

60

For you have made plain the eternal structure of the world through the works you have accomplished. You, O Lord, created the world in which we live; you are faithful from one generation to the next, upright in your judgments, spectacular in your strength and magnificence; you are wise when you create and understanding when you establish what exists; you are good in what is seen and kind to those who trust you. You who are merciful and compassionate, forgive us for our lawless acts, unjust deeds, transgressions, and faults. 2. Take into account none of the sins committed by your male slaves and female servants, but cleanse us with your truth. Set our steps straight that we

---

107 τοὺς ταπεινοὺς ἐλέησον H: om. L S C
108 σε H: om. L S C
109 χρηστὸς C L S: πιστὸς H

καρδίας πορεύεσθαι καὶ ποιεῖν τὰ καλὰ καὶ εὐάρεστα
ἐνώπιόν σου καὶ ἐνώπιον τῶν ἀρχόντων ἡμῶν. 3. ναί,
δέσποτα, ἐπίφανον τὸ πρόσωπόν σου ἐφ᾿ ἡμᾶς εἰς
ἀγαθὰ ἐν εἰρήνῃ, εἰς τὸ σκεπασθῆναι ἡμᾶς τῇ χειρί
σου τῇ κραταιᾷ καὶ ῥυσθῆναι ἀπὸ πάσης ἁμαρτίας τῷ
βραχίονί σου τῷ ὑψηλῷ, καὶ ῥῦσαι ἡμᾶς ἀπὸ τῶν
μισούντων ἡμᾶς ἀδίκως. 4. δὸς ὁμόνοιαν καὶ εἰρήνην
ἡμῖν τε καὶ πᾶσιν τοῖς κατοικοῦσιν τὴν γῆν, καθὼς
ἔδωκας τοῖς πατράσιν ἡμῶν, ἐπικαλουμένων σε αὐτῶν
ὁσίως ἐν πίστει καὶ ἀληθείᾳ, ὑπηκόους γινομένους τῷ
παντοκράτορι καὶ παναρέτῳ[110] ὀνόματί σου, τοῖς τε
ἄρχουσιν[111] καὶ ἡγουμένοις ἡμῶν ἐπὶ τῆς γῆς.

61

Σύ, δέσποτα, ἔδωκας τὴν ἐξουσίαν τῆς βασιλείας
αὐτοῖς διὰ τοῦ μεγαλοπρεποῦς καὶ ἀνεκδιηγήτου
κράτους σου, εἰς τὸ γινώσκοντας ἡμᾶς τὴν ὑπὸ σοῦ
αὐτοῖς δεδομένην δόξαν καὶ τιμὴν ὑποτάσσεσθαι
αὐτοῖς, μηδὲν ἐναντιουμένους τῷ θελήματί σου· οἷς
δός, κύριε, ὑγίειαν, εἰρήνην, ὁμόνοιαν, εὐστάθειαν, εἰς
τὸ διέπειν αὐτοὺς τὴν ὑπὸ σοῦ δεδομένην αὐτοῖς
ἡγεμονίαν ἀπροσκόπως. 2. σὺ γάρ, δέσποτα, ἐπου-
ράνιε, βασιλεῦ τῶν αἰώνων, δίδως τοῖς υἱοῖς τῶν
ἀνθρώπων δόξαν καὶ τιμὴν καὶ ἐξουσίαν τῶν ἐπὶ τῆς
γῆς ὑπαρχόντων· σύ, κύριε, διεύθυνον τὴν βουλὴν
αὐτῶν κατὰ τὸ καλὸν καὶ εὐάρεστον ἐνώπιόν σου,
ὅπως διέποντες ἐν εἰρήνῃ καὶ πραΰτητι εὐσεβῶς τὴν

may go forward with devout hearts, to do what is good and pleasing to you and to those who rule us. 3. Yes, Master, make your face shine on us in peace, for our own good, that we may be protected by your powerful hand and rescued from our every sin by your exalted arm. And rescue us from those who hate us without cause. 4. Give harmony and peace both to us and to all those who inhabit the earth, just as you gave it to our ancestors when they called upon you in a holy way, in faith and truth; and allow us to be obedient to your all powerful and all virtuous name, and to those who rule and lead us here on earth.

61

You have given them, O Master, the authority to rule through your magnificent and indescribable power, that we may both recognize the glory and honor you have given them and subject ourselves to them, resisting nothing that conforms to your will. Give to them, O Lord, health, peace, harmony, and stability, so that without faltering they may administer the rule that you have given to them. 2. For you, O Master, Heavenly King forever, give humans glory, honor, and authority over the creatures of the earth. O Lord, make their plan conform with what is good and acceptable before you, that when they administer with piety

---

110 παναρέτῳ H: ἐνδόξῳ C L S
111 τοῖς τε ἄρχουσιν κτλ. H C link with c. 61.1

145

ὑπὸ σοῦ αὐτοῖς δεδομένην ἐξουσίαν ἵλεώ σου τυγ-
χάνωσιν. 3. ὁ μόνος δυνατὸς ποιῆσαι ταῦτα καὶ
περισσότερα ἀγαθὰ μεθ' ἡμῶν, σοὶ ἐξομολογούμεθα
διὰ τοῦ ἀρχιερέως καὶ προστάτου τῶν ψυχῶν ἡμῶν
Ἰησοῦ Χριστοῦ, δι' οὗ σοι ἡ δόξα καὶ ἡ μεγαλωσύνη
καὶ νῦν καὶ εἰς γενεὰν γενεῶν καὶ εἰς τοὺς αἰῶνας τῶν
αἰώνων. ἀμήν.

62

Περὶ μὲν τῶν ἀνηκόντων τῇ θρησκείᾳ ἡμῶν καὶ τῶν
ὠφελιμωτάτων εἰς ἐνάρετον βίον τοῖς θέλουσιν εὐσεβῶς καὶ δικαίως διευθύνειν, ἱκανῶς ἐπεστείλαμεν
ὑμῖν, ἄνδρες ἀδελφοί. 2. περὶ γὰρ πίστεως καὶ μετανοίας καὶ γνησίας ἀγάπης καὶ ἐγκρατείας καὶ σωφρο-
σύνης καὶ ὑπομονῆς πάντα τόπον[112] ἐψηλαφήσαμεν,
ὑπομιμνήσκοντες δεῖν ὑμᾶς ἐν δικαιοσύνῃ καὶ ἀληθείᾳ καὶ μακροθυμίᾳ τῷ παντοκράτορι θεῷ ὁσίως
εὐαρεστεῖν,[113] ὁμονοοῦντας ἀμνησικάκως ἐν ἀγάπῃ
καὶ εἰρήνῃ μετὰ ἐκτενοῦς ἐπιεικείας, καθὼς καὶ οἱ
προδεδηλωμένοι πατέρες ἡμῶν εὐηρέστησαν ταπεινοφρονοῦντες τὰ πρὸς τὸν πατέρα καὶ θεὸν καὶ κτίστην
καὶ πάντας ἀνθρώπους. 3. καὶ ταῦτα τοσούτῳ ἥδιον
ὑπεμνήσαμεν, ἐπειδὴ σαφῶς ᾔδειμεν γράφειν ἡμᾶς
ἀνδράσιν πιστοῖς καὶ ἐλλογιμωτάτοις καὶ ἐγκεκυ-
φόσιν εἰς τὰ λόγια τῆς παιδείας τοῦ θεοῦ.

the authority you have given them, in peace and meekness, they may attain your mercy. 3. You who alone can to do these things for us, and do what is more abundantly good, we praise you through the high priest and benefactor of our souls, Jesus Christ, through whom the glory and majesty be yours both now and for all generations and forever. Amen.

62

Brothers, we have written you enough about what is fitting for our worship and what is most profitable for the virtuous life, for those who want to conduct themselves in a pious and upright way. 2. For we have touched on every aspect of faith, repentance, genuine love, self-restraint, moderation, and endurance, reminding you that you must be pleasing, in a holy way, both to the all-powerful God—by acting in righteousness, truth, and patience, living in harmony, holding no grudges, living in love and peace with fervent gentleness, just as our ancestors, whom we mentioned before, were pleasing to God by being humble-minded toward the Father, who is both God and Creator—and to all people. 3. And we were all the more happy to bring these things to mind, since we knew full well that we were writing to faithful and highly respectable men, who have gazed into the sayings of God's teaching.

---

112 τόπον H L: add τῆς γραφῆς S C
113 εὐαρεστεῖν L S C: εὐχαριστεῖν H

63

Θεμιτὸν οὖν ἐστιν τοῖς τοιούτοις καὶ τοσούτοις ὑποδείγμασιν προσελθόντας ὑποθεῖναι τὸν τράχηλον καὶ
τὸν τῆς ὑπακοῆς τόπον ἀναπληρῶσαι, ὅπως ἡσυ-
χάσαντες τῆς ματαίας στάσεως ἐπὶ τὸν προκείμενον
ἡμῖν ἐν ἀληθείᾳ σκοπὸν δίχα παντὸς μώμου κατα-
ντήσωμεν. 2. χαρὰν γὰρ καὶ ἀγαλλίασιν ἡμῖν
παρέξετε, ἐὰν ὑπήκοοι γενόμενοι τοῖς ὑφ' ἡμῶν γεγραμμένοις διὰ τοῦ ἁγίου πνεύματος ἐκκόψητε τὴν
ἀθέμιτον τοῦ ζήλους ὑμῶν ὀργὴν κατὰ τὴν ἔντευξιν,
ἣν ἐποιησάμεθα περὶ εἰρήνης καὶ ὁμονοίας ἐν τῇδε τῇ
ἐπιστολῇ. 3. ἐπέμψαμεν δὲ ἄνδρας πιστοὺς καὶ σώ-
φρονας ἀπὸ νεότητος ἀναστραφέντας ἕως γήρους
ἀμέμπτως ἐν ἡμῖν, οἵτινες καὶ μάρτυρες ἔσονται
μεταξὺ ὑμῶν καὶ ἡμῶν. 4. τοῦτο δὲ ἐποιήσαμεν, ἵνα
εἰδῆτε ὅτι πᾶσα ἡμῖν φροντὶς καὶ γέγονεν καὶ ἔστιν
εἰς τὸ ἐν τάχει ὑμᾶς εἰρηνεῦσαι.

64

Λοιπὸν[114] ὁ παντεπόπτης θεὸς καὶ δεσπότης τῶν
πνευμάτων καὶ κύριος πάσης σαρκός, ὁ ἐκλεξάμενος
τὸν κύριον Ἰησοῦν Χριστὸν καὶ ἡμᾶς δι' αὐτοῦ εἰς
λαὸν περιούσιον, δῴη πάσῃ ψυχῇ ἐπικεκλημένῃ τὸ
μεγαλοπρεπὲς καὶ ἅγιον ὄνομα αὐτοῦ πίστιν, φόβον,
εἰρήνην, ὑπομονὴν καὶ μακροθυμίαν, ἐγκράτειαν,
ἁγνείαν καὶ σωφροσύνην, εἰς εὐαρέστησιν τῷ ὀνόματι

63

Now that we have considered such great and so many examples, it is right for us to bow our necks in submission and assume a position of obedience. In this way, by putting a halt to the futile faction, we will truly reach the goal set before us, with no blame attached. 2. For you will make us joyful and happy if you become obedient to what we have written through the Holy Spirit and excise the wanton anger expressed through your jealousy, in accordance with the request we have made in this letter for your peace and harmony. 3. And we have sent faithful and temperate men who have lived blamelessly among us from youth to old age; these also will serve as witnesses between you and us. 4. We have done this that you may know that our every concern has been—and is—for you to establish the peace quickly.

64

And finally, may the God who observes all things, the Master of spirits and Lord of all flesh, who chose both the Lord Jesus Christ and us through him to be his special people— may he grant to every soul that is called by his magnificent and holy name faith, reverential awe, peace, endurance and patience, self-restraint, purity, and moderation, that they may be found pleasing to his name through our high

---

[114] . . . ιπον etc. found in A (cf. c. 57.6)

αὐτοῦ διὰ τοῦ ἀρχιερέως καὶ προστάτου ἡμῶν Ἰησοῦ Χριστοῦ, δι' οὗ αὐτῷ δόξα καὶ μεγαλωσύνη, κράτος καὶ τιμή, καὶ νῦν καὶ εἰς πάντας[115] τοὺς αἰῶνας τῶν αἰώνων. ἀμήν.

65

Τοὺς δὲ ἀπεσταλμένους ἀφ' ἡμῶν Κλαύδιον Ἔφηβον καὶ Οὐαλέριον Βίτωνα σὺν καὶ Φορτουνάτῳ ἐν εἰρήνῃ μετὰ χαρᾶς ἐν τάχει ἀναπέμψατε πρὸς ἡμᾶς, ὅπως θᾶττον τὴν εὐκταίαν καὶ ἐπιποθήτην ἡμῖν εἰρήνην καὶ ὁμόνοιαν ἀπαγγέλλωσιν, εἰς τὸ τάχιον καὶ ἡμᾶς χαρῆναι περὶ τῆς εὐσταθείας ὑμῶν. 2. ἡ χάρις τοῦ κυρίου ἡμῶν Ἰησοῦ Χριστοῦ μεθ' ὑμῶν καὶ μετὰ πάντων πανταχῇ τῶν κεκλημένων ὑπὸ τοῦ θεοῦ δι' αὐτοῦ, δι' οὗ αὐτῷ δόξα, τιμή, κράτος, καὶ μεγαλωσύνη, θρόνος αἰώνιος, ἀπὸ τῶν αἰώνων εἰς τοὺς αἰῶνας τῶν αἰώνων. ἀμήν.

Κλήμεντος πρὸς Κορινθίους ἐπιστολὴ ᾱ.[116]

115 παντας A H: om. L S C

116 Κλήμεντος—α' A: epistola Clementis ad Corinthios explicit L: finita est epistula prima Clementis quae fuit scripta ab eo ad Corinthios e Roma S: ἐπιστολὴ τῶν Ῥωμαίων πρὸς τοὺς Κορινθίους C

priest and benefactor, Jesus Christ. Through whom to him be glory and greatness, power and honor, both now and forevermore. Amen.

65

But send back to us quickly our envoys Claudius Ephebus and Valerius Bito, along with Fortunatus, in peace and with joy, that they may inform us without delay about the peace and harmony that we have prayed and desired for you. Then we will rejoice more quickly in your stability. 2. The grace of our Lord Jesus Christ be with you and with all those everywhere who are called by God through him. Through whom be to him all glory, honor, power, greatness, and the eternal throne, forever and ever. Amen.

The First Epistle of Clement to the Corinthians

SECOND LETTER OF CLEMENT
TO THE CORINTHIANS

INTRODUCTION

Second Clement is probably the most overlooked and least appreciated of the writings of the Apostolic Fathers. This is somewhat to be regretted, as it is in some ways a historically significant work.

As with 1 Clement, the book is misnamed—even more so, since in addition to being written by a different author, who cannot be identified as Clement of Rome, it is not even a letter. Readers have long recognized that the book appears in fact to be an early Christian homily, a written exposition of Scripture with an accompanying set of exhortations, delivered to a congregation gathered for worship. The service of worship—whether a weekly meeting or a special baptismal service (see Stewart-Sykes)—evidently included the reading of Scripture, an expositional homily based on the biblical text, and injunctions to moral behavior by the church presbyters (2.1; 17.3; 19.1). If this widely shared understanding of the work's genre is correct, then in 2 Clement we have the earliest instance of a Christian homily from outside the canon of the New Testament (several are preserved in the book of Acts, e.g., 3:12–26 and 20:18–35; some scholars think that the book of Hebrews may have originated as a homily as well).

INTRODUCTION

Overview

After a rather abrupt beginning, which may embody a high christology ("we must think about Jesus Christ as we think about God," 1.1), the homily immediately sets the themes of its exposition: members of the congregation are to react with awe, wonder, and gratitude for the act of salvation that God has mercifully wrought for them, former worshipers of pagan gods. The author then launches into an expository explanation of the Scripture text, Isaiah 54:1, which he interprets not in reference to its own historical context, but as a word from God that speaks directly to the situation of the members of his congregation. *Mutatis mutandis*, this explicitly Christian exegesis of the biblical text is comparable to modes of interpretation practiced by such Jewish interpreters as those who produced the Dead Sea Scrolls, in which ancient texts were taken to speak directly to the situation at hand, and, of course, by earlier Christian authors such as Paul.

The scriptural exegesis then sets the stage for the overarching points of the sermon: followers of Christ should recognize the enormous debt they owe to God for the salvation he has wrought. In response, they should repent of their sins, recognize that their new lives cannot be closely tied to this sinful world in which they temporarily reside as aliens, and commit themselves to good works and self-control in light of the judgment of God that is sure to come.

In the course of making his sundry moral exhortations, the author has occasion to cite numerous sacred authorities, principally passages from the "Old Testament" (in

Greek) and traditions of the sayings of Jesus. Some of these latter will be familiar to readers of the New Testament ("you will be like sheep in the midst of wolves" 5.2); others are somewhat startling ("Peter replied to him, 'And what if the wolves rip apart the sheep?' Jesus said to Peter, 'After they are dead, the sheep should fear the wolves no longer'" 5.3–4). In one place, the author cites and then provides a careful interpretation of a saying of Jesus closely connected with words now known from the *Gospel of Thomas*: "For when the Lord himself was asked by someone when his kingdom would come, he said, 'When the two are one and the outside like the inside, and the male with the female is neither male nor female'" (12.2; cf. *Gos. Thom.* 22. On the basis of a quotation of Clement of Alexandria, some have thought that the saying could also be found in the now lost *Gospel of the Egyptians*).

Even though the author appears to be working, in part, from oral traditions about Jesus available to him, rather than from a clearly delineated set of written Gospels, it is evident that he has some notion of collections of sacred authorities, since he at one point appeals to the authority of "the Bible [or the books] and the apostles" (14:2). He also appears to allude to the writings of Paul (e.g., in the image of the athlete in ch. 7 [cf. 1 Cor 9:24–27] and of the potter and clay in ch. 8 [cf. Rom 9:19–24]), but does not cite any of his books explicitly. It appears, then, that the author is an early witness to the idea vigorously stressed by later proto-orthodox Christians, that the Old Testament and the words and writings of the apostles (eventually, the "New Testament") represent the bipartite sacred authority for Christian faith and practice.

156

INTRODUCTION

Author

The identity of this author is almost completely obscured by the ancient record. Eusebius mentions a belief held by some that Clement of Rome had written the book as a second letter—Eusebius almost certainly means our 2 Clement—but he rejects it as improbable, noting that this other book did not receive wide acceptance in the Christian churches in earlier times or in his own day (*Eccl. Hist.* 3.37). The book is never mentioned by any earlier author (including Hegesippus and Dionysius of Corinth, who do mention 1 Clement), and is quoted later only by Monophysite Christians who welcomed some of its teachings (see Lightfoot); the few other writers who refer to the book (Rufinus, Jerome) do so in order to reject it, apart from the fourth-century *Apostolic Constitutions*, which lists it, along with 1 Clement, as part of the canon. Our principal record of its existence, then, is in the manuscript witnesses that happen to preserve it, all of them witnesses to 1 Clement as well: both of the Greek manuscripts and the solitary Syriac manuscript. In all three manuscripts the book is connected to Clement of Rome; in two of them, evidently, it is regarded as part of the Christian Scriptures.

On stylistic grounds, however, it is quite clear that the same person did not pen both works. And as this book is a homily that makes no concrete references to any persons or events that could establish its date or location, it has proved notoriously difficult to determine who wrote it, when, or where.

Adolf von Harnack popularized the view proposed by

A. Hilgenfeld that it is the letter Eusebius mentions as having been sent from the Roman bishop Soter (166–74 CE) to the congregation in Corinth. This theory has the virtue of explaining why the book came to be associated with 1 Clement: both were letters from Rome to Corinth, presumably kept then in the archives of the church there. But it founders on the circumstance that 2 Clement is neither a letter (see Holmes) nor an address from one community to another (Lightfoot).

About the most that can be said of the author is that he is a Greek-speaking Christian who was raised in and (probably) converted directly out of a pagan environment (see 1.6; 3.1). In contrast to the hypothesis that he sent the homily from Rome, some have thought that his evident connections with the *Gospel of Thomas* or the *Gospel of the Egyptians* and Clement of Alexandria indicate that he must have been from Alexandria. Others have insisted that the way he refers to "those who set sail for earthly competitions" (7.1) suggests an intimate familiarity with the Isthmian games held in Corinth during the first and third year of each Olympiad (Lightfoot). This view would have the additional benefit of explaining the ultimate association of the book with 1 Clement: both books would have been kept in the library of the church in Corinth. Donfried has argued even more specifically that this is a homily written by one of the Corinthian presbyters who had been deposed during the ecclesiastical coup described in 1 Clement, who was then restored to his position as a result of the earlier letter.

All such theories about the author and even his location, however, must remain speculative; there simply is not enough evidence for a firm determination.

Date

The situation is unfortunately not much better when it comes to establishing the date of the book. Eusebius knows of its existence in the early fourth century, even though in his judgment it was not written by Clement or widely used in the early Christian churches. In any event, Eusebius's comments show that the book was in some limited circulation by the end of the third century (since he knows of others who claimed it was written by Clement). Scholars are virtually unanimous, however, in thinking that it must have been written much earlier, sometime during the second century, a judgment necessarily made on general considerations involving its theological outlook and presupposed historical situation. There is a clear movement toward the establishment of a set of Christian textual authorities here, for example, but no indication of a recognized canon. The words of Jesus are actually called Scripture (2.40) but are nonetheless drawn from oral traditions rather than written Gospels. Some of the perspectives preserved in these traditions were later condemned as heretical (e.g., the Gnostic-like quotation of ch. 12).

Moreover, there is reference to a group of presbyters (17.3) but not to a single bishop over them. Nor does the author himself assume this role, as he seems to differentiate himself from the presbyters (17.3). Finally, the author is concerned about theological issues—for example, the relationship of Jesus and God (1.1) and the proper understanding of the flesh and Spirit, both of Christ and of the church—but does not address them in the nuanced terms more familiar from later theological discussions.

While none of these data is compelling on its own, to-

159

gether they suggest that the homily was written some time in the middle part of the second century, possibly in the 140s.

Historical Significance

Second Clement would obviously be *more* historically significant if we could pinpoint its date and location. Some scholars who have situated the book in Egypt (e.g., Koester) have seen in it the first recorded attack on burgeoning Gnosticism there. But (as Koester acknowledges) there are too many uncertainties to accept this formulation without reservations. What can be said must be of a more general nature. Given its probable mid-second century date, the book is significant as the first surviving homily outside the New Testament canon. From it one can reconstruct at least one homilist's approach to the task, including his assumptions about the authority of the Greek Old Testament (its very words are significant and speak to the present day) and the traditions in circulation about Jesus (these too are authoritative, even when passed along in oral traditions from a range of sources, some of which would later have been branded heretical). There is, in other words, a kind of movement towards a Christian canon evidenced in this author, but nothing like a narrowly defined list of sacred and authoritative writings.

The letter is significant as well for giving some hints about the nature of the worship services in its time and place: Scripture was read, a (written) sermon was based on the text, exhortations were delivered by the elders (presbyters) of the church to the congregation. The admonitions and ultimate concerns of this particular sermon are almost entirely ethical in nature. That is to say, while there is some theological reflection, especially about the nature of Christ and his church, it is ethically right behavior rather than closely nuanced theology that concerns the author and, presumably, his congregation (or at least its leaders). This author was principally concerned that, in light of God's gracious act of salvation, his community repent of their sins, live in ways that differentiated them from their pagan neighbors, with whom, therefore, they were presumably still in contact, engage in good deeds such as prayer, fasting, and especially giving to charity, and prepare for the judgment that was coming.

Textual Tradition and Editions

Neither of the Coptic manuscripts that attests 1 Clement contains 2 Clement, but the remaining three manuscripts of 1 Clement do: the solitary Syriac manuscript (dated 1169), Codex Alexandrinus (fifth century, which contains only 1.1–12.5a), and Codex Hierosolymitanus (1056).

The *editio princeps* was published by Patrick Young in 1633, based on the Codex Alexandrinus (see Introduction to 1 Clement).

Surviving Manuscripts and Abbreviations

A   Codex Alexandrinus (5th c.; missing 12.5b–end)
H   Codex Hierosolymitanus (1056)
S   Syriac manuscript of the New Testament dated 1169,

with 1 and 2 Clement located after the Catholic epistles, edited by R. L. Bensly (possibly representing an
eighth-century translation)

SELECT BIBLIOGRAPHY

Baasland, Ernst. "Der 2 Klemensbrief und frühchristliche
Rhetorik: 'Die erste christliche Predigt' im Lichte der
neueren Forschung." *ANRW* II.27.1 (1993) 78–157.

Bartlett, Vernon. "The Origin and Date of 2 Clement."
ZNW 7 (1906) 123–35.

Donfried, Karl P. *The Setting of Second Clement in Early
Christianity.* Leiden: Brill, 1974.

———— "The Theology of Second Clement." *HTR* 66
(1973) 487–501.

Grant, Robert M., and H. H. Graham. *First and Second
Clement.* Vol. 2 of *The Apostolic Fathers: A New Trans-
lation and Commentary*, ed. Robert M. Grant. Camden,
N.J.: Thomas Nelson, 1965.

Harris, J. Rendel. "The Authorship of the So-Called Second Epistle of Clement." *ZNW* 23 (1924) 193–200.

Holmes, Michael W., ed. *The Apostolic Fathers: Greek
Texts and English Translations of Their Writings.* Trans.
J. B. Lightfoot and J. R. Harmer, 2nd edition. London
and New York, 1990.

Kennett, R. H., and R. L. Bensly, *The Epistles of S. Clement to the Corinthians in Syriac. Edited from the manuscript with notes by the late R. L. Bensly.* Cambridge:
University Press, 1899.

Kenyon, F. G. *The Codex Alexandrinus (Royal ms. 1 D v-
viii) in Reduced Photographic Facsimile.* London: British Museum, 1909.

Knopf, Rudolf. *Die apostolischen Väter. Die Lehre der zwölf Apostol, Die zwei Clemensbriefe*. Vol. 1. HNTSup. Tübingen: Mohr-Siebeck, 1920.

Koester, Helmut. *Introduction to the New Testament. Vol. 2, History and Literature of Early Christianity.* Philadelphia: Fortress, 1984; 233–36.

Lightfoot, Joseph Barber. *The Apostolic Fathers: Clement, Ignatius, and Polycarp.* Part I: *Clement.* 2 vols. London: Macmillan 1889; reprinted Peabody, Mass.: Hendrickson, 1989.

Lindemann, Andreas. *Die Clemensbriefe.* Tübingen: Mohr-Siebeck, 1992.

Morin, G. *Sancti Clementis Romani ad Corinthos epistulae versio latina antiquissima. Anecdota Maredsolana* II. Maredsous, Belgium, 1894.

Stewart-Sykes, Alistair. *From Prophecy to Preaching: A Search for the Origins of the Christian Homily.* Leiden: Brill, 2001.

Thompson, E. Maunde. *Facsimile of the Codex Alexandrinus.* London: British Museum, 1879–83.

Warns, Rüdiger. *Untersuchungen zum 2. Clemens-Brief.* Marburg: Philipps-Universität, 1985.

ΚΛΕΜΕΝΤΟΣ ΠΡΟΣ
ΚΟΡΙΝΘΙΟΥΣ Β΄[1]

1

Ἀδελφοί, οὕτως δεῖ ἡμᾶς φρονεῖν περὶ Ἰησοῦ Χριστοῦ, ὡς περὶ θεοῦ, ὡς περὶ κριτοῦ ζώντων καὶ νεκρῶν· καὶ οὐ δεῖ ἡμᾶς μικρὰ φρονεῖν περὶ τῆς σωτηρίας ἡμῶν. 2. ἐν τῷ γὰρ φρονεῖν ἡμᾶς μικρὰ περὶ αὐτοῦ μικρὰ καὶ ἐλπίζομεν λαβεῖν· καὶ οἱ ἀκού-οντες ὡς περὶ[2] μικρῶν[3] ἁμαρτάνομεν οὐκ εἰδότες, πόθεν ἐκλήθημεν καὶ ὑπὸ τίνος καὶ εἰς ὃν τόπον, καὶ ὅσα ὑπέμεινεν Ἰησοῦς Χριστὸς παθεῖν ἕνεκα ἡμῶν. 3. τίνα οὖν ἡμεῖς αὐτῷ δώσομεν ἀντιμισθίαν, ἢ τίνα καρπὸν ἄξιον οὗ ἡμῖν αὐτὸς ἔδωκεν; πόσα δὲ αὐτῷ ὀφείλομεν ὅσια; 4. τὸ φῶς γὰρ ἡμῖν ἐχαρίσατο, ὡς πατὴρ υἱοὺς ἡμᾶς προσηγόρευσεν, ἀπολλυμένους ἡμᾶς ἔσωσεν. 5. ποῖον οὖν αἶνον αὐτῷ δώσομεν ἢ μισθὸν ἀντιμισθίας ὧν ἐλάβομεν; 6. πηροὶ[4] ὄντες τῇ διανοίᾳ, προσκυνοῦντες λίθους καὶ ξύλα καὶ χρυσὸν

¹ ΚΛ. ΠΡ. Κ. β΄ H S (before Κλ. add τοῦ αὐτοῦ S): om. A (but at the end of the index of New Testament Scriptures A reads Κλήμεντος ε[πιστολ]η β)

SECOND LETTER OF CLEMENT
TO THE CORINTHIANS

1

Brothers, we must think about Jesus Christ as we think
about God, as about the judge of the living and the dead.[1]
And we must not give little thought to our salvation. 2. For
when we think little about him, we also hope to receive
but little. And we who listen as if these were little things
sin, not realizing where we have been called from, by
whom, and to what place, nor how many sufferings Jesus
Christ endured for us. 3. What then shall we give to him in
exchange? How can we produce anything comparable to
what he has given us? And how many holy deeds do we owe
him? 4. For he graciously bestowed light upon us. Like a
father, he called us children; while we were perishing, he
saved us. 5. What praise, then, shall we give him, or what
can we pay in exchange for what we have received? 6. We
were maimed in our understanding, worshiping stones and

1 Acts 10:42; 1 Pet 4:5.

2 ὡς περὶ H S: ὥσπερ A
3 μικρῶν A H: add ἁμαρτάνουσιν, καὶ ἡμεῖς S
4 πηροὶ A S: πονηροὶ H

καὶ ἄργυρον καὶ χαλκόν, ἔργα ἀνθρώπων· καὶ ὁ βίος
ἡμῶν ὅλος ἄλλο οὐδὲν ἦν εἰ μὴ θάνατος. ἀμαύρωσιν
οὖν περικείμενοι καὶ τοιαύτης ἀχλύος γέμοντες ἐν τῇ
ὁράσει, ἀνεβλέψαμεν ἀποθέμενοι ἐκεῖνο ὃ περικείμεθα
νέφος τῇ αὐτοῦ θελήσει. 7. ἠλέησεν γὰρ ἡμᾶς καὶ
σπλαγχνισθεὶς ἔσωσεν, θεασάμενος ἐν ἡμῖν πολλὴν
πλάνην καὶ ἀπώλειαν, καὶ μηδεμίαν ἐλπίδα ἔχοντας
σωτηρίας, εἰ μὴ τὴν παρ' αὐτοῦ. 8. ἐκάλεσεν γὰρ ἡμᾶς
οὐκ ὄντας καὶ ἠθέλησεν ἐκ μὴ ὄντος εἶναι ἡμᾶς.

2

Εὐφράνθητι, στεῖρα ἡ οὐ τίκτουσα, ῥῆξον καὶ βόησον
ἡ οὐκ ὠδίνουσα, ὅτι πολλὰ τὰ τέκνα τῆς ἐρήμου
μᾶλλον ἢ τῆς ἐχούσης τὸν ἄνδρα. ὃ εἶπεν· εὐφράνθητι, στεῖρα ἡ οὐ τίκτουσα, ἡμᾶς εἶπεν· στεῖρα γὰρ
ἦν ἡ ἐκκλησία ἡμῶν πρὸ τοῦ δοθῆναι αὐτῇ τέκνα. 2. ὃ
δὲ εἶπεν· βόησον, ἡ οὐκ ὠδίνουσα, τοῦτο λέγει· τὰς
προσευχὰς ἡμῶν ἁπλῶς ἀναφέρειν πρὸς τὸν θεόν, μὴ
ὡς αἱ ὠδίνουσαι ἐγκακῶμεν. 3. ὃ δὲ εἶπεν· ὅτι πολλὰ
τὰ τέκνα τῆς ἐρήμου μᾶλλον ἢ τῆς ἐχούσης τὸν
ἄνδρα· ἐπεὶ ἔρημος ἐδόκει εἶναι ἀπὸ τοῦ θεοῦ ὁ λαὸς
ἡμῶν, νυνὶ δὲ πιστεύσαντες πλείονες ἐγενόμεθα τῶν
δοκούντων ἔχειν θεόν. 4. καὶ ἑτέρα δὲ γραφὴ λέγει, ὅτι
οὐκ ἦλθον καλέσαι δικαίους, ἀλλὰ ἁμαρτωλούς.

pieces of wood and gold and silver and copper—all of them made by humans. And our entire life was nothing other than death. Then when we were beset by darkening gloom, our vision blurred by such mist, we regained our sight through his will by setting aside the cloud that enveloped us. 7. For he showed mercy on us and through his compassion saved us. For he saw that a great error and destruction was in us, and that we had not the slightest hope of being saved, unless it came through him. 8. For he called us while we did not exist, and he wished us to come into being from nonbeing.

2

"Be jubilant, you who are infertile and who do not bear children! Let your voice burst forth and cry out, you who experience no pains of labor! For the one who has been deserted has more children than the one who has a husband."[2] Now when it says, "Be jubilant, you who are infertile and who do not bear children," it is referring to us. For our church was infertile before children were given to it. 2. And when it says, "Cry out, you who experience no pains of labor," it means this: we should raise our prayers up to God sincerely and not grow weary like women in labor. 3. And when it says, "For the one who has been deserted has more children than the one who has a husband," it is because our people appeared to be deserted by God, but now that we believe we have become more numerous than those who appear to have God. 4. And also another Scripture says, "I did not come to call the upright, but

[2] Isa 54:1; cf. Gal 4:27.

5. τοῦτο λέγει, ὅτι δεῖ τοὺς ἀπολλυμένους σώζειν. 6. ἐκεῖνο γάρ ἐστιν μέγα καὶ θαυμαστόν, οὐ τὰ ἑστῶτα στηρίζειν, ἀλλὰ τὰ πίπτοντα. 7. οὕτως καὶ ὁ Χριστὸς ἠθέλησεν σῶσαι τὰ ἀπολλύμενα, καὶ ἔσωσεν πολλούς, ἐλθὼν καὶ καλέσας ἡμᾶς ἤδη ἀπολλυμένους.

3

Τοσοῦτον οὖν ἔλεος ποιήσαντος αὐτοῦ εἰς ἡμᾶς—πρῶτον μέν, ὅτι ἡμεῖς οἱ ζῶντες τοῖς νεκροῖς θεοῖς οὐ θύομεν καὶ οὐ προσκυνοῦμεν αὐτοῖς,[5] ἀλλὰ ἔγνωμεν δι᾿ αὐτοῦ τὸν πατέρα τῆς ἀληθείας—τίς ἡ γνῶσις ἡ πρὸς αὐτόν,[6] ἢ τὸ μὴ ἀρνεῖσθαι δι᾿ οὗ ἔγνωμεν αὐτόν; 2. λέγει δὲ καὶ αὐτός· τὸν ὁμολογήσαντά με ἐνώπιον τῶν ἀνθρώπων, ὁμολογήσω αὐτὸν ἐνώπιον τοῦ πατρός μου. 3. οὗτος οὖν ἐστιν ὁ μισθὸς ἡμῶν, ἐὰν οὖν ὁμολογήσωμεν δι᾿ οὗ ἐσώθημεν. 4. ἐν τίνι δὲ αὐτὸν ὁμολογοῦμεν; ἐν τῷ ποιεῖν ἃ λέγει καὶ μὴ παρακούειν αὐτοῦ τῶν ἐντολῶν, καὶ μὴ μόνον χείλεσιν αὐτὸν τιμᾶν, ἀλλὰ ἐξ ὅλης καρδίας καὶ ἐξ ὅλης τῆς διανοίας. 5. λέγει δὲ καὶ ἐν τῷ Ἠσαΐᾳ· ὁ λαὸς οὗτος τοῖς χείλεσίν με τιμᾷ, ἡ δὲ καρδία αὐτῶν πόρρω ἄπεστιν ἀπ᾿ ἐμοῦ.

[5] καὶ οὐ π. αὐτ. A S: om. H
[6] ἡ πρὸς αὐτὸν A S: τῆς ἀληθείας H

sinners."[3] 5. This means that he was to save those who were perishing. 6. For it is a great and astonishing feat to fix in place something that is toppling over, not something that is standing. 7. Thus also Christ wished to save what was perishing. And he did save many; for he came and called us while we were on the brink of destruction.

3

He has shown us such mercy since, to begin with, we who are living do not sacrifice to dead gods or worship them; instead, through him we know the Father of truth. What then is the knowledge that is directed toward to him? Is it not refusing to deny the one through whom we have come to know him? 2. For even he himself says, "I will acknowledge before my Father the one who acknowledges me before others."[4] 3. This then is our reward, if we acknowledge the one through whom we were saved. 4. But how do we acknowledge him? By doing the things he says, not disobeying his commandments, and not honoring him only with our lips but from our whole heart and our whole understanding.[5] 5. For he also says in Isaiah, "This people honors me with their lips, but their heart is far removed from me."[6]

[3] Matt 9:13; Mark 2:17; Luke 5:32.
[4] Matt 10:32; Luke 12:8.
[5] Mark 12:30.
[6] Isa 29:13; cf. Matt 15:8; Mark 7:6; 1 Clem 15:2.

4

Μὴ μόνον οὖν αὐτὸν καλῶμεν κύριον· οὐ γὰρ τοῦτο
σώσει ἡμᾶς. 2. λέγει γάρ· οὐ πᾶς ὁ λέγων μοι· κύριε
κύριε, σωθήσεται, ἀλλ᾽ ὁ ποιῶν τὴν δικαιοσύνην.
3. ὥστε οὖν, ἀδελφοί, ἐν τοῖς ἔργοις αὐτὸν ὁμολογῶμεν, ἐν τῷ ἀγαπᾶν ἑαυτούς, ἐν τῷ μὴ μοιχᾶσθαι
μηδὲ καταλαλεῖν ἀλλήλων μηδὲ ζηλοῦν, ἀλλ᾽ ἐγκρατεῖς εἶναι, ἐλεήμονας, ἀγαθούς· καὶ συμπάσχειν ἀλλήλοις ὀφείλομεν, καὶ μὴ φιλαργυρεῖν. ἐν τούτοις τοῖς
ἔργοις ὁμολογῶμεν αὐτὸν καὶ μὴ ἐν τοῖς ἐναντίοις·
4. καὶ οὐ δεῖ ἡμᾶς φοβεῖσθαι τοὺς ἀνθρώπους μᾶλλον, ἀλλὰ τὸν θεόν. 5. διὰ τοῦτο, ταῦτα ὑμῶν[7] πρασ-
σόντων, εἶπεν ὁ κύριος·[8] ἐὰν ἦτε μετ᾽ ἐμοῦ συνηγμένοι
ἐν τῷ κόλπῳ μου καὶ μὴ ποιῆτε τὰς ἐντολάς μου,
ἀποβαλῶ ὑμᾶς καὶ ἐρῶ ὑμῖν· ὑπάγετε ἀπ᾽ ἐμοῦ, οὐκ
οἶδα ὑμᾶς, πόθεν ἐστέ, ἐργάται ἀνομίας.

5

Ὅθεν, ἀδελφοί, καταλείψαντες τὴν παροικίαν τοῦ
κόσμου τούτου ποιήσωμεν τὸ θέλημα τοῦ καλέσαντος
ἡμᾶς, καὶ μὴ φοβηθῶμεν ἐξελθεῖν ἐκ τοῦ κόσμου
τούτου. 2. λέγει γὰρ ὁ κύριος· ἔσεσθε ὡς ἀρνία ἐν
μέσῳ λύκων. 3. ἀποκριθεὶς δὲ ὁ Πέτρος αὐτῷ λέγει·
ἐὰν οὖν διασπαράξωσιν οἱ λύκοι τὰ ἀρνία; 4. εἶπεν ὁ

[7] ὑμῶν A: ἡμῶν H S
[8] κύριος A H: add Ἰησοῦς S

4

For this reason we should not merely call him Lord; for this will not save us. 2. For he says, "Not everyone who says to me, 'Lord, Lord' will be saved, but only the one who practices righteousness."[7] 3. So then, brothers, we should acknowledge him by what we do, by loving one another, by not committing adultery or slandering one another or showing envy. We should be restrained, charitable, and good. We should be sympathetic with one another and not be attached to money. By doing such deeds we acknowledge him, not by doing their opposites. 4. And we must not fear people, but God. 5. For this reason, when you do these things, the Lord has said, "Even if you were nestled close to my breast but did not do what I have commanded, I would cast you away and say to you, 'Leave me! I do not know where you are from, you who do what is lawless.'"[8]

5

Therefore, brothers, having abandoned our temporary residence in this world, we should do the will of the one who called us and not fear departing from this world. 2. For the Lord said, "You will be like sheep in the midst of wolves."[9] 3. But Peter replied to him, "What if the wolves rip apart the sheep?" 4. Jesus said to Peter, "After they are

7 Matt 7:21.
8 Source unknown.
9 Cf. Matt 10:16; Luke 10:3.

Ἰησοῦς τῷ Πέτρῳ· μὴ φοβείσθωσαν τὰ ἀρνία τοὺς
λύκους μετὰ τὸ ἀποθανεῖν αὐτά· καὶ ὑμεῖς μὴ φοβεῖσθε τοὺς ἀποκτέννοντας ὑμᾶς καὶ μηδὲν ὑμῖν
δυναμένους ποιεῖν, ἀλλὰ φοβεῖσθε τὸν μετὰ τὸ ἀποθανεῖν ὑμᾶς ἔχοντα ἐξουσίαν ψυχῆς καὶ σώματος τοῦ
βαλεῖν εἰς γέενναν πυρός. 5. καὶ γινώσκετε, ἀδελφοί,
ὅτι ἡ ἐπιδημία ἡ ἐν τῷ κόσμῳ τούτῳ τῆς σαρκὸς
ταύτης μικρά ἐστιν καὶ ὀλιγοχρόνιος, ἡ δὲ ἐπαγγελία
τοῦ Χριστοῦ μεγάλη καὶ θαυμαστή ἐστιν, καὶ⁹
ἀνάπαυσις τῆς μελλούσης βασιλείας καὶ ζωῆς αἰωνίου. 6. τί οὖν ἐστιν ποιήσαντας ἐπιτυχεῖν αὐτῶν, εἰ
μὴ τὸ ὁσίως καὶ δικαίως ἀναστρέφεσθαι καὶ τὰ
κοσμικὰ ταῦτα ὡς ἀλλότρια ἡγεῖσθαι καὶ μὴ ἐπιθυμεῖν αὐτῶν; 7. ἐν γὰρ τῷ ἐπιθυμεῖν ἡμᾶς κτήσασθαι
ταῦτα ἀποπίπτομεν τῆς ὁδοῦ τῆς δικαίας.

6

Λέγει δὲ ὁ κύριος· οὐδεὶς οἰκέτης δύναται δυσὶ κυρίοις
δουλεύειν. ἐὰν ἡμεῖς θέλωμεν καὶ θεῷ δουλεύειν καὶ
μαμωνᾷ, ἀσύμφορον ἡμῖν ἐστιν. 2. τί γὰρ τὸ ὄφελος,
ἐάν τις τὸν κόσμον ὅλον κερδήσῃ, τὴν δὲ ψυχὴν
ζημιωθῇ; 3. ἔστιν δὲ οὗτος ὁ αἰὼν καὶ ὁ μέλλων δύο
ἐχθροί. 4. οὗτος λέγει μοιχείαν καὶ φθορὰν καὶ φιλαρ-
γυρίαν καὶ ἀπάτην, ἐκεῖνος δὲ τούτοις ἀποτάσσεται.
5. οὐ δυνάμεθα οὖν τῶν δύο φίλοι εἶναι· δεῖ δὲ ἡμᾶς
τούτῳ ἀποταξαμένους ἐκείνῳ χρᾶσθαι. 6. οἰόμεθα, ὅτι
βέλτιόν ἐστιν τὰ ἐνθάδε μισῆσαι, ὅτι μικρὰ καὶ

dead, the sheep should fear the wolves no longer. So too you: do not fear those who kill you and then can do nothing more to you; but fear the one who, after you die, has the power to cast your body and soul into the hell of fire."[10] 5. You should realize, brothers, that our visit in this realm of the flesh is brief and short-lived, but the promise of Christ is great and astounding—namely, a rest in the coming kingdom and eternal life. 6. What then must we do to obtain these things, except conduct ourselves in a holy and upright way and consider these worldly affairs foreign to us, and not yearn after them? 7. For when we yearn to obtain these things we fall away from the right path.

6

But the Lord says, "No household servant can serve as the slave of two masters."[11] If we wish to serve as slaves of both God and wealth, it is of no gain to us. 2. "For what is the advantage of acquiring the whole world while forfeiting your life?"[12] 3. But this age and the age to come are two enemies. 4. This one preaches adultery, depravity, avarice, and deceit, but that one renounces these things. 5. We cannot, therefore, be friends of both. We must renounce this world to obtain that one. 6. We think it better to despise the things that are here, since they are brief, short-lived, and

10 Source unknown. Cf. Matt 10:28; Luke 12:4–5.
11 Luke 16:13; Matt 6:24.
12 Matt 16:26; Mark 8:36; Luke 9:25.

9 καὶ add ἡ H

ὀλιγοχρόνια καὶ φθαρτά, ἐκεῖνα δὲ ἀγαπῆσαι, τὰ
ἀγαθὰ τὰ ἄφθαρτα. 7. ποιοῦντες γὰρ τὸ θέλημα τοῦ
Χριστοῦ εὑρήσομεν ἀνάπαυσιν· εἰ δὲ μήγε, οὐδὲν
ἡμᾶς ῥύσεται ἐκ τῆς αἰωνίου κολάσεως, ἐὰν
παρακούσωμεν τῶν ἐντολῶν αὐτοῦ. 8. λέγει δὲ καὶ ἡ
γραφὴ ἐν τῷ Ἰεζεκιήλ, ὅτι ἐὰν ἀναστῇ Νῶε καὶ Ἰὼβ
καὶ Δανιήλ, οὐ ῥύσονται τὰ τέκνα αὐτῶν ἐν τῇ
αἰχμαλωσίᾳ. 9. εἰ δὲ καὶ οἱ τοιοῦτοι δίκαιοι οὐ δύνανται ταῖς ἑαυτῶν δικαιοσύναις ῥύσασθαι τὰ τέκνα
αὐτῶν, ἡμεῖς, ἐὰν μὴ τηρήσωμεν τὸ βάπτισμα ἁγνὸν
καὶ ἀμίαντον, ποίᾳ πεποιθήσει εἰσελευσόμεθα εἰς τὸ
βασίλειον τοῦ θεοῦ; ἢ τίς ἡμῶν παράκλητος ἔσται,
ἐὰν μὴ εὑρεθῶμεν ἔργα ἔχοντες ὅσια καὶ δίκαια;

7

Ὥστε οὖν, ἀδελφοί μου, ἀγωνισώμεθα εἰδότες, ὅτι ἐν
χερσὶν ὁ ἀγὼν καὶ ὅτι εἰς τοὺς φθαρτοὺς ἀγῶνας
καταπλέουσιν πολλοί, ἀλλ᾽ οὐ πάντες στεφανοῦνται,
εἰ μὴ οἱ πολλὰ κοπιάσαντες καὶ καλῶς ἀγωνισάμενοι.
2. ἡμεῖς οὖν ἀγωνισώμεθα, ἵνα πάντες στεφανωθῶμεν.
3. ὥστε θέωμεν[10] τὴν ὁδὸν τὴν εὐθεῖαν, ἀγῶνα τὸν
ἄφθαρτον, καὶ πολλοὶ εἰς αὐτὸν καταπλεύσωμεν καὶ
ἀγωνισώμεθα, ἵνα καὶ στεφανωθῶμεν· καὶ εἰ μὴ
δυνάμεθα πάντες στεφανωθῆναι, κἂν ἐγγὺς τοῦ στεφάνου γενώμεθα. 4. εἰδέναι ἡμᾶς δεῖ, ὅτι ὁ τὸν φθαρ-
τὸν ἀγῶνα ἀγωνιζόμενος, ἐὰν εὑρεθῇ φθείρων, μαστι-
γωθεὶς αἴρεται καὶ ἔξω βάλλεται τοῦ σταδίου. 5. τί

perishable, and to love those other things, which are good and imperishable. 7. For by doing the will of Christ we will find a place of rest; on the other hand, nothing will deliver us from eternal punishment if we disobey his commandments. 8. And the Scripture also says in Ezekiel, "Even if Noah, Job, and Daniel should arise, they will not deliver their children from captivity."[13] 9. But if even such upright men as these cannot deliver their children through acts of righteousness, with what confidence can we enter into the kingdom of God if we do not keep our baptism pure and undefiled? Or who will serve as our advocate, if we are not found doing what is holy and upright?

7

So then, my brothers, we should compete in the games, knowing that the competition is at hand. Many set sail for earthly competitions but not all receive the crown—only those who labor hard and compete well. 2. We should therefore compete that we all may be crowned. 3. And so we should run the straight course, the eternal competition. Many of us should sail to it and compete, that we may receive the crown. And if all of us cannot receive the crown, we should at least come close to it. 4. We must realize that if someone is caught cheating while competing in an earthly contest, he is flogged and thrown out of the sta-

13 Ezek 14:14ff.

---

10 θέωμεν S: θῶμεν A H

δοκεῖτε; ὁ τὸν τῆς ἀφθαρσίας ἀγῶνα φθείρας τί
παθεῖται;[11] 6. τῶν γὰρ μὴ τηρησάντων, φησίν, τὴν
σφραγῖδα ὁ σκώληξ αὐτῶν οὐ τελευτήσει καὶ τὸ πῦρ
αὐτῶν οὐ σβεσθήσεται, καὶ ἔσονται εἰς ὅρασιν πάσῃ
σαρκί.

8

Ὡς οὖν ἐσμὲν ἐπὶ γῆς, μετανοήσωμεν. 2. πηλὸς γάρ
ἐσμεν εἰς τὴν χεῖρα τοῦ τεχνίτου· ὃν τρόπον γὰρ ὁ
κεραμεύς, ἐὰν ποιῇ σκεῦος καὶ ἐν ταῖς χερσὶν αὐτοῦ
διαστραφῇ ἢ συντριβῇ, πάλιν αὐτὸ ἀναπλάσσει, ἐὰν
δὲ προφθάσῃ εἰς τὴν κάμινον τοῦ πυρὸς αὐτὸ βαλεῖν,
οὐκέτι βοηθήσει αὐτῷ· οὕτως καὶ ἡμεῖς, ἕως ἐσμὲν ἐν
τούτῳ τῷ κόσμῳ, ἐν τῇ σαρκὶ ἃ ἐπράξαμεν πονηρὰ
μετανοήσωμεν ἐξ ὅλης τῆς καρδίας, ἵνα σωθῶμεν ὑπὸ
τοῦ κυρίου, ἕως ἔχομεν καιρὸν μετανοίας.[12] 3. μετὰ
γὰρ τὸ ἐξελθεῖν ἡμᾶς ἐκ τοῦ κόσμου οὐκέτι δυνάμεθα
ἐκεῖ ἐξομολογήσασθαι ἢ μετανοεῖν ἔτι. 4. ὥστε,
ἀδελφοί, ποιήσαντες τὸ θέλημα τοῦ πατρὸς καὶ τὴν
σάρκα ἁγνὴν τηρήσαντες καὶ τὰς ἐντολὰς τοῦ κυρίου
φυλάξαντες λῃψόμεθα ζωὴν αἰώνιον. 5. λέγει γὰρ ὁ
κύριος ἐν τῷ εὐαγγελίῳ· εἰ τὸ μικρὸν οὐκ ἐτηρήσατε,
τὸ μέγα τίς ὑμῖν δώσει; λέγω γὰρ ὑμῖν, ὅτι ὁ πιστὸς
ἐν ἐλαχίστῳ καὶ ἐν πολλῷ πιστός ἐστιν. 6. ἄρα οὖν
τοῦτο λέγει· τηρήσατε τὴν σάρκα ἁγνὴν καὶ τὴν
σφραγῖδα ἄσπιλον, ἵνα τὴν αἰώνιον ζωὴν ἀπολάβωμεν.[13]

dium. 5. What do you suppose? What will happen to the one who cheats in the eternal competition? 6. As for those who do not keep the seal of their baptism, he says: "Their worm will not die nor their fire be extinguished; and they will be a spectacle for all to see."[14]

8

And so we should repent while we are still on earth. 2. For we are clay in the hand of the artisan. As in the case of a potter: if he is making a vessel that becomes misshapened or crushed in his hands, he then remolds it; but if he has already put it in the kiln, he can no longer fix it. So too with us. While we are still in the world, we should repent from our whole heart of the evil we have done in the flesh, so the Lord will save us—while there is still time for repentance. 3. For after we leave the world we will no longer be able to make confession or repent in that place. 4. So then, brothers, if we do the will of the Father and keep our flesh pure and guard the commandments of the Lord we will receive eternal life. 5. For the Lord says in the Gospel, "If you do not keep what is small, who will give you what is great? For I say to you that the one who is faithful in very little is faithful also in much."[15] 6. This then is what he means: you should keep the flesh pure and the seal of baptism stainless, so that we may receive eternal life.

14 Isa 66:24; cf. Mark 9:44, 46, 48.   15 Luke 16:10–12.

---

11 παθεῖται A: πείσεται H
12 μετανοίας: om. H
13 ἀπολάβωμεν A: ἀπολάβητε H S

9

Καὶ μὴ λεγέτω τις ὑμῶν, ὅτι αὕτη ἡ σὰρξ οὐ κρίνεται
οὐδὲ ἀνίσταται. 2. γνῶτε· ἐν τίνι ἐσώθητε, ἐν τίνι
ἀνεβλέψατε, εἰ μὴ ἐν τῇ σαρκὶ ταύτῃ ὄντες; 3. δεῖ οὖν
ἡμᾶς ὡς ναὸν θεοῦ φυλάσσειν τὴν σάρκα. 4. ὃν
τρόπον γὰρ ἐν τῇ σαρκὶ ἐκλήθητε, καὶ ἐν τῇ σαρκὶ
ἐλεύσεσθε. 5. εἰ Ἰησοῦς[14] Χριστὸς ὁ κύριος ὁ σώσας
ἡμᾶς, ὢν μὲν τὸ πρῶτον πνεῦμα,[15] ἐγένετο σὰρξ καὶ
οὕτως ἡμᾶς ἐκάλεσεν, οὕτως καὶ ἡμεῖς ἐν ταύτῃ τῇ
σαρκὶ ἀποληψόμεθα τὸν μισθόν. 6. ἀγαπῶμεν οὖν
ἀλλήλους, ὅπως ἔλθωμεν πάντες εἰς τὴν βασιλείαν
τοῦ θεοῦ. 7. ὡς ἔχομεν καιρὸν τοῦ ἰαθῆναι, ἐπιδῶμεν
ἑαυτοὺς τῷ θεραπεύοντι θεῷ, ἀντιμισθίαν αὐτῷ διδόντες. 8. ποίαν; τὸ μετανοῆσαι ἐξ εἰλικρινοῦς καρδίας.
9. προγνώστης γάρ ἐστιν τῶν πάντων καὶ εἰδὼς ἡμῶν
τὰ ἐν καρδίᾳ. 10. δῶμεν οὖν αὐτῷ αἶνον, μὴ ἀπὸ
στόματος μόνον, ἀλλὰ καὶ ἀπὸ καρδίας, ἵνα ἡμᾶς
προσδέξηται ὡς υἱούς. 11. καὶ γὰρ εἶπεν ὁ κύριος·
ἀδελφοί μου οὗτοί εἰσιν οἱ ποιοῦντες τὸ θέλημα τοῦ
πατρός μου.

10

Ὥστε, ἀδελφοί μου, ποιήσωμεν τὸ θέλημα τοῦ
πατρὸς τοῦ καλέσαντος ἡμᾶς, ἵνα ζήσωμεν· καὶ διώ-

---

[14] εἰ Ἰησοῦς (= ΕΠϹ) cj. Ehrman: εἰς A H S: εἰ Syr. Frag.

9

And none of you should say that this flesh is neither judged nor raised. 2. Think about it! In what state were you saved? In what state did you regain your sight? Was it not while you were in this flesh? 3. And so we must guard the flesh like the temple of God. 4. For just as you were called in the flesh, so also you will come in the flesh. 5. Since Jesus Christ[16]—the Lord who saved us—was first a spirit and then became flesh, and in this way called us, so also we will receive the reward in this flesh. 6. And so we should love one another, that we may all enter the Kingdom of God. 7. While we have time to be healed, let us give ourselves over to the God who brings healing, paying him what is due. 8. And what is that? Repentance from a sincere heart. 9. For he knows all things in advance and recognizes what is in our hearts. 10. And so we should give him praise, not from our mouth alone but also from our heart, that he may welcome us as children. 11. For the Lord also said, "My brothers are these who do the will of my Father."[17]

10

So my brothers, let us do the will of the Father who called us, that we may live; even more, let us pursue virtue. But

[16] Translating an emendation that makes sense in context and in light of the variant readings. See Greek apparatus.

[17] Matt 12:50; Mark 3:35; Luke 8:21.

---

[15] πνεῦμα A S: λόγος H

ξωμεν μᾶλλον τὴν ἀρετήν. τὴν δὲ κακίαν κατα-
λείψωμεν ὡς προοδοιπόρον τῶν ἁμαρτιῶν ἡμῶν· καὶ
φύγωμεν τὴν ἀσέβειαν, μὴ ἡμᾶς καταλάβῃ κακά.
2. ἐὰν γὰρ σπουδάσωμεν ἀγαθοποιεῖν, διώξεται ἡμᾶς
εἰρήνη. 3. διὰ ταύτην γὰρ τὴν αἰτίαν οὐκ ἔστιν εἰρηνεύειν[16] ἄνθρωπον, οἵτινες παράγουσι φόβους ἀνθρω-
πίνους, προῃρημένοι μᾶλλον τὴν ἐνθάδε ἀπόλαυσιν[17]
ἢ τὴν μέλλουσαν ἐπαγγελίαν. 4. ἀγνοοῦσιν γάρ,
ἡλίκην ἔχει βάσανον ἡ ἐνθάδε ἀπόλαυσις,[18] καὶ οἵαν
τρυφὴν ἔχει ἡ μέλλουσα ἐπαγγελία. 5. καὶ εἰ μὲν
αὐτοὶ μόνοι ταῦτα ἔπρασσον, ἀνεκτὸν ἦν· νῦν δὲ
ἐπιμένουσιν κακοδιδασκαλοῦντες τὰς ἀναιτίους ψυ-
χάς, οὐκ εἰδότες, ὅτι δισσὴν ἕξουσιν τὴν κρίσιν, αὐτοί
τε καὶ οἱ ἀκούοντες αὐτῶν.

11

Ἡμεῖς οὖν ἐν καθαρᾷ καρδίᾳ δουλεύσωμεν τῷ θεῷ,
καὶ ἐσόμεθα δίκαιοι· ἐὰν δὲ μὴ δουλεύσωμεν διὰ τὸ μὴ
πιστεύειν ἡμᾶς τῇ ἐπαγγελίᾳ τοῦ θεοῦ, ταλαίπωροι
ἐσόμεθα. 2. λέγει γὰρ καὶ ὁ προφητικὸς λόγος· ταλαίπωροί εἰσιν οἱ δίψυχοι, οἱ διστάζοντες τῇ καρδίᾳ, οἱ
λέγοντες· ταῦτα πάλαι ἠκούσαμεν καὶ ἐπὶ τῶν
πατέρων ἡμῶν, ἡμεῖς δὲ ἡμέραν ἐξ ἡμέρας προσ-
δεχόμενοι οὐδὲν τούτων ἑωράκαμεν. 3. ἀνόητοι, συμβάλετε ἑαυτοὺς ξύλῳ· λάβετε ἄμπελον· πρῶτον μὲν
φυλλοροεῖ, εἶτα βλαστὸς γίνεται, μετὰ ταῦτα ὄμφαξ,
εἶτα σταφυλὴ παρεστηκυῖα· 4. οὕτως καὶ ὁ λαός μου

we should abandon evil as a forerunner of our sins; and we should flee from impiety, lest evil overtake us. 2. For if we are eager to do good, peace will pursue us. 3. For this reason no one can find peace when they bring forward human fears and prefer the pleasure of the present to the promise that is yet to come. 4. For they do not realize the kind of torment brought by present pleasure or the kind of delight coming with the future promise. 5. It would be tolerable if they alone were doing these things; but now they persist in teaching such evil notions to innocent people, not knowing that they will bear a double penalty—both they and those who listen to them.

11

For this reason we should be enslaved to God with a pure heart, and then we will be upright. But if we choose not to be enslaved to God, not believing in his promise, we will be miserable. 2. For the prophetic word also says, "How miserable are those of two minds, who doubt in their hearts, who say, 'We heard these things long ago, in the time of our parents, but though we have waited day after day, we have seen none of them.' 3. Fools! Compare yourselves to a tree. Take a vine: first it sheds its leaves, then a bud appears, and after these things an unripe grape, and then an entire bunch fully grown. 4. So too my people is now disorderly

---

16 εἰρηνεύειν cj. Knopf: εὑρεῖν A H S
17 ἀπόλαυσιν A S: ἀνάπαυσιν H
18 ἀνάπαυσις H

ἀκαταστασίας καὶ θλίψεις ἔσχεν· ἔπειτα ἀπολήψεται
τὰ ἀγαθά. 5. ὥστε, ἀδελφοί μου, μὴ διψυχῶμεν, ἀλλὰ
ἐλπίσαντες ὑπομείνωμεν, ἵνα καὶ τὸν μισθὸν κομισώ-
μεθα. 6. πιστὸς γάρ ἐστιν ὁ ἐπαγγειλάμενος τὰς
ἀντιμισθίας ἀποδιδόναι ἑκάστῳ τῶν ἔργων αὐτοῦ.
7. ἐὰν οὖν ποιήσωμεν τὴν δικαιοσύνην ἐναντίον τοῦ
θεοῦ, εἰσήξομεν εἰς τὴν βασιλείαν αὐτοῦ καὶ ληψόμεθα τὰς ἐπαγγελίας, ἃς οὓς οὐκ ἤκουσεν οὐδὲ
ὀφθαλμὸς εἶδεν, οὐδὲ ἐπὶ καρδίαν ἀνθρώπου ἀνέβη.

12

Ἐκδεχώμεθα οὖν καθ᾽ ὥραν τὴν βασιλείαν τοῦ θεοῦ
ἐν ἀγάπῃ καὶ δικαιοσύνῃ, ἐπειδὴ οὐκ οἴδαμεν τὴν
ἡμέραν τῆς ἐπιφανείας τοῦ θεοῦ. 2. ἐπερωτηθεὶς γὰρ
αὐτὸς ὁ κύριος ὑπό τινος, πότε ἥξει αὐτοῦ ἡ βασιλεία,
εἶπεν· ὅταν ἔσται τὰ δύο ἕν, καὶ τὸ ἔξω ὡς τὸ[19] ἔσω,
καὶ τὸ ἄρσεν μετὰ τῆς θηλείας, οὔτε ἄρσεν οὔτε θῆλυ.
3. τὰ δύο δὲ ἕν ἐστιν, ὅταν λαλῶμεν ἑαυτοῖς ἀλήθειαν
καὶ ἐν δυσὶ σώμασιν ἀνυποκρίτως εἴη μία ψυχή.
4. καὶ τὸ ἔξω ὡς τὸ ἔσω, τοῦτο λέγει· τὴν ψυχὴν λέγει
τὸ ἔσω, τὸ δὲ ἔξω[20] τὸ σῶμα λέγει. ὃν τρόπον οὖν σου
τὸ σῶμα φαίνεται, οὕτως καὶ ἡ ψυχή σου δῆλος ἔστω
ἐν τοῖς καλοῖς ἔργοις. 5. καὶ τὸ ἄρσεν μετὰ τῆς
θηλείας, οὔτε ἄρσεν οὔτε θῆλυ, τοῦτο[21] λέγει· ἵνα

---

[19] τὸ . . . ὡς τὸ A: τὰ . . . ὡς τὰ H
[20] ἔσω . . . ἔξω: ἔξω . . . ἔσω H

and afflicted; but then it will receive what is good."[18] 5. So my brothers, we should not be of two minds but should remain hopeful, that we may receive the reward. 6. For the one who has promised to reward each according to his deeds is faithful.[19] 7. If, therefore, we do what is righteous before God, we will enter into his kingdom and receive his promises, which no ear has heard nor eye seen, nor has it entered into the human heart.[20]

12

For this reason, we should await the kingdom of God with love and righteousness every hour, since we do not know the day when God will appear. 2. For when the Lord himself was asked by someone when his kingdom would come, he said, "When the two are one, and the outside like the inside, and the male with the female is neither male nor female."[21] 3. Now "the two are one" when we speak truth to one another and when one soul exists in two bodies with no posturing *[Or: with no hypocrisy]*. 4. And "the outside like the inside" means this: the "inside" refers to the soul and the "outside" to the body. Just as your body is visible, so too your soul should be clearly seen in your good deeds. 5. And the words "the male with the female is neither male nor female" mean this, that a brother who sees a sister

[18] Source unknown. Cf. 1 Clem 23:3–4.
[19] Heb 10:23.   [20] 1 Cor 2:9.   [21] Cf. *Gosp. Thom.* 22; also quoted in Clement of Alexandria, *Stromateis* 3:13, where it is attributed to the otherwise lost *Gospel of the Egyptians*.

[21] after τοῦτο A is lacking

ἀδελφὸς ἰδὼν ἀδελφὴν οὐδὲν φρονῇ περὶ αὐτῆς θηλυ-
κόν, μηδὲ[22] φρονῇ τι περὶ αὐτοῦ ἀρσενικόν. 6. ταῦτα
ὑμῶν ποιούντων, φησίν, ἐλεύσεται ἡ βασιλεία τοῦ
πατρός μου.

13

Ἀδελφοὶ οὖν, ἤδη ποτὲ μετανοήσωμεν, νήψωμεν ἐπὶ τὸ
ἀγαθόν· μεστοὶ γάρ ἐσμεν πολλῆς ἀνοίας καὶ πονηρίας. ἐξαλείψωμεν ἀφ᾽ ἡμῶν τὰ πρότερα ἁμαρτήματα
καὶ μετανοήσαντες ἐκ ψυχῆς σωθῶμεν. καὶ μὴ γινώ-
μεθα ἀνθρωπάρεσκοι μηδὲ θέλωμεν μόνον ἑαυτοῖς
ἀρέσκειν, ἀλλὰ καὶ τοῖς ἔξω ἀνθρώποις ἐπὶ τῇ δικαι-
οσύνῃ, ἵνα τὸ ὄνομα δι᾽ ἡμᾶς μὴ βλασφημῆται. 2. λέγει γὰρ ὁ κύριος· διὰ παντὸς τὸ ὄνομά μου
βλασφημεῖται ἐν πᾶσιν τοῖς ἔθνεσιν, καὶ πάλιν· οὐαὶ
δι᾽ ὃν[23] βλασφημεῖται τὸ ὄνομά μου. ἐν τίνι βλασφημεῖται; ἐν τῷ μὴ ποιεῖν ὑμᾶς ἃ βούλομαι.[24] 3. τὰ ἔθνη
γὰρ ἀκούοντα ἐκ τοῦ στόματος ἡμῶν τὰ λόγια τοῦ
θεοῦ ὡς καλὰ καὶ μεγάλα θαυμάζει· ἔπειτα κατα-
μαθόντα τὰ ἔργα ἡμῶν ὅτι οὐκ ἔστιν ἄξια τῶν
ῥημάτων ὧν λέγομεν, ἔνθεν εἰς βλασφημίαν τρέπον-
ται, λέγοντες εἶναι μῦθόν τινα καὶ πλάνην. 4. ὅταν
γὰρ ἀκούσωσιν παρ᾽ ἡμῶν, ὅτι λέγει ὁ θεός· οὐ χάρις
ὑμῖν, εἰ ἀγαπᾶτε τοὺς ἀγαπῶντας ὑμᾶς, ἀλλὰ χάρις

[22] μηδὲ H: cum soror videbit fratrem S
[23] πάλιν· οὐαὶ δι᾽ ὃν S: διὸ H

should think nothing about her being female and she *[Or: he]* should think nothing about his being male. 6. When you do these things, he says, "the kingdom of my Father will come."

13

And so brothers, now at last we should repent and be alert for the good. For we are filled with great foolishness and evil. We should wipe our former sins away from ourselves; and if we repent from deep within we will be saved. We should not be crowd-pleasers nor wish to please only ourselves, but through our righteous activity we should be pleasing as well to those outside the fold, that the name not be blasphemed because of us. 2. For the Lord says, "My name is constantly blasphemed among all the outsiders *[Literally: Gentiles, or nations]*."[22] And again he says, "Woe to the one who causes my name to be blasphemed."[23] How is it blasphemed? When you fail to do what I wish. 3. For when outsiders hear the sayings of God from our mouths, they are astonished at their beauty and greatness. Then when they discover that our actions do not match our words, they turn from astonishment to blasphemy, saying that our faith is some kind of myth and error. 4. For, on the one hand, they hear from us that God has said, "It is no great accomplishment for you to love those who love you; it

[22] Isa 52:5.
[23] Source unknown.

---

[24] ὑμᾶς ἃ βούλομαι H: ἡμᾶς ἃ λέγομεν S

ὑμῖν, εἰ ἀγαπᾶτε τοὺς ἐχθροὺς καὶ τοὺς μισοῦντας
ὑμᾶς· ταῦτα ὅταν ἀκούσωσιν, θαυμάζουσιν τὴν ὑπερ-
βολὴν τῆς ἀγαθότητος· ὅταν δὲ ἴδωσιν, ὅτι οὐ μόνον
τοὺς μισοῦντας οὐκ ἀγαπῶμεν, ἀλλ' ὅτι οὐδὲ τοὺς
ἀγαπῶντας, καταγελῶσιν ἡμῶν, καὶ βλασφημεῖται τὸ
ὄνομα.

14

Ὥστε, ἀδελφοί, ποιοῦντες τὸ θέλημα τοῦ πατρὸς
ἡμῶν θεοῦ ἐσόμεθα ἐκ τῆς ἐκκλησίας τῆς πρώτης, τῆς
πνευματικῆς, τῆς πρὸ ἡλίου καὶ σελήνης ἐκτισμένης·
ἐὰν δὲ μὴ ποιήσωμεν τὸ θέλημα κυρίου, ἐσόμεθα ἐκ
τῆς γραφῆς τῆς λεγούσης· ἐγενήθη ὁ οἶκός μου
σπήλαιον λῃστῶν. ὥστε οὖν αἱρετισώμεθα ἀπὸ τῆς
ἐκκλησίας τῆς ζωῆς εἶναι, ἵνα σωθῶμεν. 2. οὐκ οἴομαι
δὲ ὑμᾶς ἀγνοεῖν, ὅτι ἐκκλησία ζῶσα σῶμά ἐστιν
Χριστοῦ· λέγει γὰρ ἡ γραφή· ἐποίησεν ὁ θεὸς τὸν
ἄνθρωπον ἄρσεν καὶ θῆλυ· τὸ ἄρσεν ἐστὶν ὁ Χριστός,
τὸ θῆλυ ἡ ἐκκλησία· καὶ ὅτι[25] τὰ βιβλία[26] καὶ οἱ
ἀπόστολοι τὴν ἐκκλησίαν οὐ νῦν εἶναι, ἀλλὰ ἄνωθεν.
ἦν γὰρ πνευματική, ὡς καὶ ὁ Ἰησοῦς ἡμῶν.
ἐφανερώθη δὲ ἐπ' ἐσχάτων τῶν ἡμερῶν, ἵνα ἡμᾶς
σώσῃ. 3. ἡ ἐκκλησία δὲ πνευματικὴ οὖσα ἐφανερώθη
ἐν τῇ σαρκὶ Χριστοῦ, δηλοῦσα ἡμῖν, ὅτι ἐάν τις ἡμῶν
τηρήσῃ αὐτὴν ἐν τῇ σαρκὶ καὶ μὴ φθείρῃ, ἀπολήψεται

[25] ὅτι H: ἔτι S

186

is great if you love your enemies and those who hate you."[24] And when they hear these things, they are astonished by their extraordinary goodness. But then when they see that we fail to love not only those who hate us, but even those who love us, they ridicule us and the name is blasphemed.

14

So then, brothers, if we do the will of God our Father we will belong to the first church, the spiritual church, the church that was created before the sun and moon. But if we do not do what the Lord wants, we will belong to the Scripture that says, "My house has become a cave of thieves."[25] So then, let us choose to belong to the church of life, that we may be saved. 2. But I cannot imagine that you do not realize that the living church is the body of Christ. For the Scripture says, "God made the human male and female."[26] The male is Christ, the female the church. And, as you know, the Bible *[Or: the books]* and the apostles indicate that the church has not come into being just now, but has existed from the beginning. For it existed spiritually, as did our Jesus; but he *[Or: it]* became manifest here in the final days so that he *[Or: it]* might save us. 3. And even though the church was spiritual, it became manifest in Christ's flesh, showing us that any of us who protects the church in the flesh, without corrupting it, will receive it in

24 Luke 6:32, 35.
25 Jer 7:11; cf. Matt 21:13; Mark 11:17; Luke 19:46.
26 Gen 1:27.

---

26 βιβλία H: add τῶν προφητῶν S

αὐτὴν ἐν τῷ πνεύματι τῷ ἁγίῳ· ἡ γὰρ σὰρξ αὕτη
ἀντίτυπός ἐστιν τοῦ πνεύματος· οὐδεὶς οὖν τὸ ἀντίτυ-
πον φθείρας τὸ αὐθεντικὸν μεταλήψεται. ἄρα οὖν
τοῦτο λέγει, ἀδελφοί· τηρήσατε τὴν σάρκα, ἵνα τοῦ
πνεύματος μεταλάβητε. 4. εἰ δὲ λέγομεν εἶναι τὴν
σάρκα τὴν ἐκκλησίαν καὶ τὸ πνεῦμα Χριστόν, ἄρα
οὖν ὁ ὑβρίσας τὴν σάρκα ὕβρισεν τὴν ἐκκλησίαν. ὁ
τοιοῦτος οὖν οὐ μεταλήψεται τοῦ πνεύματος, ὅ ἐστιν ὁ
Χριστός. 5. τοσαύτην δύναται ἡ σὰρξ αὕτη μετα-
λαβεῖν ζωὴν καὶ ἀφθαρσίαν κολληθέντος αὐτῇ τοῦ
πνεύματος τοῦ ἁγίου, οὔτε ἐξειπεῖν τις δύναται οὔτε
λαλῆσαι, ἃ ἡτοίμασεν ὁ κύριος τοῖς ἐκλεκτοῖς αὐτοῦ.

15

Οὐκ οἴομαι δέ, ὅτι μικρὰν συμβουλίαν ἐποιησάμην
περὶ ἐγκρατείας, ἣν ποιήσας τις οὐ μετανοήσει, ἀλλὰ
καὶ ἑαυτὸν σώσει κἀμὲ τὸν συμβουλεύσαντα. μισθὸς
γὰρ οὐκ ἔστιν μικρὸς πλανωμένην ψυχὴν καὶ ἀπολ-
λυμένην ἀποστρέψαι εἰς τὸ σωθῆναι. 2. ταύτην γὰρ
ἔχομεν τὴν ἀντιμισθίαν ἀποδοῦναι τῷ θεῷ τῷ κτί-
σαντι ἡμᾶς, ἐὰν ὁ λέγων καὶ ἀκούων μετὰ πίστεως καὶ
ἀγάπης καὶ λέγῃ καὶ ἀκούῃ. 3. ἐμμείνωμεν οὖν ἐφ᾽ οἷς
ἐπιστεύσαμεν δίκαιοι καὶ ὅσιοι, ἵνα μετὰ παρρησίας
αἰτῶμεν τὸν θεὸν τὸν λέγοντα· ἔτι λαλοῦντός σου ἐρῶ·
ἰδοὺ πάρειμι. 4. τοῦτο γὰρ τὸ ῥῆμα μεγάλης ἐστὶν
ἐπαγγελίας σημεῖον· ἑτοιμότερον γὰρ ἑαυτὸν λέγει ὁ
κύριος εἰς τὸ διδόναι τοῦ αἰτοῦντος. 5. τοσαύτης οὖν

the Holy Spirit. For this flesh is the mirror image of the Spirit. No one, therefore, who corrupts the mirror image will receive the reality that it represents. And so, brothers, he says this: "Protect the flesh that you may receive the Spirit."[27] 4. But if we say that the flesh is the church and the Spirit is Christ, then the one who abuses the flesh abuses the church. Such a person, therefore, will not receive the Spirit, which is Christ. 5. This flesh is able to receive such a great and incorruptible life when the Holy Spirit clings to it; nor can anyone proclaim or speak about the things that the Lord has prepared for those he has chosen.

15

I do not think that I have given trivial advice about self-restraint. And whoever takes my advice will have no regrets, but will instead save both himself and me, the one who has given the advice. There is no small reward for the one who converts a person who is going astray toward destruction, that he may be saved. 2. For this is what we can offer back to the God who created us—so long as the one who speaks and hears does so with faith and love. 3. For this reason we should continue as upright and holy in the things we have believed, that we may make our requests known to God with bold confidence. For he says, "While you are still speaking I will say, 'See, here I am.'"[28] 4. For this word is a token of a great promise; for the Lord says that he is more ready to give than we are to ask. 5. And so,

27 Source unknown.
28 Isa 58:9.

χρηστότητος μεταλαμβάνοντες μὴ φθονήσωμεν ἑαυτοῖς τυχεῖν τοσούτων ἀγαθῶν. ὅσην γὰρ ἡδονὴν ἔχει
τὰ ῥήματα ταῦτα τοῖς ποιήσασιν αὐτά, τοσαύτην
κατάκρισιν ἔχει τοῖς παρακούσασιν.

16

Ὥστε, ἀδελφοί, ἀφορμὴν λαβόντες οὐ μικρὰν εἰς τὸ
μετανοῆσαι, καιρὸν ἔχοντες ἐπιστρέψωμεν ἐπὶ τὸν
καλέσαντα ἡμᾶς θεόν, ἕως ἔτι ἔχομεν τὸν παραδεχόμενον[27] ἡμᾶς. 2. ἐὰν γὰρ ταῖς ἡδυπαθείαις ταύταις
ἀποταξώμεθα καὶ τὴν ψυχὴν ἡμῶν νικήσωμεν ἐν τῷ
μὴ ποιεῖν τὰς ἐπιθυμίας αὐτῆς τὰς πονηράς, μετα-
ληψόμεθα τοῦ ἐλέους Ἰησοῦ.[28] 3. γινώσκετε δέ, ὅτι
ἔρχεται ἤδη ἡ ἡμέρα τῆς κρίσεως ὡς κλίβανος
καιόμενος, καὶ τακήσονταί τινες τῶν οὐρανῶν καὶ
πᾶσα ἡ γῆ ὡς μόλιβος ἐπὶ πυρὶ τηκόμενος· καὶ τότε
φανήσεται τὰ κρύφια καὶ φανερὰ ἔργα τῶν ἀνθρώπων. 4. καλὸν οὖν ἐλεημοσύνη ὡς μετάνοια ἁμαρτίας·
κρείσσων νηστεία προσευχῆς, ἐλεημοσύνη δὲ ἀμφο-
τέρων· ἀγάπη δὲ καλύπτει πλῆθος ἁμαρτιῶν, προσευχὴ δὲ ἐκ καλῆς συνειδήσεως ἐκ θανάτου ῥύεται.
μακάριος πᾶς ὁ εὑρεθεὶς ἐν τούτοις πλήρης· ἐλεημοσύνη γὰρ κούφισμα ἁμαρτίας γίνεται.

[27] παραδεχόμενον H: patrem qui accipit (π̅ρ̅α̅ δεχόμενον) S
[28] Ἰησοῦ: domini nostri Iesu Christi S

since we have received such generosity, we should not begrudge one another when we receive such good things. For the pleasure these words bring to those who do them is matched by the condemnation they bring to those who disobey.

16

So then, brothers, since we have received no trivial opportunity to repent, we should turn back to the God who called us, while there is still time—while, that is, we still have one who accepts us. 2. For if we bid farewell to these sweet pleasures and conquer our soul through not doing its evil desires, we will receive mercy from Jesus. 3. But you know that the day of judgment is already coming like a blazing furnace,[29] and some of the heavens and all of the earth will melt like lead in the fire;[30] and then the hidden and secret works that people have done will be made visible. 4. Giving to charity, therefore, is good as a repentance from sin *[Or: is good; so too is repentance from sin]*. Fasting is better than prayer, but giving to charity is better than both. Love covers a multitude of sins,[31] and prayer from a good conscience will rescue a person from death. How fortunate is everyone found to be full of these things. For giving to charity lightens the load of sin.

[29] Mal 4:1.
[30] Cf. Isa 34:4.
[31] 1 Pet 4:8; cf. Prov 10:12.

17

Μετανοήσωμεν οὖν ἐξ ὅλης καρδίας, ἵνα μή τις ἡμῶν παραπόληται. εἰ γὰρ ἐντολὰς ἔχομεν καὶ τοῦτο πράσσομεν,[29] ἀπὸ τῶν εἰδώλων ἀποσπᾶν καὶ κατηχεῖν, πόσῳ μᾶλλον ψυχὴν ἤδη γινώσκουσαν τὸν θεὸν οὐ δεῖ ἀπόλλυσθαι; 2. συλλάβωμεν οὖν ἑαυτοῖς καὶ τοὺς ἀσθενοῦντας ἀνάγειν περὶ τὸ ἀγαθόν, ὅπως σωθῶμεν ἅπαντες καὶ ἐπιστρέψωμεν ἀλλήλους καὶ νουθετήσωμεν. 3. καὶ μὴ μόνον ἄρτι δοκῶμεν πιστεύειν καὶ προσέχειν ἐν τῷ νουθετεῖσθαι ἡμᾶς ὑπὸ τῶν πρεσβυτέρων, ἀλλὰ καὶ ὅταν εἰς οἶκον ἀπαλλαγῶμεν, μνημονεύωμεν τῶν τοῦ κυρίου ἐνταλμάτων καὶ μὴ ἀντιπαρελκώμεθα ἀπὸ τῶν κοσμικῶν ἐπιθυμιῶν, ἀλλὰ πυκνότερον προσερχόμενοι[30] πειρώμεθα προκόπτειν ἐν ταῖς ἐντολαῖς τοῦ κυρίου, ἵνα πάντες τὸ αὐτὸ φρονοῦντες συνηγμένοι ὦμεν ἐπὶ τὴν ζωήν. 4. εἶπεν γὰρ ὁ κύριος· ἔρχομαι συναγαγεῖν πάντα τὰ ἔθνη, φυλὰς καὶ γλώσσας. τοῦτο δὲ λέγει τὴν ἡμέραν τῆς ἐπιφανείας αὐτοῦ, ὅτε ἐλθὼν λυτρώσεται ἡμᾶς, ἕκαστον κατὰ τὰ ἔργα αὐτοῦ. 5. καὶ ὄψονται τὴν δόξαν αὐτοῦ καὶ τὸ κράτος οἱ ἄπιστοι, καὶ ξενισθήσονται ἰδόντες τὸ βασίλειον τοῦ κόσμου ἐν τῷ Ἰησοῦ, λέγοντες· οὐαὶ ἡμῖν, ὅτι σὺ ἦς, καὶ οὐκ ᾔδειμεν καὶ οὐκ ἐπιστεύομεν καὶ οὐκ ἐπειθόμεθα τοῖς πρεσβυτέ-

[29] καὶ τοῦτο πράσσομεν H: ἵνα καὶ τοῦτο πράσσωμεν S
[30] προσερχόμενοι H: προσευχόμενοι S

17

And so we should repent from our whole heart, lest any of us perish. For since we have his commandment and drag people from idols, giving them instruction, how much more must we keep a person from destruction when he has already come to know God? 2. For this reason we should help one another and bring those who are weak back to what is good, so that we may all be saved and turn one another around and admonish one another. 3. And not only should we appear to believe and pay attention now, while being admonished by the presbyters, but also when we return home we should remember the commandments of the Lord and not be dragged away by worldly desires. But by coming together for worship more frequently we should try to progress in the Lord's commandments, so that all of us, being unified in what we think, may be gathered together to inherit life. 4. For the Lord said, "I am coming to gather all the nations, tribes, and tongues."[32] And this is what he calls the "day of his appearance," when he comes to redeem each of us, according to our deeds. 5. And the unbelievers will see his glory and power and be shocked when they see that the rulership of this world has been given to Jesus. And they will say, "Woe to us! You were here, and we did not know or believe; and we were

[32] Isa 66:18.

ροις τοῖς ἀναγγέλλουσιν ἡμῖν περὶ τῆς σωτηρίας
ἡμῶν· καὶ ὁ σκώληξ αὐτῶν οὐ τελευτήσει καὶ τὸ πῦρ
αὐτῶν οὐ σβεσθήσεται, καὶ ἔσονται εἰς ὅρασιν πάσῃ
σαρκί. 6. τὴν ἡμέραν ἐκείνην λέγει τῆς κρίσεως, ὅταν
ὄψονται τοὺς ἐν ἡμῖν ἀσεβήσαντας καὶ παραλογι-
σαμένους τὰς ἐντολὰς Ἰησοῦ Χριστοῦ. 7. οἱ δὲ δίκαιοι
εὐπραγήσαντες καὶ ὑπομείναντες τὰς βασάνους καὶ
μισήσαντες τὰς ἡδυπαθείας τῆς ψυχῆς, ὅταν θεάσων-
ται τοὺς ἀστοχήσαντας καὶ ἀρνησαμένους διὰ τῶν
λόγων ἢ διὰ τῶν ἔργων τὸν Ἰησοῦν, ὅπως κολάζονται
δειναῖς βασάνοις πυρὶ ἀσβέστῳ, ἔσονται[31] δόξαν
διδόντες[32] τῷ θεῷ αὐτῶν λέγοντες, ὅτι ἔσται ἐλπὶς τῷ
δεδουλευκότι θεῷ ἐξ ὅλης καρδίας.

18

Καὶ ἡμεῖς οὖν γενώμεθα ἐκ τῶν εὐχαριστούντων, τῶν
δεδουλευκότων τῷ θεῷ, καὶ μὴ ἐκ τῶν κρινομένων
ἀσεβῶν. 2. καὶ γὰρ αὐτὸς πανθαμαρτωλὸς ὢν καὶ
μήπω φεύγων[33] τὸν πειρασμόν, ἀλλ' ἔτι ὢν ἐν μέσοις
τοῖς ὀργάνοις τοῦ διαβόλου σπουδάζω τὴν δικαιοσύνην διώκειν, ὅπως ἰσχύσω κἂν ἐγγὺς αὐτῆς γενέσθαι, φοβούμενος τὴν κρίσιν τὴν μέλλουσαν.

---

[31] ἔσονται add ἐν ἀγαλλιάσει S
[32] διδόντες S: δόντες H
[33] φεύγων H: φυγὼν S(?)

not persuaded by the presbyters who announced your salvation to us." And their worm will not die nor their fire be extinguished, and they will be a spectacle for all to see.[33] 6. He calls that the day of judgment, when others see those who have acted with impiety among us and distorted the commandments of Jesus Christ. 7. But those who are upright, who have acted well, endured torments, and hated the sweet pleasures of the soul, when they observe those who have deviated from the right path and denied Jesus through their words or deeds are punished with terrible torments in a fire that cannot be extinguished, they, the upright, will give glory to their God, saying "there will be hope for the one who has served as God's slave from his whole heart."

18

For this reason we should be among those who give thanks, who serve as the slaves of God, not among the impious who are condemned. 2. For even I myself am completely sinful and have not yet fled temptation and am still surrounded by the instruments of the Devil; nonetheless I am eager to pursue righteousness, that I may be made strong enough to approach it, for fear of the coming judgment.

[33] Isa 66:18, 24; cf. Mark 9:48.

19

Ὥστε, ἀδελφοὶ καὶ ἀδελφαί, μετὰ τὸν θεὸν τῆς ἀληθείας ἀναγινώσκω ὑμῖν ἔντευξιν εἰς τὸ προσέχειν τοῖς
γεγραμμένοις, ἵνα καὶ ἑαυτοὺς σώσητε καὶ τὸν ἀνα-
γινώσκοντα ἐν ὑμῖν·[34] μισθὸν γὰρ αἰτῶ ὑμᾶς τὸ
μετανοῆσαι ἐξ ὅλης καρδίας, σωτηρίαν ἑαυτοῖς καὶ
ζωὴν διδόντας. τοῦτο γὰρ ποιήσαντες σκοπὸν[35] πᾶσιν
τοῖς νέοις θήσομεν, τοῖς βουλομένοις περὶ τὴν εὐσέβειαν καὶ τὴν χρηστότητα τοῦ θεοῦ φιλοπονεῖν. 2. καὶ
μὴ ἀηδῶς ἔχωμεν καὶ ἀγανακτῶμεν οἱ ἄσοφοι, ὅταν
τις ἡμᾶς νουθετῇ καὶ ἐπιστρέφῃ ἀπὸ τῆς ἀδικίας εἰς
τὴν δικαιοσύνην. ἐνίοτε γὰρ πονηρὰ πράσσοντες οὐ
γινώσκομεν διὰ τὴν διψυχίαν καὶ ἀπιστίαν τὴν ἐνοῦ-
σαν ἐν τοῖς στήθεσιν ἡμῶν, καὶ ἐσκοτίσμεθα τὴν
διάνοιαν ὑπὸ τῶν ἐπιθυμιῶν τῶν ματαίων. 3. πράξω-
μεν οὖν τὴν δικαιοσύνην, ἵνα εἰς τέλος σωθῶμεν.
μακάριοι οἱ τούτοις ὑπακούοντες τοῖς προστάγμα-
σιν· κἂν ὀλίγον χρόνον κακοπαθήσωσιν ἐν τῷ κόσμῳ
τούτῳ, τὸν ἀθάνατον[36] τῆς ἀναστάσεως καρπὸν τρυγήσουσιν.[37] 4. μὴ οὖν λυπείσθω ὁ εὐσεβής, ἐὰν ἐπὶ
τοῖς νῦν χρόνοις ταλαιπωρῇ· μακάριος αὐτὸν ἀναμένει
χρόνος· ἐκεῖνος ἄνω μετὰ τῶν πατέρων ἀναβιώσας
εὐφρανθήσεται εἰς τὸν ἀλύπητον αἰῶνα.

[34] ὑμῖν: add verba Dei S
[35] σκοπὸν S: κόπον H
[36] ἀθάνατον S: δὲ θάνατον H
[37] τρυγήσουσιν: τρυφήσουσιν S

19

So then, brothers and sisters, now that we have heard this word from the God of Truth *[Literally: after the God of Truth]*, I am reading you a request to pay attention to what has been written, so that you may save yourselves and the one who is your reader. As a reward I ask that you repent from your whole heart, giving yourselves salvation and life. For when we do this we set a goal for those who are younger, who wish to devote themselves to the piety and generosity that come from God. 2. We who are foolish should not be displeased and indignant when someone admonishes us and turns us away from injustice to righteousness. For sometimes, because we are of two minds and disbelieving in our hearts, we do not realize that we are doing evil; and we are darkened in our understanding[34] through vain desires. 3. And so we should practice righteousness, that we may be saved in the end. How fortunate are those who obey these commandments! Even if they suffer evil for a brief time in this world, they will reap the imperishable fruit of the resurrection. 4. And so the one who is pious should not be despondent over miseries suffered at present. A more fortunate time awaits him! When he is restored to life with our ancestors he will be jubilant, in an age removed from sorrow.

[34] Cf. Eph. 4:18.

20

Ἀλλὰ μηδὲ ἐκεῖνο τὴν διάνοιαν ὑμῶν ταρασσέτω, ὅτι βλέπομεν τοὺς ἀδίκους πλουτοῦντας καὶ στενοχωρου-μένους τοὺς τοῦ θεοῦ δούλους. 2. πιστεύωμεν οὖν, ἀδελφοὶ καὶ ἀδελφαί· θεοῦ ζῶντος πεῖραν ἀθλοῦμεν καὶ γυμναζόμεθα τῷ νῦν βίῳ, ἵνα τῷ μέλλοντι στεφα-νωθῶμεν. 3. οὐδεὶς τῶν δικαίων ταχὺν καρπὸν ἔλαβεν, ἀλλ᾽ ἐκδέχεται αὐτόν. 4. εἰ γὰρ τὸν μισθὸν τῶν δικαίων ὁ θεὸς συντόμως ἀπεδίδου, εὐθέως ἐμπορίαν ἠσκοῦμεν καὶ οὐ θεοσέβειαν· ἐδοκοῦμεν γὰρ εἶναι δίκαιοι, οὐ τὸ εὐσεβές, ἀλλὰ τὸ κερδαλέον διώκοντες. καὶ διὰ τοῦτο θεία κρίσις ἔβλαψεν πνεῦμα μὴ ὂν δίκαιον, καὶ ἐβάρυνεν δεσμοῖς.[38]

5. Τῷ μόνῳ θεῷ ἀοράτῳ, πατρὶ τῆς ἀληθείας, τῷ ἐξαποστείλαντι ἡμῖν τὸν σωτῆρα καὶ ἀρχηγὸν τῆς ἀφθαρσίας, δι᾽ οὗ καὶ ἐφανέρωσεν ἡμῖν τὴν ἀλήθειαν καὶ τὴν ἐπουράνιον ζωήν, αὐτῷ ἡ δόξα εἰς τοὺς αἰῶνας τῶν αἰώνων. ἀμήν.

Κλήμεντος πρὸς Κορινθίους ἐπιστολὴ β΄.[39]

[38] δεσμοῖς S: δεσμός H
[39] subscription after the example of the First Letter of Clem-ent: *hic finitur secunda epistula Clementis ad Corinthios* S: στίχοι χ̅ ῥητὰ κ̅ε̅ H

20

But neither should this thought disturb you, that we see the unjust becoming rich while the slaves of God suffer in dire straights. 2. We need to have faith, brothers and sisters! We are competing in the contest of the living God, training in the present life that we may be crowned in the one to come. 3. No one who is upright receives the fruit of his labor quickly; he instead waits for it. 4. For if God were to reward the upright immediately, we would straightaway be engaged in commerce rather than devotion to God. For we would appear to be upright not for the sake of piety but for a profit. And for this reason, a divine judgment harms the spirit that is not upright and burdens it with chains.

5. To the only invisible God,[35] the Father of truth, who sent us the savior and founder of incorruptibility, through whom he also revealed to us the truth and the heavenly life—to him be the glory forever and ever. Amen.

The Second Epistle of Clement to the Corinthians

[35] Cf. 1 Tim 1:17.

LETTERS OF IGNATIUS

INTRODUCTION

The letters of Ignatius have received far more scholarly attention than any of the other writings of the Apostolic Fathers. In part this is because of the inherent intrigue surrounding their composition: these are letters written by an early second-century church leader, the bishop of Antioch, who was literally en route to his martyrdom in Rome. In part the scholarly interest derives from the letters' historical significance: they embody concerns that came to characterize the early Christian movement towards orthodoxy—in particular the quest to root out heresy from the churches and to stress the importance of the church's hierarchy, with a sole bishop exercising ultimate authority and presbyters and deacons serving beneath him.

In the early modern period it was precisely this witness to the monepiscopacy at such an early date that drove scholars to determine whether Ignatius of Antioch had in fact penned all, some, or any of the letters that appear under his name, and if so, to ascertain which of the several forms of these letters transmitted in the manuscript tradition is authentic.

Overview

In his letters Ignatius indicates that he was the bishop of Antioch of Syria (*Ign. Rom.* 2.2); early tradition holds that he was the second bishop there, after Peter (Origen, *Hom. 6 in Luke*) or the third, following Peter and Euodius (Eusebius, *Eccl. Hist.* 3.22.36).

The context for his surviving writings is relatively clear. Ignatius was arrested as part of a persecution against Christians in Antioch and sent to Rome, probably with other prisoners, under armed guard (he refers to the squad of soldiers as ten "leopards," *Ign. Rom.* 5.1). Taking the land route over Asia Minor, he had a brief stay in Smyrna, where he became acquainted with the church and its bishop, Polycarp. He also came to know representatives of several other churches of the region, who had come expressly to meet with him and tender their support. In response he wrote brief letters to three of these communities—Ephesus, Magnesia, and Tralles—urging them to seek church unity, to root out heretical teachings, and above all to remain faithful to their bishop. He also asks for prayers for his home church in Antioch, which was undergoing some kind of unspecified but serious difficulty. In addition, he wrote a letter to the Christians in Rome, urging them not to intervene with the legal proceedings against him once he arrived, since he passionately sought martyrdom by facing the wild beasts in the amphitheater, so that by suffering a violent death he might "attain to God."

After leaving Smyrna, Ignatius traveled to Troas, where again he dashed off several letters, one to Philadelphia (which he had passed through on the way), one back to Smyrna, and another to its bishop Polycarp. In broad terms, these letters deal with issues similar to the earlier ones: church unity, heresy, the authority of the bishop. In the interim, however, Ignatius had learned that the situation in his home church had been resolved, and he urges the churches to send representatives to Antioch in order to celebrate with them the renewed peace they now enjoy.

In his final letter, to Polycarp, Ignatius indicates that he is to set sail immediately, and asks the bishop to send letters ahead to the churches that lie before him. That is the last we hear of Ignatius from his own pen. But in a later letter by Polycarp himself (see *Polycarp to the Philippians*) we learn that Ignatius had stopped off in Philippi and spent time with the Christians there. After he left, the Philippians wrote Polycarp, asking him to send the letters of Ignatius he had available to him. These would presumably include the ones received in Smyrna (*Smyrneans* and *Polycarp*) and at least the four he had written while with them, possibly from copies made before they were sent. This would account, at the least, for all of the surviving letters apart from *Philadelphians* (written to a church nearby); it may well be that our present collection of all seven letters derives from this collection made by Polycarp himself.

Polycarp's letter to the Philippians mentions Ignatius's martyrdom (*Pol. Phil.* 9), but provides no details. Eusebius indicates that it occurred midway through the reign of Trajan (98–117 CE; *Eccl. Hist.* 3.36). This coincides well with certain aspects of the letters (but see below). We know, for example, of other Christian martyrdoms in the period from the correspondence of Trajan with Pliny, governor of Bithynia, in close proximity to the cities that Ignatius himself addresses. Later accounts of Ignatius's own death, however, are purely legendary.

Major Issues in the Letters

Although some scholars have argued that the issues Ignatius addresses in these letters are entirely those he faced while bishop of Antioch (see Donahue; cf. Corwin), most maintain that he is dealing with problems of the individual churches that he addressed, as he had learned them either during his visits (Smyrna and Philadelphia) or from the representatives they had sent to meet him (Ephesus, Magnesia, Tralles). He refers explicitly to encounters with false teachers in Philadelphia, for example, and the different letters appear to address different problems, especially the problems of heresy.

There have been long and hard debates over the nature of the heresy or heresies that Ignatius attacks. Some scholars have maintained that there was only one heretical group, a kind of judaizing Gnosticism (Zahn, Lightfoot, Molland, Barnard). Others have argued that since it is only in *Philadelphians* and *Magnesians* that he deals with the problem of Judaizers (those who insisted on the ongoing validity of the Jewish law for followers of Christ) whereas it is only in *Trallians* and *Smyrneans* that he directly addresses the problem of docetism (the view that Christ was not really a human, but only "appeared" to be so, from the Greek word δοκέω, "to seem" or "to appear"), he is dealing with two different groups that had exerted their influence in different places (e.g., Richardson, Corwin, Donahue). Some others have thought that in addition to Judaizers and docetists, Ignatius was confronting a third group who stood in opposition to his notion of monepiscopacy (Trevett). It is not clear, however, if his polemic in this case is directed against a specific group or a general tendency found throughout the early Christian communities (cf. Sumney).

Other recent scholars have argued that Ignatius is attacking specific Gnostic groups that we know about from a later period (Valentinus and his followers), and that, as a result, the letters must be re-dated to the second half of the second century (Lechner; cf. Hübner). Most scholars, however, have remained unpersuaded by this thesis, and find sufficient grounds for accepting the traditional date.

What is clear is that Ignatius insisted on doctrinal purity: he praises the Philadelphians, for example, for not having division in their ranks, but a "filter" (*Ign. Phil.* 3.1). For him this meant understanding, on the one hand, that Jesus was fully human ("he was truly born, both ate and drank, was truly persecuted at the time of Pontius Pilate, was truly crucified and died . . . was also truly raised from the dead" *Ign. Trall.* 9.1–2) and that, on the other hand, he was the fulfillment of the Jewish law, making it unnecessary for Christians to continue to adhere to the ways of Judaism ("It is outlandish to proclaim Jesus Christ and practice Judaism. For Christianity did not believe in Judaism, but Judaism in Christianity," *Ign. Magn.* 10.1). Moreover, this quest for purity is related to his insistence on the unity of the church—a resounding theme of his letters—which is secured through submitting to the ruling bishop at all times and engaging in no church activities (for example, baptism or eucharist) without him: "Be subject to the bishop as to the commandment" (*Ign. Trall.* 13.2); "we are clearly obliged to look upon the bishop as the Lord himself" (*Ign. Eph.* 6.1); "you should do nothing apart from the bishop" (*Ign. Magn.* 7.1).

Two issues that are less clear-cut involve the situation

that Ignatius left behind in Antioch and the reason he was being sent to Rome to face execution. Traditionally it has been assumed that Ignatius was concerned for the church in Antioch because it continued to suffer persecution, and that when he learned that hostilities had ceased, he urged churches to send letters of congratulations and personal representatives to express best wishes (Lightfoot, Camelot). More recently, however, scholars have noted that Ignatius never actually speaks about antagonism from non-Christian opponents in Antioch. Moreover, the terms he uses to describe the resolution of the problem—the church had its "peace" restored—are more commonly used in Christian texts to refer to situations of internal conflict. Given Ignatius's overarching concern over heretical forms of Christianity and the circumstance that Antioch was home to a range of theological perspectives (Jewish-Christian, Gnostic), some scholars have suggested that the problems involved struggles within the community itself. Others have thought that the struggle was not just over right belief, if it was over that at all, but over leadership in the church (see Hammond Bammel; Schoedel). Possibly Ignatius's own leadership had proved divisive, for example his claim to have the right, as bishop, to exercise ultimate authority over the church. In this scenario, the happy resolution of the situation (from Ignatius's perspective) may have involved the appointment of a like-minded person as his successor.

Matters are equally unclear with regard to the reasons for his removal to Rome. It has sometimes been claimed that he was arrested for Christian activities (much like his contemporaries in Bithynia, under Pliny), but that, like the apostle Paul, he was a Roman citizen and appealed his case to the emperor, and so was being sent to stand trial in the capital city. But Ignatius speaks of himself as already "condemned," not just charged (*Ign. Rom.* 4. 3). Moreover, he was eager, not reluctant, to experience his death in the arena, so as to imitate Christ's own passion and thus show himself to be a true disciple, and thereby to "attain to God": "May I have the full pleasure of the wild beasts prepared for me; I pray they will be found ready for me. Indeed, I will coax them to devour me quickly . . . And even if they do not wish to do so willingly, I will force them to it . . . Fire and cross and packs of wild beasts, cuttings and being torn apart, the scattering of bones, the mangling of limbs, the grinding of the whole body, the evil torments of the devil—let them come upon me, only that I may attain to Jesus Christ" (*Ign. Rom.* 5). The fact that he pleads with the Roman Christians not to intervene on his behalf suggests that he was not going to Rome under appeal.

Some scholars have thought, then, that Ignatius was being sent to Rome either because the chief administrator of Syria at the time of his arrest did not have imperium (i.e., authority to sentence him to death) or, perhaps more likely, that, as sometimes happened, he was being sent as a "gift" by the Syrian governor, a criminal donated for the violent hunting games of the Roman amphitheater.

Recensions of the Letters

The letters of Ignatius were known from the earliest of times (Polycarp, Irenaeus, Origen); Eusebius explicitly mentions the seven that are today accepted as authentic (*Eccl. Hist.* 3.36). But a much larger corpus of Ignatian letters was in circulation throughout the Middle Ages. The

Greek manuscript tradition gives the familiar seven letters in a different, expanded form, and includes six additional letters: one from Mary of Cassabola to Ignatius, along with his reply to her; letters sent to the churches of Tarsus, Antioch, and Philippi; and one to Hero, his successor as bishop in Antioch. This expanded form of the Ignatian corpus, known today as the "long" recension, embodied even more fully the theological and ecclesiastical interests and perspectives of later (fourth-century) orthodoxy, particularly as these can be seen in the so-called *Apostolic Constitutions*, whose author is sometimes thought to have forged the additional elements of the long recension. As virtually the only corpus of Ignatius known until modern times, this group of thirteen letters was subjected to serious critical scrutiny early in modern scholarship, especially in the seventeenth century, when proponents of both the Roman and Anglican ecclesiastical hierarchies could point to Ignatius as evidence for the antiquity of their systems, whereas Puritans, nonconformists, and others insisted that the Ignatian letters had been forged.

It was an Anglican archbishop, James Ussher, who found a way out of the impasse in the 1640s. Having noted that several late medieval writers, including the famed thirteenth-century patristic scholar Robert Grosseteste of Lincoln, cited the text of Ignatius (in Latin) in a different, shorter form from that otherwise known, Ussher reasoned that another textual tradition of the letters must once have existed, at least in England. He embarked on a mission to find remnants of this other tradition, and was rewarded in uncovering two Latin manuscripts that contained the seven Eusebian letters in a shorter form, which coincided with the medieval citations of the text, lacking the passages so obviously tied to the theological and ecclesiastical concerns of the fourth century (although these manuscripts included the additional letters as well). On the basis of his discovery, in 1644 Ussher published a new Latin edition of the Ignatian corpus: just the Eusebian letters in their non-interpolated form (although Ussher considered the letter to Polycarp spurious). Two years later his views were confirmed by Isaac Voss's publication of a Greek manuscript from Florence that preserved six of the Eusebian letters in their shortened form—all but *Romans,* which had a separate history of transmission. Finally, in 1689 a French scholar, T. Ruinart, published the Greek text of *Romans* as part of the Acts of the Martyrs, from a tenth-century manuscript from Paris, making then the original form of the authentic corpus completely available.

By the end of the seventeenth century, most scholars recognized the persuasiveness of the arguments for the noninterpolated form of the seven letters and the inauthenticity of those not mentioned by Eusebius. In 1845, however, the waters were disturbed when William Cureton uncovered yet another form of the Ignatian epistles in a Syriac manuscript, which contained condensed versions of the letters to Polycarp, the Ephesians, and the Romans. Cureton maintained that this shorter version was authentic and that a later forger had fabricated the additional letters mentioned by Eusebius. This view was accepted as persuasive for a time; but eventually a consensus emerged, based largely on the compelling arguments advanced by T. Zahn and J. B. Lightfoot, that the middle recension was authentic and that Cureton's corpus of three letters was an abridgment of the original seven.

As a result, scholars today speak of three recensions of

Ignatius's letters: the "long" recension, which includes the thirteen letters (twelve by Ignatius, and one addressed to him) found throughout most of the Greek and Latin manuscript tradition (there are several other letters in the Latin tradition as well, including letters to and from Mary, the mother of Jesus, and to the disciple John); the "middle" recension, which comprises the seven letters mentioned by Eusebius in their noninterpolated form as found in only a few Greek and Latin witnesses (all of which include the additional letters as well); and the "short" recension, which contains the abbreviated forms of three of the letters in the Syriac tradition, as uncovered by Cureton (Polycarp, Ephesians, and Romans). The middle recension is generally regarded as original; the long recension is thought to have been created in the fourth century by a forger who interpolated passages into the original Ignatian letters and composed six additional writings; the short recension is thought to have been a condensed version also created in the fourth century.

There were several challenges to the consensus during the second half of the twentieth century—some scholars maintaining that the entire corpus was forged (Weijenborg, Joly), others that some of the seven letters were altered and others fabricated (Rius-Camps), and others arguing that the letters must date not from the early second century but from a later period, when full-blown Gnosticism was threatening the proto-orthodox church (Lechner; cf. Hübner). While these studies are erudite and effectively point out some of the difficulties of the Ignatian corpus—syntactical anacoloutha, internal discrepancies, views and vocabulary otherwise difficult to document in this early period—most scholars have not found their arguments convincing (on Joly and Rius-Camps, see esp. Hammond Bammel), and argued that (a) in some ways, their "solutions" create more problems than they solve, and (b) many of the difficulties they cite (for example, inconsistencies and grammatical problems) may have derived from the trying circumstances presupposed by the letters, written in comparative haste by someone facing his own violent death. Moreover, given the scarcity of our sources for the period, it is difficult to evaluate claims that certain terms in these letters ("Christianity") or views they embrace (the monepiscopacy) are anachronistic.

Editions, Manuscripts, Abbreviations

The long recension was published in Latin as early as 1498 by Jacques Lefèvre d'Étaples; the Greek by Valentinus Hartunk (also known as Frid or Pacaeus) in 1558. The Greek text of the seven authentic letters (though still in their interpolated form) was published by Nicolaus Vedelius in 1623.

The Latin of the middle recension was first published by James Ussher, *Polycarpi et Ignatii epistolae* (Oxford: Lichfield, 1644). Isaac Voss published the uninterpolated Greek texts of the letters of the middle recension, except *Romans*, in 1646 (*Epistolae genuinae S. Ignatii martyris*, Amsterdam: Blaev); T. Ruinart published the uninterpolated Greek text of *Romans* in 1689, as part of his *Acta primorum martyrum sincere et selecta* (Paris: Muget).

The short recension was published by William Cureton, *The Ancient Syriac Version of Saint Ignatius* (London: Rivington, 1845).

The majority of manuscripts, both Greek and Latin,

along with Armenian, Syriac, and Coptic versions, contain the interpolated texts of the seven letters mentioned by Eusebius as well as some or all of the additional forged letters. The following are the surviving witnesses to the middle recension.

For the letters except *Romans*:

Greek MSS:

  Mediceo-Laurentianus 57,7 (11th c.)

  Berlin papyrus, Codex 10581(5th c., Smyr. 3.3–12:1)

Latin MSS:

  Caiensis 395 (= L1)

  Montacutianus (now lost) (= L2)

There are also three Syriac fragments, an Armenian extraction from the Syriac, an Arabic extraction from the Syriac, and two Coptic fragments (*Trallians*, *Philippians*, *Romans* 1–5.2; 2–9.1, *Smyrneans* 1–6, *Polycarp* 7.2–8.3) along with quotations in Eusebius.

Romans had a separate history of transmission. See below under abbreviations.

Abbreviations in the Apparatus

For All the Letters Except Romans

G   Greek text of the middle recension (Codex Medicio-Laurentianus)

g   Greek text of the long recension (i.e., the interpolated manuscripts)

P   Berlin Papyrus (middle recension, of Smyrn. 3.3 - 12.1)

L   Latin text of the middle recension

l   Latin text of the long recension (i.e., the interpolated manuscripts)

A	Armenian version
C	Coptic version
S	Syriac text of the short recension (of Ephesians, Romans, and Polycarp)
Sf	fragments of the Syriac version

For Romans

G	Codex Parisiensis (10th-11th c.)
H	Codex Hierosolymitanus (10th c.)
K	Codex Siniaiticus (10th c.)
T	Codex Taurinensis (13th c.)
z	combined witness of GHKT
M	Greek text of the letter, as found in the Martyrdom of Ignatius by Metaphrastes
Sm	Syriac version of the letter, as preserved in the Martyrdom of Ignatius
Am	Armenian version of the letter, as preserved in the Martyrdom of Ignatius

g L l A C S Sf: same as for the other letters

SELECT BIBLIOGRAPHY

Barnard, Leslie W. "The Background of St. Ignatius of Antioch." *VC* 17 (1963) 193–206.

Barrett, Charles K. "Jews and Judaizers in the Epistles of Ignatius." In *Jews, Greeks and Christians: Religious Cultures in Late Antiquity*, ed. R. Hammerton-Kelly and R. Scroggs. Leiden: Brill, 1976; 220–44.

Camelot, P. T. *Ignace d'Antioche: Lettres. Lettres et Martyre de. Polycarpe de Smyrne*. 4th ed. SC, 10. Paris: Cerf, 1969.

Corwin, Virginia. *St. Ignatius and Christianity in Antioch.* New Haven: Yale University Press, 1960.

Donahue, Paul J. "Jewish Christianity in the Letters of Ignatius of Antioch." *VC* 32 (1978) 81–93.

Grant, Robert M. *Ignatius of Antioch.* Vol. 4 of *The Apostolic Fathers: A New Translation and Commentary*, ed. Robert M. Grant. Camden, N.J.: Thomas Nelson, 1967.

Hammond Bammel, C. P. "Ignatian Problems." *JTS* n.s. 33 (1982) 62–97.

Hübner, R. M. "Thesen zur Echtheit und Datierung der sieben Briefe des Ignatius Antiochien." *ZAC* 1 (1997) 44–72.

Joly, Robert. *Le Dossier d'Ignace d'Antioche.* Université libre de Bruxelles, Faculté de Philosophie et Lettres 69. Brussels: Éditions de l'université de Bruxelles, 1979.

Lechner, Thomas. *Ignatius adversus Valentinianos? Chronologische und theologiegeschichtliche Studien zu den Briefen des Ignatius von Antiochen.* VCSup 47. Leiden: Brill, 1999.

Lightfoot, Joseph Barber. *The Apostolic Fathers: Clement, Ignatius, and Polycarp.* Part II: *Ignatius and Polycarp.* 3 vols. London: Macmillan, 1889; reprinted Peabody, Mass.: Hendrickson, 1989.

Molland, Einar. "The Heretics Combatted by Ignatius of Antioch." *JEH* 5 (1954) 1–6.

Munier, Charles. "Où en est la question d'Ignace d'Antioche? Bilan d'un siècle de recherches 1870–1988." *ANRW* II.27.1 (1993) 359–484.

Paulsen, Henning. *Die Briefe des Ignatius von Antiochia und der Brief des Polykarp von Smyrna*, 2. neubearbeitete Aufl. der Auslegung von Walter Bauer. Tübingen: Mohr-Siebeck, 1985.

———— *Studien zur Theologie des Ignatius von Antiochien.* Forschungen zur Kirchen- und Dogmengeschichte 29. Göttingen: Vandenhoeck and Ruprecht, 1978.

Richardson, Cyril. *The Christianity of Ignatius of Antioch.* New York: Columbia University Press, 1935.

Rius-Camps, Josep. *The Four Authentic Letters of Ignatius.* Rome: Pontificium Institutum Orientalium Studiorum, 1980.

Schoedel, William R. *Ignatius of Antioch: A Commentary on the Letters of Ignatius of Antioch.* Philadelphia: Fortress Press, 1985.

———— "Polycarp of Smyrna and Ignatius of Antioch." *ANRW* II.27.1 (1993) 272–358.

Sumney, Jerry L. "Those Who 'Ignorantly Deny Him': The Opponents of Ignatius of Antioch (Identified in Three Letters)." *JECS* 1 (1993) 345–65.

Trevett, Christine. "Prophecy and Anti-Episcopal Activity: A Third Error Combatted by Ignatius?" *JEH* (1983) 1–18.

Weijenborg, Reinoud. *Les lettres d'Ignace d'Antioche.* Leiden: Brill, 1969.

Zahn, Theodor. *Ignatius von Antiochien.* Gotha: Perthes, 1873.

ΤΟΥ ΑΓΙΟΥ ΙΓΝΑΤΙΟΥ
ΕΠΙΣΤΟΛΑΙ

ΠΡΟΣ ΕΦΕΣΙΟΥΣ ΙΓΝΑΤΙΟΣ

Ἰγνάτιος, ὁ καὶ Θεοφόρος, τῇ εὐλογημένῃ ἐν μεγέθει
θεοῦ πατρὸς πληρώματι, τῇ προωρισμένῃ πρὸ αἰώνων
εἶναι διὰ παντὸς εἰς δόξαν παράμονον ἄτρεπτον, ἡνω-
μένην καὶ ἐκλελεγμένην[1] ἐν πάθει ἀληθινῷ, ἐν θελήματι τοῦ πατρὸς καὶ Ἰησοῦ Χριστοῦ, τοῦ θεοῦ ἡμῶν,
τῇ ἐκκλησίᾳ τῇ ἀξιομακαρίστῳ, τῇ οὔσῃ ἐν Ἐφέσῳ
τῆς Ἀσίας, πλεῖστα ἐν Ἰησοῦ Χριστῷ καὶ ἐν ἀμώμῳ
χαρᾷ[2] χαίρειν.

1

Ἀποδεξάμενος ὑμῶν ἐν θεῷ τὸ πολυαγάπητον ὄνομα,[3]
ὃ κέκτησθε φύσει δικαίᾳ κατὰ πίστιν καὶ ἀγάπην ἐν
Χριστῷ Ἰησοῦ, τῷ σωτῆρι ἡμῶν· μιμηταὶ ὄντες θεοῦ,
ἀναζωπυρήσαντες ἐν αἵματι θεοῦ τὸ συγγενικὸν ἔργον τελείως ἀπηρτίσατε. 2. ἀκούσαντες γὰρ δεδεμέ-
νον ἀπὸ Συρίας ὑπὲρ τοῦ κοινοῦ ὀνόματος καὶ ἐλπίδος,

---

[1] καὶ ἐκλελεγμένη S: om. A

LETTERS OF IGNATIUS

TO THE EPHESIANS

Ignatius, who is also called God-bearer, to the church that is blessed with greatness by the fullness of God the Father, a church foreordained from eternity past to obtain a constant glory which is enduring and unchanging, a church that has been unified and chosen in true suffering *[Or: a glory which is enduring, unchanging, unified, and chosen through true suffering]* by the will of the Father and of Jesus Christ, our God; to the church in Ephesus of Asia, which is worthy of all good fortune. Warmest greetings in Jesus Christ and in blameless joy!

1

Now that I have received in God your greatly loved name, which you have obtained because of your upright nature, according to the faith and love that is in Christ Jesus our Savior—for you are imitators of God and have rekindled, through the blood of God, the work we share as members of the same family, and brought it to perfect completion. 2. For you were eager to see me, since you heard that I was

---

² χαρᾷ S A g: χάριτι G L
³ ὑμῶν ἐν . . . ὄνομα g l (S A): ἐν . . . σου ὄνομα G L

ἐλπίζοντα τῇ προσευχῇ ὑμῶν ἐπιτυχεῖν ἐν Ῥώμῃ
θηριομαχῆσαι, ἵνα διὰ τοῦ ἐπιτυχεῖν δυνηθῶ μαθητὴς
εἶναι,[4] ἰδεῖν ἐσπουδάσατε.[5] 3. ἐπεὶ οὖν τὴν πολυπλη-
θίαν ὑμῶν ἐν ὀνόματι θεοῦ ἀπείληφα ἐν Ὀνησίμῳ, τῷ
ἐν ἀγάπῃ ἀδιηγήτῳ, ὑμῶν δὲ ἐν σαρκὶ ἐπισκόπῳ, ὃν
εὔχομαι κατὰ Ἰησοῦν Χριστὸν ὑμᾶς ἀγαπᾶν καὶ πάντας ὑμᾶς αὐτῷ ἐν ὁμοιότητι εἶναι. εὐλογητὸς γὰρ ὁ
χαρισάμενος ὑμῖν ἀξίοις οὖσι τοιοῦτον ἐπίσκοπον
κεκτῆσθαι.

2

Περὶ δὲ τοῦ συνδούλου μου Βούρρου, τοῦ κατὰ θεὸν
διακόνου ὑμῶν ἐν πᾶσιν εὐλογημένου, εὔχομαι παρα-
μεῖναι αὐτὸν εἰς τιμὴν ὑμῶν καὶ τοῦ ἐπισκόπου· καὶ
Κρόκος δέ, ὁ θεοῦ ἄξιος καὶ ὑμῶν, ὃν ἐξεμπλάριον τῆς
ἀφ' ὑμῶν ἀγάπης ἀπέλαβον, κατὰ πάντα με ἀνέπαυσεν, ὡς καὶ αὐτὸν ὁ πατὴρ Ἰησοῦ Χριστοῦ ἀναψύξαι
ἅμα Ὀνησίμῳ καὶ Βούρρῳ καὶ Εὔπλῳ καὶ Φρόντωνι,
δι' ὧν πάντας ὑμᾶς κατὰ ἀγάπην εἶδον. 2. ὀναίμην
ὑμῶν διὰ παντός, ἐάνπερ ἄξιος ὦ. πρέπον οὖν ἐστιν
κατὰ πάντα τρόπον δοξάζειν Ἰησοῦν Χριστὸν τὸν
δοξάσαντα ὑμᾶς, ἵνα ἐν μιᾷ ὑποταγῇ κατηρτισμένοι,[6]
ὑποτασσόμενοι τῷ ἐπισκόπῳ καὶ τῷ πρεσβυτερίῳ,
κατὰ πάντα ἦτε ἡγιασμένοι.

[4] μαθητὴς εἶναι L: add dei S A: add τοῦ ὑπὲρ ἡμῶν ἑαυτὸν
ἀνενεγκόντος θεῷ προσφορὰν καὶ θυσίαν G g

being brought in chains from Syria because of the name and hope we share, and that I was hoping, through your prayer, to be allowed to fight the beasts in Rome, that by doing so I might be able to be a disciple. 3. Since, then, I have received your entire congregation in the name of God through Onesimus, who abides in a love that defies description and serves as your bishop in the flesh—and I ask by Jesus Christ that you love him, and that all of you be like him. For blessed is the one who has graciously granted you, who are worthy, to obtain such a bishop.

2

But as to my fellow slave Burrhus, your godly deacon who is blessed in all things, I ask that he stay here for the honor of both you and the bishop. And Crocus as well—who is worthy of God and of you, whom I received as an embodiment of your love—has revived me in every way. So may the Father of Jesus Christ refresh him, along with Onesimus, Burrhus, Euplus, and Fronto, those through whom I lovingly saw all of you. 2. I hope to enjoy you at all times, if indeed I am worthy. For it is fitting for you in every way to give glory to Jesus Christ, the one who glorified you, so that you may be holy in all respects, being made complete through a single subjection, being subject to the bishop and the presbytery.

---

5 ἰδεῖν ἐσπουδάσατε: om. G g

6 κατηρτισμένοι L: ἦτε κατηρτισμένοι τῷ αὐτῷ νοΐ καὶ τῇ αὐτῇ γνώμῃ καὶ τὸ αὐτὸ λέγητε πάντες περὶ τοῦ αὐτοῦ, ἵνα G g

3

Οὐ διατάσσομαι ὑμῖν ὡς ὤν τις.[7] εἰ γὰρ καὶ δέδεμαι ἐν τῷ ὀνόματι, οὔπω ἀπήρτισμαι ἐν Ἰησοῦ Χριστῷ. νῦν γὰρ ἀρχὴν ἔχω τοῦ μαθητεύεσθαι καὶ προσλαλῶ ὑμῖν ὡς συνδιδασκαλίταις μου. ἐμὲ γὰρ ἔδει ὑφ᾽ ὑμῶν ὑπαλειφθῆναι[8] πίστει, νουθεσίᾳ, ὑπομονῇ, μακροθυμίᾳ. 2. ἀλλ᾽ ἐπεὶ ἡ ἀγάπη οὐκ ἐᾷ με σιωπᾶν περὶ ὑμῶν, διὰ τοῦτο προέλαβον παρακαλεῖν ὑμᾶς, ὅπως συντρέχητε τῇ γνώμῃ τοῦ θεοῦ. καὶ γὰρ Ἰησοῦς Χριστός, τὸ ἀδιάκριτον ἡμῶν ζῆν, τοῦ πατρὸς ἡ γνώμη, ὡς καὶ οἱ ἐπίσκοποι, οἱ κατὰ τὰ πέρατα ὁρισθέντες, ἐν Ἰησοῦ Χριστοῦ γνώμῃ εἰσίν.

4

Ὅθεν πρέπει ὑμῖν συντρέχειν τῇ τοῦ ἐπισκόπου γνώμῃ, ὅπερ καὶ ποιεῖτε. τὸ γὰρ ἀξιονόμαστον ὑμῶν πρεσβυτέριον, τοῦ θεοῦ ἄξιον, οὕτως συνήρμοσται τῷ ἐπισκόπῳ, ὡς χορδαὶ κιθάρᾳ. διὰ τοῦτο ἐν τῇ ὁμονοίᾳ ὑμῶν καὶ συμφώνῳ ἀγάπῃ Ἰησοῦς Χριστὸς ᾄδεται. 2. καὶ οἱ κατ᾽ ἄνδρα δὲ χορὸς γίνεσθε, ἵνα σύμφωνοι ὄντες ἐν ὁμονοίᾳ, χρῶμα θεοῦ λαβόντες ἐν ἑνότητι, ᾄδητε ἐν φωνῇ μιᾷ διὰ Ἰησοῦ Χριστοῦ τῷ πατρί, ἵνα ὑμῶν καὶ ἀκούσῃ καὶ ἐπιγινώσκῃ δι᾽ ὧν εὖ πράσσετε, μέλη ὄντας τοῦ υἱοῦ αὐτοῦ. χρήσιμον οὖν ἐστίν, ὑμᾶς ἐν ἀμώμῳ ἑνότητι εἶναι, ἵνα καὶ θεοῦ πάντοτε μετέχητε.

3

I am not giving you orders as if I were someone. For even though I have been bound in the name, I have not yet been perfected in Jesus Christ. For now I have merely begun to be a disciple and am speaking to you as my fellow learners. For I have needed you to prepare me for the struggle in faith, admonishment, endurance, and patience. 2. But since love does not allow me to be silent concerning you, I decided to encourage you, that you may run together in harmony with the mind of God. For also Jesus Christ, who cannot be distinguished from our life, is the Father's mind, just as also the bishops who have been appointed throughout the world share the mind of Jesus Christ.

4

For this reason it is fitting for you to run together in harmony with the mind of the bishop, which is exactly what you are doing. For your presbytery, which is both worthy of the name and worthy of God, is attuned to the bishop as strings to the lyre. Therefore Jesus Christ is sung in your harmony and symphonic love. 2. And each of you should join the chorus, that by being symphonic in your harmony, taking up God's pitch in unison, you may sing in one voice through Jesus Christ to the Father, that he may both hear and recognize you through the things you do well, since you are members of his Son. Therefore it is useful for you to be in flawless unison, that you may partake of God at all times as well.

---

⁷ τις G L: τι A g   ⁸ ὑποληφθῆναι L

5

Εἰ γὰρ ἐγὼ ἐν μικρῷ χρόνῳ τοιαύτην συνήθειαν
ἔσχον πρὸς τὸν ἐπίσκοπον ὑμῶν, οὐκ ἀνθρωπίνην
οὖσαν, ἀλλὰ πνευματικήν, πόσῳ μᾶλλον ὑμᾶς μακα-
ρίζω τοὺς ἐγκεκραμένους οὕτως,[9] ὡς ἡ ἐκκλησία
Ἰησοῦ Χριστῷ καὶ ὡς Ἰησοῦς Χριστὸς τῷ πατρί, ἵνα
πάντα ἐν ἑνότητι σύμφωνα ᾖ; 2. μηδεὶς πλανάσθω·
ἐὰν μή τις ᾖ ἐντὸς τοῦ θυσιαστηρίου, ὑστερεῖται τοῦ
ἄρτου τοῦ θεοῦ.[10] εἰ γὰρ ἑνὸς καὶ δευτέρου προσευχὴ
τοσαύτην ἰσχὺν ἔχει, πόσῳ μᾶλλον ἥ τε τοῦ ἐπισκόπου καὶ πάσης τῆς ἐκκλησίας; 3. ὁ οὖν μὴ ἐρχόμενος ἐπὶ τὸ αὐτό, οὗτος ἤδη ὑπερηφανεῖ καὶ ἑαυτὸν
διέκρινεν. γέγραπται γάρ· ὑπερηφάνοις ὁ θεὸς ἀντιτάσσεται. σπουδάσωμεν οὖν μὴ ἀντιτάσσεσθαι τῷ
ἐπισκόπῳ, ἵνα ὦμεν θεῷ ὑποτασσόμενοι.

6

Καὶ ὅσον βλέπει τις σιγῶντα ἐπίσκοπον, πλειόνως
αὐτὸν φοβείσθω· πάντα γάρ, ὃν πέμπει ὁ οἰκοδεσπό-
της εἰς ἰδίαν οἰκονομίαν, οὕτως δεῖ ἡμᾶς αὐτὸν
δέχεσθαι, ὡς αὐτὸν τὸν πέμψαντα. τὸν οὖν ἐπίσκοπον
δῆλον ὅτι ὡς αὐτὸν τὸν κύριον δεῖ προσβλέπειν.
2. αὐτὸς μὲν οὖν Ὀνήσιμος ὑπερεπαινεῖ ὑμῶν τὴν ἐν
θεῷ εὐταξίαν, ὅτι πάντες κατὰ ἀλήθειαν ζῆτε καὶ ὅτι
ἐν ὑμῖν οὐδεμία αἵρεσις κατοικεῖ· ἀλλ' οὐδὲ ἀκούετέ

5

For since I was able to establish such an intimacy with your bishop so quickly (an intimacy that was not human but spiritual), how much more do I consider you fortunate, you who are mingled together with him as the church is mingled with Jesus Christ and Jesus Christ with the Father, so that all things may be symphonic in unison. 2. Let no one be deceived. Anyone who is not inside the sanctuary lacks the bread of God. For if the prayer of one or two persons has such power, how much more will that of the bishop and the entire church? 3. Therefore the one who does not join the entire congregation is already haughty and passes judgment on himself. For it is written, "God opposes the haughty."[1] And so we should be eager not to oppose the bishop, that we may be subject to God.

6

The more one notices that the bishop is silent, the more he should stand in awe of him. For we must receive everyone that the master of the house sends to take care of his affairs as if he were the sender himself. And so we are clearly obliged to look upon the bishop as the Lord himself. 2. Thus Onesimus himself praises you highly for being so well ordered in God, because all of you live according to the truth and no heresy resides among you. On the

---

1 Prov 3:34; cf. Jas 4:6; 1 Pet 5:5.

---

9 οὕτως G L: αὐτῷ A g

10 τοῦ θεοῦ: om. A

τινος πλέον ἢ περὶ[11] Ἰησοῦ Χριστοῦ λαλοῦντος ἐν
ἀληθείᾳ.

7

Εἰώθασιν γάρ τινες δόλῳ πονηρῷ τὸ ὄνομα περι-
φέρειν, ἄλλα τινὰ πράσσοντες ἀνάξια θεοῦ· οὓς δεῖ
ὑμᾶς ὡς θηρία ἐκκλίνειν. εἰσὶν γὰρ κύνες λυσσῶντες,
λαθροδῆκται· οὓς δεῖ ὑμᾶς φυλάσσεσθαι ὄντας
δυσθεραπεύτους. 2. εἷς ἰατρός ἐστιν, σαρκικός τε καὶ
πνευματικός, γεννητὸς καὶ ἀγέννητος, ἐν σαρκὶ γενόμενος[12] θεός, ἐν θανάτῳ[13] ζωὴ ἀληθινή, καὶ ἐκ Μαρίας
καὶ ἐκ θεοῦ, πρῶτον παθητὸς καὶ τότε ἀπαθής, Ἰησοῦς
Χριστὸς ὁ κύριος ἡμῶν.[14]

8

Μὴ οὖν τις ὑμᾶς ἐξαπατάτω, ὥσπερ οὐδὲ ἐξαπατᾶσθε,
ὅλοι ὄντες θεοῦ. ὅταν γὰρ μηδεμία ἔρις ἐνήρεισται ἐν
ὑμῖν ἡ δυναμένη ὑμᾶς βασανίσαι, ἄρα κατὰ θεὸν
ζῆτε. περίψημα ὑμῶν καὶ ἁγνίζομαι ὑμῶν Ἐφεσίων,
ἐκκλησίας τῆς διαβοήτου τοῖς αἰῶσιν. 2. οἱ σαρκικοὶ
τὰ πνευματικὰ πράσσειν οὐ δύνανται οὐδὲ οἱ πνευμα-
τικοὶ τὰ σαρκικά, ὥσπερ οὐδὲ ἡ πίστις τὰ τῆς
ἀπιστίας οὐδὲ ἡ ἀπιστία τὰ τῆς πίστεως. ἃ δὲ καὶ

---

11 ἢ περὶ cj. Lightfoot: ἥπερ L: εἴπερ G: εἰ μὴ περὶ A
12 ἐν σαρκὶ γενόμενος G L: ἐν ἀνθρώπῳ Sf

contrary, you no longer listen to anyone, except one who speaks truthfully about Jesus Christ.

7

For some are accustomed to bear the name in wicked deceit, while acting in ways that are unworthy of God. You must shun them as wild animals. For they are raving dogs who bite when no one is looking. You must guard against them, for they are hard to tame. 2. For there is one physician, both fleshly and spiritual, born and unborn, God come in the flesh, true life in death, from both Mary and God, first subject to suffering and then beyond suffering, Jesus Christ our Lord.

8

And so let no one deceive you, just as you are not deceived, since you belong entirely to God. For when no strife that is able to torment you is rooted within you, then you are living as God wants. I am your lowly scapegoat; I give myself as a sacrificial offering for you Ephesians, a church of eternal renown. 2. Those who belong to the flesh cannot do spiritual things, nor can those who belong to the spirit do fleshly things;[2] so too, faith cannot do what is faithless nor can faithlessness do what is faithful. But even what you do

2 Rom 8:5, 8.

---

13 ἐν ἀθανάτῳ G L
14 Ἰησοῦς . . . ἡμῶν A (L) Sf: om. G

κατὰ σάρκα πράσσετε, ταῦτα πνευματικά ἐστιν, ἐν
Ἰησοῦ γὰρ Χριστῷ πάντα πράσσετε.

9

Ἔγνων δὲ παροδεύσαντάς τινας ἐκεῖθεν, ἔχοντας κακὴν διδαχήν· οὓς οὐκ εἰάσατε σπεῖραι εἰς ὑμᾶς,
βύσαντες τὰ ὦτα, εἰς τὸ μὴ παραδέξασθαι τὰ σπει-
ρόμενα ὑπ' αὐτῶν, ὡς ὄντες λίθοι ναοῦ πατρός, ἡτοι-
μασμένοι¹⁵ εἰς οἰκοδομὴν θεοῦ πατρός, ἀναφερόμενοι
εἰς τὰ ὕψη διὰ τῆς μηχανῆς Ἰησοῦ Χριστοῦ, ὅς ἐστιν
σταυρός, σχοινίῳ χρώμενοι τῷ πνεύματι τῷ ἁγίῳ· ἡ
δὲ πίστις ὑμῶν ἀναγωγεὺς ὑμῶν, ἡ δὲ ἀγάπη ὁδὸς ἡ
ἀναφέρουσα εἰς θεόν. 2. ἐστὲ οὖν καὶ σύνοδοι πάντες,
θεοφόροι καὶ ναοφόροι, χριστοφόροι, ἁγιοφόροι, κατὰ
πάντα κεκοσμημένοι ἐν ταῖς ἐντολαῖς Ἰησοῦ Χρι-
στοῦ· οἷς καὶ ἀγαλλιῶμαι, ὅτι ἠξιώθην δι' ὧν γράφω
προσομιλῆσαι ὑμῖν καὶ συγχαρῆναι, ὅτι κατ' ἀνθρώ-
πινον¹⁶ βίον οὐδὲν ἀγαπᾶτε εἰ μὴ μόνον τὸν θεόν.

10

Καὶ ὑπὲρ τῶν ἄλλων δὲ ἀνθρώπων ἀδιαλείπτως προσ-
εύχεσθε· ἔστιν γὰρ ἐν αὐτοῖς ἐλπὶς μετανοίας, ἵνα
θεοῦ τύχωσιν. ἐπιτρέψατε οὖν αὐτοῖς κἂν ἐκ τῶν

according to the flesh is spiritual, for you do all things in Jesus Christ.

9

I have learned that some people have passed through on their way from there with an evil teaching. But you did not permit them to sow any seeds among you, plugging your ears so as not to receive anything sown by them. You are stones of the Father's temple, prepared for the building of God the Father. For you are being carried up to the heights by the crane of Jesus Christ, which is the cross, using as a cable the Holy Spirit; and your faith is your hoist, and love is the path that carries you up to God. 2. And so you are all traveling companions bearing God, bearing the temple, bearing Christ, and bearing the holy things, adorned in every way with the commandments of Jesus Christ. I exult in you, since I have been deemed worthy through the things that I write to speak with you and to rejoice together with you; for you love nothing in human life but God alone.

10

Constantly pray for others; for there is still hope that they may repent so as to attain to God. And so, allow them

---

15 πατρὸς ἡτοιμασμένοι G L A: προητοιμασμένοι cj. Lightfoot

16 ἀνθρώπινον (cj. Lightfoot): ἀνθρώπων cj. Lightfoot: ὅλον cj. Zahn: ἄλλον G L (A)

ἔργων ὑμῖν μαθητευθῆναι. 2. πρὸς τὰς ὀργὰς αὐτῶν
ὑμεῖς πραεῖς, πρὸς τὰς μεγαλορημοσύνας αὐτῶν
ὑμεῖς ταπεινόφρονες, πρὸς τὰς βλασφημίας αὐτῶν
ὑμεῖς τὰς προσευχάς, πρὸς τὴν πλάνην αὐτῶν ὑμεῖς
ἑδραῖοι τῇ πίστει, πρὸς τὸ ἄγριον αὐτῶν ὑμεῖς ἥμεροι,
μὴ σπουδάζοντες ἀντιμιμήσασθαι αὐτούς. 3. ἀδελφοὶ
αὐτῶν εὑρεθῶμεν τῇ ἐπιεικείᾳ· μιμηταὶ δὲ τοῦ κυρίου
σπουδάζωμεν εἶναι, τίς πλέον ἀδικηθῇ, τίς ἀπο-
στερηθῇ, τίς ἀθετηθῇ; ἵνα μὴ τοῦ διαβόλου βοτάνη
τις εὑρεθῇ ἐν ὑμῖν, ἀλλ' ἐν πάσῃ ἁγνείᾳ καὶ
σωφροσύνῃ μένητε ἐν Ἰησοῦ Χριστῷ σαρκικῶς καὶ
πνευματικῶς.

11

Ἔσχατοι καιροί· λοιπὸν αἰσχυνθῶμεν, φοβηθῶμεν
τὴν μακροθυμίαν τοῦ θεοῦ, ἵνα μὴ ἡμῖν εἰς κρίμα
γένηται. ἢ γὰρ τὴν μέλλουσαν ὀργὴν φοβηθῶμεν, ἢ
τὴν ἐνεστῶσαν χάριν ἀγαπήσωμεν, ἓν τῶν δύο· μόνον
ἐν Χριστῷ Ἰησοῦ εὑρεθῆναι εἰς τὸ ἀληθινὸν ζῆν.
2. χωρὶς τούτου μηδὲν ὑμῖν πρεπέτω, ἐν ᾧ τὰ δεσμὰ
περιφέρω, τοὺς πνευματικοὺς μαργαρίτας, ἐν οἷς γένοιτό μοι ἀναστῆναι τῇ προσευχῇ ὑμῶν, ἧς γένοιτό
μοι ἀεὶ μέτοχον εἶναι, ἵνα ἐν κλήρῳ Ἐφεσίων εὑρεθῶ
τῶν Χριστιανῶν, οἳ καὶ τοῖς ἀποστόλοις πάντοτε
συνήνεσαν[17] ἐν δυνάμει Ἰησοῦ Χριστοῦ.

[17] συνήνεσαν G L: συνῆσαν A g

to learn from you, at least by your deeds. 2. In response to their anger, show meekness; to their boasting, be humble; to their blasphemies, offer up prayers; to their wandering in error, be firmly rooted in faith; to their savage behavior, act civilized. Do not be eager to imitate their example. 3. Through gentleness we should be their brothers. And we should be seen to be eager to imitate the Lord. Who was mistreated more than he? Or defrauded? Or rejected? Do this, so that no weed planted by the Devil may be found in you and you may abide in Jesus Christ both in the flesh and in the spirit, with all holiness and self-control.

11

These are the end times. And so we should feel shame and stand in fear of God's patience, that it not turn into our judgment. For we should either fear the wrath that is coming or love the gracious gift that is already here—one or the other, so long as we acquire true life by being found in Christ Jesus. 2. Apart from him nothing should seem right to you. In him I am bearing my chains, which are spiritual pearls; in them I hope to rise again, through your prayer. May I always have a share of it! Then I will be found to share the lot of the Ephesian Christians, who have always agreed with the apostles by the power of Jesus Christ.

12

Οἶδα, τίς εἰμι καὶ τίσιν γράφω. ἐγὼ κατάκριτος, ὑμεῖς ἠλεημένοι· ἐγὼ ὑπὸ κίνδυνον, ὑμεῖς ἐστηριγμένοι. 2. πάροδός ἐστε τῶν εἰς θεὸν ἀναιρουμένων, Παύλου συμμύσται, τοῦ ἡγιασμένου, τοῦ μεμαρτυρημένου, ἀξιομακαρίστου, οὗ γένοιτό μοι ὑπὸ τὰ ἴχνη εὑρεθῆναι, ὅταν θεοῦ ἐπιτύχω, ὃς ἐν πάσῃ ἐπιστολῇ μνημονεύει ὑμῶν ἐν Χριστῷ Ἰησοῦ.

13

Σπουδάζετε οὖν πυκνότερον συνέρχεσθαι εἰς εὐχαριστίαν θεοῦ καὶ εἰς δόξαν. ὅταν γὰρ πυκνῶς ἐπὶ τὸ αὐτὸ γίνεσθε, καθαιροῦνται αἱ δυνάμεις τοῦ σατανᾶ, καὶ λύεται ὁ ὄλεθρος αὐτοῦ ἐν τῇ ὁμονοίᾳ ὑμῶν τῆς πίστεως. 2. οὐδέν ἐστιν ἄμεινον εἰρήνης, ἐν ᾗ πᾶς πόλεμος καταργεῖται ἐπουρανίων καὶ ἐπιγείων.

14

Ὧν οὐδὲν λανθάνει ὑμᾶς, ἐὰν τελείως εἰς Ἰησοῦν Χριστὸν ἔχητε τὴν πίστιν καὶ τὴν ἀγάπην, ἥτις ἐστὶν ἀρχὴ ζωῆς καὶ τέλος· ἀρχὴ μὲν πίστις, τέλος δὲ ἀγάπη. τὰ δὲ δύο ἐν ἑνότητι γενόμενα θεός[18] ἐστιν, τὰ δὲ ἄλλα πάντα εἰς καλοκαγαθίαν ἀκόλουθά ἐστιν. 2. οὐδεὶς πίστιν ἐπαγγελλόμενος ἁμαρτάνει, οὐδὲ ἀγάπην κεκτημένος μισεῖ. φανερὸν τὸ δένδρον ἀπὸ

12

I know who I am and to whom I am writing. I am condemned, you have been shown mercy; I am in danger, you are secure. 2. You are a passageway for those slain for God; you are fellow initiates with Paul, the holy one who received a testimony and proved worthy of all fortune. When I attain to God, may I be found in his footsteps, this one who mentions you in every epistle in Christ Jesus.

13

Be eager, therefore, to come together more frequently to give thanks and glory *[Or: to celebrate the eucharist and give glory]* to God. For when you frequently gather as a congregation, the powers of Satan are destroyed, and his destructive force is vanquished by the harmony of your faith. 2. Nothing is better than peace, by which every battle is abolished, whether waged by those in heaven or by those on earth.

14

None of these things escapes your notice if you completely adhere to the faith and love that are in Jesus Christ. This is the beginning and end of life: faith is the beginning, love is the end. And the two together in unity are God; all other things that lead to nobility of character follow. 2. No one who professes faith sins, nor does anyone hate after acquir-

---

18 θεός L Sf A: θεοῦ G

τοῦ καρποῦ αὐτοῦ· οὕτως οἱ ἐπαγγελλόμενοι Χριστοῦ[19] εἶναι δι᾽ ὧν πράσσουσιν ὀφθήσονται. οὐ γὰρ
νῦν ἐπαγγελίας τὸ ἔργον, ἀλλ᾽ ἐν δυνάμει πίστεως ἐάν
τις εὑρεθῇ εἰς τέλος.

15

Ἄμεινόν ἐστιν σιωπᾶν καὶ εἶναι, ἢ λαλοῦντα μὴ εἶναι.
καλὸν τὸ διδάσκειν, ἐὰν ὁ λέγων ποιῇ. εἷς οὖν
διδάσκαλος, ὃς εἶπεν, καὶ ἐγένετο· καὶ ἃ σιγῶν δὲ
πεποίηκεν, ἄξια τοῦ πατρός ἐστιν. 2. ὁ λόγον Ἰησοῦ
κεκτημένος ἀληθῶς δύναται καὶ τῆς ἡσυχίας αὐτοῦ
ἀκούειν, ἵνα τέλειος ᾖ, ἵνα δι᾽ ὧν λαλεῖ πράσσῃ καὶ δι᾽
ὧν σιγᾷ γινώσκηται. 3. οὐδὲν λανθάνει τὸν κύριον,
ἀλλὰ καὶ τὰ κρυπτὰ ἡμῶν ἐγγὺς αὐτῷ ἐστιν. πάντα
οὖν ποιῶμεν ὡς αὐτοῦ ἐν ἡμῖν κατοικοῦντος, ἵνα ὦμεν
αὐτοῦ ναοὶ καὶ αὐτὸς ἐν ἡμῖν θεὸς ἡμῶν, ὅπερ καὶ
ἔστιν. καὶ φανήσεται πρὸ προσώπου ἡμῶν ἐξ ὧν
δικαίως ἀγαπῶμεν αὐτόν.

16

Μὴ πλανᾶσθε, ἀδελφοί μου· οἱ οἰκοφθόροι βασιλείαν
θεοῦ οὐ κληρονομήσουσιν. 2. εἰ οὖν οἱ κατὰ σάρκα
ταῦτα πράσσοντες ἀπέθανον, πόσῳ μᾶλλον, ἐὰν
πίστιν θεοῦ ἐν κακῇ διδασκαλίᾳ φθείρῃ, ὑπὲρ ἧς

---

[19] Χριστοῦ A g: χριστιανός G L

ing love. The tree is known by its fruit;[3] so those who profess to belong to Christ will be seen by what they do. For the deed is not a matter of professing in the present but of being found in the power of faith at the end.

15

It is better to be silent and to exist than to speak and not exist. It is good to teach, if the one who speaks also acts. For there was one teacher who spoke and it happened.[4] And the things he has done while remaining silent are worthy of the Father. 2. The one who truly possesses the word of Jesus is able to hear his silence as well. He will, as a result, be perfect, acting through what he says and being understood through what he does not say. 3. Nothing escapes the notice of the Lord, but even what we have kept hidden is near to him. And so, we should do everything knowing that he is dwelling within us, that we may be his temples and he our God in us,[5] as in fact he is. And he will be made visible before our eyes. For these reasons, let us love him in an upright way.

16

Do not be deceived, my brothers; those who corrupt their households will not inherit the kingdom of God.[6] 2. If then those who do such things according to the flesh die, how much more the one who corrupts the faith of God through

3 Matt 12:33.   4 Ps 33:9.
5 Cf. 1 Cor 3:16.   6 Cf. 1 Cor 6:9.

Ἰησοῦς Χριστὸς ἐσταυρώθη; ὁ τοιοῦτος, ῥυπαρὸς
γενόμενος, εἰς τὸ πῦρ τὸ ἄσβεστον χωρήσει, ὁμοίως
καὶ ὁ ἀκούων αὐτοῦ.

17

Διὰ τοῦτο μύρον ἔλαβεν ἐπὶ τῆς κεφαλῆς αὐτοῦ ὁ
κύριος, ἵνα πνέῃ τῇ ἐκκλησίᾳ ἀφθαρσίαν. μὴ ἀλεί-
φεσθε δυσωδίαν τῆς διδασκαλίας τοῦ ἄρχοντος τοῦ
αἰῶνος τούτου, μὴ αἰχμαλωτίσῃ ὑμᾶς ἐκ τοῦ προ-
κειμένου ζῆν. 2. διὰ τί δὲ οὐ πάντες φρόνιμοι γινόμεθα
λαβόντες θεοῦ γνῶσιν, ὅ ἐστιν Ἰησοῦς Χριστός; τί
μωρῶς ἀπολλύμεθα, ἀγνοοῦντες τὸ χάρισμα ὃ πέπομ-
φεν ἀληθῶς ὁ κύριος;

18

Περίψημα τὸ ἐμὸν πνεῦμα τοῦ σταυροῦ, ὅ ἐστιν σκάνδαλον τοῖς ἀπιστοῦσιν, ἡμῖν δὲ σωτηρία καὶ ζωὴ
αἰώνιος. ποῦ σοφός; ποῦ συζητητής; ποῦ καύχησις
τῶν λεγομένων συνετῶν; 2. ὁ γὰρ θεὸς ἡμῶν Ἰησοῦς ὁ
Χριστὸς ἐκυοφορήθη ὑπὸ[20] Μαρίας κατ᾽ οἰκονομίαν
θεοῦ ἐκ σπέρματος μὲν Δαυίδ, πνεύματος δὲ ἁγίου· ὃς
ἐγεννήθη καὶ ἐβαπτίσθη, ἵνα τῷ πάθει τὸ ὕδωρ
καθαρίσῃ.

[20] ὑπὸ G Cod. Paris. graec. 950 (containing Eph. 18.2–19.3):
ἐκ L g

an evil teaching, the faith for which Jesus Christ was crucified? Such a person is filthy and will depart into the unquenchable fire; so too the one who listens to him.

17

For this reason the Lord received perfumed ointment on his head,[7] that he might breathe immortality into the church. Do not be anointed with the stench of the teaching of the ruler of this age, lest he take you captive from the life set before you. 2. Why do we all not become wise by receiving the knowledge of God, which is Jesus Christ? Why do we foolishly perish, remaining ignorant of the gracious gift the Lord has truly sent?

18

My spirit is a sacrificial offering bound to the cross, which is a scandal to those who do not believe but salvation and eternal life to us. Where is the one who is wise? Where is the debater?[8] Where is the boast of those called intelligent? 2. For our God, Jesus Christ, was conceived by Mary according to the plan of God; he was from the seed of David, but also from the Holy Spirit. He was born and baptized, that he might cleanse the water by his suffering.

[7] Matt 26:7; Mark 14:3.
[8] 1 Cor 1:20, 23.

19

Καὶ ἔλαθεν τὸν ἄρχοντα τοῦ αἰῶνος τούτου ἡ παρ-
θενία Μαρίας καὶ ὁ τοκετὸς αὐτῆς, ὁμοίως καὶ ὁ
θάνατος τοῦ κυρίου· τρία μυστήρια κραυγῆς, ἅτινα ἐν
ἡσυχίᾳ θεοῦ ἐπράχθη. 2. πῶς οὖν ἐφανερώθη τοῖς
αἰῶσιν; ἀστὴρ ἐν οὐρανῷ ἔλαμψεν ὑπὲρ πάντας τοὺς
ἀστέρας, καὶ τὸ φῶς αὐτοῦ ἀνεκλάλητον ἦν καὶ
ξενισμὸν παρεῖχεν ἡ καινότης αὐτοῦ. τὰ δὲ λοιπὰ
πάντα ἄστρα ἅμα ἡλίῳ καὶ σελήνῃ χορὸς ἐγένετο τῷ
ἀστέρι, αὐτὸς δὲ ἦν ὑπερβάλλων τὸ φῶς αὐτοῦ ὑπὲρ
πάντα· ταραχή τε ἦν, πόθεν ἡ καινότης ἡ ἀνόμοιος
αὐτοῖς. 3. ὅθεν ἐλύετο πᾶσα μαγεία καὶ πᾶς δεσμὸς
ἠφανίζετο κακίας· ἄγνοια καθῃρεῖτο, παλαιὰ βασιλεία διεφθείρετο θεοῦ ἀνθρωπίνως φανερουμένου εἰς
καινότητα ἀϊδίου ζωῆς· ἀρχὴν δὲ ἐλάμβανεν τὸ παρὰ
θεῷ ἀπηρτισμένον. ἔνθεν τὰ πάντα συνεκινεῖτο διὰ τὸ
μελετᾶσθαι θανάτου κατάλυσιν.

20

Ἐάν με καταξιώσῃ Ἰησοῦς Χριστὸς ἐν τῇ προσευχῇ
ὑμῶν καὶ θέλημα ᾖ, ἐν τῷ δευτέρῳ βιβλιδίῳ, ὃ μέλλω
γράφειν ὑμῖν, προσδηλώσω ὑμῖν, ἧς ἠρξάμην οἰκονο-
μίας εἰς τὸν καινὸν ἄνθρωπον Ἰησοῦν Χριστόν, ἐν τῇ
αὐτοῦ πίστει καὶ ἐν τῇ αὐτοῦ ἀγάπῃ, ἐν πάθει αὐτοῦ
καὶ ἀναστάσει· 2. μάλιστα ἐὰν ὁ κύριός μοι ἀποκαλύψῃ, ὅτι[21] οἱ κατ' ἄνδρα κοινῇ πάντες ἐν χάριτι ἐξ

19

The virginity of Mary and her giving birth escaped the notice of the ruler of this age; so too did the death of the Lord—three mysteries of a cry which were accomplished in the silence of God. 2. How then did he become manifest to the aeons *[Or: ages; or: world]*? A star in the sky shone brighter than all the stars. Its light was indescribable and its novelty created astonishment. All the other stars, along with the sun and the moon, formed a chorus to that star, and its light surpassed all the others. And there was a disturbance over whence it had come, this novel thing, so different from the others. 3. Hence all magic was vanquished and every bondage of evil came to nought. Ignorance was destroyed and the ancient realm was brought to ruin, when God became manifest in a human way, for the newness of eternal life. And that which had been prepared by God received its beginning. From that time on, all things were put in commotion because the dissolution of death was taking place.

20

If Jesus Christ finds me worthy through your prayer and it be his will, in the second small book that I am about to write you I will show you plainly what I have begun to discuss about the divine plan that leads to the new person Jesus Christ, involving his faithfulness and love, his suffering and resurrection. 2. I will especially do so if the Lord shows me that all of you to a person are gathering together one by

---

21 ἀποκαλύψῃ ὅτι G L (A): ἀποκαλύψῃ τι cj. Zahn

ὀνόματος συνέρχεσθε ἐν μιᾷ πίστει καὶ ἐν Ἰησοῦ
Χριστῷ, τῷ κατὰ σάρκα ἐκ γένους Δαυίδ, τῷ υἱῷ
ἀνθρώπου καὶ υἱῷ θεοῦ, εἰς τὸ ὑπακούειν ὑμᾶς τῷ
ἐπισκόπῳ καὶ τῷ πρεσβυτερίῳ ἀπερισπάστῳ διανοίᾳ,
ἕνα ἄρτον κλῶντες, ὅς ἐστιν φάρμακον ἀθανασίας,
ἀντίδοτος τοῦ μὴ ἀποθανεῖν, ἀλλὰ ζῆν ἐν Ἰησοῦ
Χριστῷ διὰ παντός.

21

Ἀντίψυχον ὑμῶν ἐγὼ καὶ ὧν[22] ἐπέμψατε εἰς θεοῦ τιμὴν
εἰς Σμύρναν, ὅθεν καὶ γράφω ὑμῖν, εὐχαριστῶν τῷ
κυρίῳ, ἀγαπῶν Πολύκαρπον ὡς καὶ ὑμᾶς. μνημονεύετέ μου, ὡς καὶ ὑμῶν Ἰησοῦς Χριστός. 2. προσ-
εὔχεσθε ὑπὲρ τῆς ἐκκλησίας τῆς ἐν Συρίᾳ, ὅθεν
δεδεμένος εἰς Ῥώμην ἀπάγομαι, ἔσχατος ὢν τῶν ἐκεῖ
πιστῶν, ὥσπερ ἠξιώθην εἰς τιμὴν θεοῦ εὑρεθῆναι.
ἔρρωσθε ἐν θεῷ πατρὶ καὶ ἐν Ἰησοῦ Χριστῷ, τῇ κοινῇ
ἐλπίδι ἡμῶν.

ΜΑΓΝΗΣΙΕΤΣΙΝ ΙΓΝΑΤΙΟΣ

Ἰγνάτιος, ὁ καὶ Θεοφόρος, τῇ εὐλογημένῃ ἐν χάριτι
θεοῦ πατρὸς ἐν Χριστῷ Ἰησοῦ τῷ σωτῆρι ἡμῶν, ἐν ᾧ
ἀσπάζομαι τὴν ἐκκλησίαν τὴν οὖσαν ἐν Μαγνησίᾳ τῇ
πρὸς Μαιάνδρῳ καὶ εὔχομαι ἐν θεῷ πατρὶ καὶ ἐν
Ἰησοῦ Χριστῷ πλεῖστα χαίρειν.

one in God's grace, in one faith and in Jesus Christ—who is from the race of David according to the flesh, and is both son of man and son of God—so that you may obey the bishop and the presbytery (which is undistracted in mind), breaking one bread, which is a medicine that brings immortality, an antidote that allows us not to die but to live at all times in Jesus Christ.

21

I am giving my life for you, and for those you sent to Smyrna for the honor of God. I am writing you from there, giving thanks to the Lord and loving Polycarp as also I love you. Remember me as Jesus Christ remembers you. 2. Pray on behalf of the church in Syria; I am being taken from there to Rome in chains—even though I am the least of those who believe there—since I have been deemed worthy to be found honorable to God. Farewell in God the Father and in Jesus Christ, our mutual hope.

TO THE MAGNESIANS

Ignatius, who is also called God-bearer, to the one that has been blessed by the gracious gift of God the Father in Christ Jesus our Savior, in whom I greet the church that is in Magnesia on the Meander and extend warmest greetings in God the Father and in Jesus Christ.

---

22 ὧν g: ὃν G L A l

1

Γνοὺς ὑμῶν τὸ πολυεύτακτον τῆς κατὰ θεὸν ἀγάπης,
ἀγαλλιώμενος προειλόμην ἐν πίστει Ἰησοῦ Χριστοῦ
προσλαλῆσαι ὑμῖν. 2. καταξιωθεὶς γὰρ ὀνόματος
θεοπρεπεστάτου, ἐν οἷς περιφέρω δεσμοῖς ᾄδω τὰς
ἐκκλησίας, ἐν αἷς ἕνωσιν εὔχομαι σαρκὸς καὶ πνεύματος Ἰησοῦ Χριστοῦ, τοῦ διὰ παντὸς ἡμῶν ζῆν,
πίστεώς τε καὶ ἀγάπης, ἧς οὐδὲν προκέκριται, τὸ δὲ
κυριώτερον Ἰησοῦ καὶ πατρός· ἐν ᾧ ὑπομένοντες τὴν
πᾶσαν ἐπήρειαν τοῦ ἄρχοντος τοῦ αἰῶνος τούτου καὶ
διαφυγόντες θεοῦ τευξόμεθα.

2

Ἐπεὶ οὖν ἠξιώθην ἰδεῖν ὑμᾶς διὰ Δαμᾶ τοῦ ἀξιοθέου
ὑμῶν ἐπισκόπου καὶ πρεσβυτέρων ἀξίων Βάσσου καὶ
Ἀπολλωνίου καὶ τοῦ συνδούλου μου διακόνου Ζωτίω-
νος, οὗ ἐγὼ ὀναίμην, ὅτι ὑποτάσσεται τῷ ἐπισκόπῳ ὡς
χάριτι θεοῦ καὶ τῷ πρεσβυτερίῳ ὡς νόμῳ Ἰησοῦ
Χριστοῦ.

3

Καὶ ὑμῖν δὲ πρέπει μὴ συγχρᾶσθαι τῇ ἡλικίᾳ τοῦ
ἐπισκόπου, ἀλλὰ κατὰ δύναμιν θεοῦ πατρὸς πᾶσαν
ἐντροπὴν αὐτῷ ἀπονέμειν, καθὼς ἔγνων καὶ τοὺς ἁγίους πρεσβυτέρους οὐ προσειληφότας τὴν φαινομένην

1

Knowing the great orderliness of your godly love, I have joyfully decided to speak with you in the faith of Jesus Christ. 2. For since I have been made worthy of a most godly name, by the bonds that I bear I sing the praises of the churches, praying that they may experience the unity of the flesh and spirit of Jesus Christ—our constant life— and of faith and love, to which nothing is preferred, and (more important still) of Jesus and the Father. If we endure in him all the abusive treatment of the ruler of this age and escape, we will attain to God.

2

Since, then, I have been found worthy to see you through Damas, your bishop who is worthy of God, through your worthy presbyters Bassus and Apollonius, and through my fellow slave, the deacon Zotion—whom I hope to enjoy, for he is subject to the bishop as to the grace of God, and to the presbytery as to the law of Jesus Christ.

3

But it is not right for you to take advantage of your bishop because of his age. You should render him all due respect according to the power of God the Father, just as I have learned that even your holy presbyters have not exploited

νεωτερικὴν τάξιν, ἀλλ᾿ ὡς φρονίμῳ[23] ἐν θεῷ συγχω-
ροῦντας αὐτῷ, οὐκ αὐτῷ δέ, ἀλλὰ τῷ πατρὶ Ἰησοῦ
Χριστοῦ, τῷ πάντων ἐπισκόπῳ. 2. εἰς τιμὴν οὖν ἐκεί-
νου τοῦ θελήσαντος ἡμᾶς πρέπον ἐστὶν ἐπακούειν[24]
κατὰ μηδεμίαν ὑπόκρισιν· ἐπεὶ οὐχ ὅτι τὸν ἐπίσκοπον
τοῦτον τὸν βλεπόμενον πλανᾷ τις, ἀλλὰ τὸν ἀόρατον
παραλογίζεται. τὸ δὲ τοιοῦτον οὐ πρὸς σάρκα ὁ λόγος,
ἀλλὰ πρὸς θεὸν τὸν τὰ κρύφια εἰδότα.

4

Πρέπον οὖν ἐστὶν μὴ μόνον καλεῖσθαι Χριστιανούς,
ἀλλὰ καὶ εἶναι· ὥσπερ καί τινες ἐπίσκοπον μὲν καλοῦ-
σιν, χωρὶς δὲ αὐτοῦ πάντα πράσσουσιν. οἱ τοιοῦτοι δὲ
οὐκ εὐσυνείδητοί μοι εἶναι φαίνονται διὰ τὸ μὴ βεβαίως κατ᾿ ἐντολὴν συναθροίζεσθαι.

5

Ἐπεὶ οὖν τέλος τὰ πράγματα ἔχει καὶ πρόκειται τὰ
δύο ὁμοῦ, ὅ τε θάνατος καὶ ἡ ζωή, καὶ ἕκαστος εἰς τὸν
ἴδιον τόπον μέλλει χωρεῖν. 2. ὥσπερ γάρ ἐστιν νο-
μίσματα δύο, ὃ μὲν θεοῦ, ὃ δὲ κόσμου, καὶ ἕκαστον
αὐτῶν ἴδιον χαρακτῆρα ἐπικείμενον ἔχει, οἱ ἄπιστοι
τοῦ κόσμου τούτου, οἱ δὲ πιστοὶ ἐν ἀγάπῃ χαρακτῆρα
θεοῦ πατρὸς διὰ Ἰησοῦ Χριστοῦ, δι᾿ οὗ ἐὰν μὴ αὐθαι-

---

[23] φρονίμῳ A (g): φρονίμους G L

his seemingly youthful appearance *[Or: rank; or: position]*; but they have deferred to him as one who is wise in God—and not to him, but to the Father of Jesus Christ, the bishop of all. 2. And so it is fitting for us to be obedient apart from all hypocrisy, for the honor of the one who has desired us. For it is not that a person deceives this bishop who is seen, but he deals falsely with the one who is invisible. In such a case, an account must be rendered not to human flesh, but to God, who knows the things that are hidden.

4

And so it is fitting not only to be called Christians, but also to be Christians, just as there are some who call a person the bishop but do everything without him. Such persons do not seem to me to be acting in good conscience, because they do not hold valid meetings in accordance with the commandment.

5

Since, then, these matters have an end, and the two things are set together, death and life, and each person is about to depart to his own place—2. for just as there are two kinds of coin, one from God and the other from the world, and each of them has its own stamp set upon it: the unbelievers the stamp of this world and the believers the stamp of God the Father, in love, through Jesus Christ. If we do

---

24 ἐπακούειν G: ὑπακούειν (g)

ρέτως ἔχομεν[25] τὸ ἀποθανεῖν εἰς τὸ αὐτοῦ πάθος, τὸ
ζῆν αὐτοῦ οὐκ ἔστιν ἐν ἡμῖν.

6

Ἐπεὶ οὖν ἐν τοῖς προγεγραμμένοις προσώποις τὸ πᾶν
πλῆθος ἐθεώρησα ἐν πίστει καὶ ἠγάπησα,[26] παραινῶ,
ἐν ὁμονοίᾳ θεοῦ σπουδάζετε πάντα πράσσειν, προ-
καθημένου τοῦ ἐπισκόπου εἰς τόπον θεοῦ καὶ τῶν
πρεσβυτέρων εἰς τόπον[27] συνεδρίου τῶν ἀποστόλων,
καὶ τῶν διακόνων τῶν ἐμοὶ γλυκυτάτων πεπιστευ-
μένων διακονίαν Ἰησοῦ Χριστοῦ, ὃς πρὸ αἰώνων παρὰ
πατρὶ ἦν καὶ ἐν τέλει ἐφάνη. 2. πάντες οὖν ὁμοήθειαν
θεοῦ λαβόντες ἐντρέπεσθε ἀλλήλους καὶ μηδεὶς κατὰ
σάρκα βλεπέτω τὸν πλησίον, ἀλλ᾽ ἐν Ἰησοῦ Χριστῷ
ἀλλήλους διὰ παντὸς ἀγαπᾶτε. μηδὲν ἔστω ἐν ὑμῖν, ὃ
δυνήσεται ὑμᾶς μερίσαι, ἀλλ᾽ ἑνώθητε τῷ ἐπισκόπῳ
καὶ τοῖς προκαθημένοις εἰς τύπον καὶ διδαχὴν ἀφθαρσίας.

7

Ὥσπερ οὖν ὁ κύριος ἄνευ τοῦ πατρὸς οὐδὲν ἐποίησεν,
ἡνωμένος ὤν,[28] οὔτε δι᾽ ἑαυτοῦ οὔτε διὰ τῶν ἀπο-
στόλων· οὕτως μηδὲ ὑμεῖς ἄνευ τοῦ ἐπισκόπου καὶ τῶν
πρεσβυτέρων μηδὲν πράσσετε· μηδὲ πειράσητε εὔλο-

---

[25] ἔχομεν G: ἔχωμεν g L

246

not choose to die voluntarily in his suffering, his life is not in us.

6

Since, then, I have observed, by the eyes of faith, your entire congregation through those I have already mentioned, and loved it, I urge you to hasten to do all things in the harmony of God, with the bishop presiding in the place of God and the presbyters in the place of the council of the apostles, and the deacons, who are especially dear to me, entrusted with the ministry of Jesus Christ, who was with the Father before the ages and has been manifest at the end. 2. You should assume the character of God and all respect one another. No one should consider his neighbor in a fleshly way, but you should love one another in Jesus Christ at all times. Let there be nothing among you that can divide you, but be unified with the bishop and with those who preside according to the model and teaching of incorruptibility.

7

And so, just as the Lord did nothing apart from the Father—being united with him—neither on his own nor through the apostles, so too you should do nothing apart from the bishop and the presbyters. Do not try to maintain

---

26 ἠγάπησα G g: ἀγάπῃ L A Sf l
27 τόπον . . . τόπον G L g l: τύπον . . . τύπον S A
28 ἡνωμένος ὤν G L: om. Sf A (g)

γόν τι φαίνεσθαι ἰδίᾳ ὑμῖν, ἀλλ' ἐπὶ τὸ αὐτό· μία προσευχή, μία δέησις, εἷς νοῦς, μία ἐλπὶς ἐν ἀγάπῃ, ἐν τῇ χαρᾷ τῇ ἀμώμῳ, ὅ[29] ἐστιν Ἰησοῦς Χριστός, οὗ ἄμεινον οὐθέν ἐστιν. 2. πάντες ὡς εἰς ἕνα ναὸν συντρέχετε θεοῦ, ὡς ἐπὶ ἓν θυσιαστήριον, ἐπὶ ἕνα Ἰησοῦν Χριστόν, τὸν ἀφ' ἑνὸς πατρὸς προελθόντα καὶ εἰς ἕνα ὄντα καὶ χωρήσαντα.

8

Μὴ πλανᾶσθε ταῖς ἑτεροδοξίαις μηδὲ μυθεύμασιν τοῖς παλαιοῖς ἀνωφελέσιν οὖσιν. εἰ γὰρ μέχρι νῦν κατὰ Ἰουδαϊσμὸν[30] ζῶμεν, ὁμολογοῦμεν χάριν μὴ εἰληφέναι. 2. οἱ γὰρ θειότατοι προφῆται κατὰ Χριστὸν Ἰησοῦν ἔζησαν. διὰ τοῦτο καὶ ἐδιώχθησαν, ἐμπνεόμενοι ὑπὸ τῆς χάριτος αὐτοῦ εἰς τὸ πληροφορηθῆναι τοὺς ἀπειθοῦντας, ὅτι εἷς θεός ἐστιν, ὁ φανερώσας ἑαυτὸν διὰ Ἰησοῦ Χριστοῦ τοῦ υἱοῦ αὐτοῦ, ὅς ἐστιν αὐτοῦ λόγος[31] ἀπὸ σιγῆς προελθών, ὃς κατὰ πάντα εὐηρέστησεν τῷ πέμψαντι αὐτόν.

9

Εἰ οὖν οἱ ἐν παλαιοῖς πράγμασιν[32] ἀναστραφέντες εἰς καινότητα ἐλπίδος ἦλθον, μηκέτι σαββατίζοντες,

---

29 ὅ L: εἷς G: ὅς cj. Lightfoot   30 Ἰουδαϊσμὸν L: νόμον ἰουδαϊσμὸν G: νόμον ἰουδαϊκὸν g A

that it is reasonable for you to do something among yourselves in private; instead, for the common purpose, let there be one prayer, one petition, one mind, one hope in love and in blameless joy, which is Jesus Christ. Nothing is superior to him. 2. You should all run together, as into one temple of God, as upon one altar, upon one Jesus Christ, who came forth from one Father and was with the one *[Or: and was one with him]* and returned to the one.[9]

8

Do not be deceived by false opinions or old fables that are of no use. For if we have lived according to Judaism until now, we admit that we have not received God's gracious gift. 2. For the most divine prophets lived according to Jesus Christ. For this reason also they were persecuted. But they were inspired by his gracious gift, so that the disobedient became fully convinced that there is one God, who manifested himself through Jesus Christ his Son, who is his Word that came forth from silence, who was pleasing in every way to the one who sent him.

9

And so those who lived according to the old ways came to a new hope, no longer keeping the Sabbath but living ac-

[9] Cf. John 16:28.

---

31 λόγος A: add ἀΐδιος οὐκ G L
32 πράγμασιν: γράμμασιν g

ἀλλὰ κατὰ κυριακὴν[33] ζῶντες, ἐν ᾗ καὶ ἡ ζωὴ ἡμῶν
ἀνέτειλεν δι᾽ αὐτοῦ καὶ τοῦ θανάτου αὐτοῦ, ὅ τινες
ἀρνοῦνται, δι᾽ οὗ μυστηρίου ἐλάβομεν τὸ πιστεύειν,
καὶ διὰ τοῦτο ὑπομένομεν, ἵνα εὑρεθῶμεν μαθηταὶ
Ἰησοῦ Χριστοῦ τοῦ μόνου διδασκάλου ἡμῶν· 2. πῶς
ἡμεῖς δυνησόμεθα ζῆσαι χωρὶς αὐτοῦ, οὗ καὶ οἱ προφῆται μαθηταὶ ὄντες τῷ πνεύματι ὡς διδάσκαλον
αὐτὸν προσεδόκων; καὶ διὰ τοῦτο, ὃν δικαίως ἀνέμε-
νον, παρὼν ἤγειρεν αὐτοὺς ἐκ νεκρῶν.

10

Μὴ οὖν ἀναισθητῶμεν τῆς χρηστότητος αὐτοῦ. ἐὰν
γὰρ ἡμᾶς μιμήσηται[34] καθὰ πράσσομεν, οὐκ ἔτι
ἐσμέν. διὰ τοῦτο, μαθηταὶ αὐτοῦ γενόμενοι, μάθωμεν
κατὰ Χριστιανισμὸν ζῆν. ὃς γὰρ ἄλλῳ ὀνόματι καλεῖ-
ται πλέον τούτου, οὐκ ἔστιν τοῦ θεοῦ. 2. ὑπέρθεσθε
οὖν τὴν κακὴν ζύμην, τὴν παλαιωθεῖσαν καὶ ἐνοξίσα-
σαν, καὶ μεταβάλεσθε εἰς νέαν ζύμην, ὅ ἐστιν Ἰησοῦς
Χριστός. ἁλίσθητε ἐν αὐτῷ, ἵνα μὴ διαφθαρῇ τις ἐν
ὑμῖν, ἐπεὶ ἀπὸ τῆς ὀσμῆς[35] ἐλεγχθήσεσθε. 3. ἄτοπόν
ἐστιν, Ἰησοῦν Χριστὸν λαλεῖν καὶ ἰουδαΐζειν. ὁ γὰρ
Χριστιανισμὸς οὐκ εἰς Ἰουδαϊσμὸν ἐπίστευσεν, ἀλλ᾽
Ἰουδαϊσμὸς εἰς Χριστιανισμόν, εἰς ὃν[36] πᾶσα γλῶσσα
πιστεύσασα εἰς θεὸν συνήχθη.

[33] κυριακὴν L (A g): add ζωὴν G
[34] -σηται g L: -σεται G

cording to the Lord's day, on which also our life arose through him and his death—which some deny. Through this mystery we came to believe, and for this reason we endure, that we may be found to be disciples of Jesus Christ, our only teacher. 2. How then are we able to live apart from him? Even the prophets who were his disciples in the spirit awaited him as their teacher. And for this reason, the one they righteously expected raised them from the dead when he arrived.

10

We should not fail to perceive his kindness. For if he were to imitate our actions, we would no longer exist. For this reason, since we are his disciples, let us learn to live according to Christianity. For whoever is called by a name other than this does not belong to God. 2. So lay aside the bad yeast, which has grown old and sour, and turn to the new yeast, which is Jesus Christ. Be salted in him, that no one among you become rotten; for you will be shown for what you are by your smell. 3. It is outlandish to proclaim Jesus Christ and practice Judaism. For Christianity did not believe in Judaism, but Judaism in Christianity—in which every tongue that believes in God has been gathered together.[10]

---

[10] Cf. Isa 66:18.

---

35 ὀσμῆς L: ὁρμῆς G
36 εἰς ὃν g Sf A: ὡς G (L?): ᾧ cj. Lightfoot

11

Ταῦτα δέ, ἀγαπητοί μου, οὐκ ἐπεὶ ἔγνων τινὰς ἐξ ὑμῶν οὕτως ἔχοντας, ἀλλ' ὡς μικρότερος ὑμῶν θέλω προφυλάσσεσθαι ὑμᾶς, μὴ ἐμπεσεῖν εἰς τὰ ἄγκιστρα τῆς κενοδοξίας, ἀλλὰ πεπληροφορῆσθαι ἐν τῇ γεννήσει καὶ τῷ πάθει καὶ τῇ ἀναστάσει τῇ γενομένῃ ἐν καιρῷ τῆς ἡγεμονίας Ποντίου Πιλάτου· πραχθέντα ἀληθῶς καὶ βεβαίως ὑπὸ Ἰησοῦ Χριστοῦ τῆς ἐλπίδος ἡμῶν, ἧς ἐκτραπῆναι μηδενὶ ὑμῶν γένοιτο.

12

Ὀναίμην ὑμῶν κατὰ πάντα, ἐάνπερ ἄξιος ὦ. εἰ γὰρ καὶ δέδεμαι, πρὸς ἕνα τῶν λελυμένων ὑμῶν οὐκ εἰμί. οἶδα ὅτι οὐ φυσιοῦσθε· Ἰησοῦν γὰρ Χριστὸν ἔχετε ἐν ἑαυτοῖς· καὶ μᾶλλον, ὅταν ἐπαινῶ ὑμᾶς, οἶδα ὅτι ἐντρέπεσθε, ὡς γέγραπται, ὅτι ὁ δίκαιος ἑαυτοῦ κατήγορος.

13

Σπουδάζετε οὖν βεβαιωθῆναι ἐν τοῖς δόγμασιν τοῦ κυρίου καὶ τῶν ἀποστόλων, ἵνα πάντα ὅσα ποιεῖτε, κατευοδωθῆτε σαρκὶ καὶ πνεύματι, πίστει καὶ ἀγάπῃ, ἐν υἱῷ καὶ πατρὶ καὶ ἐν πνεύματι, ἐν ἀρχῇ καὶ ἐν τέλει, μετὰ τοῦ ἀξιοπρεπεστάτου ἐπισκόπου ὑμῶν καὶ ἀξιοπλόκου πνευματικοῦ στεφάνου τοῦ πρεσβυτερίου

11

I am not writing these things, my beloved, because I have learned that some of you are behaving like this. But as one who is less important than you I want to protect you from being snagged by the fish hooks of worthless ideas. You should be fully convinced of the birth and suffering and resurrection that occurred in the time of the governor Pontius Pilate. These things were truly and certainly done by Jesus Christ, our hope. From this hope may none of you turn away.

12

May I enjoy you in every way, if I should be worthy. For even though I am in chains, I am not worth one of you who is free. I know you are not haughty; for you have Jesus Christ in you. On the contrary, when I praise you, I know you are respectful. As it is written, "the one who is upright is his own accuser."[11]

13

Be eager therefore to stand securely in the decrees of the Lord and the apostles, that you may prosper in everything you do in flesh and spirit, in faith and love, in the Son and the Father and in the Spirit, in the beginning and end, along with your most worthy bishop and your presbytery, which is a spiritual crown worthily woven, and your godly deacons. 2. Be submissive to the bishop and to one an-

[11] Prov 18:17.

ὑμῶν καὶ τῶν κατὰ θεὸν διακόνων. 2. ὑποτάγητε τῷ
ἐπισκόπῳ καὶ ἀλλήλοις, ὡς Ἰησοῦς Χριστὸς τῷ πατρὶ
κατὰ σάρκα καὶ οἱ ἀπόστολοι τῷ Χριστῷ καὶ τῷ
πατρί,[37] ἵνα ἕνωσις ᾖ σαρκική τε καὶ πνευματική.

14

Εἰδὼς, ὅτι θεοῦ γέμετε, συντόμως παρεκέλευσα[38]
ὑμᾶς. μνημονεύετέ μου ἐν ταῖς προσευχαῖς ὑμῶν, ἵνα
θεοῦ ἐπιτύχω, καὶ τῆς ἐν Συρίᾳ ἐκκλησίας, ὅθεν οὐκ
ἄξιός εἰμι καλεῖσθαι· ἐπιδέομαι γὰρ τῆς ἡνωμένης
ὑμῶν ἐν θεῷ προσευχῆς καὶ ἀγάπης, εἰς τὸ ἀξιωθῆναι
τὴν ἐν Συρίᾳ ἐκκλησίαν διὰ τῆς ἐκκλησίας ὑμῶν δρο-
σισθῆναι.

15

Ἀσπάζονται ὑμᾶς Ἐφέσιοι ἀπὸ Σμύρνης, ὅθεν καὶ
γράφω ὑμῖν, παρόντες εἰς δόξαν θεοῦ ὥσπερ καὶ
ὑμεῖς, οἳ κατὰ πάντα με ἀνέπαυσαν ἅμα Πολυκάρπῳ,
ἐπισκόπῳ Σμυρναίων. καὶ αἱ λοιπαὶ δὲ ἐκκλησίαι ἐν
τιμῇ Ἰησοῦ Χριστοῦ ἀσπάζονται ὑμᾶς. ἔρρωσθε ἐν
ὁμονοίᾳ θεοῦ κεκτημένοι ἀδιάκριτον πνεῦμα, ὅς ἐστιν
Ἰησοῦς Χριστός.

[37] πατρὶ A: add καὶ τῷ πνεύματι G L
[38] -ευσα G: -εσα g

other—as Jesus Christ was to the Father, according to the flesh, and as the apostles were to Christ and to the Father and to the Spirit—so that there may be unity in both flesh and spirit.

14

Because I know that you are filled with God, I have exhorted you briefly. Remember me in your prayers, that I may attain to God; and remember the church in Syria, from which I am not worthy to be called. For I am in need of your unified prayer and love in God, that the church in Syria may be deemed worthy to be refreshed with dew through your church.

15

The Ephesians greet you from Smyrna; I am writing you from there. They are here for the glory of God, as you are as well. They have refreshed me in every way, along with Polycarp, the bishop of the Smyrnaeans. And the other churches also greet you in the honor of Jesus Christ. In the harmony of God, farewell to you who have obtained a spirit *[Or: Spirit]* that is not divided, which is Jesus Christ.

ΤΡΑΛΛΙΑΝΙΟΣ ΙΓΝΑΤΙΟΣ

Ἰγνάτιος, ὁ καὶ Θεοφόρος, ἠγαπημένῃ θεῷ, πατρὶ
Ἰησοῦ Χριστοῦ, ἐκκλησίᾳ ἁγίᾳ τῇ οὔσῃ ἐν Τράλ-
λεσιν τῆς Ἀσίας, ἐκλεκτῇ καὶ ἀξιοθέῳ, εἰρηνευούσῃ ἐν
σαρκὶ καὶ πνεύματι[39] τῷ πάθει[40] Ἰησοῦ Χριστοῦ, τῆς
ἐλπίδος ἡμῶν ἐν τῇ εἰς αὐτὸν ἀναστάσει· ἣν καὶ
ἀσπάζομαι ἐν τῷ πληρώματι ἐν ἀποστολικῷ χαρα-
κτῆρι καὶ εὔχομαι πλεῖστα χαίρειν.

1

Ἄμωμον διάνοιαν καὶ ἀδιάκριτον ἐν ὑπομονῇ ἔγνων
ὑμᾶς ἔχοντας οὐ κατὰ χρῆσιν, ἀλλὰ κατὰ φύσιν,
καθὼς ἐδήλωσέν μοι Πολύβιος, ὁ ἐπίσκοπος ὑμῶν, ὃς
παρεγένετο θελήματι θεοῦ καὶ Ἰησοῦ Χριστοῦ ἐν
Σμύρνῃ καὶ οὕτως μοι συνεχάρη δεδεμένῳ ἐν Χριστῷ
Ἰησοῦ, ὥστε με τὸ πᾶν πλῆθος ὑμῶν ἐν αὐτῷ θεωρεῖσθαι. 2. ἀποδεξάμενος οὖν τὴν κατὰ θεὸν εὔνοιαν
δι᾽ αὐτοῦ ἐδόξασα,[41] εὑρὼν ὑμᾶς, ὡς ἔγνων, μιμητὰς
ὄντας θεοῦ.

2

Ὅταν γὰρ τῷ ἐπισκόπῳ ὑποτάσσησθε ὡς Ἰησοῦ
Χριστῷ, φαίνεσθέ μοι οὐ κατὰ ἄνθρωπον ζῶντες,
ἀλλὰ κατὰ Ἰησοῦν Χριστὸν τὸν δι᾽ ἡμᾶς ἀποθανόντα,
ἵνα πιστεύσαντες εἰς τὸν θάνατον αὐτοῦ τὸ ἀποθανεῖν

TO THE TRALLIANS

Ignatius, who is also called God-bearer, to the holy church
in Tralles of Asia, beloved of God, the Father of Jesus
Christ, chosen and worthy of God, a church made at peace
in flesh and spirit by the suffering of Jesus Christ, who is
our hope for a resurrection that leads to him, a church
which I also greet in fullness in the apostolic manner and
to which I extend warmest greetings.

1

I have learned that your way of thinking is blameless and
unwavering in endurance, not by force of habit but by
your very nature, just as Polybius, your bishop, showed me.
He arrived in Smyrna by the will of God and Jesus Christ,
and so rejoiced together with me, who am in chains in
Christ Jesus, so that I saw your entire congregation in him.
2. I was exultant when I received your act of godly kindness
through him, for I found that you were imitators of God, as
I had known.

2

For when you are subject to the bishop as to Jesus Christ,
you appear to me to live not in a human way but according
to Jesus Christ, who died for us that you may escape dying

---

39 πνεύματι g: αἵματι G L (add καὶ) A C
40 τῷ πάθει: om. A C
41 ἐδόξασα L A C: ἔδοξα G g

ἐκφύγητε. 2. ἀναγκαῖον οὖν ἐστίν, ὥσπερ ποιεῖτε, ἄνευ
τοῦ ἐπισκόπου μηδὲν πράσσειν ὑμᾶς, ἀλλ᾽ ὑποτάσσεσθαι καὶ τῷ πρεσβυτερίῳ ὡς τοῖς ἀποστόλοις
Ἰησοῦ Χριστοῦ τῆς ἐλπίδος ἡμῶν, ἐν ᾧ διάγοντες
εὑρεθησόμεθα. 3. δεῖ δὲ καὶ τοὺς διακόνους ὄντας
μυστηρίων Ἰησοῦ Χριστοῦ κατὰ πάντα τρόπον πᾶσιν
ἀρέσκειν. οὐ γὰρ βρωμάτων καὶ ποτῶν εἰσιν διάκονοι,
ἀλλ᾽ ἐκκλησίας θεοῦ ὑπηρέται. δέον οὖν αὐτοὺς φυλάσσεσθαι τὰ ἐγκλήματα ὡς πῦρ.

3

Ὁμοίως πάντες ἐντρεπέσθωσαν τοὺς διακόνους ὡς
Ἰησοῦν Χριστόν,[42] ὡς καὶ τὸν ἐπίσκοπον[43] ὄντα τύπον[44] τοῦ πατρός, τοὺς δὲ πρεσβυτέρους ὡς συνέδριον
θεοῦ καὶ ὡς σύνδεσμον ἀποστόλων. χωρὶς τούτων
ἐκκλησία οὐ καλεῖται· 2. περὶ ὧν πέπεισμαι ὑμᾶς
οὕτως ἔχειν. τὸ γὰρ ἐξεμπλάριον τῆς ἀγάπης ὑμῶν
ἔλαβον καὶ ἔχω μεθ᾽ ἑαυτοῦ ἐν τῷ ἐπισκόπῳ ὑμῶν, οὗ
αὐτὸ τὸ κατάστημα μεγάλη μαθητεία, ἡ δὲ πραότης
αὐτοῦ δύναμις· ὃν λογίζομαι καὶ τοὺς ἀθέους ἐντρέ-
πεσθαι. 3. ἀγαπῶν ὑμᾶς φείδομαι,[45] συντονώτερον
δυνάμενος γράφειν ὑπὲρ τούτου. οὐκ[46] εἰς τοῦτο
ᾠήθην, ἵνα ὢν κατάκριτος ὡς ἀπόστολος ὑμῖν διατάσ-
σωμαι.

---

[42] Ἰησοῦν Χριστὸν G Sf A g: ἐντολὴν Ἰησοῦ Χριστοῦ L
[43] ἐπίσκοπον: add ut Iesum Christum L

by believing in his death. 2. And so—as is already the case—you must not engage in any activity apart from the bishop, but be subject also to the presbytery as to the apostles of Jesus Christ, our hope. If we live in him, we will be found in him. 3. And those who are deacons of the mysteries of Jesus Christ must also be pleasing in every way to all people. For they are not deacons dealing with food and drink; they are servants of the church of God. And so they must guard themselves against accusations as against fire.

3

So too let everyone respect the deacons like Jesus Christ, and also the bishop, who is the image of the Father; and let them respect the presbyters like the council of God and the band of the apostles. Apart from these a gathering cannot be called a church. 2. I am convinced that you agree about this. For I have received the embodiment of your love and have it with me in the person of your bishop, whose very deportment is a great lesson and whose meekness is power, who is respected, I believe, even by the godless. 3. I am sparing you out of love, though I could write more sharply about this matter. But I have not thought that I, a condemned man, should give you orders like an apostle.[12]

---

[12] The text of this verse is corrupt; the translation attempts to convey the sense.

---

44 τύπον Sf C (g A): υἱὸν G L   45 ἀγαπῶν ὑμᾶς φείδομαι g A C: ἀγαπῶντας ὡς οὐ φείδομαι G L   46 οὐκ A C
(g): om. G L: ἀλλ' οὐχ ἱκανὸν ἑαυτὸν cj. Lightfoot

4

Πολλὰ φρονῶ ἐν θεῷ, ἀλλ᾿ ἐμαυτὸν μετρῶ, ἵνα μὴ ἐν
καυχήσει ἀπόλωμαι. νῦν γάρ με δεῖ πλέον φοβεῖσθαι
καὶ μὴ προσέχειν τοῖς φυσιοῦσίν με. οἱ γὰρ λέγοντές
μοι μαστιγοῦσίν με. 2. ἀγαπῶ μὲν γὰρ τὸ παθεῖν,
ἀλλ᾿ οὐκ οἶδα, εἰ ἄξιός εἰμι. τὸ γὰρ ζῆλος πολλοῖς μὲν
οὐ φαίνεται, ἐμὲ δὲ πλέον πολεμεῖ. χρήζω οὖν πραό-
τητος, ἐν ᾗ καταλύεται ὁ ἄρχων τοῦ αἰῶνος τούτου.

5

Μὴ οὐ δύναμαι ὑμῖν τὰ ἐπουράνια γράψαι; ἀλλὰ
φοβοῦμαι, μὴ νηπίοις οὖσιν ὑμῖν βλάβην παραθῶ·
καὶ συγγνωμονεῖτέ μοι, μήποτε οὐ δυνηθέντες χωρῆ-
σαι στραγγαλωθῆτε. 2. καὶ γὰρ ἐγώ, οὐ καθότι
δέδεμαι καὶ δύναμαι νοεῖν τὰ ἐπουράνια καὶ τὰς τοπο-
θεσίας τὰς ἀγγελικὰς καὶ τὰς συστάσεις τὰς ἀρχοντι-
κάς, ὁρατά τε καὶ ἀόρατα, παρὰ τοῦτο ἤδη καὶ
μαθητής εἰμι. πολλὰ γὰρ ἡμῖν λείπει, ἵνα θεοῦ μὴ
λειπώμεθα.

6

Παρακαλῶ οὖν ὑμᾶς, οὐκ ἐγώ, ἀλλ᾿ ἡ ἀγάπη Ἰησοῦ
Χριστοῦ· μόνῃ τῇ χριστιανῇ τροφῇ χρῆσθε, ἀλλοτρίας δὲ βοτάνης ἀπέχεσθε, ἥτις ἐστὶν αἵρεσις· 2. οἱ

4

I am thinking many things in God, but I take measure of myself so as not to be destroyed by my boasting. For now I must fear all the more and pay no attention to those who make me self-important. For those who speak to me flog me. 2. For indeed I love to suffer; but I do not know if I am worthy. For envy is not obvious to many, but it is escalating its war against me. And so I need humility, by which the ruler of this age is destroyed.

5

Am I not able to write to you about heavenly things? But I am afraid that I may harm you who are still infants.[13] Grant me this concession—otherwise you may choke, not being able to swallow enough. 2. For not even I am a disciple already, simply because I am in bondage and am able to understand the heavenly realms and the angelic regions and hierarchies of the cosmic rulers, both visible and invisible.[14] For many things are still lacking to us, that we may not be lacking God.

6

Therefore I am urging you—not I, but the love of Jesus Christ—make use only of Christian food and abstain from a foreign plant, which is heresy. 2. Even though such per-

13 Cf. 1 Cor 3:1–2.
14 Cf. Col 1:16.

ἑαυτοῖς[47] παρεμπλέκουσιν Ἰησοῦν Χριστὸν καταξιοπιστευόμενοι,[48] ὥσπερ θανάσιμον φάρμακον διδόντες
μετὰ οἰνομέλιτος, ὅπερ ὁ ἀγνοῶν ἡδέως λαμβάνει ἐν
ἡδονῇ κακῇ τὸ ἀποθανεῖν.

7

Φυλάττεσθε οὖν τοὺς τοιούτους. τοῦτο δὲ ἔσται ὑμῖν
μὴ φυσιουμένοις καὶ οὖσιν ἀχωρίστοις θεοῦ Ἰησοῦ
Χριστοῦ καὶ τοῦ ἐπισκόπου καὶ τῶν διαταγμάτων τῶν
ἀποστόλων. 2. ὁ ἐντὸς θυσιαστηρίου ὢν καθαρός
ἐστιν· ὁ δὲ ἐκτὸς θυσιαστηρίου ὢν οὐ καθαρός ἐστιν·
τοῦτ' ἔστιν, ὁ χωρὶς ἐπισκόπου καὶ πρεσβυτερίου καὶ
διακόνων[49] πράσσων τι, οὗτος οὐ καθαρός ἐστιν τῇ
συνειδήσει.

8

Οὐκ ἐπεὶ ἔγνων τοιοῦτόν τι ἐν ὑμῖν, ἀλλὰ προφυλάσσω ὑμᾶς ὄντας μου ἀγαπητούς, προορῶν τὰς
ἐνέδρας τοῦ διαβόλου. ὑμεῖς οὖν τὴν πραϋπάθειαν
ἀναλαβόντες ἀνακτίσασθε ἑαυτοὺς ἐν πίστει, ὅ ἐστιν
σὰρξ τοῦ κυρίου, καὶ ἐν ἀγάπῃ, ὅ ἐστιν αἷμα Ἰησοῦ
Χριστοῦ. 2. μηδεὶς ὑμῶν[50] κατὰ τοῦ πλησίον ἐχέτω.[51]
μὴ ἀφορμὰς δίδοτε τοῖς ἔθνεσιν, ἵνα μὴ δι' ὀλίγους
ἄφρονας τὸ ἐν θεῷ πλῆθος βλασφημῆται. οὐαὶ γάρ,

sons seem to be trustworthy, they mingle Jesus Christ with themselves, as if giving a deadly drug mixed with honeyed wine, which the unsuspecting gladly takes with evil pleasure, but then dies.

7

Guard against such people. You will be able to do this when you are not haughty and are inseparable from God—that is, Jesus Christ—and from the bishop and from the injunctions of the apostles. 2. The one who is inside the sanctuary is pure but the one outside the sanctuary is not pure. This means that the one who does anything apart from the bishop, the presbytery, and the deacons is not pure in conscience.

8

It is not that I know of any such problem among you, but I am protecting you, my loved ones, anticipating the snares of the devil. You should therefore take up gentleness and create yourselves anew in faith, which is the flesh of the Lord, and in love, which is the blood of Jesus Christ. 2. Let none of you hold a grudge against your neighbor. Give no occasion to the outsiders lest on account of a few foolish persons the entire congregation in God be slandered. "For

---

47 οἱ ἑαυτοῖς Sf A C: οἱ καιροὶ G: ἢ καὶ ῥυπαροῖς L: καὶ τὸν ἰὸν g: οἱ καὶ ἰοῖς cj. Voss: οἱ καὶ ἰῷ cj. Lightfoot
48 καταξιοπιστευόμενοι (Sf A C): καταξίαν πιστευόμενοι G: om. L   49 διακόνων g C: διακόνου G L: om. A
50 ὑμῶν: add τι g   51 ἐχέτω G: τι ἐχέτω L C

δι᾽ οὗ ἐπὶ ματαιότητι τὸ ὄνομά μου ἐπί τινων βλασφημεῖται.

9

Κωφώθητε οὖν, ὅταν ὑμῖν χωρὶς Ἰησοῦ Χριστοῦ λαλῇ
τις, τοῦ ἐκ γένους Δαυίδ, τοῦ ἐκ Μαρίας, ὃς ἀληθῶς
ἐγεννήθη, ἔφαγέν τε καὶ ἔπιεν, ἀληθῶς ἐδιώχθη ἐπὶ
Ποντίου Πιλάτου, ἀληθῶς ἐσταυρώθη καὶ ἀπέθανεν,
βλεπόντων τῶν ἐπουρανίων καὶ ἐπιγείων καὶ ὑποχθο-
νίων· 2. ὃς καὶ ἀληθῶς ἠγέρθη ἀπὸ νεκρῶν, ἐγεί-
ραντος αὐτὸν τοῦ πατρὸς αὐτοῦ, ὃς[52] καὶ κατὰ τὸ
ὁμοίωμα[53] ἡμᾶς τοὺς πιστεύοντας αὐτῷ οὕτως ἐγερεῖ ὁ
πατὴρ αὐτοῦ ἐν Χριστῷ Ἰησοῦ, οὗ χωρὶς τὸ ἀληθινὸν
ζῆν οὐκ ἔχομεν.

10

Εἰ δέ, ὥσπερ τινὲς ἄθεοι ὄντες, τουτέστιν ἄπιστοι,
λέγουσιν, τὸ δοκεῖν πεπονθέναι αὐτόν, αὐτοὶ ὄντες τὸ
δοκεῖν, ἐγὼ τί δέδεμαι, τί δὲ καὶ εὔχομαι θηριομαχῆσαι; δωρεὰν οὖν ἀποθνήσκω. ἄρα οὖν[54] καταψεύ-
δομαι τοῦ κυρίου.

[52] ὃς G L: ὡς C: ita ut Sf: itidem A: οὗ cj. Zahn
[53] ὃς . . . ὁμοίωμα L: κατὰ τὸ ὁμοίωμα ὃς καὶ G: ὡς C
[54] οὖν C: οὐ G L: om. g

woe to that one through whom my name is slandered in vain by some."[15]

9

And so, be deaf when someone speaks to you apart from Jesus Christ, who was from the race of David and from Mary, who was truly born, both ate and drank, was truly persecuted at the time of Pontius Pilate, was truly crucified and died, while those in heaven and on earth and under the earth looked on. 2. He was also truly raised from the dead, his Father having raised him. In the same way his Father will also raise us in Christ Jesus, we who believe in him, apart from whom we do not have true life.

10

But if, as some who are atheists—that is, unbelievers—say, that he only appeared to suffer (it is they who are the appearance), why am I in bondage, and why also do I pray to fight the wild beasts? I am then dying in vain and am, even more, lying about the Lord.

[15] Cf. Isa 52:5.

11

Φεύγετε οὖν τὰς κακὰς παραφυάδας τὰς γεννώσας καρπὸν θανατηφόρον, οὗ ἐὰν γεύσηταί τις, παραυτὰ[55] ἀποθνήσκει· οὗτοι γὰρ οὔκ εἰσιν φυτεία πατρός. 2. εἰ γὰρ ἦσαν, ἐφαίνοντο ἂν κλάδοι τοῦ σταυροῦ, καὶ ἦν ἂν ὁ καρπὸς αὐτῶν ἄφθαρτος· δι᾿ οὗ ἐν τῷ πάθει αὐτοῦ προσκαλεῖται ὑμᾶς ὄντας μέλη αὐτοῦ. οὐ δύναται οὖν κεφαλὴ χωρὶς γεννηθῆναι ἄνευ μελῶν, τοῦ θεοῦ ἕνωσιν ἐπαγγελλομένου, ὅ ἐστιν αὐτός.

12

Ἀσπάζομαι ὑμᾶς ἀπὸ Σμύρνης ἅμα ταῖς συμπαρούσαις μοι ἐκκλησίαις τοῦ θεοῦ, οἳ κατὰ πάντα με ἀνέπαυσαν σαρκί τε καὶ πνεύματι. 2. παρακαλεῖ ὑμᾶς τὰ δεσμά μου, ἃ ἕνεκεν Ἰησοῦ Χριστοῦ περιφέρω αἰτούμενος θεοῦ ἐπιτυχεῖν· διαμένετε ἐν τῇ ὁμονοίᾳ ὑμῶν καὶ τῇ μετ᾿ ἀλλήλων προσευχῇ. πρέπει γὰρ ὑμῖν τοῖς καθ᾿ ἕνα, ἐξαιρέτως καὶ τοῖς πρεσβυτέροις, ἀναψύχειν τὸν ἐπίσκοπον εἰς τιμὴν πατρὸς καὶ[56] Ἰησοῦ Χριστοῦ καὶ τῶν ἀποστόλων. 3. εὔχομαι ὑμᾶς ἐν ἀγάπῃ ἀκοῦσαί μου, ἵνα μὴ εἰς μαρτύριον ὦ ἐν ὑμῖν γράψας. καὶ περὶ ἐμοῦ δὲ προσεύχεσθε, τῆς ἀφ᾿ ὑμῶν ἀγάπης χρήζοντος ἐν τῷ ἐλέει τοῦ θεοῦ, εἰς τὸ καταξιωθῆναί με τοῦ κλήρου, οὗ περίκειμαι ἐπιτυχεῖν, ἵνα μὴ ἀδόκιμος εὑρεθῶ.

11

Flee therefore the evil offshoots that produce deadly fruit; anyone who tastes it dies at once. For these are not the Father's planting. 2. If they were, they would appear as branches of the cross and their fruit would be imperishable. Through the cross, by his suffering, he calls you who are the parts of his body. Thus the head cannot be born without the other parts, because God promises unity, which he himself is.

12

I greet you from Smyrna, along with the churches of God that are present with me and that have refreshed me in every way, in both flesh and spirit. 2. My chains exhort you; I bear them on account of Jesus Christ, asking that I may attain to God. Remain in your harmony and in prayer with one another. For it is fitting for each one of you, and especially the presbyters, to refresh the bishop for the honor of the Father and of Jesus Christ and of the apostles. 3. I ask you to hear me in love, that I may not be a witness against you by having written. And pray also for me, since I stand in need of your love by God's mercy, that I may be found worthy of the lot I am bound to obtain, lest I be discovered to have failed the test.[16]

16 Cf. 1 Cor 9:27.

---

55 παραυτὰ Lightfoot: παρ' αὐτὰ G: παραυτίκα g
56 καὶ (add εἰς τιμὴν g) A C g: om. G L

13

Ἀσπάζεται ὑμᾶς ἡ ἀγάπη Σμυρναίων καὶ Ἐφεσίων. μνημονεύετε ἐν ταῖς προσευχαῖς ὑμῶν τῆς ἐν Συρίᾳ ἐκκλησίας, ὅθεν οὐκ ἄξιός εἰμι λέγεσθαι, ὢν ἔσχατος ἐκείνων. 2. ἔρρωσθε ἐν Ἰησοῦ Χριστῷ, ὑποτασσόμενοι τῷ ἐπισκόπῳ ὡς τῇ ἐντολῇ, ὁμοίως καὶ τῷ πρεσβυτερίῳ. καὶ οἱ κατ᾽ ἄνδρα ἀλλήλους ἀγαπᾶτε ἐν ἀμερίστῳ καρδίᾳ. 3. ἁγνίζεται ὑμῶν τὸ ἐμὸν πνεῦμα οὐ μόνον νῦν, ἀλλὰ καὶ ὅταν θεοῦ ἐπιτύχω. ἔτι γὰρ ὑπὸ κίνδυνόν εἰμι· ἀλλὰ πιστὸς ὁ πατὴρ ἐν Ἰησοῦ Χριστῷ πληρῶσαί μου τὴν αἴτησιν καὶ ὑμῶν, ἐν ᾧ εὑρεθείητε ἄμωμοι.

ΠΡΟΣ ΡΩΜΑΙΟΥΣ ΙΓΝΑΤΙΟΣ

Ἰγνάτιος, ὁ καὶ Θεοφόρος, τῇ ἠλεημένῃ ἐν μεγαλειότητι πατρὸς ὑψίστου καὶ Ἰησοῦ Χριστοῦ τοῦ μόνου υἱοῦ αὐτοῦ ἐκκλησίᾳ ἠγαπημένῃ[57] καὶ πεφωτισμένῃ ἐν θελήματι τοῦ θελήσαντος τὰ πάντα, ἃ ἔστιν, κατὰ πίστιν καὶ[58] ἀγάπην Ἰησοῦ Χριστοῦ, τοῦ θεοῦ ἡμῶν, ἥτις καὶ προκάθηται ἐν τόπῳ χωρίου Ῥωμαίων, ἀξιόθεος, ἀξιοπρεπής, ἀξιομακάριστος, ἀξιέπαινος, ἀξιοεπίτευκτος, ἀξιόαγνος καὶ προκαθημένη τῆς ἀγάπης, χριστόνομος,[59] πατρώνυμος, ἣν καὶ ἀσπάζομαι ἐν ὀνόματι Ἰησοῦ Χριστοῦ, υἱοῦ πατρός· κατὰ σάρκα καὶ πνεῦμα ἡνωμένοις πάσῃ ἐντολῇ

13

The love of the Smyrnaeans and of the Ephesians greets you. Remember the church in Syria in your prayers; I am not worthy to be called from there, since I am the least of them. 2. Farewell in Jesus Christ. Be subject to the bishop as to the commandment, and to the presbytery as well. And let each of you love one another with an undivided heart. 3. My own spirit is sacrificed for you, not only now but also when I attain to God. For I am still in danger; but the Father is faithful in Jesus Christ to fulfill my request and yours. In him may you be found blameless.

TO THE ROMANS

Ignatius, who is also called God-bearer, to the church that has obtained mercy by the greatness of the Father Most High and Jesus Christ his only Son; the church that is loved and enlightened by the will of the one who has willed everything that is, according to the faith and love of Jesus Christ, our God; the church that is presiding in the land of the Romans, worthy of God, worthy of honor, worthy of blessing, worthy of praise, worthy of success, worthy of holiness, and preeminent in love, a church that keeps the law of Christ and bears the name of the Father; this is the church that I greet in the name of Jesus Christ, the Son of the Father. And I extend warmest greetings blamelessly in

---

57 ἠγαπημένη G H K L Sm Am M: ἡγιασμένη T (A) g: τετιμημένη C

58 πίστιν καὶ T A Am C g: om. G H K L Sm M

59 χριστόνομος L (S Sm A Am C l): χριστώ(-ο-)νυμος z g

αὐτοῦ, πεπληρωμένοις χάριτος θεοῦ ἀδιακρίτως, καὶ
ἀποδιϋλισμένοις ἀπὸ παντὸς ἀλλοτρίου χρώματος,
πλεῖστα ἐν Ἰησοῦ Χριστῷ, τῷ θεῷ ἡμῶν, ἀμώμως
χαίρειν.

1

Ἐπεὶ εὐξάμενος θεῷ ἐπέτυχον ἰδεῖν ὑμῶν τὰ ἀξιόθεα
πρόσωπα, ὡς καὶ πλέον ᾐτούμην λαβεῖν· δεδεμένος
γὰρ ἐν Χριστῷ Ἰησοῦ ἐλπίζω ὑμᾶς ἀσπάσασθαι,
ἐάνπερ θέλημα ᾖ τοῦ ἀξιωθῆναί με εἰς τέλος εἶναι.
2. ἡ μὲν γὰρ ἀρχὴ εὐοικονόμητός ἐστιν, ἐάνπερ χάρι-
τος⁶⁰ ἐπιτύχω εἰς τὸ τὸν κλῆρόν μου ἀνεμποδίστως
ἀπολαβεῖν. φοβοῦμαι γὰρ τὴν ὑμῶν ἀγάπην, μὴ αὐτή
με ἀδικήσῃ. ὑμῖν γὰρ εὐχερές ἐστιν, ὃ θέλετε ποιῆ-
σαι· ἐμοὶ δὲ δύσκολόν ἐστιν τοῦ θεοῦ ἐπιτυχεῖν,
ἐάνπερ ὑμεῖς μὴ⁶¹ φείσησθέ μου.

2

Οὐ γὰρ θέλω ὑμᾶς ἀνθρωπαρεσκῆσαι, ἀλλὰ θεῷ
ἀρέσαι, ὥσπερ καὶ ἀρέσκετε. οὔτε γὰρ ἐγώ ποτε ἕξω
καιρὸν τοιοῦτον θεοῦ ἐπιτυχεῖν, οὔτε ὑμεῖς, ἐὰν
σιωπήσητε, κρείττονι ἔργῳ ἔχετε ἐπιγραφῆναι. ἐὰν
γὰρ σιωπήσητε ἀπ᾽ ἐμοῦ, ἐγὼ λόγος θεοῦ· ἐὰν δὲ

---

⁶⁰ ἐάνπερ χάριτος z L g (M): ἐὰν πέρατος S A: *si finem etiam
gratiae* (*per gratiam* C) *assequar* Am C (Sm)

Jesus Christ, our God, to those who are united in both flesh and spirit in his every commandment, filled with the gracious gift of God without wavering, and filtered from every unsuitable taint.

1

Since by my prayer to God I have managed to see your faces, which are worthy of God—as indeed I have asked to receive even more, for I hope to greet you while in chains in Christ Jesus, if indeed it be the will of the one who has made me worthy to endure until the end. 2. For the beginning is auspicious, if I can indeed obtain the gracious gift I need to receive my lot without any impediment. For I am afraid of your love, that it may do me harm. For it is easy for you to do what you want, but it is difficult for me to attain to God, if you do not spare me.

2

For I do not want you to please people but to please God,[17] as indeed you are doing. For I will have no other such opportunity to attain to God, nor can you be enlisted for a better work—if, that is, you keep silent. For if you keep silent about me, I will be a word of God; but if you desire

[17] Cf. 2 Thess 2:4.

[61] μὴ L S (A) g: om. G H K Sm Am (C) M

ἐρασθῆτε τῆς σαρκός μου, πάλιν ἔσομαι φωνή.[62]
2. πλέον δέ μοι μὴ παράσχησθε τοῦ σπονδισθῆναι
θεῷ, ὡς ἔτι θυσιαστήριον ἕτοιμόν ἐστιν, ἵνα ἐν ἀγάπῃ
χορὸς γενόμενοι ᾄσητε τῷ πατρὶ ἐν Ἰησοῦ Χριστῷ,
ὅτι τὸν ἐπίσκοπον Συρίας κατηξίωσεν ὁ θεὸς εὑρεθῆναι εἰς δύσιν ἀπὸ ἀνατολῆς μεταπεμψάμενος. καλὸν
τὸ δῦναι ἀπὸ κόσμου πρὸς θεόν, ἵνα εἰς αὐτὸν ἀνα-
τείλω.

3

Οὐδέποτε ἐβασκάνατε οὐδενί,[63] ἄλλους ἐδιδάξατε. ἐγὼ
δὲ θέλω, ἵνα κἀκεῖνα βέβαια ᾖ, ἃ μαθητεύοντες ἐν-
τέλλεσθε. 2. μόνον μοι δύναμιν αἰτεῖσθε ἔσωθέν τε
καὶ ἔξωθεν, ἵνα μὴ μόνον λέγω, ἀλλὰ καὶ θέλω, ἵνα
μὴ[64] μόνον λέγωμαι Χριστιανός, ἀλλὰ καὶ εὑρεθῶ.
ἐὰν γὰρ εὑρεθῶ, καὶ λέγεσθαι δύναμαι καὶ τότε
πιστὸς εἶναι, ὅταν κόσμῳ μὴ φαίνωμαι. 3. οὐδὲν
φαινόμενον καλόν.[65] ὁ γὰρ θεὸς ἡμῶν Ἰησοῦς Χριστὸς ἐν πατρὶ ὢν μᾶλλον φαίνεται. οὐ πεισμονῆς τὸ
ἔργον, ἀλλὰ μεγέθους ἐστὶν ὁ Χριστιανισμός,[66] ὅταν
μισῆται ὑπὸ κόσμου.

62 φωνή L S Sm (Am) C: τρέχων z A g M
63 οὐδενί T C g M: οὐδένα G H l: in aliquo L
64 ἵνα μὴ G H Sm (C g) M: μὴ ἵνα T L S
65 καλὸν S Sm L A Am: αἰώνιον· τὰ γὰρ βλεπόμενα
(φαινόμενα T) πρόσκαιρα, τὰ δὲ μὴ βλεπόμενα αἰώνια G H T
g (M)

my flesh, I will once again be a mere noise. 2. But grant me
nothing more than to be poured out as a libation to God
while there is still an altar at hand, that by becoming a chorus in love, you may sing forth to the Father in Jesus Christ,
saying that God has deemed the bishop of Syria worthy to
be found at the setting of the sun, after sending him from
where it rises. For it is good for me to set from the world to
God, that I may rise up to him.

3

At no time have you been envious of anyone; instead you
have taught others. But my wish is that the instructions you
enjoin on others be firm, when you make them disciples.
2. For me, ask only that I have power both inside and out,
that I not only speak but also have the desire, that I not
only be called a Christian but also be found one. For if I
be found a Christian, I can also be called one and then
be faithful—when I am no longer visible in the world.
3. Nothing that is visible is good. For our God Jesus Christ,
since he is in the Father, is all the more visible. The work is
not a matter of persuasion, but Christianity is a matter of
greatness, when it is hated by the world.

---

66 Χριστιανισμός G H T S A Am l: χριστιανός L Sm (g)

4

Ἐγὼ γράφω πάσαις ταῖς ἐκκλησίαις καὶ ἐντέλλομαι
πᾶσιν, ὅτι ἐγὼ ἑκὼν ὑπὲρ θεοῦ ἀποθνῄσκω, ἐάνπερ
ὑμεῖς μὴ κωλύσητε. παρακαλῶ ὑμᾶς, μὴ εὔνοια
ἄκαιρος γένησθέ μοι. ἄφετέ με θηρίων εἶναι βοράν,
δι' ὧν ἔνεστιν θεοῦ ἐπιτυχεῖν. σῖτός εἰμι θεοῦ καὶ δι'
ὀδόντων θηρίων ἀλήθομαι, ἵνα καθαρὸς ἄρτος εὑρεθῶ
τοῦ Χριστοῦ.[67] 2. μᾶλλον κολακεύσατε τὰ θηρία, ἵνα
μοι τάφος γένωνται καὶ μηθὲν καταλίπωσι τῶν τοῦ
σώματός μου, ἵνα μὴ κοιμηθεὶς βαρύς τινι γένωμαι.
τότε ἔσομαι μαθητὴς ἀληθῶς Ἰησοῦ Χριστοῦ, ὅτε
οὐδὲ τὸ σῶμά μου ὁ κόσμος ὄψεται. λιτανεύσατε τὸν
Χριστὸν ὑπὲρ ἐμοῦ, ἵνα διὰ τῶν ὀργάνων τούτων
θεοῦ[68] θυσία εὑρεθῶ. 3. οὐχ ὡς Πέτρος καὶ Παῦλος
διατάσσομαι ὑμῖν. ἐκεῖνοι ἀπόστολοι, ἐγὼ κατά-
κριτος· ἐκεῖνοι ἐλεύθεροι, ἐγὼ δὲ μέχρι νῦν δοῦλος.
ἀλλ' ἐὰν πάθω, ἀπελεύθερος γενήσομαι Ἰησοῦ
Χριστοῦ καὶ ἀναστήσομαι ἐν αὐτῷ ἐλεύθερος. καὶ νῦν
μανθάνω δεδεμένος μηδὲν ἐπιθυμεῖν.[69]

5

Ἀπὸ Συρίας μέχρι Ῥώμης θηριομαχῶ, διὰ γῆς καὶ
θαλάσσης, νυκτὸς καὶ ἡμέρας, ἐνδεδεμένος δέκα λεο-
πάρδοις, ὅ ἐστιν στρατιωτικὸν τάγμα· οἳ καὶ εὐεργε-
τούμενοι χείρους γίνονται. ἐν δὲ τοῖς ἀδικήμασιν

4

I am writing all the churches and giving instruction to all, that I am willingly dying for God, unless you hinder me. I urge you, do not become an untimely kindness to me. Allow me to be bread for the wild beasts; through them I am able to attain to God. I am the wheat of God and am ground by the teeth of the wild beasts, that I may be found to be the pure bread of Christ. 2. Rather, coax the wild beasts, that they may become a tomb for me and leave no part of my body behind, that I may burden no one once I have died. Then I will truly be a disciple of Jesus Christ, when the world does not see even my body. Petition Christ on my behalf, that I may be found a sacrifice through these instruments of God. 3. I am not enjoining you as Peter and Paul did. They were apostles, I am condemned; they were free, until now I have been a slave. But if I suffer, I will become a freed person who belongs to Jesus Christ, and I will rise up, free, in him. In the meantime I am learning to desire nothing while in chains.

5

From Syria to Rome I have been fighting the wild beasts, through land and sea, night and day, bound to ten leopards, which is a company of soldiers, who become worse when treated well. But I am becoming more of a disciple by their

---

67 τοῦ Χριστοῦ G H T L Sm M: θεοῦ S A Am (Sf C g)

68 θεοῦ L (A Am) g (cod. n): θεῷ S Sf Sm (C) g (codd. c m v): καθαρὰ (after θυσία) M: om. z l   69 ἐπιθυμεῖν L S Sm A Am: add κοσμικὸν (om. H) ἢ μάταιον z g H M

αὐτῶν μᾶλλον μαθητεύομαι, ἀλλ' οὐ παρὰ τοῦτο
δεδικαίωμαι. 2. ὀναίμην τῶν θηρίων τῶν ἐμοὶ ἡτοι-
μασμένων καὶ εὔχομαι σύντομά μοι εὑρεθῆναι· ἃ καὶ
κολακεύσω, συντόμως με καταφαγεῖν, οὐχ ὥσπερ
τινῶν δειλαινόμενα οὐχ ἥψαντο. κἂν αὐτὰ δὲ ἑκόντα[70]
μὴ θέλῃ, ἐγὼ προσβιάσομαι. 3. συγγνώμην μοι
ἔχετε· τί μοι συμφέρει, ἐγὼ γινώσκω. νῦν ἄρχομαι
μαθητὴς εἶναι. μηθέν με ζηλῶσαι τῶν ὁρατῶν καὶ
ἀοράτων, ἵνα Ἰησοῦ Χριστοῦ ἐπιτύχω. πῦρ καὶ
σταυρὸς θηρίων τε συστάσεις, ἀνατομαί, διαιρέσεις,[71]
σκορπισμοὶ ὀστέων, συγκοπὴ[72] μελῶν, ἀλεσμοὶ ὅλου
τοῦ σώματος, κακαὶ κολάσεις τοῦ διαβόλου ἐπ' ἐμὲ
ἐρχέσθωσαν, μόνον ἵνα Ἰησοῦ Χριστοῦ ἐπιτύχω.

6

Οὐδέν μοι ὠφελήσει τὰ πέρατα τοῦ κόσμου οὐδὲ αἱ
βασιλεῖαι τοῦ αἰῶνος τούτου. καλόν μοι ἀποθανεῖν
εἰς[73] Ἰησοῦν Χριστόν, ἢ βασιλεύειν τῶν περάτων τῆς
γῆς.[74] ἐκεῖνον ζητῶ, τὸν ὑπὲρ ἡμῶν ἀποθανόντα·
ἐκεῖνον θέλω, τὸν δι' ἡμᾶς ἀναστάντα. ὁ δὲ τοκετός
μοι ἐπίκειται. 2. σύγγνωτέ μοι, ἀδελφοί· μὴ ἐμποδί-
σητέ μοι ζῆσαι, μὴ θελήσητέ με ἀποθανεῖν, τὸν τοῦ
θεοῦ θέλοντα εἶναι κόσμῳ μὴ χαρίσησθε μηδὲ ὕλῃ

---

[70] ἑκόντα L g: ἄκοντα z M   [71] ἀνατομαί,   διαιρέσεις
G H T (Sm) Am g M: διαίρεσις καὶ Sf A: om. L S
[72] συγκοπή G H L M: συγκοπαὶ T g

mistreatment. Still, it is not because of this that I have been made upright.[18] 2. May I have the full pleasure of the wild beasts prepared for me; I pray they will be found ready for me. Indeed, I will coax them to devour me quickly—not as happens with some, whom they are afraid to touch. And even if they do not wish to do so willingly, I will force them to it. 3. Grant this to me; I know what benefits me. Now I am beginning to be a disciple. May nothing visible or invisible show any envy toward me, that I may attain to Jesus Christ. Fire and cross and packs of wild beasts, cuttings and being torn apart, the scattering of bones, the mangling of limbs, the grinding of the whole body, the evil torments of the devil—let them come upon me, only that I may attain to Jesus Christ.

6

Neither the ends of the world nor the kingdoms of this age will benefit me in the least. It is better for me to die in Jesus Christ than to rule the ends of the earth. That is the one I seek, who died on our behalf; that is the one I desire, who arose for us. But pains of birth have come upon me. 2. Grant this to me, brothers: do not keep me from living; do not wish me to die; do not hand over to the world the one who wants to belong to God or deceive him by what is

---

[18] 1 Cor 4:4.

---

[73] εἰς G H T: ἐν M: in (= εἰς or ἐν) Sf A Am l: *cum* Sm: διὰ L g
[74] γῆς L Sf Sm A Am: add τί γὰρ ὠφελεῖται ἄνθρωπος, ἐὰν κερδήσῃ τὸν κόσμον ὅλον, τὴν δὲ ψυχὴν αὐτοῦ ζημιωθῇ G H (T) g M

ἐξαπατήσητε.[75] ἄφετέ με καθαρὸν φῶς λαβεῖν· ἐκεῖ
παραγενόμενος ἄνθρωπος[76] ἔσομαι. 3. ἐπιτρέψατέ μοι
μιμητὴν εἶναι τοῦ πάθους τοῦ θεοῦ μου. εἴ τις αὐτὸν ἐν
ἑαυτῷ ἔχει, νοησάτω, ὃ θέλω, καὶ συμπαθείτω μοι,
εἰδὼς τὰ συνέχοντά με.

7

Ὁ ἄρχων τοῦ αἰῶνος τούτου διαρπάσαι με βούλεται
καὶ τὴν εἰς θεόν μου γνώμην διαφθεῖραι. μηδεὶς οὖν
τῶν παρόντων ὑμῶν βοηθείτω αὐτῷ· μᾶλλον ἐμοῦ
γίνεσθε, τουτέστιν τοῦ θεοῦ. μὴ λαλεῖτε Ἰησοῦν
Χριστόν, κόσμον δὲ ἐπιθυμεῖτε. 2. βασκανία ἐν ὑμῖν
μὴ κατοικείτω. μηδ' ἂν ἐγὼ παρὼν παρακαλῶ ὑμᾶς,
πείσθητέ μοι· τούτοις δὲ μᾶλλον πείσθητε, οἷς γράφω
ὑμῖν. ζῶν γὰρ γράφω ὑμῖν, ἐρῶν τοῦ ἀποθανεῖν. ὁ
ἐμὸς ἔρως ἐσταύρωται, καὶ οὐκ ἔστιν ἐν ἐμοὶ πῦρ
φιλόϋλον· ὕδωρ δὲ ζῶν καὶ λαλοῦν ἐν ἐμοί, ἔσωθέν μοι
λέγον· δεῦρο πρὸς τὸν πατέρα. 3. οὐχ ἥδομαι τροφῇ
φθορᾶς οὐδὲ ἡδοναῖς τοῦ βίου τούτου. ἄρτον θεοῦ
θέλω,[77] ὅ ἐστιν σὰρξ Ἰησοῦ Χριστοῦ, τοῦ ἐκ
σπέρματος Δαυίδ,[78] καὶ πόμα[79] θέλω τὸ αἷμα αὐτοῦ, ὅ
ἐστιν ἀγάπη ἄφθαρτος.[80]

[75] μηδὲ ὕλῃ ἐξαπατήσητε (seducatis) L (Am): μ. ὔ.
κολακεύσητε (Sf Sm A): μ. ὔ. κηλήσητε cj. Hilgenfeld: om. z g
[76] ἄνθρωπος L Sm C: add θεοῦ z g M: add τέλειος Sf A: ange-
lus Am   [77] θέλω L S Sm A Am C: add ἄρτον οὐράνιον
ἄρτον ζωῆς z g M

material. Allow me to receive the pure light; when I have arrived there, I will be a human. 3. Allow me to be an imitator of the suffering of my God. If anyone has him within himself, let him both understand what I want and sympathize with me, realizing the things that constrain me.

7

The ruler of this age wishes to snatch me away and corrupt my mind, which is directed toward God. And so let none of you who are present assist him; rather be on my side—that is, on God's. Do not speak about Jesus Christ but long for the world. 2. Let no envy dwell among you. Even if I urge you otherwise when I arrive, do not be persuaded; instead be persuaded by what I am writing you now. For I write to you while living, desiring to die. My passion has been crucified[19] and there is no burning love within me for material things; instead there is living water,[20] which also is speaking in me, saying to me from within: "Come to the Father." 3. I have no pleasure in the food that perishes nor in the pleasures of this life. I desire the bread of God, which is the flesh of Jesus Christ, from the seed of David; and for drink I desire his blood, which is imperishable love.

[19] Cf. Gal 6:14.
[20] Cf. John 4:10, 14.

---

[78] τοῦ ἐκ σπ. Δ. (add κατὰ σάρκα C) L Sm A Am C: τοῦ (om. T) υἱοῦ (om. T) τοῦ θεοῦ τοῦ γενομένου ἐν ὑστέρῳ ἐκ σπ. Δ. καὶ Ἀβραάμ z g M

[79] πόμα L S Sm A Am C g: add θεοῦ z M

[80] ἄφθαρτος L S Sm A C: add καὶ ἀέναος ζωή z g M

8

Οὐκέτι θέλω κατὰ ἀνθρώπους ζῆν. τοῦτο δὲ ἔσται, ἐὰν
ὑμεῖς θελήσητε. θελήσατε, ἵνα καὶ ὑμεῖς θεληθῆτε.
2. δι᾿ ὀλίγων γραμμάτων αἰτοῦμαι ὑμᾶς· πιστεύσατέ
μοι· Ἰησοῦς δὲ Χριστὸς ὑμῖν ταῦτα φανερώσει, ὅτι
ἀληθῶς λέγω· τὸ ἀψευδὲς στόμα, ἐν ᾧ ὁ πατὴρ ἀληθῶς ἐλάλησεν. 3. αἰτήσασθε περὶ ἐμοῦ, ἵνα ἐπιτύχω.[81]
οὐ κατὰ σάρκα ὑμῖν ἔγραψα, ἀλλὰ κατὰ γνώμην θεοῦ.
ἐὰν πάθω, ἠθελήσατε· ἐὰν ἀποδοκιμασθῶ, ἐμισήσατε.

9

Μνημονεύετε ἐν τῇ προσευχῇ ὑμῶν τῆς ἐν Συρίᾳ
ἐκκλησίας, ἥτις ἀντὶ ἐμοῦ ποιμένι τῷ θεῷ χρῆται.
μόνος αὐτὴν Ἰησοῦς Χριστὸς[82] ἐπισκοπήσει καὶ ἡ
ὑμῶν ἀγάπη. 2. ἐγὼ δὲ αἰσχύνομαι ἐξ αὐτῶν λέγε-
σθαι· οὐδὲ γὰρ ἄξιός εἰμι, ὢν ἔσχατος αὐτῶν καὶ
ἔκτρωμα· ἀλλ᾿ ἠλέημαί τις εἶναι, ἐὰν θεοῦ ἐπιτύχω.
3. ἀσπάζεται ὑμᾶς τὸ ἐμὸν πνεῦμα καὶ ἡ ἀγάπη τῶν
ἐκκλησιῶν τῶν δεξαμένων με εἰς ὄνομα Ἰησοῦ Χριστοῦ, οὐχ ὡς παροδεύοντα. καὶ γὰρ αἱ μὴ προσήκου-
σαί μοι τῇ ὁδῷ τῇ κατὰ σάρκα, κατὰ πόλιν με
προῆγον.

[81] ἐπιτύχω G H T L Sm Am C M: add ἐν πνεύματι ἁγίῳ g A
[82] Ἰησοῦς Χριστὸς: Χριστὸς ὁ θεὸς H

8

I no longer desire to live like a human; and I will succeed, if you also desire it. Desire it, that you may also be desired. 2. Through just a few words I ask you: trust me! Jesus Christ will show you that I speak the truth. He is the mouth that does not lie, by whom the Father spoke the truth. 3. Pray for me, that I may attain to God. I have not written you according to the flesh but according to the mind of God. If I suffer, you have desired it; if I am rejected, you have hated me.

9

In your prayer remember the church of Syria, which has God as its shepherd in my place. Jesus Christ alone will oversee it *[Or: be its bishop]*, along with your love. 2. But I am ashamed to be called one of them; for I am not at all worthy, as the least of them and a miscarriage.[21] But I have found mercy to be someone, if I attain to God. 3. My spirit greets you, as does the love of the churches that received me in the name of Jesus Christ, and not just as one passing by. For even those that did not lie on my actual route went ahead of me from city to city.

[21] 1 Cor 15:8–9.

10

Γράφω δὲ ὑμῖν ταῦτα ἀπὸ Σμύρνης δι᾿ Ἐφεσίων τῶν ἀξιομακαρίστων. ἔστιν δὲ καὶ ἅμα ἐμοὶ σὺν ἄλλοις πολλοῖς καὶ Κρόκος, τὸ ποθητόν μοι ὄνομα. 2. περὶ τῶν προελθόντων[83] με[84] ἀπὸ Συρίας εἰς Ῥώμην εἰς δόξαν θεοῦ πιστεύω ὑμᾶς ἐπεγνωκέναι, οἷς καὶ δηλώσατε ἐγγύς με ὄντα. πάντες γάρ εἰσιν ἄξιοι θεοῦ καὶ ὑμῶν· οὓς πρέπον ὑμῖν ἐστὶν κατὰ πάντα ἀναπαῦσαι. 3. ἔγραψα δὲ ὑμῖν ταῦτα τῇ πρὸ ἐννέα καλανδῶν Σεπτεμβρίων. ἔρρωσθε εἰς τέλος ἐν ὑπομονῇ Ἰησοῦ Χριστοῦ.

ΦΙΛΑΔΕΛΦΕΥΣΙΝ ΙΓΝΑΤΙΟΣ

Ἰγνάτιος, ὁ καὶ Θεοφόρος, ἐκκλησίᾳ θεοῦ πατρὸς καὶ κυρίου[85] Ἰησοῦ Χριστοῦ τῇ οὔσῃ ἐν Φιλαδελφίᾳ τῆς Ἀσίας, ἠλεημένῃ καὶ ἡδρασμένῃ ἐν ὁμονοίᾳ θεοῦ καὶ ἀγαλλιωμένῃ ἐν τῷ πάθει τοῦ κυρίου ἡμῶν ἀδιακρίτως καὶ ἐν τῇ ἀναστάσει αὐτοῦ πεπληροφορημένῃ ἐν παντὶ ἐλέει, ἣν ἀσπάζομαι ἐν αἵματι Ἰησοῦ Χριστοῦ, ἥτις ἐστὶν χαρὰ αἰώνιος καὶ παράμονος, μάλιστα ἐὰν ἐν ἑνὶ ὦσιν σὺν τῷ ἐπισκόπῳ καὶ τοῖς σὺν αὐτῷ[86] πρεσβυτέροις καὶ διακόνοις ἀποδεδειγμένοις ἐν γνώμῃ Ἰησοῦ Χριστοῦ, οὓς κατὰ τὸ ἴδιον θέλημα ἐστήριξεν ἐν βεβαιωσύνῃ τῷ ἁγίῳ αὐτοῦ πνεύματι.

10

I am writing this to you from Smyrna, through the Ephesians, who are worthy to be blessed. Along with many others, Crocus is with me, a name that is dear to me. 2. I believe you know about those who have preceded me from Syria to Rome for the glory of God. Tell them I am near. For they are all worthy of God and of you. It is fitting for you to refresh them in every way. 3. I am writing this to you on August 24. Farewell until the end, in the endurance of Jesus Christ.

TO THE PHILADELPHIANS

Ignatius, who is also called God-bearer, to the church of God the Father and of the Lord Jesus Christ that is in Philadelphia of Asia, that has received mercy and been founded in the harmony that comes from God, that rejoices without wavering in the suffering of our Lord and that is fully convinced by all mercy in his resurrection; this is the church that I greet by the blood of Jesus Christ, which is an eternal and enduring joy, especially if they are at one with the bishop and with the presbyters with him, and with the deacons who have been appointed in accordance with the mind of Jesus Christ—those who have been securely set in place by his Holy Spirit according to his own will.

---

83 προελθόντων G H T A: προσελθ. L (Am) g: συνελθ. M

84 με G H T Sm A: μοι L M: om. Am g

85 κυρίου G g (A): om. L C

86 σὺν αὐτῷ: om. A g

1

Ὃν ἐπίσκοπον ἔγνων οὐκ ἀφ᾿ ἑαυτοῦ οὐδὲ δι᾿ ἀνθρώπων κεκτῆσθαι τὴν διακονίαν τὴν εἰς τὸ κοινὸν ἀνήκουσαν οὐδὲ κατὰ κενοδοξίαν, ἀλλ᾿ ἐν ἀγάπῃ θεοῦ
πατρὸς καὶ κυρίου Ἰησοῦ Χριστοῦ· οὗ καταπέ-
πληγμαι τὴν ἐπιείκειαν, ὃς σιγῶν πλείονα δύναται
τῶν μάταια[87] λαλούντων. 2. συνευρύθμισται γὰρ ταῖς
ἐντολαῖς ὡς χορδαῖς κιθάρα. διὸ μακαρίζει μου ἡ
ψυχὴ τὴν εἰς θεὸν αὐτοῦ γνώμην, ἐπιγνοὺς ἐνάρετον
καὶ τέλειον οὖσαν, τὸ ἀκίνητον αὐτοῦ καὶ τὸ ἀόργητον
αὐτοῦ ἐν πάσῃ ἐπιεικείᾳ θεοῦ ζῶντος.

2

Τέκνα οὖν φωτὸς ἀληθείας, φεύγετε τὸν μερισμὸν καὶ
τὰς κακοδιδασκαλίας· ὅπου δὲ ὁ ποιμήν ἐστιν, ἐκεῖ ὡς
πρόβατα ἀκολουθεῖτε. 2. πολλοὶ γὰρ λύκοι ἀξιόπιστοι
ἡδονῇ κακῇ αἰχμαλωτίζουσιν τοὺς θεοδρόμους· ἀλλ᾿
ἐν τῇ ἑνότητι ὑμῶν οὐχ ἕξουσιν[88] τόπον.

3

Ἀπέχεσθε τῶν κακῶν βοτανῶν, ἅστινας οὐ γεωργεῖ
Ἰησοῦς Χριστός, διὰ τὸ μὴ εἶναι αὐτοὺς φυτείαν
πατρός· οὐχ ὅτι παρ᾿ ὑμῖν μερισμὸν εὗρον, ἀλλ᾿
ἀποδιϋλισμόν. 2. ὅσοι γὰρ θεοῦ εἰσιν καὶ Ἰησοῦ
Χριστοῦ, οὗτοι μετὰ τοῦ ἐπισκόπου εἰσίν· καὶ ὅσοι ἂν

1

I have learned that your bishop did not obtain his ministry to the community from himself, nor through humans, nor according to pure vanity, but by the love of God the Father and the Lord Jesus Christ. I have been amazed at his gentleness; by being silent he can do more than those who speak idle thoughts. 2. For he is attuned to the commandments like a lyre to the strings. For this reason my soul blesses his mind fixed in God—knowing it to be virtuous and perfect—along with his solid and anger-free character, manifest in all gentleness, which comes from the living God.

2

Therefore, children of the light of truth, flee division and evil teachings. Where the shepherd is, there you should follow as sheep. 2. For many seemingly trustworthy wolves use wicked pleasure to capture those who run in God's race; but they will have no place in your unity.

3

Abstain from evil plants which Jesus Christ does not cultivate, since they are not a planting of the Father. Not that I found a division among you, but a filter. 2. For all who belong to God and Jesus Christ are with the bishop; and all

---

87 μάταια G L C: πλέον g: om. A
88 ἔξουσιν G g (C): ἔχουσιν L (A)

μετανοήσαντες ἔλθωσιν ἐπὶ τὴν ἑνότητα τῆς ἐκκλησίας, καὶ οὗτοι θεοῦ ἔσονται, ἵνα ὦσιν κατὰ Ἰησοῦν
Χριστὸν ζῶντες. 3. μὴ πλανᾶσθε, ἀδελφοί μου· εἴ τις
σχίζοντι ἀκολουθεῖ, βασιλείαν θεοῦ οὐ κληρονομεῖ· εἴ
τις ἐν ἀλλοτρίᾳ γνώμῃ περιπατεῖ, οὗτος τῷ πάθει οὐ
συγκατατίθεται.

4

Σπουδάσατε οὖν μιᾷ εὐχαριστίᾳ χρῆσθαι· μία γὰρ
σὰρξ τοῦ κυρίου ἡμῶν Ἰησοῦ Χριστοῦ καὶ ἓν ποτή-
ριον εἰς ἕνωσιν τοῦ αἵματος αὐτοῦ, ἓν θυσιαστήριον,
ὡς εἷς ἐπίσκοπος ἅμα τῷ πρεσβυτερίῳ καὶ διακόνοις,
τοῖς συνδούλοις μου· ἵνα, ὃ ἐὰν πράσσητε, κατὰ θεὸν
πράσσητε.

5

Ἀδελφοί μου, λίαν ἐκκέχυμαι ἀγαπῶν ὑμᾶς καὶ ὑπερ-
αγαλλόμενος ἀσφαλίζομαι ὑμᾶς· οὐκ ἐγὼ δέ, ἀλλ᾽
Ἰησοῦς Χριστός, ἐν ᾧ δεδεμένος φοβοῦμαι μᾶλλον,
ὡς ἔτι ὢν ἀναπάρτιστος· ἀλλ᾽ ἡ προσευχὴ ὑμῶν εἰς
θεόν με ἀπαρτίσει, ἵνα ἐν ᾧ κλήρῳ ἠλεήθην ἐπιτύχω,
προσφυγὼν τῷ εὐαγγελίῳ ὡς σαρκὶ Ἰησοῦ καὶ τοῖς
ἀποστόλοις ὡς πρεσβυτερίῳ ἐκκλησίας. 2. καὶ τοὺς
προφήτας δὲ ἀγαπῶμεν,[89] διὰ τὸ καὶ αὐτοὺς εἰς τὸ
εὐαγγέλιον κατηγγελκέναι καὶ εἰς αὐτὸν ἐλπίζειν καὶ
αὐτὸν ἀναμένειν, ἐν ᾧ καὶ πιστεύσαντες ἐσώθησαν, ἐν

those who come into the unity of the church through repentance will belong to God, so that they may live according to Jesus Christ. 3. Do not be deceived my brothers; no one who follows someone creating a schism will inherit the kingdom of God;[22] anyone who thinks otherwise does not agree with the Passion.

4

And so be eager to celebrate just one eucharist. For there is one flesh of our Lord Jesus Christ and one cup that brings the unity of his blood, and one altar, as there is one bishop together with the presbytery and the deacons, my fellow slaves. Thus, whatever you do, do according to God.

5

My brothers, I am completely overflowing with love for you and out of extreme joy am I watching over you—not I, but Jesus Christ. Even though I bear my chains in him, I am even more afraid, since I am still not perfected. But your prayer to God will perfect me, so that I may attain to God by the lot that I have been mercifully assigned, when I flee to the gospel as to the flesh of Jesus and to the apostles as to the presbytery of the church. 2. And we should also love the prophets, because their proclamation anticipated the gospel and they hoped in him and awaited him. And they were saved by believing in him, because they stood in

[22] Cf. 1 Cor 6:9–10.

---

89 ἀγαπῶμεν G L C: ἀγαπῶ A g

ἑνότητι Ἰησοῦ Χριστοῦ ὄντες, ἀξιαγάπητοι καὶ ἀξιο-
θαύμαστοι ἅγιοι, ὑπὸ Ἰησοῦ Χριστοῦ μεμαρτυρη-
μένοι καὶ συνηριθμημένοι ἐν τῷ εὐαγγελίῳ τῆς κοινῆς
ἐλπίδος.

6

Ἐὰν δέ τις Ἰουδαϊσμὸν ἑρμηνεύῃ ὑμῖν, μὴ ἀκούετε
αὐτοῦ. ἄμεινον γάρ ἐστιν παρὰ ἀνδρὸς περιτομὴν
ἔχοντος Χριστιανισμὸν ἀκούειν, ἢ παρὰ ἀκροβύστου
Ἰουδαϊσμόν. ἐὰν δὲ ἀμφότεροι περὶ Ἰησοῦ Χριστοῦ
μὴ λαλῶσιν, οὗτοι ἐμοὶ στῆλαί εἰσιν καὶ τάφοι
νεκρῶν, ἐφ᾽ οἷς γέγραπται μόνον ὀνόματα ἀνθρώπων.
2. φεύγετε οὖν τὰς κακοτεχνίας καὶ ἐνέδρας τοῦ ἄρχοντος τοῦ αἰῶνος τούτου, μήποτε θλιβέντες τῇ
γνώμῃ αὐτοῦ ἐξασθενήσετε ἐν τῇ ἀγάπῃ· ἀλλὰ πάντες
ἐπὶ τὸ αὐτὸ γίνεσθε ἐν ἀμερίστῳ καρδίᾳ. 3. εὐχαριστῶ
δὲ τῷ θεῷ μου, ὅτι εὐσυνείδητός εἰμι ἐν ὑμῖν καὶ οὐκ
ἔχει τις καυχήσασθαι οὔτε λάθρα οὔτε φανερῶς, ὅτι
ἐβάρησά τινα ἐν μικρῷ ἢ ἐν μεγάλῳ. καὶ πᾶσι δέ, ἐν
οἷς ἐλάλησα, εὔχομαι, ἵνα μὴ εἰς μαρτύριον αὐτὸ
κτήσωνται.

7

Εἰ γὰρ καὶ κατὰ σάρκα μέ τινες ἠθέλησαν πλανῆσαι,
ἀλλὰ τὸ πνεῦμα οὐ πλανᾶται ἀπὸ θεοῦ ὄν. οἶδεν γάρ,
πόθεν ἔρχεται καὶ ποῦ ὑπάγει, καὶ τὰ κρυπτὰ ἐλέγχει.

the unity of Jesus Christ, saints who were worthy of love and admiration, who were testified to by Jesus Christ and counted as belonging to the gospel of our mutual hope.

6

But if anyone should interpret Judaism to you, do not hear him. For it is better to hear Christianity from a man who is circumcised than Judaism from one who is uncircumcised. But if neither one speaks about Jesus Christ, they both appear to me as monuments and tombs of the dead, on which are written merely human names. 2. And so flee the evil designs and snares of the ruler of this age, lest being oppressed by his way of thinking you be weakened in love. But all of you should stand in agreement with an undivided heart. 3. I thank my God that I have a good conscience among you and that no one can boast against me, whether in secret or in public, that I burdened anyone in either a trifling matter or great. But I pray that none of those who heard me speak may encounter my word as a witness against himself.

7

For even if some people have wanted to deceive me according to the flesh, the Spirit is not deceived, since it comes from God. For it knows whence it comes and where it is going, and it exposes the things that are hidden.[23] I

[23] Cf. John 3:8; 1 Cor 2:10.

ἐκραύγασα μεταξὺ ὤν, ἐλάλουν μεγάλῃ φωνῇ, θεοῦ
φωνῇ· τῷ ἐπισκόπῳ προσέχετε καὶ τῷ πρεσβυτερίῳ
καὶ διακόνοις. 2. οἱ[90] δὲ ὑποπτεύσαντές με ὡς
προειδότα τὸν μερισμόν τινων λέγειν ταῦτα· μάρτυς
δέ μοι, ἐν ᾧ δέδεμαι, ὅτι ἀπὸ σαρκὸς ἀνθρωπίνης οὐκ
ἔγνων. τὸ δὲ πνεῦμα ἐκήρυσσεν λέγον τάδε· χωρὶς τοῦ
ἐπισκόπου μηδὲν ποιεῖτε, τὴν σάρκα ὑμῶν ὡς ναὸν
θεοῦ τηρεῖτε, τὴν ἕνωσιν ἀγαπᾶτε, τοὺς μερισμοὺς
φεύγετε, μιμηταὶ γίνεσθε Ἰησοῦ Χριστοῦ, ὡς καὶ
αὐτὸς τοῦ πατρὸς αὐτοῦ.

8

Ἐγὼ μὲν οὖν τὸ ἴδιον ἐποίουν ὡς ἄνθρωπος εἰς ἕνωσιν
κατηρτισμένος. οὗ δὲ μερισμός ἐστιν καὶ ὀργή, θεὸς
οὐ κατοικεῖ. πᾶσιν οὖν μετανοοῦσιν ἀφίει ὁ κύριος,
ἐὰν μετανοήσωσιν εἰς ἑνότητα θεοῦ καὶ συνέδριον τοῦ
ἐπισκόπου. πιστεύω τῇ χάριτι Ἰησοῦ Χριστοῦ, ὃς
λύσει ἀφ᾽ ὑμῶν πάντα δεσμόν. 2. παρακαλῶ δὲ ὑμᾶς
μηδὲν κατ᾽ ἐρίθειαν πράσσειν, ἀλλὰ κατὰ χριστομα-
θίαν. ἐπεὶ ἤκουσά τινων λεγόντων ὅτι, ἐὰν μὴ ἐν τοῖς
ἀρχείοις[91] εὕρω, ἐν τῷ εὐαγγελίῳ οὐ πιστεύω· καὶ
λέγοντός μου αὐτοῖς, ὅτι γέγραπται, ἀπεκρίθησάν
μοι, ὅτι πρόκειται. ἐμοὶ δὲ ἀρχεῖά[92] ἐστιν Ἰησοῦς
Χριστός, τὰ ἄθικτα ἀρχεῖα,[93] ὁ σταυρὸς αὐτοῦ καὶ ὁ
θάνατος καὶ ἡ ἀνάστασις αὐτοῦ καὶ ἡ πίστις ἡ δι᾽
αὐτοῦ, ἐν οἷς θέλω ἐν τῇ προσευχῇ ὑμῶν δικαιωθῆναι.

cried out while among you, speaking in a great voice, the voice of God, "Pay attention to the bishop and the presbytery and the deacons." 2. But some suspected that I said these things because I knew in advance that there was a division among you. But the one in whom I am bound is my witness that I knew it from no human source; but the Spirit was preaching, saying: "Do nothing apart from the bishop; keep your flesh as the Temple of God; love unity; flee divisions; be imitators of Jesus Christ as he is of his Father."

8

I was therefore acting on my own accord as a person set on unity. But where there is division and anger, God does not dwell. Thus the Lord forgives all who repent, if they return to the unity of God and the council of the bishop. I believe in the gracious gift that comes from Jesus Christ, who will loose every bond from you. 2. But I urge you to do nothing in a contentious way, but in accordance with what you have learned in Christ. For I heard some saying: "If I do not find it in the ancient records, I do not believe in the gospel." And when I said to them, "It is written," they replied to me, "That is just the question." But for me, Jesus Christ is the ancient records; the sacred ancient records are his cross and death, and his resurrection, and the faith that comes through him—by which things I long to be made righteous by your prayer.

---

90 οἱ G L C (Sf A): εἰ g scripturis antiquis (prioribus) A cipium L: scriptura prior A   91 ἀρχείοις g: ἀρχαίοις G L: 92 ἀρχεῖα G C g: principium L: scriptura prior A   93 τὰ ἄθικτα ἀρχεῖα: καὶ C ἀρχεῖα G: principia L: ἀρχεῖον g: om. A

9

Καλοὶ καὶ οἱ ἱερεῖς, κρεῖσσον δὲ ὁ ἀρχιερεὺς ὁ πεπι-
στευμένος τὰ ἅγια τῶν ἁγίων, ὃς μόνος πεπίστευται
τὰ κρυπτὰ τοῦ θεοῦ, αὐτὸς ὢν θύρα τοῦ πατρός, δι᾽ ἧς
εἰσέρχονται Ἀβραὰμ καὶ Ἰσαὰκ καὶ Ἰακὼβ καὶ οἱ
προφῆται καὶ οἱ ἀπόστολοι καὶ ἡ ἐκκλησία. πάντα
ταῦτα εἰς ἑνότητα θεοῦ. 2. ἐξαίρετον δέ τι ἔχει τὸ
εὐαγγέλιον, τὴν παρουσίαν τοῦ σωτῆρος, κυρίου
ἡμῶν Ἰησοῦ Χριστοῦ, τὸ πάθος αὐτοῦ καὶ τὴν
ἀνάστασιν. οἱ γὰρ ἀγαπητοὶ προφῆται κατήγγειλαν
εἰς αὐτόν· τὸ δὲ εὐαγγέλιον ἀπάρτισμά ἐστιν ἀφθαρσίας. πάντα ὁμοῦ καλά ἐστιν, ἐὰν ἐν ἀγάπῃ
πιστεύητε.

10

Ἐπειδὴ κατὰ τὴν προσευχὴν ὑμῶν καὶ κατὰ τὰ
σπλάγχνα, ἃ ἔχετε ἐν Χριστῷ Ἰησοῦ, ἀπηγγέλη μοι,
εἰρηνεύειν τὴν ἐκκλησίαν τὴν ἐν Ἀντιοχείᾳ τῆς Συρίας, πρέπον ἐστὶν ὑμῖν, ὡς ἐκκλησίᾳ θεοῦ, χειροτονῆσαι διάκονον εἰς τὸ πρεσβεῦσαι ἐκεῖ θεοῦ
πρεσβείαν, εἰς τὸ συγχαρῆναι αὐτοῖς ἐπὶ τὸ αὐτὸ
γενομένοις καὶ δοξάσαι τὸ ὄνομα. 2. μακάριος ἐν
Ἰησοῦ Χριστῷ, ὃς καταξιωθήσεται τῆς τοιαύτης διακονίας, καὶ ὑμεῖς δοξασθήσεσθε. θέλουσιν δὲ ὑμῖν
οὐκ ἔστιν ἀδύνατον ὑπὲρ ὀνόματος θεοῦ, ὡς καὶ αἱ
ἔγγιστα ἐκκλησίαι ἔπεμψαν ἐπισκόπους, αἱ δὲ
πρεσβυτέρους καὶ διακόνους.

9

The priests are good, but the high priest who has been entrusted with the holy of holies is better; he alone is entrusted with the hidden things that belong to God. He is the door of the Father,[24] through which Abraham and Isaac and Jacob and the prophets and the apostles and the church enter. All these things are bound together in the unity of God. 2. But there is something distinct about the gospel—that is, the coming of the Savior, our Lord Jesus Christ, his suffering, and resurrection. For the beloved prophets made their proclamation looking ahead to him; but the gospel is the finished work that brings immortality. All things together are good, if you believe while showing forth love.

10

Since it has been reported to me that the church of God in Antioch of Syria is at peace—in accordance with your prayer and the compassion that you have in Christ Jesus—it is fitting for you as the church of God to elect a deacon to go as an ambassador of God there, that you may rejoice together with those who have achieved a common purpose and so give glory to the name. 2. Most fortunate in Jesus Christ is the one who will be considered worthy of this ministry, and you too will be glorified. And for you who wish to do this, on behalf of the name of God, it is not an impossible task, since the churches that are nearer have even sent bishops, while others have sent presbyters and deacons.

[24] Cf. John 10:7, 9.

11

Περὶ δὲ Φίλωνος τοῦ διακόνου ἀπὸ Κιλικίας, ἀνδρὸς
μεμαρτυρημένου, ὃς καὶ νῦν ἐν λόγῳ θεοῦ ὑπηρετεῖ
μοι ἅμα Ῥέῳ[94] Ἀγαθόποδι, ἀνδρὶ ἐκλεκτῷ, ὃς ἀπὸ
Συρίας μοι ἀκολουθεῖ ἀποταξάμενος τῷ βίῳ, οἳ καὶ
μαρτυροῦσιν ὑμῖν, κἀγὼ τῷ θεῷ εὐχαριστῶ ὑπὲρ
ὑμῶν, ὅτι ἐδέξασθε αὐτούς, ὡς καὶ ὑμᾶς ὁ κύριος. οἱ δὲ
ἀτιμάσαντες αὐτοὺς λυτρωθείησαν ἐν τῇ χάριτι τοῦ
Ἰησοῦ Χριστοῦ. 2. ἀσπάζεται ὑμᾶς ἡ ἀγάπη τῶν
ἀδελφῶν τῶν ἐν Τρῳάδι, ὅθεν καὶ γράφω ὑμῖν διὰ
Βούρρου πεμφθέντος ἅμα ἐμοὶ ἀπὸ Ἐφεσίων καὶ
Σμυρναίων εἰς λόγον τιμῆς. τιμήσει αὐτοὺς ὁ κύριος
Ἰησοῦς Χριστός, εἰς ὃν ἐλπίζουσιν σαρκί, ψυχῇ,
πνεύματι,[95] πίστει, ἀγάπῃ, ὁμονοίᾳ. ἔρρωσθε ἐν
Χριστῷ Ἰησοῦ, τῇ κοινῇ ἐλπίδι ἡμῶν.

ΣΜΥΡΝΑΙΟΙΣ ΙΓΝΑΤΙΟΣ

Ἰγνάτιος, ὁ καὶ Θεοφόρος, ἐκκλησίᾳ θεοῦ πατρὸς καὶ
τοῦ ἠγαπημένου Ἰησοῦ Χριστοῦ, ἠλεημένῃ ἐν παντὶ
χαρίσματι, πεπληρωμένῃ ἐν πίστει καὶ ἀγάπῃ, ἀνυσ-
τερήτῳ οὔσῃ παντὸς χαρίσματος, θεοπρεπεστάτῃ καὶ
ἁγιοφόρῳ, τῇ οὔσῃ ἐν Σμύρνῃ τῆς Ἀσίας, ἐν ἀμώμῳ
πνεύματι καὶ λόγῳ θεοῦ πλεῖστα χαίρειν.

[94] Ῥέῳ G L A: Γαυΐᾳ καὶ g: Gaio et C l: Ῥαίῳ cj. Lightfoot:
add ἀδελφῷ καὶ A
[95] πνεύματι L (A) C g: om. G

11

But concerning Philo, the deacon from Cilicia, a man who has received a good testimony and who now serves me in the word of God along with Rheus Agathopous, one of the elect who is following me from Syria, who has bid farewell to life—these also bear testimony to you. And I thank God for you that you welcomed them as also the Lord welcomed you. But may those who dishonored them be redeemed by the gracious gift that comes from Jesus Christ. 2. The love of the brothers in Troas greets you; it is from there that I am writing you through Burrhus, who has been sent together with me from the Ephesians and Smyrneans as a pledge of honor. The Lord Jesus Christ will honor them; in him they hope, in flesh, soul, spirit, faith, love, and harmony. Farewell in Christ Jesus, our mutual hope.

TO THE SMYRNEANS

Ignatius, who is also called God-bearer, to the church of God the Father and the beloved Jesus Christ which is in Smyrna of Asia, which has been shown mercy in every gracious gift, filled with faith and love, and lacking no gracious gift, a church that is most worthy of God and bears what is holy. Warmest greetings in a blameless spirit and the word of God.

1

Δοξάζω Ἰησοῦν Χριστὸν τὸν θεὸν τὸν οὕτως ὑμᾶς
σοφίσαντα· ἐνόησα γὰρ ὑμᾶς κατηρτισμένους ἐν
ἀκινήτῳ πίστει, ὥσπερ καθηλωμένους ἐν τῷ σταυρῷ
τοῦ κυρίου Ἰησοῦ Χριστοῦ σαρκί τε καὶ πνεύματι, καὶ
ἡδρασμένους ἐν ἀγάπῃ ἐν τῷ αἵματι Χριστοῦ, πεπλη-
ροφορημένους εἰς τὸν κύριον ἡμῶν, ἀληθῶς ὄντα ἐκ
γένους Δαυὶδ κατὰ σάρκα, υἱὸν θεοῦ κατὰ θέλημα καὶ
δύναμιν θεοῦ, γεγεννημένον ἀληθῶς ἐκ παρθένου,
βεβαπτισμένον ὑπὸ Ἰωάννου, ἵνα πληρωθῇ πᾶσα
δικαιοσύνη ὑπ᾽ αὐτοῦ· 2. ἀληθῶς ἐπὶ Ποντίου Πιλάτου
καὶ Ἡρώδου τετράρχου καθηλωμένον ὑπὲρ ἡμῶν ἐν
σαρκί, ἀφ᾽ οὗ καρποῦ ἡμεῖς ἀπὸ τοῦ θεομακαρίστου
αὐτοῦ πάθους, ἵνα ἄρῃ σύσσημον εἰς τοὺς αἰῶνας διὰ
τῆς ἀναστάσεως εἰς τοὺς ἁγίους καὶ πιστοὺς αὐτοῦ,
εἴτε ἐν Ἰουδαίοις εἴτε ἐν ἔθνεσιν, ἐν ἑνὶ σώματι τῆς
ἐκκλησίας αὐτοῦ.

2

Ταῦτα γὰρ πάντα ἔπαθεν δι᾽ ἡμᾶς, ἵνα σωθῶμεν·[96] καὶ
ἀληθῶς ἔπαθεν, ὡς καὶ ἀληθῶς ἀνέστησεν ἑαυτόν,
οὐχ ὥσπερ ἄπιστοί τινες λέγουσιν, τὸ δοκεῖν αὐτὸν
πεπονθέναι· αὐτοὶ τὸ δοκεῖν ὄντες, καὶ καθὼς φρονοῦσιν, καὶ συμβήσεται αὐτοῖς, οὖσιν ἀσωμάτοις καὶ
δαιμονικοῖς.

1

I give glory to Jesus Christ, the God who has made you so wise. For I know that you have been made complete in a faith that cannot be moved—as if you were nailed to the cross of the Lord Jesus Christ in both flesh and spirit—and that you have been established in love by the blood of Christ. For you are fully convinced about our Lord, that he was truly from the family of David according to the flesh, Son of God according to the will and power of God, truly born from a virgin, and baptized by John that all righteousness might be fulfilled by him.[25] 2. In the time of Pontius Pilate and the tetrarch Herod, he was truly nailed for us in the flesh—we ourselves come from the fruit of his divinely blessed suffering—so that through his resurrection he might eternally lift up the standard for his holy and faithful ones, whether among Jews or Gentiles, in the one body of his church.

2

For he suffered all these things for our sake, that we might be saved; and he truly suffered, just as he also truly raised himself—not as some unbelievers say, that he suffered only in appearance. They are the ones who are only an appearance; and it will happen to them just as they think, since they are without bodies, like the daimons.

[25] Cf. Matt 3:15.

---

96 ἵνα σωθῶμεν: om. C g

3

Ἐγὼ γὰρ καὶ μετὰ τὴν ἀνάστασιν ἐν σαρκὶ αὐτὸν
οἶδα καὶ πιστεύω ὄντα. 2. καὶ ὅτε πρὸς τοὺς περὶ
Πέτρον ἦλθεν, ἔφη αὐτοῖς· λάβετε, ψηλαφήσατέ με
καὶ ἴδετε, ὅτι οὐκ εἰμὶ δαιμόνιον ἀσώματον. καὶ εὐθὺς
αὐτοῦ ἥψαντο καὶ ἐπίστευσαν, κραθέντες τῇ σαρκὶ
αὐτοῦ καὶ τῷ πνεύματι.97 διὰ τοῦτο καὶ θανάτου κατ-
εφρόνησαν, ηὑρέθησαν δὲ ὑπὲρ θάνατον. 3. μετὰ δὲ
τὴν ἀνάστασιν συνέφαγεν αὐτοῖς καὶ συνέπιεν ὡς
σαρκικός, καίπερ πνευματικῶς98 ἡνωμένος τῷ πατρί.

4

Ταῦτα δὲ παραινῶ ὑμῖν, ἀγαπητοί, εἰδὼς ὅτι καὶ ὑμεῖς
οὕτως ἔχετε. προφυλάσσω δὲ ὑμᾶς ἀπὸ τῶν θηρίων
τῶν ἀνθρωπομόρφων, οὓς οὐ μόνον δεῖ ὑμᾶς μὴ παρα-
δέχεσθαι, ἀλλ' εἰ δυνατὸν μηδὲ συναντᾶν, μόνον δὲ
προσεύχεσθαι ὑπὲρ αὐτῶν, ἐάν πως μετανοήσωσιν,
ὅπερ δύσκολον. τούτου δὲ ἔχει ἐξουσίαν Ἰησοῦς Χριστός, τὸ ἀληθινὸν ἡμῶν ζῆν. 2. εἰ γὰρ τὸ δοκεῖν ταῦτα
ἐπράχθη ὑπὸ τοῦ κυρίου ἡμῶν, κἀγὼ τὸ δοκεῖν
δέδεμαι. τί δὲ καὶ ἑαυτὸν ἔκδοτον δέδωκα τῷ θανάτῳ,
πρὸς πῦρ, πρὸς μάχαιραν, πρὸς θηρία; ἀλλ' ἐγγὺς99
μαχαίρας ἐγγὺς θεοῦ, μεταξὺ θηρίων μεταξὺ θεοῦ·

97 πνεύματι G L C: αἵματι A   98 σαρκικός, καίπερ
πνευματικῶς G L: σαρκικ . . . καὶ πνευματικῶς P: σαρκικῶς
καὶ πνευματικῶς (A): σαρκικὸς καὶ πνευματικὸς C

3

For I know and believe that he was in the flesh even after the resurrection. 2. And when he came to those who were with Peter, he said to them, "Reach out, touch me and see that I am not a bodiless daimon."[26] And immediately they touched him and believed, having been intermixed with his flesh and spirit. For this reason they also despised death, for they were found to be beyond death. 3. And after his resurrection he ate and drank with them as a fleshly being, even though he was spiritually united with the Father.

4

I am advising you about these things, beloved, even though I know that you already agree. But I am guarding you ahead of time from the wild beasts in human form. Not only should you refrain from welcoming such people, if possible you should not even meet with them. Instead pray for them that they might somehow repent, though even this is difficult. But Jesus Christ, our true life, has authority over this. 2. For if these things were accomplished by our Lord only in appearance, I also am in chains only in appearance. But why then have I handed myself over to death, to fire, to the sword, to wild beasts? But to be near the sword is to be near God, to be in the presence of the wild beasts is to be in the presence of God—so long as it is

[26] Cf. Luke 24:39.

---

99 ἐγγὺς G P L: ὁ ἐγγὺς Sf A C

μόνον ἐν τῷ ὀνόματι Ἰησοῦ Χριστοῦ. εἰς τὸ συμπαθεῖν αὐτῷ πάντα ὑπομένω, αὐτοῦ με ἐνδυναμοῦντος τοῦ τελείου ἀνθρώπου γενομένου.[100]

5

Ὅν τινες ἀγνοοῦντες ἀρνοῦνται, μᾶλλον δὲ ἠρνήθησαν ὑπ᾽ αὐτοῦ, ὄντες συνήγοροι τοῦ θανάτου μᾶλλον ἢ τῆς ἀληθείας· οὓς οὐκ ἔπεισαν αἱ προφητεῖαι οὐδὲ ὁ νόμος Μωϋσέως, ἀλλ᾽ οὐδὲ μέχρι νῦν τὸ εὐαγγέλιον οὐδὲ τὰ ἡμέτερα τῶν κατ᾽ ἄνδρα παθήματα. 2. καὶ γὰρ περὶ ἡμῶν τὸ αὐτὸ φρονοῦσιν. τί γάρ με ὠφελεῖ τις, εἰ ἐμὲ ἐπαινεῖ, τὸν δὲ κύριόν μου βλασφημεῖ, μὴ ὁμολογῶν αὐτὸν σαρκοφόρον; ὁ δὲ τοῦτο μὴ[101] λέγων τελείως αὐτὸν ἀπήρνηται, ὢν νεκροφόρος. 3. τὰ δὲ ὀνόματα αὐτῶν, ὄντα ἄπιστα, οὐκ ἔδοξέν μοι ἐγγράψαι. ἀλλὰ μηδὲ γένοιτό μοι αὐτῶν μνημονεύειν, μέχρις οὗ μετανοήσωσιν εἰς τὸ πάθος, ὅ ἐστιν ἡμῶν ἀνάστασις.

6

Μηδεὶς πλανάσθω· καὶ τὰ ἐπουράνια καὶ ἡ δόξα τῶν ἀγγέλων καὶ οἱ ἄρχοντες ὁρατοί τε καὶ ἀόρατοι, ἐὰν μὴ πιστεύσωσιν εἰς τὸ αἷμα Χριστοῦ,[102] κἀκείνοις κρίσις ἐστίν. ὁ χωρῶν χωρείτω. τόπος μηδένα φυσι-

---

[100] γενομένου G L: om. P C

in the name of Jesus Christ. I am enduring all things in order to suffer along with him, while he, the one who became the perfect human, empowers me.

5

Some deny him out of ignorance, or rather, they are denied by him: these are public advocates of death, not truth. They have been convinced neither by the words of the prophets nor the Law of Moses, nor, until now, by the gospel nor by the suffering each of us has experienced. 2. For they think the same things about us. For how does anyone benefit me if he praises me but blasphemes my Lord, not confessing that he bore flesh? The one who refuses to say this denies him completely, as one who bears a corpse. 3. But I see no point in recording their disbelieving names. I do not even want to recall them, until they repent concerning the Passion, which is our resurrection.

6

Let no one be deceived. Judgment is prepared even for the heavenly beings, for the glory of the angels, and for the rulers both visible and invisible, if they do not believe in the blood of Christ. Let the one who can receive this receive it.[27] Let no one become haughty because of his position.

---

[27] Matt 19:12.

---

[101] μὴ: om. P C
[102] Χριστοῦ G P L A C: add ὁ θεός ἐστιν Sf: add τοῦ θεοῦ cj. Lightfoot

οὕτω· τὸ γὰρ ὅλον ἐστὶν πίστις καὶ ἀγάπη, ὧν οὐδὲν
προκέκριται. 2. καταμάθετε δὲ τοὺς ἑτεροδοξοῦντας εἰς
τὴν χάριν Ἰησοῦ Χριστοῦ τὴν εἰς ἡμᾶς ἐλθοῦσαν,
πῶς ἐναντίοι εἰσὶν τῇ γνώμῃ τοῦ θεοῦ. περὶ ἀγάπης οὐ
μέλει αὐτοῖς, οὐ περὶ χήρας, οὐ περὶ ὀρφανοῦ, οὐ περὶ
θλιβομένου, οὐ περὶ δεδεμένου ἢ λελυμένου,[103] οὐ περὶ
πεινῶντος ἢ διψῶντος.

7

Εὐχαριστίας καὶ προσευχῆς ἀπέχονται, διὰ τὸ μὴ
ὁμολογεῖν τὴν εὐχαριστίαν σάρκα εἶναι τοῦ σωτῆρος
ἡμῶν Ἰησοῦ Χριστοῦ τὴν ὑπὲρ τῶν ἁμαρτιῶν ἡμῶν
παθοῦσαν, ἣν τῇ χρηστότητι ὁ πατὴρ ἤγειρεν. οἱ οὖν
ἀντιλέγοντες τῇ δωρεᾷ τοῦ θεοῦ συζητοῦντες ἀπο-
θνήσκουσιν. συνέφερεν δὲ αὐτοῖς ἀγαπᾶν, ἵνα καὶ
ἀναστῶσιν. 2. πρέπον οὖν ἐστιν ἀπέχεσθαι τῶν τοιούτων καὶ μήτε κατ᾽ ἰδίαν περὶ αὐτῶν λαλεῖν μήτε
κοινῇ, προσέχειν δὲ τοῖς προφήταις, ἐξαιρέτως δὲ τῷ
εὐαγγελίῳ, ἐν ᾧ τὸ πάθος ἡμῖν δεδήλωται καὶ ἡ
ἀνάστασις τετελείωται. τοὺς δὲ μερισμοὺς φεύγετε ὡς
ἀρχὴν κακῶν.

8

Πάντες τῷ ἐπισκόπῳ ἀκολουθεῖτε, ὡς Ἰησοῦς Χριστὸς τῷ πατρί, καὶ τῷ πρεσβυτερίῳ ὡς τοῖς ἀπο-
στόλοις· τοὺς δὲ διακόνους ἐντρέπεσθε ὡς θεοῦ ἐντο-

For faith and love are everything; nothing is preferable to them. 2. But take note of those who spout false opinions about the gracious gift of Jesus Christ that has come to us, and see how they are opposed to the mind of God. They have no interest in love, in the widow, the orphan, the oppressed, the one who is in chains or the one set free, the one who is hungry or the one who thirsts.

7

They abstain from the eucharist and prayer, since they do not confess that the eucharist is the flesh of our savior Jesus Christ, which suffered on behalf of our sins and which the Father raised in his kindness. And so, those who dispute the gift of God perish while still arguing the point. It would be better for them to engage in acts of love, that they might also rise up. 2. And so it is fitting to avoid such people and not even to speak about them, either privately or in public, but instead to pay attention to the prophets, and especially to the gospel, in which the passion is clearly shown to us and the resurrection is perfected. But flee divisions as the beginning of evils.

8

All of you should follow the bishop as Jesus Christ follows the Father; and follow the presbytery as you would the apostles. Respect the deacons as the commandment of

---

103 ἢ λελυμένου G P L: om. A C (g)

λήν. μηδεὶς χωρὶς[104] τοῦ ἐπισκόπου τι πρασσέτω τῶν
ἀνηκόντων εἰς τὴν ἐκκλησίαν. ἐκείνη βεβαία εὐχαρι-
στία ἡγείσθω, ἡ ὑπὸ ἐπίσκοπον οὖσα ἢ ᾧ ἂν αὐτὸς
ἐπιτρέψῃ. 2. ὅπου ἂν φανῇ ὁ ἐπίσκοπος, ἐκεῖ τὸ
πλῆθος ἔστω, ὥσπερ ὅπου ἂν ᾖ Χριστὸς Ἰησοῦς, ἐκεῖ
ἡ καθολικὴ ἐκκλησία. οὐκ ἐξόν ἐστιν χωρὶς[105]
ἐπισκόπου οὔτε βαπτίζειν οὔτε ἀγάπην ποιεῖν· ἀλλ᾽ ὃ
ἂν ἐκεῖνος δοκιμάσῃ, τοῦτο καὶ τῷ θεῷ εὐάρεστον, ἵνα
ἀσφαλὲς ᾖ καὶ βέβαιον πᾶν ὃ πράσσετε.

9

Εὔλογόν ἐστιν λοιπὸν ἀνανῆψαι ἡμᾶς, ὡς ἔτι[106] καιρὸν ἔχομεν εἰς θεὸν μετανοεῖν. καλῶς ἔχει, θεὸν καὶ
ἐπίσκοπον εἰδέναι. ὁ τιμῶν ἐπίσκοπον ὑπὸ θεοῦ τετί-
μηται· ὁ λάθρα ἐπισκόπου τι πράσσων τῷ διαβόλῳ
λατρεύει. 2. πάντα οὖν ὑμῖν ἐν χάριτι περισσευέτω·
ἄξιοι γάρ ἐστε. κατὰ πάντα με ἀνεπαύσατε, καὶ ὑμᾶς
Ἰησοῦς Χριστός. ἀπόντα με καὶ παρόντα ἠγαπήσατε.
ἀμοιβὴ[107] ὑμῖν ὁ θεός, δι᾽ ὃν πάντα ὑπομένοντες αὐτοῦ
τεύξεσθε.

10

Φίλωνα καὶ Ῥέον[108] Ἀγαθόπουν, οἳ ἐπηκολούθησάν
μοι εἰς λόγον θεοῦ, καλῶς ἐποιήσατε ὑποδεξάμενοι ὡς

---

[104] χωρὶς P g: add τοῦ G   [105] χωρὶς P: add τοῦ G g

God. Let no one do anything involving the church without the bishop. Let that eucharist be considered valid that occurs under the bishop or the one to whom he entrusts it. 2. Let the congregation be wherever the bishop is; just as wherever Jesus Christ is, there also is the universal church. It is not permitted either to baptize or to hold a love feast without the bishop. But whatever he approves is acceptable to God, so that everything you do should be secure and valid.

9

Finally, it is reasonable for us to return to sobriety, while we still have time to repent to God. It is good to know both God and the bishop. The one who honors the bishop is honored by God; the one who does anything behind the bishop's back serves the devil. 2. Let all things abound to you in grace, for you are worthy. You have refreshed me in every way and Jesus Christ has refreshed you. You have loved me when absent as well as when present. God is your recompense; if you endure all things for his sake, you will attain to him.

10

You did well to receive Philo and Rheus Agathopous as deacons of the Christ of God *[Or: of Christ, who is God]*;

---

106 ἔτι G P L g: om. Sf A   107 ἀμοιβὴ P: ἀμοίβει G:
retribuat L: ἀμεύψεται g (A): ἀμείβοι cj. Jacobson
108 Ῥέον L: Ῥέων G: Γάϊον P g A: add καὶ L A g

διακόνους Χριστοῦ[109] θεοῦ· οἳ καὶ εὐχαριστοῦσιν τῷ
κυρίῳ ὑπὲρ ὑμῶν, ὅτι αὐτοὺς ἀνεπαύσατε κατὰ πάντα
τρόπον. οὐδὲν ὑμῖν οὐ μὴ ἀπολεῖται. 2. ἀντίψυχον
ὑμῶν τὸ πνεῦμά μου καὶ τὰ δεσμά μου, ἃ οὐχ ὑπερ-
ηφανήσατε οὐδὲ ἐπῃσχύνθητε. οὐδὲ ὑμᾶς ἐπαισχυν-
θήσεται ἡ τελεία ἐλπίς,[110] Ἰησοῦς Χριστός.

11

Ἡ προσευχὴ ὑμῶν ἀπῆλθεν ἐπὶ τὴν ἐκκλησίαν τὴν ἐν
Ἀντιοχείᾳ τῆς Συρίας, ὅθεν δεδεμένος θεοπρεπε-
στάτοις δεσμοῖς πάντας ἀσπάζομαι, οὐκ ὢν ἄξιος
ἐκεῖθεν εἶναι, ἔσχατος αὐτῶν ὤν· κατὰ θέλημα δὲ
κατηξιώθην, οὐκ ἐκ συνειδότος, ἀλλ' ἐκ χάριτος θεοῦ,
ἣν εὔχομαι τελείαν μοι δοθῆναι, ἵνα ἐν τῇ προσευχῇ
ὑμῶν θεοῦ ἐπιτύχω. 2. ἵνα οὖν τέλειον ὑμῶν γένηται τὸ
ἔργον καὶ ἐπὶ γῆς καὶ ἐν οὐρανῷ, πρέπει εἰς τιμὴν
θεοῦ χειροτονῆσαι τὴν ἐκκλησίαν ὑμῶν θεοπρεσβευ-
τήν, εἰς τὸ γενόμενον ἕως Συρίας συγχαρῆναι αὐτοῖς,
ὅτι εἰρηνεύουσιν καὶ ἀπέλαβον τὸ ἴδιον μέγεθος καὶ
ἀπεκατεστάθη αὐτοῖς τὸ ἴδιον σωματεῖον. 3. ἐφάμην
μοι οὖν θεοῦ[111] ἄξιον πρᾶγμα, πέμψαι τινὰ τῶν ὑμετέ-
ρων μετ' ἐπιστολῆς, ἵνα συνδοξάσῃ τὴν κατὰ θεὸν
αὐτοῖς γενομένην εὐδίαν, καὶ ὅτι λιμένος ἤδη ἔτυχον
ἐν τῇ προσευχῇ ὑμῶν. τέλειοι ὄντες τέλεια καὶ φρο-

---

[109] Χριστοῦ G L: om. P A

they have followed me in the word of God. And they give thanks to the Lord for you, because you refreshed them in every way. Nothing will be lost to you. 2. My spirit is given in exchange for yours, as are my chains, which you did not treat with haughtiness or shame. Neither will the perfect hope, Jesus Christ, be ashamed of you.

11

Your prayer has gone out to the church in Antioch of Syria. I greet everyone, having come from there bound in chains that are most acceptable to God; but I am not worthy to be from there, since I am the least of them. Still, I have been deemed worthy according to God's will—not by my own conscience but by the gracious gift of God. I ask that it may be given to me perfectly, that I may attain to God by your prayer. 2. So then, that your work may be made perfect both on earth and in heaven, it is fitting for the honor of God that your church elect an ambassador of God to go to Syria and rejoice together with them. For they have found peace and have recovered their own greatness, and their own corporate body has been restored to them. 3. And so it seems to me a matter worthy of God that you send one of your own with a letter, that he may exult with them in the tranquility that has come to them from God, because they have already reached a harbor by your prayer. As those who are perfect, you should also think perfect things.[28] For

28 Cf. Phil 3:15.

---

110 ἐλπίς P A g: πίστις G L
111 θεοῦ P L (A): om. G g

νεῖτε. θέλουσιν γὰρ ὑμῖν εὐπράσσειν θεὸς ἕτοιμος εἰς
τὸ παρασχεῖν.

12

Ἀσπάζεται ὑμᾶς ἡ ἀγάπη τῶν ἀδελφῶν τῶν ἐν Τρω-
άδι, ὅθεν καὶ γράφω ὑμῖν διὰ Βούρρου, ὃν ἀπεστεί-
λατε μετ' ἐμοῦ ἅμα Ἐφεσίοις, τοῖς ἀδελφοῖς[112] ὑμῶν,
ὃς κατὰ πάντα με ἀνέπαυσεν. καὶ ὄφελον πάντες
αὐτὸν ἐμιμοῦντο, ὄντα ἐξεμπλάριον θεοῦ διακονίας.
ἀμείψεται αὐτὸν ἡ χάρις κατὰ πάντα. 2. ἀσπάζομαι
τὸν ἀξιόθεον ἐπίσκοπον καὶ θεοπρεπὲς πρεσβυτέριον
καὶ τοὺς συνδούλους μου διακόνους καὶ τοὺς κατ'
ἄνδρα καὶ κοινῇ πάντας ἐν ὀνόματι Ἰησοῦ Χριστοῦ
καὶ τῇ σαρκὶ αὐτοῦ καὶ τῷ αἵματι, πάθει τε καὶ
ἀναστάσει, σαρκικῇ τε καὶ πνευματικῇ, ἐν ἑνότητι
θεοῦ καὶ ὑμῶν. χάρις ὑμῖν, ἔλεος, εἰρήνη, ὑπομονὴ διὰ
παντός.

13

Ἀσπάζομαι τοὺς οἴκους τῶν ἀδελφῶν μου σὺν γυναιξὶ
καὶ τέκνοις καὶ τὰς παρθένους τὰς λεγομένας χήρας.
ἔρρωσθέ μοι ἐν δυνάμει πατρός.[113] ἀσπάζεται ὑμᾶς
Φίλων σὺν ἐμοὶ ὤν. 2. ἀσπάζομαι τὸν οἶκον Ταουΐας,
ἣν εὔχομαι ἑδρᾶσθαι πίστει καὶ ἀγάπῃ σαρκικῇ τε
καὶ πνευματικῇ. ἀσπάζομαι Ἄλκην, τὸ ποθητόν μοι
ὄνομα, καὶ Δάφνον τὸν ἀσύγκριτον καὶ Εὔτεκνον καὶ
πάντας κατ' ὄνομα. ἔρρωσθε ἐν χάριτι θεοῦ.

God is ready to supply what is needed for you who wish to do good.

12

The love of the brothers who are in Troas greets you; from there I am writing to you through Burrhus, whom you sent along with me, together with your brothers the Ephesians. He has refreshed me in every way. Would that everyone imitated him, as he is the embodiment of the ministry of God. But the gracious gift of God will reward him in every way. 2. I greet the bishop who is worthy of God, the godly presbytery, the deacons who are my fellow slaves, and all individually and together in the name of Jesus Christ, in his flesh and blood, in his passion and resurrection, which pertains to both flesh and spirit, in unity with God and with you. May grace, mercy, peace, and endurance be yours at all times.

13

I greet the households of my brothers, along with their wives and children, and the virgins who are called widows. I wish you farewell in the power of the Father. Philo, who is with me, greets you. 2. I greet the household of Tavia, whom I pray will be firm in faith and in a love that pertains to both flesh and spirit. I greet Alce, a name dear to me, and the incomparable Daphnus and Eutecnus, and all by name. Farewell in the gracious gift of God.

---

112 P breaks off here.
113 πατρός L A l: πνεύματος G g

ΠΡΟΣ ΠΟΛΥΚΑΡΠΟΝ ΙΓΝΑΤΙΟΣ

Ἰγνάτιος, ὁ καὶ Θεοφόρος, Πολυκάρπῳ ἐπισκόπῳ ἐκκλησίας Σμυρναίων, μᾶλλον ἐπισκοπημένῳ ὑπὸ θεοῦ πατρὸς καὶ κυρίου Ἰησοῦ Χριστοῦ, πλεῖστα χαίρειν.

1

Ἀποδεχόμενός σου τὴν ἐν θεῷ γνώμην, ἡδρασμένην ὡς ἐπὶ πέτραν ἀκίνητον, ὑπερδοξάζω,[114] καταξιωθεὶς τοῦ προσώπου σου τοῦ ἀμώμου,[115] οὗ ὀναίμην ἐν θεῷ. 2. παρακαλῶ σε ἐν χάριτι, ᾗ ἐνδέδυσαι, προσθεῖναι τῷ δρόμῳ σου καὶ πάντας παρακαλεῖν, ἵνα σώζωνται. ἐκδίκει σου τὸν τόπον ἐν πάσῃ ἐπιμελείᾳ σαρκικῇ τε καὶ πνευματικῇ· τῆς ἑνώσεως φρόντιζε, ἧς οὐδὲν ἄμεινον. πάντας βάσταζε, ὡς καὶ σὲ ὁ κύριος· πάντων ἀνέχου ἐν ἀγάπῃ, ὥσπερ καὶ ποιεῖς. 3. προσευχαῖς σχόλαζε ἀδιαλείπτοις· αἰτοῦ σύνεσιν πλείονα ἧς ἔχεις· γρηγόρει ἀκοίμητον πνεῦμα κεκτημένος. τοῖς κατ' ἄνδρα κατὰ ὁμοήθειαν[116] θεοῦ λάλει· πάντων τὰς νόσους βάσταζε ὡς τέλειος ἀθλητής. ὅπου πλείων κόπος, πολὺ κέρδος.

114 ὑπερδοξάζω G L g: add θεὸν S A
115 τοῦ ἀμώμου: om. S A
116 ὁμοήθειαν L g: βοήθειαν G: voluntatem S Sf A

TO POLYCARP

Ignatius, who is also called God-bearer, to Polycarp, bishop of the church of the Smyrnaeans—rather, the one who has God the Father and the Lord Jesus Christ as his bishop—warmest greetings.

1

I welcome your godly way of thinking, which is fixed firmly as upon an unmovable rock; and I exult all the more, having been found worthy of your blameless face. I hope to enjoy it in God! 2. But I urge you by the gracious gift with which you are clothed, to forge ahead in your race and urge all to be saved. Vindicate your position *[Or: office]* with all fleshly and spiritual diligence. Consider unity, for nothing is better. Bear with all people, just as the Lord bears with you. Tolerate everyone in love, just as you are already doing.[29] 3. Be assiduous in constant prayers; ask for greater understanding than you have. Be alert, as one who has obtained a spirit that never slumbers. Speak to each one according to God's own character. Bear the illnesses of all as a perfect athlete. Where there is more toil, there is great gain.

[29] Cf. Eph 4:2.

2

Καλοὺς μαθητὰς ἐὰν φιλῇς, χάρις σοι οὐκ ἔστιν·
μᾶλλον τοὺς λοιμοτέρους ἐν πραότητι ὑπότασσε. οὐ
πᾶν τραῦμα τῇ αὐτῇ ἐμπλάστρῳ θεραπεύεται. τοὺς
παροξυσμοὺς ἐμβροχαῖς παῦε. 2. φρόνιμος γίνου ὡς
ὄφις ἐν ἅπασιν καὶ ἀκέραιος εἰς ἀεὶ[117] ὡς ἡ περιστερά.
διὰ τοῦτο σαρκικὸς εἶ καὶ πνευματικός, ἵνα τὰ
φαινόμενά σου εἰς πρόσωπον κολακεύῃς· τὰ δὲ
ἀόρατα αἴτει ἵνα σοι φανερωθῇ, ὅπως μηδενὸς λείπῃ
καὶ παντὸς χαρίσματος περισσεύῃς. 3. ὁ καιρὸς ἀπαι-
τεῖ σε, ὡς κυβερνῆται ἀνέμους καὶ ὡς χειμαζόμενος
λιμένα, εἰς τὸ θεοῦ ἐπιτυχεῖν. νῆφε ὡς θεοῦ ἀθλητής·
τὸ θέμα ἀφθαρσία καὶ ζωὴ αἰώνιος, περὶ ἧς καὶ σὺ
πέπεισαι. κατὰ πάντα σου ἀντίψυχον ἐγὼ καὶ τὰ
δεσμά μου, ἃ ἠγάπησας.

3

Οἱ δοκοῦντες ἀξιόπιστοι[118] εἶναι καὶ ἑτεροδιδασκα-
λοῦντες μή σε καταπλησσέτωσαν. στῆθι ἑδραῖος ὡς
ἄκμων[119] τυπτόμενος. μεγάλου ἐστὶν ἀθλητοῦ τὸ
δέρεσθαι καὶ νικᾶν. μάλιστα δὲ ἕνεκεν θεοῦ πάντα
ὑπομένειν ἡμᾶς δεῖ, ἵνα καὶ αὐτὸς ἡμᾶς ὑπομείνῃ.
2. πλέον σπουδαῖος γίνου οὗ εἶ. τοὺς καιροὺς κατα-
μάνθανε. τὸν ὑπὲρ καιρὸν προσδόκα, τὸν ἄχρονον, τὸν

[117] εἰς ἀεὶ g (S A): om. G L

2

It is nothing special for you to love good disciples; instead, gently bring those who are more pestiferous into subjection. Not every wound is cured with the same plaster. Soothe paroxysms of fever with cold compresses. 2. Be wise as a serpent in all things and always pure as the dove.[30] You are fleshly and spiritual for this reason, that you may deal gently with what is visible before you. But ask that what is unseen be made visible to you, that you may lack nothing and abound in every gracious gift. 3. The season seeks for you—as sailors at the helm seek for winds and the one driven by storm a harbor—so that you may attain to God. Be sober as an athlete of God. The prize is immortality and eternal life, about which you have already been convinced. I am given in exchange for you in every way, as are the bonds I bear, which you have loved.

3

Do not allow those who appear trustworthy yet who deliver contrary teachings daze you. Stand firm as an anvil that is struck. It is the mark of a great athlete to bear up under blows and still claim the victory. But we must endure everything especially for God's sake, that he may endure us. 2. Be more eager than you are. Take note of the seasons. Await the one who is beyond the season, the one

[30] Matt 10:16.

---

[118] ἀξιόπιστοι G L g: *aliquid* S Sf A
[119] ἄκμων: *vir fortis* Sf A: *athleta* S

ἀόρατον, τὸν δι᾽ ἡμᾶς ὁρατόν, τὸν ἀψηλάφητον, τὸν
ἀπαθῆ, τὸν δι᾽ ἡμᾶς παθητόν, τὸν κατὰ πάντα τρόπον
δι᾽ ἡμᾶς ὑπομείναντα.

4

Χῆραι μὴ ἀμελείσθωσαν· μετὰ τὸν κύριον σὺ αὐτῶν
φροντιστὴς ἔσο. μηδὲν ἄνευ γνώμης σου γινέσθω,
μηδὲ σὺ ἄνευ θεοῦ[120] τι πρᾶσσε, ὅπερ οὐδὲ πράσσεις·
εὐστάθει. 2. πυκνότερον συναγωγαὶ γινέσθωσαν· ἐξ
ὀνόματος πάντας ζήτει. 3. δούλους καὶ δούλας μὴ
ὑπερηφάνει· ἀλλὰ μηδὲ αὐτοὶ φυσιούσθωσαν, ἀλλ᾽ εἰς
δόξαν θεοῦ πλέον δουλευέτωσαν, ἵνα κρείττονος ἐλευ-
θερίας ἀπὸ θεοῦ τύχωσιν. μὴ ἐράτωσαν ἀπὸ τοῦ
κοινοῦ ἐλευθεροῦσθαι, ἵνα μὴ δοῦλοι εὑρεθῶσιν ἐπιθυμίας.

5

Τὰς κακοτεχνίας φεῦγε, μᾶλλον δὲ περὶ τούτων
ὁμιλίαν ποιοῦ. ταῖς ἀδελφαῖς μου προσλάλει, ἀγαπᾶν
τὸν κύριον καὶ τοῖς συμβίοις ἀρκεῖσθαι σαρκὶ καὶ
πνεύματι. ὁμοίως καὶ τοῖς ἀδελφοῖς μου παράγγελλε
ἐν ὀνόματι Ἰησοῦ Χριστοῦ, ἀγαπᾶν τὰς συμβίους ὡς
ὁ κύριος τὴν ἐκκλησίαν. 2. εἴ τις δύναται ἐν ἁγνείᾳ
μένειν εἰς τιμὴν τῆς σαρκὸς τοῦ κυρίου, ἐν ἀκαυχησίᾳ

[120] θεοῦ G L: add γνώμης S A g

who is timeless, the one who is invisible, who became visible for us, the one who cannot be handled, the one who is beyond suffering, who suffered for us, enduring in every way on our account.

4

Do not allow the widows to be neglected. After the Lord, it is you who must be mindful of them. Let nothing be done apart from your consent, and do nothing apart from God. You are already acting in this way. Be imperturbable. 2. Let there be more frequent gatherings; seek out everyone by name. 3. Do not be arrogant towards male and female slaves, but neither let them become haughty; rather, let them serve even more as slaves for the glory of God, that they may receive a greater freedom from God. And they should not long to be set free through the common fund, lest they be found slaves of passion.

5

Flee the evil arts; indeed, deliver a sermon about them. Instruct my sisters to love the Lord and to be satisfied with their husbands in flesh and spirit. So too enjoin my brothers in the name of Jesus Christ to love their wives as the Lord loves the church.[31] 2. If anyone is able to honor the flesh of the Lord by maintaining a state of purity, let him do

[31] Eph 5:25, 29.

μενέτω. ἐὰν καυχήσηται, ἀπώλετο, καὶ ἐὰν γνωσθῇ
πλέον[121] τοῦ ἐπισκόπου, ἔφθαρται. πρέπει δὲ τοῖς
γαμοῦσι καὶ ταῖς γαμουμέναις[122] μετὰ γνώμης τοῦ
ἐπισκόπου τὴν ἕνωσιν ποιεῖσθαι, ἵνα ὁ γάμος ᾖ κατὰ
κύριον[123] καὶ μὴ κατ' ἐπιθυμίαν. πάντα εἰς τιμὴν θεοῦ
γινέσθω.

6

Τῷ ἐπισκόπῳ προσέχετε, ἵνα καὶ ὁ θεὸς ὑμῖν. ἀντίψυχον ἐγὼ τῶν ὑποτασσομένων τῷ ἐπισκόπῳ,
πρεσβυτέροις, διακόνοις· καὶ μετ' αὐτῶν μοι τὸ μέρος
γένοιτο σχεῖν ἐν θεῷ. συγκοπιᾶτε ἀλλήλοις, συν-
αθλεῖτε, συντρέχετε, συμπάσχετε, συγκοιμᾶσθε,
συνεγείρεσθε ὡς θεοῦ οἰκονόμοι καὶ πάρεδροι καὶ
ὑπηρέται. 2. ἀρέσκετε ᾧ στρατεύεσθε, ἀφ' οὗ καὶ τὰ
ὀψώνια κομίζεσθε· μή τις ὑμῶν δεσέρτωρ εὑρεθῇ. τὸ
βάπτισμα ὑμῶν μενέτω ὡς ὅπλα, ἡ πίστις ὡς περι-
κεφαλαία, ἡ ἀγάπη ὡς δόρυ, ἡ ὑπομονὴ ὡς πανοπλία·
τὰ δεπόσιτα ὑμῶν τὰ ἔργα ὑμῶν, ἵνα τὰ ἄκκεπτα ὑμῶν
ἄξια κομίσησθε. μακροθυμήσατε οὖν μετ' ἀλλήλων ἐν
πραότητι, ὡς ὁ θεὸς μεθ' ὑμῶν. ὀναίμην ὑμῶν διὰ
παντός.

[121] πλέον G L: πλὴν g S A
[122] γαμουμέναις G L: γαμούσαις g
[123] κύριον L S A g: θεὸν G

so without boasting. If he boasts, he has been destroyed, and if it becomes known to anyone beyond the bishop, he is ruined. But it is right for men and women who marry to make their union with the consent of the bishop, that their marriage may be for the Lord and not for passion. Let all things be done for the honor of God.

6

All of you should pay attention to the bishop, that God may pay attention to you. I am giving my life in exchange for those who are subject to the bishop, the presbyters, and the deacons. And I hope to have my lot together with them in God. Labor together with one another, compete together, run together, suffer together, lie down together, and be raised together as the household slaves, attendants, and servants of God. 2. Be pleasing to the one in whose army you serve,[32] from whom also you receive your wages. Let none of you be found a deserter. Let your baptism remain as your weaponry, your faith as a helmet, your love as a spear, your endurance as a full set of armor.[33] Let your works be a down payment on your wages, that you may receive the back pay you deserve. Be patient therefore with one another in gentleness, as God is with you. May I enjoy you at all times.

[32] Cf. 2 Tim 2:4.
[33] Cf. Eph 6:11–17.

7

Ἐπειδὴ ἡ ἐκκλησία ἡ ἐν Ἀντιοχείᾳ τῆς Συρίας
εἰρηνεύει, ὡς ἐδηλώθη μοι, διὰ τὴν προσευχὴν ὑμῶν,
κἀγὼ εὐθυμότερος ἐγενόμην ἐν ἀμεριμνίᾳ θεοῦ, ἐάνπερ διὰ τοῦ παθεῖν θεοῦ ἐπιτύχω, εἰς τὸ εὑρεθῆναί με
ἐν τῇ ἀναστάσει[124] ὑμῶν μαθητήν.[125] 2. πρέπει, Πολύκαρπε θεομακαριστότατε, συμβούλιον ἀγαγεῖν θεο-
πρεπέστατον καὶ χειροτονῆσαί τινα, ὃν ἀγαπητὸν
λίαν ἔχετε καὶ ἄοκνον, ὃς δυνήσεται θεοδρόμος καλεῖ-
σθαι· τοῦτον καταξιῶσαι, ἵνα πορευθεὶς εἰς Συρίαν
δοξάσῃ ὑμῶν τὴν ἄοκνον ἀγάπην εἰς δόξαν θεοῦ.
3. Χριστιανὸς[126] ἑαυτοῦ ἐξουσίαν οὐκ ἔχει, ἀλλὰ θεῷ
σχολάζει. τοῦτο τὸ ἔργον θεοῦ ἐστιν καὶ ὑμῶν, ὅταν
αὐτὸ ἀπαρτίσητε. πιστεύω γὰρ τῇ χάριτι, ὅτι ἕτοιμοί
ἐστε εἰς εὐποιΐαν θεῷ ἀνήκουσαν. εἰδὼς ὑμῶν τὸ
σύντονον τῆς ἀληθείας, δι' ὀλίγων ὑμᾶς γραμμάτων
παρεκάλεσα.

8

Ἐπεὶ οὖν πάσαις ταῖς ἐκκλησίαις οὐκ ἠδυνήθην
γράψαι διὰ τὸ ἐξαίφνης πλεῖν με ἀπὸ Τρωάδος εἰς
Νεάπολιν, ὡς τὸ θέλημα προστάσσει, γράψεις ταῖς
ἔμπροσθεν[127] ἐκκλησίαις, ὡς θεοῦ γνώμην κεκτη-

---

124 ἀναστάσει G L: αἰτήσει g (A)
125 μαθητήν L A g: παθητήν G

7

Since the church in Antioch of Syria is now at peace because of your prayer, as has been shown to me, I too, having been removed from all earthly cares by God, have become more eager to be found your disciple in the resurrection, if indeed I attain to God through suffering. 2. It is fitting, O Polycarp, most blessed by God, for you to call a council that is pleasing to God and to elect someone whom you hold most dear and resolved, who can be called the runner of God. Deem this one worthy to go to Syria and glorify your resolute love for the glory of God. 3. A Christian has no authority over himself, but is diligent for God. When you bring it to completion, this work belongs to both God and you. For by grace I believe that you are prepared to do the good deeds that are appropriate to God. Because I know the zeal you have for the truth, I have urged you through just these few words.

8

Because I have not been able to write to all the churches—since, as the divine will enjoins, I am unexpectedly to set sail from Troas to Neapolis—you are to write to the churches that lie before me *[Or: "on this side"],*[34] as one

---

[34] Possibly referring to the churches that lie between Smyrna and Antioch, or between Troas and Rome.

---

126 χριστιανὸς G: ὁ χριστιανὸς C g
127 ἔμπροσθεν G g (A): *aliis* L: om. C

μένος, εἰς τὸ καὶ αὐτοὺς τὸ αὐτὸ ποιῆσαι, οἱ μὲν
δυνάμενοι πεζοὺς πέμψαι, οἱ δὲ ἐπιστολὰς διὰ τῶν ὑπὸ
σου πεμπομένων, ἵνα δοξασθῆτε[128] αἰωνίῳ ἔργῳ,[129] ὡς
ἄξιος ὤν. 2. ἀσπάζομαι πάντας ἐξ ὀνόματος καὶ τὴν
τοῦ Ἐπιτρόπου σὺν ὅλῳ τῷ οἴκῳ αὐτῆς καὶ τῶν
τέκνων. ἀσπάζομαι Ἄτταλον τὸν ἀγαπητόν μου.
ἀσπάζομαι τὸν μέλλοντα καταξιοῦσθαι τοῦ εἰς Συρίαν πορεύεσθαι. ἔσται ἡ χάρις μετ᾽ αὐτοῦ διὰ παντὸς
καὶ τοῦ πέμποντος αὐτὸν Πολυκάρπου. 3. ἐρρῶσθαι
ὑμᾶς διὰ παντὸς ἐν θεῷ ἡμῶν Ἰησοῦ Χριστῷ εὔχομαι,
ἐν ᾧ διαμείνητε ἐν ἑνότητι θεοῦ καὶ ἐπισκοπῇ.[130]
ἀσπάζομαι Ἄλκην, τὸ ποθητόν μοι ὄνομα. ἔρρωσθε ἐν
κυρίῳ.[131]

[128] δοξασθῆς L: δοξάσωσιν C
[129] αἰωνίῳ ἔργῳ G L: ἐν αἰωνίῳ ἔργῳ g (A): θεὸν αἰώνιον ἐν
ἔργῳ C
[130] ἐπισκόπου A
[131] κυρίῳ: add πρὸς Πολύκαρπον G

who has the mind of God, that they may do the same thing as well. Some can send messengers by foot; but others can send letters through those whom you send yourself, so that all of you may be glorified by an eternal work, since you yourself are worthy. 2. I greet all by name, and the wife of Epitropus, along with the entire household of her and her children. I greet Attalus, my beloved. I greet the one who is about to be deemed worthy to go to Syria. God's grace will be with him constantly, and with Polycarp who sends him. 3. I bid you constant farewell in our God Jesus Christ. May you remain in him, in the unity and care that comes from God. I greet Alce, a name dear to me. Farewell in the Lord.

LETTER OF POLYCARP
TO THE PHILIPPIANS

INTRODUCTION

In some ways we are better informed about Polycarp of
Smyrna than any other Christian of the early second century. Among the writings of the Apostolic Fathers, there
is one text written *to* him (by Ignatius), another written
about him (the *Martyrdom of Polycarp*), and yet another
written *by* him, a letter sent to the Christians of Philippi.

Overview

It must be admitted that this letter has rarely ranked
high in the estimation of most students of the Apostolic Fathers. It is commonly judged to lack originality and insight,
consisting, as it does, of a pastiche of early Christian traditions, written and oral, related just loosely to the evident
occasion of the letter. Other readers, however, have found
the letter significant, both for what it says and for the circumstances that appear to have occasioned it.

The letter appears to respond to several concerns. Most
obviously, Polycarp indicates that the Philippians had sent
him a request for the letters of Ignatius, those "that he sent
to us, along with all the others we had with us" (13.2). This
then is a cover letter being sent back to the Philippians
with the collection of Ignatian writings that Polycarp had
gathered, a collection that would have included the letters

to the Smyrnean church and to Polycarp himself as well as those Ignatius wrote while staying in Smyrna on his way to martyrdom in Rome (the letters to the Ephesians, Magnesians, Trallians, and Romans, of which copies may have been made before being sent off). It is hard to tell whether it would have also included the letter to the Philadelphians, but many scholars believe that the surviving group of seven of Ignatius's letters (the so-called "middle recension": see Introduction to the Letters of Ignatius) ultimately stems from this collection that Polycarp forwarded to the Philippians.

Polycarp mentions several other reasons for this cover letter.

(1) Both the Philippians and Ignatius, when he had been among them, had expressed a wish for Polycarp to forward a letter from the Philippians to Antioch when he had the opportunity to do so (see Introduction to the Letters of Ignatius). Polycarp uses the present letter, in part, to indicate how he plans to respond to the request (13.1).

(2) Polycarp has learned of some kind of malfeasance by one of the former presbyters of Philippi, a man named Valens. It appears that Valens, along with his wife, had engaged in some shady dealings, possibly involving the church's finances. Polycarp writes to express his sorrow, to suggest how to deal with the situation, and to urge his readers not to be caught up in the "love of money" (11.1–4).

(3) Polycarp appears concerned that heretical teachings are making an inroad into the church in Philippi, and he urges his readers to shun anyone who refuses to say that Christ was fully human and who, as a consequence, denies the reality of the future resurrection and judgment (7.1). The one who takes this view, he avers, is the "firstborn of

Satan"—a term that, according to the later witness of
Irenaeus, Polycarp explicitly applied to Marcion, the
infamous heretic of the mid-second century (possibly
around 140 CE; Iren. *Adv. Haer.* 3.3.4).

(4) Most of the letter, rather than dealing directly with
these sundry issues, urges the Philippians to engage in upright behavior; Polycarp himself says he is writing in response to the Philippians' request for some words about
"righteousness" (3.1). The ultimate purpose of Polycarp's
letter, in other words, appears to be to encourage and admonish his readers to lead moral and respectable lives. To
accomplish this aim, he cites a large number of early Christian traditions and commonplaces, in quotations and remi-
niscences of the words of Jesus (probably from written
texts, such as the Gospel of Matthew; see *Pol. Phil.* 2.3),
the letters of Paul (esp. 1 Corinthians, Ephesians, and the
Pastoral epistles; see 4.1; 5.2, 3, and 12.1), and other early
Christian texts such as 1 Peter (see, e.g., 1.3 and 8.1).

Critical Issues in the Letter

Despite these relatively straightforward reasons for
writing, Polycarp's letter to the Philippians has puzzled
careful readers. Among the various problems it presents,
none has proved so thorny as the apparent discrepancy between chapters 9 and 13, and its implications for both the
date and the integrity of the letter. In chapter 13, Polycarp
indicates that Ignatius and the Philippians had asked him
to take along a letter from the Philippians to Syria; he then
gives the Philippians a request of his own, to let him know
if they have learned anything more definite about Ignatius
and "those who are with him" (*qui cum eo sunt.* This por-

tion of the letter is preserved only in Latin; see below). Both these requests suggest that Ignatius had recently passed through Philippi and that, to Polycarp's knowledge at least, he had not yet reached Rome and attained his goal of martyrdom. Polycarp wants to know what happened.

In chapter 9, however, Polycarp shows that he knows that like Paul and other apostles, Ignatius had already been martyred for his faith: "You should be convinced that none of them acted in vain, but in faith and righteousness, and that they are in the place they deserved, with the Lord, with whom they also suffered" (9. 2). This passage then suggests that the letter was written later, after Ignatius's death—possibly much later.

Since the seventeenth century scholars have pondered this evident inconsistency and its implications. Three major solutions to the problem have been proposed:

(a) Some scholars have argued that the discrepancy is only apparent, that Polycarp did indeed know that Ignatius had been martyred (thus chapter 9) but did not yet know the details (thus his request for further information in chapter 13).

(b) Others have thought the discrepancy is real, since in chapter 13 Polycarp does indeed seem to speak of Ignatius as still living (mentioning his wish for someone to go on to Syria with letters and speaking of "those who are with him"), and so have proposed that either chapter 9 or chapter 13, or both, have been interpolated into Polycarp's letter by a later Christian author, possibly by someone who wanted to show that a surviving collection of Ignatian letters derives directly from the work of his friend Polycarp.

(c) Others have thought that the discrepancy is real but that there is not sufficient evidence to indicate that either chapter 9 or chapter 13 represents an interpolation from the pen of someone other than Polycarp. The natural conclusion, then, is that Polycarp wrote both chapters, but at different times (ch. 13 while Ignatius was on the road to martyrdom, ch. 9 after his death). In this case, the letter to the Philippians that we now have was originally two separate letters that only later came to be combined into one.

This final solution was forcefully put forth by P. N. Harrison in 1936, and achieved a kind of consensus status for most of the rest of the twentieth century. More fully stated, Harrison maintained that soon after Ignatius passed through Smyrna and then Philippi on his way to Rome, around 110 CE, Polycarp wrote a letter in response to the Philippians' request for a collection of Ignatius's letters. Then, some twenty or twenty-five years later, Polycarp wrote a separate letter, again to the Philippians, in which he dealt with the problems of heresy and the sad case of Valens that had arisen in the Philippian church. Only at a later time did someone combine the two letters, which had been kept by the Philippian church, possibly in order to provide a copy of Polycarp's writings for some other community. This final editor then put the two available letters together, removing the ending of the second letter (chs. 1–12) and the opening of the first (chs. 13–14).

On the surface of it there is nothing implausible about this reconstruction. As Harrison noted, there are a number of instances among the early Christian writings in which several letters were combined into one (e.g., probably 2 Corinthians in the New Testament, and almost certainly the Epistle to Diognetus in the Apostolic Fathers). And the view would further explain why the heresy attacked in the early parts of the letter sounds so much like Marcion, who did not perpetrate his views until the late 130s at the earliest, long after the death of Ignatius (for Harrison the heretical views sound Marcionite because they *were* Marcionite). It also explains why, in the first twelve chapters of the letter, Polycarp shows such a familiarity with so many of the writings that later came to be regarded as parts of the New Testament (e.g., Matthew, 1 Corinthians, 1 Peter), when earlier writers such as Ignatius and 1 Clement show no such familiarity. This reconstruction is made even more plausible by the circumstance that Polycarp lived at least another forty years after he had met Ignatius (see Introduction to the *Martyrdom of Polycarp*).

This view continues to hold sway among the majority of scholars today, even though strong objections have been raised anew against it, both by those who subscribe to theories of interpolation (Lechner) and by those who think the integrity of the entire letter can be maintained (Schoedel).

Manuscript Tradition

The manuscript tradition for the Epistle of Polycarp is unusually deficient. There are nine surviving Greek manuscripts, but they all break off in 9.2 after the words καὶ δι' ὑμᾶς ὑπό, which are immediately followed then by Barnabas 5.7 (τὸν λαὸν τὸν καινόν) and the rest of the letter of Barnabas. Obviously all nine manuscripts go back to the same exemplar; when they differ among themselves, Codex Vaticanus Graecus 859 is usually judged as standing closest to the archetype.

The remaining portion of the letter is preserved in manuscripts of a Latin translation and in two Greek quotations by Eusebius of all of chapter 9 and all of chapter 13, except the final sentence. There are also Syriac fragments of chapter 12.

The *editio princeps* of the Latin text was published by Jacques Lefèvre d'Étaples in 1498. The Greek was first published by P. Halloix in 1633; James Ussher published an improved text of the Greek in 1644.

Abbreviations

G   the combined witness of the nine defective Greek manuscripts (11th c. and later)
    Individual Greek manuscripts: v, o, f, p, c, t, n, s, a (in terms of textual groupings, these usually stand in the following combinations: vofp / ctns / a)

L   the combined witness of the Latin manuscripts
    Individual Latin manuscripts: r, t, c, b, o, p, f, v, m

Eus Eusebius

SELECT BIBLIOGRAPHY

Barnard, L. W. "The Problem of St. Polycarp's Epistle to the Philippians." *CQR* 163 (1962) 421–30.

Bauer, Johannes B. *Die Polykarpbriefe*. KAV 5. Göttingen: Vandenhoeck and Ruprecht, 1995.

Camelot, P. T. *Ignace d'Antioche: Lettres. Lettres et Martyre de Polycarpe de Smyrne*. 4th ed. SC, 10. Paris: Cerf, 1969.

Campenhausen, Hans F. von. *Polykarp von Smyrna und die Pastoralbriefe*. Heidelberg: Carl Winter, 1951.

Dehandschutter, Boudewijn. "Polycarp's Epistle to the Philippians: An Early Example of 'Reception'." In *The*

New Testament in Early Christianity, ed. Jean-Marie Sevrin. Leuven: Peeters, 1989; 275–91.

Harrison, P. N. *Polycarp's Two Epistles to the Philippians*. Cambridge: University Press, 1936.

Lechner, Thomas. *Ignatius adversus Valentinianos? Chronologische und theologiegeschichtliche Studien zu den Briefen des Ignatius von Antiochen*. VCSup. 47. Leiden: Brill, 1999.

Lightfoot, Joseph Barber. *The Apostolic Fathers: Clement, Ignatius, and Polycarp*. Part II: *Ignatius and Polycarp*. 3 vols. London: Macmillan, 1889; reprinted Peabody, Mass.: Hendrickson, 1989.

Paulsen, Henning. *Die Briefe des Ignatius von Antiochia und der Brief des Polykarp von Smyrna*, 2. neubearbeitete Aufl. der Auslegung von Walter Bauer. Tübingen: Mohr Siebeck, 1985.

Schoedel, William R.. *Polycarp, Martyrdom of Polycarp. Fragments of Papias*. Vol. 5 of *The Apostolic Fathers: A New Translation and Commentary*, ed. Robert M. Grant. Camden, N.J.: Thomas Nelson, 1967.

——— "Polycarp of Smyrna and Ignatius of Antioch." *ANRW* II.27.1 (1993) 272–358.

ΤΟΥ ΑΓΙΟΥ ΠΟΛΥΚΑΡΠΟΥ

ΕΠΙΣΚΟΠΟΥ ΣΜΥΡΝΗΣ ΚΑΙ ΙΕΡΟΜΑΡΤΥΡΟΣ
ΠΡΟΣ ΦΙΛΙΠΠΗΣΙΟΥΣ ΕΠΙΣΤΟΛΗ[1]

Πολύκαρπος καὶ οἱ σὺν αὐτῷ πρεσβύτεροι τῇ ἐκκλησίᾳ τοῦ θεοῦ τῇ παροικούσῃ Φιλίππους· ἔλεος ὑμῖν
καὶ εἰρήνη παρὰ θεοῦ παντοκράτορος καὶ Ἰησοῦ Χριστοῦ τοῦ σωτῆρος ἡμῶν πληθυνθείη.

1

Συνεχάρην ὑμῖν μεγάλως ἐν τῷ κυρίῳ ἡμῶν Ἰησοῦ
Χριστῷ, δεξαμένοις[2] τὰ μιμήματα τῆς ἀληθοῦς ἀγάπης καὶ προπέμψασιν, ὡς ἐπέβαλεν ὑμῖν, τοὺς ἐνειλημένους[3] τοῖς ἁγιοπρεπέσιν δεσμοῖς, ἅτινά ἐστιν δια-
δήματα τῶν ἀληθῶς ὑπὸ θεοῦ καὶ τοῦ κυρίου ἡμῶν
ἐκλελεγμένων· 2. καὶ ὅτι ἡ βεβαία τῆς πίστεως ὑμῶν
ῥίζα, ἐξ ἀρχαίων καταγγελλομένη χρόνων, μέχρι νῦν
διαμένει καὶ καρποφορεῖ εἰς τὸν κύριον ἡμῶν Ἰησοῦν
Χριστόν, ὃς ὑπέμεινεν ὑπὲρ τῶν ἁμαρτιῶν ἡμῶν ἕως
θανάτου καταντῆσαι, ὃν ἤγειρεν ὁ θεός, λύσας τὰς

---

[1] του αγιου . . . επιστολη G: incipit epistola beati Policarpi

LETTER OF POLYCARP
BISHOP OF SMYRNA AND MARTYR
TO THE PHILIPPIANS

Polycarp and the presbyters who are with him to the church of God that temporarily resides in Philippi. May mercy and peace be multiplied to you from God Almighty and Jesus Christ our savior.

1

I greatly rejoice together with you in our Lord Jesus Christ. For you have received the replicas of true love and have, as was incumbent upon you, sent ahead those who were confined in chains fitting for the saints, crowns for those who have truly been chosen by God and our Lord. 2. And I rejoice that the secure root of your faith, proclaimed from ancient times, even now continues to abide and bear fruit in our Lord Jesus Christ. He persevered to the point of death on behalf of our sins; and God raised

---

Smirnaeorum ecclesiae episcopi ad Philippenses confirmantis fidem eorum L (with variations)

2 δεξαμένοις G: δεξάμενος L

3 ἐνειλημένους Gpc: ἐνειλημμένους Gv o f n a (t): ἐνειλιγμένους cj. Zahn

ὠδῖνας τοῦ ᾅδου· 3. εἰς ὃν οὐκ ἰδόντες πιστεύετε χαρᾷ
ἀνεκλαλήτῳ καὶ δεδοξασμένῃ, εἰς ἣν πολλοὶ ἐπιθυμοῦσιν εἰσελθεῖν, εἰδότες, ὅτι χάριτί ἐστε σεσωσμέ-
νοι, οὐκ ἐξ ἔργων, ἀλλὰ θελήματι θεοῦ διὰ Ἰησοῦ
Χριστοῦ.

2

Διὸ ἀναζωσάμενοι τὰς ὀσφύας ὑμῶν δουλεύσατε τῷ
θεῷ ἐν φόβῳ καὶ ἀληθείᾳ, ἀπολιπόντες τὴν κενὴν
ματαιολογίαν καὶ τὴν τῶν πολλῶν πλάνην, πιστεύσαντες εἰς τὸν ἐγείραντα τὸν κύριον ἡμῶν Ἰησοῦν
Χριστὸν ἐκ νεκρῶν καὶ δόντα αὐτῷ δόξαν καὶ θρόνον
ἐκ δεξιῶν αὐτοῦ· ᾧ ὑπετάγη τὰ πάντα ἐπουράνια καὶ
ἐπίγεια, ᾧ πᾶσα πνοὴ λατρεύσει,[4] ὃς ἔρχεται κριτὴς
ζώντων καὶ νεκρῶν, οὗ τὸ αἷμα ἐκζητήσει ὁ θεὸς ἀπὸ
τῶν ἀπειθούντων αὐτῷ. 2. ὁ δὲ ἐγείρας αὐτὸν ἐκ
νεκρῶν καὶ ἡμᾶς ἐγερεῖ, ἐὰν ποιῶμεν αὐτοῦ τὸ θέλημα
καὶ πορευώμεθα ἐν ταῖς ἐντολαῖς αὐτοῦ καὶ ἀγαπῶμεν,
ἃ ἠγάπησεν, ἀπεχόμενοι πάσης ἀδικίας, πλεονεξίας,
φιλαργυρίας, καταλαλιᾶς, ψευδομαρτυρίας· μὴ ἀπο-
διδόντες κακὸν ἀντὶ κακοῦ ἢ λοιδορίαν ἀντὶ λοιδορίας
ἢ γρόνθον ἀντὶ γρόνθου ἢ κατάραν ἀντὶ κατάρας·
3. μνημονεύοντες δὲ ὧν εἶπεν ὁ κύριος διδάσκων· μὴ
κρίνετε, ἵνα μὴ κριθῆτε· ἀφίετε, καὶ ἀφεθήσεται ὑμῖν·
ἐλεᾶτε, ἵνα ἐλεηθῆτε· ᾧ μέτρῳ μετρεῖτε, ἀντιμετρη-

---

4 λατρεύσει G⁰ f c t n a (p): λατρεύει Gᵛ L

him up after loosing the labor pains of Hades.[1] 3. Even without seeing him, you believe in him with an inexpressible and glorious joy[2] that many long to experience. For you know that you have been saved by a gracious gift—not from works[3] but by the will of God through Jesus Christ.

2

Therefore, bind up your loose robes and serve as God's slaves in reverential fear and truth, abandoning futile reasoning and the error that deceives many, and believing in the one who raised our Lord Jesus Christ from the dead and gave him glory[4] and a throne at his right hand. Everything in heaven and on earth is subject to him;[5] everything that breathes will serve him; he is coming as a judge of the living and the dead;[6] and God will hold those who disobey him accountable for his blood. 2. But the one who raised him from the dead will raise us as well,[7] if we do his will, walking in his commandments and loving the things he loved, abstaining from every kind of injustice, greed, love of money, slander, and false witness, not paying back evil for evil, or abuse for abuse,[8] or blow for blow, or curse for curse, 3. but remembering what the Lord said when he taught: "Do not judge lest you be judged; forgive and it will be forgiven you; show mercy that you may be shown mercy; the amount you dispense will be the amount you

---

[1] Acts 2:24. [2] 1 Pet 1:8.
[3] Eph 2:5, 8–9. [4] 1 Pet 1:21.
[5] Cf. 1 Cor 15:28; Phil 2:10; 3:21.
[6] Acts 10:42. [7] Cf. 2 Cor 4:14.
[8] 1 Pet 3:9.

θήσεται ὑμῖν· καὶ ὅτι μακάριοι οἱ πτωχοὶ[5] καὶ οἱ διωκόμενοι ἕνεκεν δικαιοσύνης, ὅτι αὐτῶν ἐστὶν ἡ βασιλεία τοῦ θεοῦ.

3

Ταῦτα, ἀδελφοί, οὐκ ἐμαυτῷ ἐπιτρέψας γράφω ὑμῖν περὶ τῆς δικαιοσύνης, ἀλλ᾿ ἐπεὶ ὑμεῖς προεπεκαλέσασθέ με. 2. οὔτε γὰρ ἐγὼ οὔτε ἄλλος ὅμοιος ἐμοὶ δύναται κατακολουθῆσαι τῇ σοφίᾳ τοῦ μακαρίου καὶ ἐνδόξου Παύλου, ὃς γενόμενος ἐν ὑμῖν κατὰ πρόσωπον τῶν τότε ἀνθρώπων ἐδίδαξεν ἀκριβῶς καὶ βεβαίως τὸν περὶ ἀληθείας λόγον, ὃς καὶ ἀπὼν ὑμῖν ἔγραψεν ἐπιστολάς, εἰς ἃς ἐὰν ἐγκύπτητε, δυνηθήσεσθε οἰκοδομεῖσθαι εἰς τὴν δοθεῖσαν ὑμῖν πίστιν. 3. ἥτις ἐστὶν μήτηρ πάντων ἡμῶν, ἐπακολουθούσης τῆς ἐλπίδος, προαγούσης τῆς ἀγάπης τῆς εἰς θεὸν καὶ Χριστὸν καὶ εἰς τὸν πλησίον. ἐὰν γάρ τις τούτων ἐντὸς ᾖ, πεπλήρωκεν ἐντολὴν δικαιοσύνης· ὁ γὰρ ἔχων ἀγάπην μακράν ἐστιν πάσης ἁμαρτίας.

4

Ἀρχὴ δὲ πάντων χαλεπῶν[6] φιλαργυρία. εἰδότες οὖν, ὅτι οὐδὲν εἰσηνέγκαμεν εἰς τὸν κόσμον, ἀλλ᾿ οὐδὲ ἐξενεγκεῖν τι ἔχομεν, ὁπλισώμεθα τοῖς ὅπλοις τῆς

---

[5] πτωχοὶ G: add *spiritu* L   [6] χαλεπῶν G: κακῶν L

receive in return."[9] And, "blessed are the poor and those persecuted for the sake of righteousness, because the kingdom of God belongs to them."[10]

3

I am writing these things about righteousness, brothers, not on my own initiative but at your request. 2. For neither I nor anyone like me is able to replicate the wisdom of the blessed and glorious Paul. When he was with you he accurately and reliably taught the word of truth to those who were there at the time. And when he was absent he wrote you letters. If you carefully peer into them, you will be able to be built up in the faith that was given you. 3. This faith is the mother of us all,[11] with hope following close after, and the love of God, Christ, and neighbor leading the way. For anyone centered in these has fulfilled the commandment of righteousness. For the one who has love is far removed from all sin.

4

The love of money is the beginning of all difficulties.[12] And so, since we know that we brought nothing into the world and can take nothing out of it,[13] we should arm our-

---

[9] Matt 7:1–2; Luke 6:36–38; cf. 1 Clem 13:2.
[10] Luke 6:20; Matt 5:10.
[11] Gal 4:26.
[12] Cf. 1 Tim 6:10.
[13] Cf. 1 Tim 6:7.

δικαιοσύνης καὶ διδάξωμεν ἑαυτοὺς πρῶτον πορεύεσθαι ἐν τῇ ἐντολῇ τοῦ κυρίου· 2. ἔπειτα καὶ τὰς
γυναῖκας ἡμῶν[7] ἐν τῇ δοθείσῃ αὐταῖς πίστει καὶ
ἀγάπῃ καὶ ἁγνείᾳ, στεργούσας τοὺς ἑαυτῶν ἄνδρας ἐν
πάσῃ ἀληθείᾳ καὶ ἀγαπώσας πάντας ἐξ ἴσου ἐν πάσῃ
ἐγκρατείᾳ, καὶ τὰ τέκνα παιδεύειν τὴν παιδείαν τοῦ
φόβου τοῦ θεοῦ· 3. τὰς χήρας σωφρονούσας περὶ τὴν
τοῦ κυρίου πίστιν, ἐντυγχανούσας ἀδιαλείπτως περὶ
πάντων, μακρὰν οὔσας πάσης διαβολῆς, καταλαλιᾶς,
ψευδομαρτυρίας, φιλαργυρίας καὶ παντὸς κακοῦ·
γινωσκούσας, ὅτι εἰσὶ θυσιαστήριον θεοῦ καὶ ὅτι
πάντα μωμοσκοπεῖται, καὶ λέληθεν αὐτὸν οὐδὲν οὔτε
λογισμῶν οὔτε ἐννοιῶν οὔτε τι τῶν κρυπτῶν τῆς
καρδίας.

5

Εἰδότες οὖν, ὅτι θεὸς οὐ μυκτηρίζεται, ὀφείλομεν
ἀξίως τῆς ἐντολῆς αὐτοῦ καὶ δόξης περιπατεῖν.
2. ὁμοίως διάκονοι ἄμεμπτοι κατενώπιον αὐτοῦ τῆς
δικαιοσύνης ὡς θεοῦ καὶ Χριστοῦ διάκονοι καὶ οὐκ
ἀνθρώπων· μὴ διάβολοι, μὴ δίλογοι,[8] ἀφιλάργυροι,
ἐγκρατεῖς περὶ πάντα, εὔσπλαγχνοι, ἐπιμελεῖς, πορευ-
όμενοι κατὰ τὴν ἀλήθειαν τοῦ κυρίου, ὃς ἐγένετο
διάκονος πάντων· ᾧ ἐὰν εὐαρεστήσωμεν ἐν τῷ νῦν

---

[7] ἡμῶν cj. Junius: ὑμῶν G L

[8] δίλογοι G v o f p n: δίγλωσσοι G t c a: *detractores* L

selves with the weapons of righteousness and teach one another, first of all, to walk in the commandment of the Lord. 2. Then we should teach our wives to walk in the faith given them and in love and purity; to be affectionate towards their own husbands in all truth;[14] to love everyone equally, with all self-restraint; and to discipline their children in the reverential fear of God.[15] 3. We should teach the widows to be self-controlled with respect to faith in the Lord, to pray without ceasing for everyone, and to be distant from all libel, slander, false witness, love of money, and all evil, knowing that they are God's altar and that each offering is inspected for a blemish[16] and that nothing escapes his notice, whether thoughts, ideas,[17] or any of the things hidden in the heart.[18]

5

Since we know that God is not mocked,[19] we should walk in a manner worthy of his commandment and glory. 2. So too the deacons should be blameless[20] before his righteousness as ministers of God and of Christ, not of humans. They should not be slanderous or insincere, but free from the love of money, self-restrained in every way, compassionate, attentive, and proceeding according to the truth of the Lord, who became a minister for everyone. If we are pleasing to him in the present age we will receive

[14] Cf. 1 Clem 1:3. [15] Cf. 1 Clem 21:6–8.
[16] Cf. 1 Clem 41:2. [17] Cf. 1 Clem 21:3.
[18] 1 Cor 14:25.
[19] Gal 6:7.
[20] Cf. 1 Tim 3:8–13.

αἰῶνι, ἀποληψόμεθα καὶ τὸν μέλλοντα, καθὼς ὑπ-
έσχετο ἡμῖν ἐγεῖραι ἡμᾶς ἐκ νεκρῶν, καὶ ὅτι ἐὰν
πολιτευσώμεθα ἀξίως αὐτοῦ, καὶ συμβασιλεύσομεν[9]
αὐτῷ, εἴγε πιστεύομεν. 3. ὁμοίως καὶ νεώτεροι ἄμεμπτοι ἐν πᾶσιν, πρὸ παντὸς προνοοῦντες ἁγνείας καὶ
χαλιναγωγοῦντες ἑαυτοὺς ἀπὸ παντὸς κακοῦ. καλὸν
γὰρ τὸ ἀνακόπτεσθαι ἀπὸ τῶν ἐπιθυμιῶν τῶν ἐν τῷ
κόσμῳ, ὅτι πᾶσα ἐπιθυμία κατὰ τοῦ πνεύματος στρα-
τεύεται καὶ οὔτε πόρνοι οὔτε μαλακοὶ οὔτε ἀρσενο-
κοῖται βασιλείαν θεοῦ κληρονομήσουσιν, οὔτε οἱ
ποιοῦντες τὰ ἄτοπα. διὸ δέον ἀπέχεσθαι ἀπὸ πάντων
τούτων, ὑποτασσομένους τοῖς πρεσβυτέροις καὶ διακόνοις ὡς θεῷ καὶ Χριστῷ· τὰς παρθένους ἐν ἀμώμῳ
καὶ ἁγνῇ συνειδήσει περιπατεῖν.

6

Καὶ οἱ πρεσβύτεροι δὲ εὔσπλαγχνοι, εἰς πάντας
ἐλεήμονες, ἐπιστρέφοντες τὰ ἀποπεπλανημένα, ἐπι-
σκεπτόμενοι πάντας ἀσθενεῖς, μὴ ἀμελοῦντες χήρας ἢ
ὀρφανοῦ ἢ πένητος· ἀλλὰ προνοοῦντες ἀεὶ τοῦ καλοῦ
ἐνώπιον θεοῦ καὶ ἀνθρώπων, ἀπεχόμενοι πάσης ὀρ-
γῆς, προσωποληψίας, κρίσεως ἀδίκου, μακρὰν ὄντες
πάσης φιλαργυρίας, μὴ ταχέως πιστεύοντες κατά
τινος, μὴ ἀπότομοι ἐν κρίσει, εἰδότες, ὅτι πάντες
ὀφειλέται ἐσμὲν ἁμαρτίας. 2. εἰ οὖν δεόμεθα τοῦ

---

[9] συμβασιλεύσομεν G[f]p L: -λεύσωμεν G v o t c n a

also the age that is coming, just as he promised that he would raise us from the dead and that, if we conducted ourselves worthily of him, we would also rule together with him[21]—so long as we believe. 3. So too let the young men be blameless in all things, concerned above all else for their purity, keeping themselves in check with respect to all evil. For it is good to be cut off from the passions of the world, since every passion wages war against the spirit,[22] and neither the sexually immoral, nor the effeminate, nor male prostitutes will inherit the kingdom of God;[23] nor will those who engage in aberrant behavior. Therefore we must abstain from all these things, and be subject to the presbyters and deacons as to God and Christ. And the virgins must walk in a blameless and pure conscience.

6

The presbyters also should be compassionate, merciful to all, turning back those who have gone astray, caring for all who are sick, not neglecting the widow, the orphan, or the poor, but always taking thought for what is good before both God and others,[24] abstaining from all anger, prejudice, and unfair judgment, avoiding all love of money, not quick to believe a rumor against anyone, not severe in judgment, knowing that we are all in debt because of sin. 2. And so if we ask the Lord to forgive us, we ourselves also

[21] 2 Tim 2:12.
[22] 1 Pet 2:11.
[23] 1 Cor 6:9.
[24] Prov 3:4; cf. 2 Cor 8:21.

κυρίου, ἵνα ἡμῖν ἀφῇ, ὀφείλομεν καὶ ἡμεῖς ἀφιέναι·
ἀπέναντι γὰρ τῶν τοῦ κυρίου καὶ θεοῦ ἐσμὲν ὀφθαλμῶν, καὶ πάντας δεῖ παραστῆναι τῷ βήματι τοῦ
Χριστοῦ καὶ ἕκαστον ὑπὲρ αὐτοῦ λόγον δοῦναι. 3.
οὕτως οὖν δουλεύσωμεν αὐτῷ μετὰ φόβου καὶ πάσης
εὐλαβείας, καθὼς αὐτὸς ἐνετείλατο καὶ οἱ εὐαγ-
γελισάμενοι ἡμᾶς[10] ἀπόστολοι καὶ οἱ προφῆται, οἱ
προκηρύξαντες τὴν ἔλευσιν τοῦ κυρίου ἡμῶν· ζηλωταὶ
περὶ τὸ καλόν, ἀπεχόμενοι τῶν σκανδάλων καὶ τῶν
ψευδαδέλφων καὶ τῶν ἐν ὑποκρίσει φερόντων τὸ
ὄνομα τοῦ κυρίου, οἵτινες ἀποπλανῶσι κενοὺς ἀνθρώπους.

7

Πᾶς γὰρ ὃς ἂν μὴ ὁμολογῇ, Ἰησοῦν Χριστὸν ἐν
σαρκὶ ἐληλυθέναι, ἀντίχριστός ἐστιν· καὶ ὃς ἂν μὴ
ὁμολογῇ τὸ μαρτύριον τοῦ σταυροῦ, ἐκ τοῦ διαβόλου
ἐστίν· καὶ ὃς ἂν μεθοδεύῃ τὰ λόγια τοῦ κυρίου πρὸς
τὰς ἰδίας ἐπιθυμίας καὶ λέγῃ μήτε ἀνάστασιν μήτε
κρίσιν, οὗτος πρωτότοκός ἐστι τοῦ σατανᾶ. 2. διὸ
ἀπολιπόντες τὴν ματαιότητα τῶν πολλῶν καὶ τὰς
ψευδοδιδασκαλίας ἐπὶ τὸν ἐξ ἀρχῆς ἡμῖν παραδο-
θέντα λόγον ἐπιστρέψωμεν, νήφοντες πρὸς τὰς εὐχὰς
καὶ προσκαρτεροῦντες νηστείαις, δεήσεσιν αἰτούμενοι
τὸν παντεπόπτην θεὸν μὴ εἰσενεγκεῖν ἡμᾶς εἰς
πειρασμόν, καθὼς εἶπεν ὁ κύριος· τὸ μὲν πνεῦμα
πρόθυμον, ἡ δὲ σὰρξ ἀσθενής.

ought to forgive; for we are before the eyes of the Lord and of God, and everyone must appear before the judgment seat of Christ, each rendering an account of himself.[25] 3. And so we should serve as his slaves, with reverential fear and all respect, just as he commanded, as did the apostles who proclaimed the gospel to us and the prophets who preached, in advance, the coming of our Lord. We should be zealous for what is good, avoiding stumbling blocks, false brothers, and those who carry the name of the Lord in hypocrisy, leading the empty-minded astray.

7

For anyone who does not confess that Jesus Christ has come in the flesh is an antichrist;[26] and whoever does not confess the witness of the cross is from the devil;[27] and whoever distorts the words of the Lord for his own passions, saying that there is neither resurrection nor judgment—this one is the firstborn of Satan. 2. And so, let us leave behind the idle speculation of the multitudes and false teachings and turn to the word that was delivered to us from the beginning, being alert in prayer and persistent in fasting. Through our entreaties let us ask the God who sees all things not to bring us into temptation,[28] just as the Lord said, "For the spirit is willing but the flesh is weak."[29]

[25] Cf. Rom 14:10, 12; 2 Cor 5:10.
[26] Cf. 1 John 4:2–3.
[27] Cf. 1 John 3:8.
[28] Matt 6:13.   [29] Matt 26:41.

---

10 ἡμᾶς G t c n s L: ὑμᾶς G v o f p n a

8

Ἀδιαλείπτως οὖν προσκαρτερῶμεν τῇ ἐλπίδι ἡμῶν καὶ
τῷ ἀρραβῶνι τῆς δικαιοσύνης ἡμῶν, ὅς ἐστι Χριστὸς
Ἰησοῦς, ὃς ἀνήνεγκεν ἡμῶν τὰς ἁμαρτίας τῷ ἰδίῳ
σώματι ἐπὶ τὸ ξύλον, ὃς ἁμαρτίαν οὐκ ἐποίησεν, οὐδὲ
εὑρέθη δόλος ἐν τῷ στόματι αὐτοῦ· ἀλλὰ δι᾽ ἡμᾶς, ἵνα
ζήσωμεν ἐν αὐτῷ, πάντα ὑπέμεινεν. 2. μιμηταὶ οὖν
γενώμεθα τῆς ὑπομονῆς αὐτοῦ,[11] καὶ ἐὰν πάσχομεν
διὰ τὸ ὄνομα αὐτοῦ, δοξάζωμεν αὐτόν. τοῦτον γὰρ
ἡμῖν τὸν ὑπογραμμὸν ἔθηκε δι᾽ ἑαυτοῦ, καὶ ἡμεῖς
τοῦτο ἐπιστεύσαμεν.

9

Παρακαλῶ οὖν πάντας ὑμᾶς πειθαρχεῖν τῷ λόγῳ τῆς
δικαιοσύνης καὶ ἀσκεῖν πᾶσαν ὑπομονήν,[12] ἣν καὶ
εἴδατε κατ᾽ ὀφθαλμοὺς οὐ μόνον ἐν τοῖς μακαρίοις
Ἰγνατίῳ καὶ Ζωσίμῳ καὶ Ῥούφῳ, ἀλλὰ καὶ ἐν ἄλλοις
τοῖς ἐξ ὑμῶν καὶ ἐν αὐτῷ Παύλῳ καὶ τοῖς λοιποῖς[13]
ἀποστόλοις· 2. πεπεισμένους, ὅτι οὗτοι πάντες οὐκ εἰς
κενὸν ἔδραμον, ἀλλ᾽ ἐν πίστει καὶ δικαιοσύνῃ, καὶ ὅτι
εἰς τὸν ὀφειλόμενον αὐτοῖς τόπον εἰσὶ παρὰ τῷ κυρίῳ,
ᾧ καὶ συνέπαθον. οὐ γὰρ τὸν νῦν ἠγάπησαν αἰῶνα,
ἀλλὰ τὸν ὑπὲρ ἡμῶν ἀποθανόντα καὶ δι᾽ ἡμᾶς ὑπὸ τοῦ
θεοῦ ἀναστάντα.

11 αὐτοῦ Gᶜ s t a nᵃ L: om. Gᵛ o f p n (corr.)

8

Thus we should persevere, unremitting in our hope and in the down payment of our righteousness, which is Christ Jesus, who bore our sins in his own body on the tree, who did not commit sin nor was deceit found in his mouth;[30] but he endured all things on our account, that we might live in him. 2. Therefore we should be imitators of his endurance, and if we suffer for his name, we should give him the glory. For he set this example for us through what he did,[31] and we have believed it.

9

Therefore I urge all of you to obey the word of righteousness and to practice all endurance, which you also observed with your own eyes not only in the most fortunate Ignatius, Zosimus, and Rufus, but also in others who lived among you, and in Paul himself and the other apostles. 2. You should be convinced that none of them acted in vain,[32] but in faith and righteousness, and that they are in the place they deserved, with the Lord, with whom they also suffered. For they did not love the present age;[33] they loved the one who died for us and who was raised by God for our sakes.

[30] 1 Pet 2:24, 22.   [31] Cf. 1 Pet 2:21.
[32] Phil 2:16.   [33] Cf. 2 Tim 4:10.

---

[12] ἀσκεῖν πᾶσαν ὑπομονήν Eus: ὑπομένειν πᾶσαν ὑπο-μονήν G: ὑπομονῆς L

[13] λοιποῖς G f p c t n s a o L Eus: ἄλλοις G v o*

10

In his ergo state et domini exemplar sequimini, firmi in fide et immutabiles, fraternitatis amatores, diligentes invicem, in veritate sociati, mansuetudine[14] domini alterutri praestolantes, nullum despicientes. 2. cum potestis[15] benefacere, nolite differre, quia eleemosyna de morte liberat. omnes vobis invicem subiecti estote, conversationem vestram irreprensibilem habentes in gentibus, ut ex bonis operibus vestris et vos laudem accipiatis et dominus in vobis non blasphemetur. 3. vae autem, per quem nomen domini blasphematur. sobrietatem ergo docete omnes, in qua et vos conversamini.

11

Nimis contristatus sum pro Valente, qui presbyter factus est aliquando apud vos, quod sic ignoret is locum, qui datus est ei. moneo itaque, ut abstineatis vos ab avaritia et sitis casti[16] veraces. abstinete vos ab omni malo. 2. qui autem non potest se in his gubernare, quomodo alii pronuntiat hoc? si quis non se abstinuerit ab avaritia, ab idolatria coinquinabitur et tamquam inter gentes iudicabitur, qui ignorant iudicium domini. aut nescimus, quia sancti mundum

---

14 *mansuetudine* cj. Hilgenfeld: *mansuetudinem* L
15 *potestis* L o b v c t: *possitis* L r p m f
16 *casti* L r p m v b c f t: add et L o

10

And so, you should stand firm in these things and follow the example of the Lord, secure and unmoveable in your faith, loving the brotherhood, caring for one another, united in the truth, waiting on one another in the gentleness of the Lord, looking down on no one. 2. When you are able to do good, do not put it off,[34] since giving to charity frees a person from death.[35] Let all of you be subject to one another, keeping your interactions with the outsiders above reproach, that by your good works you may receive praise and the Lord not be blasphemed because of you. 3. For woe to the one through whom the name of the Lord is blasphemed.[36] Teach all, therefore, to conduct themselves in a sober way, as you yourselves are doing.

11

I am extremely sad for Valens, once a presbyter among you, that he should so misunderstand the office that was given him. Thus I urge you to abstain from love of money and to be pure and truthful. Abstain from every kind of evil.[37] 2. For if someone cannot control himself in such things, how can he preach self-control to another?[38] Anyone who cannot avoid the love of money will be defiled by idolatry and will be judged as if among the outsiders who know nothing about the judgment of the Lord. Or do we

---

[34] Cf. Prov 3:28. [35] Tob 4:10.
[36] Cf. Isa 52:5. [37] Cf. 1 Thess 5:22.
[38] Cf. 1 Tim 3:5.

iudicabunt? sicut Paulus docet. 3. ego autem nihil tale sensi in vobis vel audivi, in quibus laboravit beatus Paulus, qui estis in principio epistulae eius. de vobis etenim gloriatur in omnibus ecclesiis, quae deum solae tunc[17] cognoverant; nos autem nondum cognoveramus. 4. valde ergo, fratres, contristor pro illo et pro coniuge eius, quibus det dominus paenitentiam veram. sobrii ergo estote et vos in hoc; et non sicut inimicos tales existimetis, sed sicut passibilia membra et errantia eos revocate, ut omnium vestrum corpus salvetis. hoc enim agentes vos ipsos aedificatis.

12

Confido enim vos bene exercitatos esse in sacris literis, et nihil vos latet; mihi autem non est concessum. modo, ut his scripturis dictum est, irascimini et nolite peccare, et sol non occidat super iracundiam vestram. beatus, qui meminerit; quod ego credo esse in vobis. 2. deus autem et pater domini nostri Iesu Christi, et ipse sempiternus pontifex, dei filius Iesus Christus, aedificet vos in fide et veritate et in omni mansuetudine et sine iracundia et in patientia et in longanimitate et tolerantia et castitate; et det vobis sortem et partem inter sanctos suos et nobis vobiscum et omnibus, qui sunt sub caelo, qui credituri sunt in dominum nostrum

---

[17] *deum solae tunc* L^r o v b c t: *solae tunc dominum* L^p m f

not realize that "the saints will judge the world?"[39] For so Paul teaches. 3. But I have neither perceived nor heard that you have any such thing in your midst, among whom the most fortunate Paul labored and who are found in the beginning of his epistle. For he exulted in you among all his churches, which alone knew God at that time; for we had not yet come to know him. 4. And so, my brothers, I am very sad for that man and his wife; may the Lord give them true repentance. And you yourselves should act in a sober way in this matter. Rather than judge such people as enemies, call them back as frail and wayward members, so as to heal your entire body. For when you do this, you build yourselves up.

12

I am confident that you are well trained in the sacred Scriptures and that nothing is hidden from you; but to me this has not been granted. Only, as it is written in these Scriptures, "Be angry and do not sin, and do not let the sun go down on your anger."[40] How fortunate is the one who remembers this; and I believe this to be the case among you. 2. So may the God and Father of our Lord Jesus Christ, and the eternal priest himself, the Son of God, Jesus Christ, build you up in faith and truth and in all gentleness, without anger, and in patience, forbearance, tolerance, and purity; and may he grant to you the lot and portion to be among his saints—and to us as well with you, and to everyone under heaven who is about to believe in

[39] 1 Cor 6:2.
[40] Eph 4:26; Ps 4:5.

et deum[18] Iesum Christum et in ipsius patrem, qui resuscitavit eum a mortuis. 3. pro omnibus sanctis orate. orate etiam pro regibus et potestatibus et principibus atque pro persequentibus et odientibus vos et pro inimicis crucis, ut fructus vester manifestus sit in omnibus, ut sitis in illo perfecti.

13

Ἐγράψατέ μοι καὶ ὑμεῖς καὶ Ἰγνάτιος, ἵν' ἐάν τις ἀπέρχηται εἰς Συρίαν, καὶ τὰ παρ' ὑμῶν ἀποκομίσῃ γράμματα· ὅπερ ποιήσω, ἐὰν λάβω καιρὸν εὔθετον, εἴτε ἐγώ, εἴτε ὃν πέμπω πρεσβεύσοντα καὶ περὶ ὑμῶν. 2. τὰς ἐπιστολὰς Ἰγνατίου τὰς πεμφθείσας ἡμῖν ὑπ' αὐτοῦ καὶ ἄλλας, ὅσας εἴχομεν παρ' ἡμῖν, ἐπέμψαμεν ὑμῖν, καθὼς ἐνετείλασθε· αἵτινες ὑποτεταγμέναι εἰσὶν τῇ ἐπιστολῇ ταύτῃ· ἐξ ὧν μεγάλα ὠφεληθῆναι δυνήσεσθε. περιέχουσι γὰρ πίστιν καὶ ὑπομονὴν καὶ πᾶσαν οἰκοδομὴν τὴν εἰς τὸν κύριον ἡμῶν ἀνήκουσαν. et de ipso Ignatio et de his, qui cum eo sunt, quod certius agnoveritis, significate.

14

Haec vobis scripsi per Crescentem, quem in praesenti commendavi vobis et nunc commendo. conversatus est

---

18 *et deum* L r p m f: om. L o v b c t

our Lord and God, Jesus Christ, and in his Father, who raised him from the dead. 3. Pray for all the saints.[41] Pray also for kings and magistrates and rulers, as well as for those who persecute and hate you[42] and for the enemies of the cross, that your fruit may be manifest to all and you may be made perfect in him.

13

Both you and Ignatius have written to me that if anyone is going to Syria he should take along your letter. I will do so if I have the opportunity—either I or someone I send as a representative on your behalf and mine. 2. We have forwarded to you the letters of Ignatius that he sent to us, along with all the others we had with us, just as you directed us to do. These accompany this letter; you will be able to profit greatly from them, for they deal with faith and endurance and all edification that is suitable in our Lord. And let us know what you have learned more definitely about Ignatius himself and those who are with him.

14

I am writing these things to you through Crescens, whom I commended to you recently *[Or: when I was with you]* and now commend again. For he has conducted himself

---

[41] Cf. Eph 6:18.
[42] Cf. Matt 5:44; Luke 6:27.

enim nobiscum inculpabiliter; credo quia et vobiscum similiter. sororem autem eius habebitis commendatam, cum venerit ad vos. incolumes estote in domino Iesu Christo in gratia cum omnibus vestris. Amen.

blamelessly among us; and I believe that he will do the same among you. And his sister will be commended to you when she comes to you. Farewell in the Lord Jesus Christ in grace, with all who are yours. Amen.

MARTYRDOM OF POLYCARP

INTRODUCTION

The Martyrdom of Polycarp has long occupied a place of special intrigue for readers of the Apostolic Fathers. This is an account, evidently based on the testimony of eyewitnesses, of the trial and execution of a prominent church leader of the first half of the second century, Polycarp, bishop of Smyrna. Known already from the letter addressed to him by Ignatius, an earlier martyr (whose own death is recounted only in later legends), and from the letter that he wrote to the church in Philippi (see the Letter of Polycarp), Polycarp was an important figure in the development of proto-orthodox Christianity. Tradition held that in his youth he was the follower of the disciple John and that later in life he became the teacher of Irenaeus, famous bishop of Gaul, forming a link between the apostles themselves and the emerging proto-orthodox community (Eusebius *Eccl. Hist.* 5.20; 4.14; see *Mart. Pol.* 22.2). In any event, this account of his death is the earliest Christian martyrology that we have outside of the New Testament description of the death of Stephen (Acts 7). It was not, however, written simply to recount the historical facts of Polycarp's arrest, trial, conviction, and execution. It was also meant to sanction a particular attitude and approach to martyrdom.

Overview

The Martyrdom of Polycarp is in the form of a letter sent by the church of Smyrna to the church of Philomelium, in Phrygia. Its actual author was an otherwise unknown Christian named Marcion (unrelated to the heretic of the same name reportedly opposed by Polycarp), who dictated the account to a scribe named Evaristus (20.1–2). This Marcion begins his account by informing his readers that Polycarp's death was no mere accident of history or miscarriage of justice: it occurred according to the will of God and happened "in conformity with the gospel" (1.1).

To illustrate the point, the account narrates numerous parallels between the deaths of Polycarp and Jesus. Like Jesus, we are told, Polycarp did not turn himself in, but waited to be betrayed (1.2); he knew about his coming execution in advance and predicted it to his followers (5.2); he prayed intensely before his arrest (7.2–3); he asked that God's will be done (7.1); the official in charge of his arrest was named Herod (6.2); he rode into town on a donkey (8.3); and so on.

This emphasis that Polycarp's martyrdom conformed to the will of God can be seen in other aspects of the account as well. Like other martyrs, who are mentioned only in passing (2.2–3), Polycarp receives such divine succor during his torture that he feels no terror and experiences no anguish (12.1; 15.2). When burned at the stake, he does not need to be secured to the upright with nails, but can stand of his own volition. When the conflagration begins, a miracle occurs: the flames do not touch his body but envelop him like a sheet. And rather than emitting a stench of burning flesh, his body exudes a sweet odor like perfume

(15.2). Since the flames cannot kill him, an executioner resorts to stabbing him with a dagger, which has the effect of releasing a dove from his side (his "holy" spirit, returning to heaven?), along with such a quantity of blood that it douses the flames (16.1).

The legendary details of the account, in other words, are designed to show God's stamp of approval on a martyrdom of this kind. The author does not want to insist, however, that every Christian is to suffer like this. Quite the contrary, one of the overarching points of the narrative is that even though a Christian brought up on charges should face death bravely, without denying Christ or performing the acts of sacrifice necessary to escape the ultimate penalty, one must not go out of the way to seek death by martyrdom. The point is stated explicitly early on in the narrative, in the brief account of Quintus, a Christian from Phrygia who volunteers for martyrdom and urges others to do so as well, only to turn coward when confronted by the beasts (ch. 4). And so the author says, "we do not praise those who hand themselves over, since this is not what the gospel teaches."

It may be, then, that this author wanted to present a moderating view of martyrdom to his Christian readership—against some groups of Gnostics on the one side, who insisted that God never calls a Christian to die for the faith (their logic, in part: since Jesus died for others, others need not die), and against some rigorist groups, on the other side, like the Montanists who later appeared in Quintus's home territory of Phyrgia and who believed in voluntary martyrdom. For this author, Polycarp did nothing to expedite his death (he actually went into hiding), and yet when his time came, he faced it faithfully and bravely, in imitation of Christ: "my king who has saved me," as he proudly announced at his interrogation, a king he had served for eighty-six years (9.3).

Several other ideas set forth in the account became standard features in the martyrological accounts that were to become increasingly popular among Christian readers: a person could be put to death simply for claiming to be Christian, and part of the crime involved "atheism," that is, not acknowledging the existence and power of the pagan gods (3.2; 9.2; 12.1); suffering martyrdom brings eternal life (which is no doubt why some Christians sought it out; 2.3); the temporary suffering at the hands of human torturers is nothing compared to the eternal torments reserved for those who oppose God (2.3); the struggle between antagonistic pagan mobs and Christians is actually a cosmic battle between the devil and God (2.4; 3.1; 17.1–2); and God's certain victory in this contest, seen above all in the fearless and proud demeanor of Christians in the face of death, could not help but attract the notice of pagan onlookers themselves (3.2; 16.1).

Also significant is (a) the claim that even though the obvious opponents of the Christians are the pagan mobs and ruling authorities (and the devil), it is the Jews who are ultimately responsible for the antagonism (13.1; 17.2); (b) the emphasis played on the sanctity of the body of the martyr, both before his death and afterwards, when his remains were preserved as relics (13.2; 17.1; 18.2); (c) the indication that celebrations were held to commemorate the martyrdoms on the anniversaries of their deaths (their "birthdays"! 18.3); and (d) the curious comment that Christians who were martyred were "no longer humans but already angels" (2.3).

Date and Integrity

Two of the most disputed issues in the modern study of the Martyrdom of Polycarp involve the integrity of its text (i.e., whether we have the original or a highly interpolated form) and the date of its composition.

Some scholars have held that the surviving text went through several stages of composition. H. von Campenhausen in particular maintained that the miraculous elements of the account, especially in the death scene itself, were added to a more straightforward description of Polycarp's death by a later pious redactor, and that someone else added the clear parallels to the passion narratives of the New Testament in order to stress that Polycarp's death conformed closely to that of Jesus (these parallels are not contained in the quotations of Eusebius). In addition, according to von Campenhausen, the anti-rigorist story about voluntary martyrs turned coward in chapter 4 was added later in opposition to Montanists.

More recent scholars have argued, however, that the book is a unified whole, written at one time by one author, with the exception, of course, of the material found in the colophon of chapter 22 concerning the history of the transmission of the text by various copyists over the years (and possibly ch. 21; see Barnard, Musurillo, Buschmann, Dehandshutter).

It appears that the letter was written soon after Polycarp was martyred; but there is no agreement about when that may have been. Chapter 21 indicates that it occurred when Philip of Tralles was the high priest of Asia and Statius Quadratus was proconsul. Unfortunately, the dates in which they each held office evidently did not overlap (Barnes). Moreover, a number of scholars believe that this chapter was added to the book only later, much as the post-script of 22.2–3 (or the alternative ending in the Moscow manuscript), so that it cannot provide a reliable guide to the dating. Eusebius locates the martyrdom in the rule of Marcus Aurelius (*Eccl. Hist.* 4. 14–15). But questions have been raised about the accuracy of his report: he may well have been making a best guess a century and a half after the fact.

A range of factors have influenced the discussions of dating, including (a) Polycarp's enigmatic statement made during the trial itself, that he had served Christ for eighty-six years (since his birth? since his baptism as an infant? since his baptism as a young adult?); (b) his documented relationship with Ignatius around 110 CE, when he was al-ready bishop of Smyrna; (c) the possibility that the text opposes a Montanist understanding of voluntary martyr-dom, and so would have to date after the appearance of Montanism in the early 170s. Weighing these data differ-ently, scholars are divided on whether the account should be dated as late as 177 (Gregoire and Orgels), some time in the late 160s (Telfer, Marrou, von Campenhausen, and Frend), or a decade earlier, possibly 155 or 156 (see Light-foot, Barnes, Musurillo, Schoedel, Bisbee, Bushmann, Dehandshutter). On balance, probably the majority of scholars favor the final view. This would mean that Poly-carp was born around 70 CE and became acquainted with Ignatius when about forty years of age, not quite half way through his long life.

Manuscripts, Abbreviations, and Editions

The epilogue (22.2–3, given differently in the Moscow manuscript), indicates the lineage of the manuscript once it was produced. A copy of the letter, we are told, was preserved in the personal library of Ireneaus; this was copied by a scribe named Gaius; the copy by Gaius was transcribed by Socrates; and this was later discovered and copied by Pionius. This is presumably the Pionius known from the third century, who was himself martyred during the persecution of Decius (ca. 250).

The text produced by Pionius is now preserved in seven Greek manuscripts, as follows:

a   Atheniensis (10th c.)
h   Hierosolymitanus (11th c.)
b   Baroccianus (11th c)
c   Chalcensis (11th c.)
p   Parisinus (10th c.)
v   Vindobonensis (11–12th c.)
m   Mosquensis (13th c.)

Of these, m stands out as distinctive in many of its readings, a good number of which agree with the quotations of Eusebius, who cites most of the document in his *Ecclesiastical History* 4.15 (although he paraphrases 2.2–7.3 and gives no citation of 19.2–22.3). In addition, there is a rather paraphrastic Latin translation (L), which occasionally provides assistance for establishing the Greek text.

The apparatus uses the following abbreviations, in addition to those of the individual manuscripts:

G   the agreement of all the Greek manuscripts
g   the agreement of all the manuscripts apart from m
Eus Eusebius

The *editio princeps* of the Martyrdom was published by James Ussher in 1647 (*Appendix Ignatiana*), based just on the eleventh-century Codex Baroccianus (b).

SELECT BIBLIOGRAPHY

Barnard, Leslie W. "In Defence of Pseudo-Pionius' Account of Polycarp's Martyrdom." In *Kyriakon: Festschrift Johannes Quasten*, ed. P. Granfield. Münster: Aschendorff, 1970; 1. 192–204.

Barnes, Timothy D. "A Note on Polycarp." *JTS* n.s. 18 (1967) 433–37.

_____ "Pre-Decian Acta Martyrium." *JTS* n.s. 19 (1968) 510–14.

Bisbee, Gary A. *Pre-Decian Acts of Martyrs and Commentarii.* Philadelphia: Fortress, 1988.

Buschmann, Gerd. *Martyrium Polycarpi: eine formkritische Studie, ein Beitrag zur Frage nach der Entstehung der Gattung Martyrerakte.* Berlin/New York: de Gruyter, 1994.

Camelot, P. T. *Ignace d'Antioche: Lettres. Lettres et Martyre de Polycarpe de Smyrne.* 4th ed. SC, 10. Paris: Cerf, 1969.

Campenhausen, Hans F. von. "Bearbeitungen und Interpolationen des Polykarpmartyriums." In *Aus der Frühzeit des Christentums.* Tübingen: Mohr-Siebeck, 1963.

Conzelmann, Hans. *Bemerkungen zum Martyrium Polykarps.* Göttingen: Vandenhoeck and Ruprecht, 1978.

Dehandschutter, Boudewijn. *Martyrium Polycarpi: een literair-kritische studie.* Leuven: Universitaire Leuven, 1979.

_____ "A 'New' Text of the Martyrdom of Polycarp." *ETL* 66 (1990) 391–94.

_____ "The Martyrium Polycarpi: A Century of Research (Bibliography)." *ANRW* II.27.1 (1993) 485–522.

Frend, W. H. C. "Note on the Chronology of the Martyrdom of Polycarp and the Outbreak of Montanism." In *Oikoumen; studi paleocristiani*, ed. J. Courcelle, et al. Catania: Universitá di Catania, 1964; 499–506.

Gregoire, H., and P. Orgels. "La veritable date du martyre de S. Polycarpe et le Corpus Polycarpianum." AnBoll 69 (1951) 1–38.

Lightfoot, Joseph Barber. *The Apostolic Fathers: Clement, Ignatius, and Polycarp.* Part II: *Ignatius and Polycarp.* 3 vols. London: Macmillan, 1889; reprinted Peabody, Mass.: Hendrickson, 1989.

Marrou, H.-I. "La Date du martyre de S. Polycarpe." AnBoll 71 (1953) 5–20.

Musurillo, H. A. *The Acts of the Christian Martyrs.* Oxford: Clarendon, 1972.

Schoedel, William. *Polycarp, Martyrdom of Polycarp. Fragments of Papias.* Vol. 5 of *The Apostolic Fathers: A New Translation and Commentary*, ed. Robert M. Grant. Camden, N.J.: Thomas Nelson, 1967.

——— "Polycarp of Smyrna and Ignatius of Antioch." ANRW II.27.1 (1993) 272–358.

Telfer, William. "The Date of the Martyrdom of Polycarp." JTS n.s. 3 (1952) 79–83.

ΜΑΡΤΥΡΙΟΝ ΤΟΥ ΑΓΙΟΥ
ΠΟΛΥΚΑΡΠΟΥ
ΕΠΙΣΚΟΠΟΥ ΣΜΥΡΝΗΣ

Ἡ ἐκκλησία τοῦ θεοῦ ἡ παροικοῦσα Σμύρναν τῇ
ἐκκλησίᾳ τοῦ θεοῦ[1] τῇ παροικούσῃ ἐν Φιλομηλίῳ[2] καὶ
πάσαις ταῖς κατὰ πάντα τόπον τῆς ἁγίας καὶ[3] καθολικῆς ἐκκλησίας παροικίαις· ἔλεος, εἰρήνη καὶ ἀγάπη
θεοῦ πατρὸς καὶ τοῦ[4] κυρίου ἡμῶν Ἰησοῦ Χριστοῦ
πληθυνθείη.

1

Ἐγράψαμεν ὑμῖν, ἀδελφοί,[5] τὰ κατὰ τοὺς μαρτυρή-
σαντας καὶ τὸν μακάριον Πολύκαρπον, ὅστις ὥσπερ
ἐπισφραγίσας διὰ τῆς μαρτυρίας αὐτοῦ κατέπαυσεν
τὸν διωγμόν. σχεδὸν γὰρ πάντα τὰ προάγοντα ἐγένετο, ἵνα ἡμῖν ὁ κύριος ἄνωθεν ἐπιδείξῃ τὸ κατὰ τὸ
εὐαγγέλιον μαρτύριον. 2. περιέμενεν γάρ, ἵνα παρα-
δοθῇ, ὡς καὶ ὁ κύριος, ἵνα μιμηταὶ καὶ ἡμεῖς αὐτοῦ
γενώμεθα, μὴ μόνον σκοποῦντες τὸ καθ᾽ ἑαυτούς,

---

[1] τῇ ἐκκλησίᾳ τοῦ θεοῦ a b m p Eus.: *ecclesiis dei* L: om. c h v

MARTYRDOM OF
SAINT POLYCARP,
BISHOP OF SMYRNA

The church of God that temporarily resides in Smyrna
to the church of God that temporarily resides in Philomelium, and to all congregations of temporary residents
everywhere, who belong to the holy and universal church.
May the mercy, peace, and love of God the Father and of
our Lord Jesus Christ be multiplied.

1

We are writing you, brothers, about those who were martyred, along with the blessed Polycarp, who put an end to
the persecution by, as it were, setting a seal on it through
his death as a martyr. For nearly everything leading up to
his death occurred so that the Lord might show us from
above a martyrdom in conformity with the gospel. 2. For
Polycarp waited to be betrayed, as also did the Lord, that
we in turn might imitate him, thinking not only of our-

---

2 Φιλομεληλίῳ: Φιλαδελφία b p

3 καὶ: om. v Eus.

4 τοῦ: om. c h Eus.

5 ἀδελφοὶ ἀγαπητοί m

ἀλλὰ καὶ τὸ κατὰ τοὺς πέλας. ἀγάπης γὰρ ἀληθοῦς
καὶ βεβαίας ἐστίν, μὴ μόνον ἑαυτὸν θέλειν σώζεσθαι,
ἀλλὰ καὶ πάντας τοὺς ἀδελφούς.

2

Μακάρια μὲν οὖν καὶ γενναῖα τὰ μαρτύρια πάντα τὰ
κατὰ τὸ θέλημα τοῦ θεοῦ γεγονότα. δεῖ γὰρ εὐλα-
βεστέρους ἡμᾶς ὑπάρχοντας τῷ θεῷ τὴν κατὰ πάντων
ἐξουσίαν ἀνατιθέναι. 2. τὸ γὰρ γενναῖον αὐτῶν[6] καὶ
ὑπομονητικὸν καὶ φιλοδέσποτον τίς οὐκ ἂν θαυ-
μάσειεν; οἳ μάστιξιν μὲν καταξανθέντες, ὥστε μέχρι
τῶν ἔσω φλεβῶν καὶ ἀρτηριῶν τὴν τῆς σαρκὸς οἰκονομίαν θεωρεῖσθαι, ὑπέμειναν, ὡς καὶ τοὺς περι-
εστῶτας ἐλεεῖν καὶ ὀδύρεσθαι· τοὺς δὲ καὶ εἰς τοσοῦτον γενναιότητος ἐλθεῖν, ὥστε μήτε γρύξαι μήτε
στενάξαι τινὰ αὐτῶν, ἐπιδεικνυμένους ἅπασιν ἡμῖν,
ὅτι ἐκείνῃ τῇ ὥρᾳ βασανιζόμενοι τῆς σαρκὸς ἀπεδή-
μουν οἱ[7] μάρτυρες τοῦ Χριστοῦ, μᾶλλον δέ, ὅτι
παρεστὼς ὁ κύριος ὡμίλει αὐτοῖς. 3. καὶ προσέχοντες
τῇ τοῦ Χριστοῦ χάριτι τῶν κοσμικῶν κατεφρόνουν
βασάνων, διὰ μιᾶς ὥρας τὴν αἰώνιον ζωὴν[8] ἐξαγο-
ραζόμενοι. καὶ τὸ πῦρ ἦν αὐτοῖς ψυχρὸν τὸ τῶν
ἀπανθρώπων[9] βασανιστῶν· πρὸ ὀφθαλμῶν γὰρ εἶχον
φυγεῖν τὸ αἰώνιον καὶ μηδέποτε σβεννύμενον,[10] καὶ

---

[6] αὐτῶν a b m: αὐτοῦ p: om. c h v
[7] οἱ b c v: add γενναιότατοι a h m p

selves, but also of our neighbors.[1] For anyone with true and certain love wants not only himself but also all the brothers to be saved.

2

Blessed and noble, therefore, are all the martyrdoms that have occurred according to the will of God. For we must be reverent and attribute the ultimate authority to God. 2. For who would not be astounded by their nobility, endurance, and love of the Master? For they endured even when their skin was ripped to shreds by whips, revealing the very anatomy of their flesh, down to the inner veins and arteries, while bystanders felt pity and wailed. But they displayed such nobility that none of them either grumbled or moaned, clearly showing us all that in that hour, while under torture, the martyrs of Christ had journeyed far away from the flesh, or rather, that the Lord was standing by, speaking to them. 3. And clinging to the gracious gift of Christ, they despised the torments of the world, in one hour purchasing for themselves eternal life. And the fire of their inhuman torturers was cold to them, because they kept their eyes on the goal of escaping the fire that is eternal and never extinguished. And with the eyes of their

---

[1] Phil 2:4.

---

8 ζωὴν m: κόλασιν g
9 ἀπανθρώπων (ἀπ$\overline{ανω}$ν) m: ἀπηνῶν (ἀπεινῶν h p) g
10 σβεννύμενον b h p: add πῦρ a c m v

τοῖς τῆς καρδίας ὀφθαλμοῖς ἀνέβλεπον[11] τὰ τηρού-
μενα τοῖς ὑπομείνασιν ἀγαθά, ἃ οὔτε οὖς ἤκουσεν
οὔτε ὀφθαλμὸς εἶδεν οὔτε ἐπὶ καρδίαν ἀνθρώπου ἀνέβη, ἐκείνοις δὲ ὑπεδείκνυτο ὑπὸ τοῦ κυρίου, οἵπερ[12]
μηκέτι[13] ἄνθρωποι, ἀλλ᾽ ἤδη ἄγγελοι ἦσαν. 4. ὁμοίως
δὲ καὶ οἱ εἰς τὰ θηρία κατακριθέντες ὑπέμειναν δεινὰς
κολάσεις, κήρυκας[14] μὲν ὑποστρωννύμενοι καὶ ἄλλαις
ποικίλων βασάνων ἰδέαις κολαφιζόμενοι,[15] ἵνα, εἰ δυνηθείη,[16] διὰ τῆς ἐπιμόνου κολάσεως εἰς ἄρνησιν
αὐτοὺς τρέψῃ.

3

Πολλὰ γὰρ ἐμηχανᾶτο κατ᾽ αὐτῶν ὁ διάβολος. ἀλλὰ
χάρις τῷ θεῷ· κατὰ πάντων γὰρ οὐκ ἴσχυσεν. ὁ γὰρ
γενναιότατος Γερμανικὸς ἐπερρώννυεν αὐτῶν τὴν δει-
λίαν διὰ τῆς ἐν αὐτῷ ὑπομονῆς· ὃς καὶ ἐπισήμως
ἐθηριομάχησεν. βουλομένου γὰρ τοῦ ἀνθυπάτου πεί-
θειν αὐτὸν καὶ λέγοντος, τὴν ἡλικίαν αὐτοῦ κατοι-
κτεῖραι, ἑαυτῷ ἐπεσπάσατο τὸ θηρίον προσβια-
σάμενος, τάχιον τοῦ ἀδίκου καὶ ἀνόμου βίου αὐτῶν
ἀπαλλαγῆναι βουλόμενος. 2. ἐκ τούτου οὖν πᾶν τὸ
πλῆθος, θαυμάσαν τὴν γενναιότητα τοῦ θεοφιλοῦς καὶ
θεοσεβοῦς γένους τῶν Χριστιανῶν, ἐπεβόησεν· αἶρε
τοὺς ἀθέους· ζητείσθω Πολύκαρπος.

11 ἀνέβλεπον b c v h p: ἐνέβλεπον a m
12 οἵπερ b: εἵπερ a c h p v: οἵτινες m
13 μηκέτι a b c h v: μὴ p: λοιπὸν οὐκέτι m

hearts they looked above to the good things preserved for those who endure, which no ear has heard nor eye seen, which have never entered into the human heart,[2] but which the Lord revealed to them, who were no long humans but already angels. 4. In a similar way, those who were condemned to the wild beasts endured horrible torments, stretched out on sharp shells and punished with various other kinds of tortures, that, if possible, he[3] might force them to make a denial through continuous torment.

3

For the devil devised many torments against them. But thanks be to God: he had no power over any of them. For the most noble Germanicus strengthened their cowardice through his endurance, and he fought the wild beasts impressively. For when the proconsul wanted to persuade him, saying "Take pity on your age," he forcefully dragged the wild beast onto himself, wanting to leave their unjust and lawless life without delay. 2. Because of this, the entire multitude, astounded by the great nobility of the godly and reverent race of the Christians, cried out, "Away with the atheists! Find Polycarp!"

[2] 1 Cor 2:9.
[3] I.e., the devil; see 3.1

---

[14] κήρυκας b m (Eus.): ξίφη c p v: ξίφει a h
[15] κολαφιζόμενοι g: κολαζόμενοι m
[16] δυνηθείη m: add ὁ τύραννος g

4

Εἷς δέ, ὀνόματι Κόϊντος, Φρύξ, προσφάτως ἐληλυθὼς
ἀπὸ τῆς Φρυγίας, ἰδὼν τὰ θηρία ἐδειλίασεν. οὗτος δὲ
ἦν ὁ παραβιασάμενος ἑαυτόν τε καί τινας προσελθεῖν
ἑκόντας. τοῦτον ὁ ἀνθύπατος πολλὰ ἐκλιπαρήσας
ἔπεισεν ὀμόσαι καὶ ἐπιθῦσαι. διὰ τοῦτο οὖν, ἀδελφοί,
οὐκ ἐπαινοῦμεν τοὺς προδιδόντας[17] ἑαυτούς,[18] ἐπειδὴ
οὐχ οὕτως διδάσκει τὸ εὐαγγέλιον.

5

Ὁ δὲ θαυμασιώτατος Πολύκαρπος τὸ μὲν πρῶτον
ἀκούσας οὐκ ἐταράχθη, ἀλλ᾽ ἐβούλετο κατὰ πόλιν
μένειν· οἱ δὲ πλείους ἔπειθον αὐτὸν ὑπεξελθεῖν. καὶ
ὑπεξῆλθεν εἰς ἀγρίδιον οὐ μακρὰν ἀπέχον ἀπὸ τῆς
πόλεως καὶ διέτριβεν μετ᾽ ὀλίγων,[19] νύκτα καὶ ἡμέραν
οὐδὲν ἕτερον ποιῶν ἢ προσευχόμενος περὶ πάντων καὶ
τῶν κατὰ τὴν οἰκουμένην ἐκκλησίων, ὅπερ ἦν σύνηθες
αὐτῷ. 2. καὶ προσευχόμενος ἐν ὀπτασίᾳ γέγονεν πρὸ
τριῶν ἡμερῶν τοῦ συλληφθῆναι αὐτόν, καὶ εἶδεν τὸ
προσκεφάλαιον αὐτοῦ ὑπὸ πυρὸς κατακαιόμενον· καὶ
στραφεὶς εἶπεν πρὸς τοὺς σὺν αὐτῷ·[20] δεῖ με ζῶντα
καυθῆναι.[21]

---

[17] προδιδόντας a h v: προσιόντας b m p: δίδοντας c: (se)
offerunt L
[18] ἑαυτοὺς a h m: ἑαυτοῖς b c p v L
[19] ὀλίγων ἀδελφῶν c v

4

But there was a person named Quintus, a Phrygian who
had recently come from Phrygia, who was overcome with
cowardice once he saw the wild beasts. This is the one
who compelled both himself and several others to turn
themselves in. But the insistent pleas of the proconsul convinced him to take the oath and offer a sacrifice. Because
of this, brothers, we do not praise those who hand themselves over, since this is not what the gospel teaches.

5

Now when the most marvelous Polycarp first heard, he was
not disturbed, but wanted to remain in the city. But most
of the others were persuading him to leave. And so he left
for a small country house not far from the city and stayed
there with a few others, night and day doing nothing but
pray for everyone and for the churches throughout the
world, as was his custom. 2. Three days before he was
arrested, while praying, he had a vision and saw his pillow
being consumed by fire. Then he turned to those with him
and said, "I must be burned alive."

---

20 αὐτῷ m L: add προφητικῶς g
21 καυθῆναι b c h p v: κατακαυθῆναι a: καῆναι m

6

Καὶ ἐπιμενόντων τῶν ζητούντων αὐτὸν μετέβη εἰς
ἕτερον ἀγρίδιον, καὶ εὐθέως ἐπέστησαν οἱ ζητοῦντες
αὐτόν· καὶ μὴ εὑρόντες συνελάβοντο παιδάρια δύο, ὧν
τὸ ἕτερον βασανιζόμενον ὡμολόγησεν.[22] 2. ἦν γὰρ καὶ
ἀδύνατον λαθεῖν αὐτόν, ἐπεὶ καὶ οἱ προδιδόντες αὐτὸν
οἰκεῖοι ὑπῆρχον. καὶ ὁ εἰρήναρχος, ὁ κεκληρωμένος τὸ
αὐτὸ ὄνομα, Ἡρώδης ἐπιλεγόμενος, ἔσπευδεν εἰς τὸ
στάδιον αὐτὸν εἰσαγαγεῖν, ἵνα ἐκεῖνος μὲν τὸν ἴδιον
κλῆρον ἀπαρτίσῃ, Χριστοῦ κοινωνὸς γενόμενος, οἱ δὲ
προδόντες αὐτὸν τὴν αὐτοῦ τοῦ Ἰούδα ὑπόσχοιεν
τιμωρίαν.[23]

7

Ἔχοντες οὖν τὸ παιδάριον,[24] τῇ παρασκευῇ περὶ
δείπνου ὥραν ἐξῆλθον διωγμῖται καὶ ἱππεῖς μετὰ τῶν
συνήθων αὐτοῖς ὅπλων ὡς ἐπὶ λῃστὴν τρέχοντες. καὶ
ὀψὲ τῆς ὥρας συνεπελθόντες ἐκεῖνον μὲν εὗρον ἔν τινι
δωματίῳ κατακείμενον ἐν ὑπερῴῳ· κἀκεῖθεν δὲ ἠδύνα-
το εἰς ἕτερον χωρίον ἀπελθεῖν, ἀλλ᾽ οὐκ ἠβουλήθη
εἰπών· τὸ θέλημα τοῦ θεοῦ[25] γενέσθω. 2. ἀκούσας οὖν
αὐτοὺς παρόντας, καταβὰς διελέχθη αὐτοῖς, θαυμα-
ζόντων τῶν παρόντων τὴν ἡλικίαν αὐτοῦ καὶ τὸ

[22] ὧν . . . ὡμολόγησεν b p m: ἃ καὶ βασανιζόμενα ὡμολόγησεν (a) c v (h)
[23] καὶ ὁ εἰρήναρχος . . . τιμωρίαν om. c v

6

While they continued searching for him, he moved to a different country house—just as those who were seeking him arrived at the other. Since they could not find him, they arrested two young slaves, one of whom made a confession under torture. 2. For it was impossible for him to keep in hiding, since the ones who betrayed him were members of his household. And the chief of police, who was called by the same name—for his name was Herod—was eager to lead him into the stadium, that he might fulfill his special destiny as a partner with Christ, while those who betrayed him might suffer the punishment of Judas himself.

7

And so, taking the young slave, on the Day of Preparation around the dinner hour, the mounted police and horsemen went out with their usual weapons, as if running down a thief.[4] And when the hour was late, they converged and found Polycarp lying down in a small room upstairs. He could have fled elsewhere even from there, but he chose not to, saying, "God's will be done."[5] 2. And so, when he heard them come in, he came downstairs and talked with them; and those who were there were astonished at how

[4] Matt 26:55. The Day of Preparation is Friday.
[5] Acts 21:14; cf. Luke 22:42; Matt 6:10.

---

24 τὰ παιδάρια c v
25 θεοῦ a c h p v Eus. L: κυρίου b m

εὐσταθές, καὶ[26] εἰ[27] τοσαύτη σπουδὴ ἦν τοῦ συλληφθῆναι τοιοῦτον[28] πρεσβύτην ἄνδρα. εὐθέως οὖν αὐτοῖς ἐκέλευσεν παρατεθῆναι φαγεῖν καὶ πιεῖν ἐν ἐκείνῃ τῇ ὥρᾳ ὅσον ἂν βούλωνται, ἐξῃτήσατο δὲ αὐτούς, ἵνα δῶσιν αὐτῷ ὥραν πρὸς τὸ προσεύξασθαι ἀδεῶς. 3. τῶν δὲ ἐπιτρεψάντων, σταθεὶς[29] προσηύξατο πλήρης ὢν τῆς χάριτος τοῦ θεοῦ οὕτως, ὡς[30] ἐπὶ δύο ὥρας[31] μὴ δύνασθαι σιωπῆσαι καὶ ἐκπλήττεσθαι τοὺς ἀκούοντας, πολλούς[32] τε μετανοεῖν ἐπὶ τῷ ἐληλυθέναι ἐπὶ τοιοῦτον θεοπρεπῆ πρεσβύτην.

8

Ἐπεὶ δέ ποτε κατέπαυσεν τὴν προσευχήν, μνημονεύσας ἁπάντων καὶ τῶν[33] πώποτε συμβεβληκότων αὐτῷ, μικρῶν τε καὶ μεγάλων, ἐνδόξων τε καὶ ἀδόξων καὶ πάσης τῆς κατὰ τὴν οἰκουμένην καθολικῆς ἐκκλησίας, τῆς ὥρας ἐλθούσης τοῦ ἐξιέναι, ὄνῳ καθίσαντες αὐτὸν ἤγαγον εἰς τὴν πόλιν, ὄντος σαββάτου μεγάλου.[34] 2. καὶ ὑπήντα αὐτῷ ὁ εἰρήναρχος Ἡρώδης[35] καὶ ὁ πατὴρ αὐτοῦ[36] Νικήτης, οἳ καὶ μεταθέντες αὐτὸν ἐπὶ τὴν καροῦχαν ἔπειθον παρακαθεζόμενοι καὶ λέγοντες· τί γὰρ κακόν ἐστιν εἰπεῖν· Κύριος Καῖσαρ, καὶ ἐπιθῦσαι καὶ τὰ τούτοις ἀκόλουθα καὶ διασώζεσθαι; ὁ δὲ τὰ μὲν πρῶτα οὐκ ἀπεκρίνατο αὐτοῖς, ἐπιμενόντων δὲ αὐτῶν ἔφη· οὐ μέλλω ποιεῖν, ὃ συμ-

---

[26] καὶ p Eus.: τινὲς ἔλεγον b: om. a c h m v

old and composed he was, and they wondered why there was so much haste to arrest an old man like him. Straight away he ordered them to be given everything they wanted to eat and drink, then and there. And he asked them for an hour to pray without being disturbed. 3. When they gave their permission, he stood and prayed, being so filled with God's grace that for two hours he could not be silent. Those who heard him were amazed, and many of them regretted coming out for such a godly old man.

8

Then he finished his prayer, having remembered everyone he had ever met, both small and great, reputable and disreputable, as well as the entire universal church throughout the world; and when it came time for him to leave, they seated him on a donkey and led him into the city. It was a great Sabbath.[6] 2. The chief of police Herod, along with his father Nicetas, met him and transferred him to their carriage. Sitting on either side, they were trying to persuade him, saying, "Why is it so wrong to save yourself by saying 'Caesar is Lord,' making a sacrifice, and so on?" He did not answer them at first; but when they persisted, he said, "I

6 Cf. John 19:31.

---

27 εἰ m Eus.: ἥ b c h v: ᾗ cj. Ussher: ὅτι p
28 τοιοῦτον θεοφιλεῖ m   29 σταθεὶς πρὸς ἀνατολὴν m
30 ὡς m Eus.: ὥστε g   31 ὥρας ἢ τρεῖς a
32 πολλούς om. c v   33 καὶ τῶν g Eus.: τῶν καὶ m
34 μεγάλου: om. p
35 Ἡρώδης: ὁ ἐπικληθεὶς Ἡρώδης c v
36 αὐτοῦ ὀνόματι c v

βουλεύετέ μοι. 3. οἱ δὲ ἀποτυχόντες τοῦ πεῖσαι αὐτὸν
δεινὰ ῥήματα ἔλεγον καὶ μετὰ[37] σπουδῆς καθῇρουν
αὐτόν, ὡς κατιόντα ἀπὸ τῆς καρούχας[38] ἀποσῦραι τὸ
ἀντικνήμιον. καὶ μὴ[39] ἐπιστραφείς, ὡς οὐδὲν πεπον-
θὼς προθύμως μετὰ σπουδῆς[40] ἐπορεύετο, ἀγόμενος
εἰς τὸ στάδιον, θορύβου τηλικούτου ὄντος ἐν τῷ σταδίῳ, ὡς μηδὲ ἀκουσθῆναί τινα δύνασθαι.

9

Τῷ δὲ Πολυκάρπῳ εἰσιόντι εἰς τὸ στάδιον φωνὴ ἐξ
οὐρανοῦ ἐγένετο· ἴσχυε, Πολύκαρπε, καὶ ἀνδρίζου.[41]
καὶ τὸν μὲν εἰπόντα οὐδεὶς εἶδεν, τὴν δὲ φωνὴν τῶν
ἡμετέρων οἱ παρόντες ἤκουσαν. καὶ λοιπὸν προσ-
αχθέντος αὐτοῦ, θόρυβος ἦν μέγας ἀκουσάντων, ὅτι
Πολύκαρπος συνείληπται. 2. προσαχθέντα οὖν αὐτὸν
ἀνηρώτα ὁ ἀνθύπατος, εἰ αὐτὸς εἴη Πολύκαρπος.[42] τοῦ
δὲ ὁμολογοῦντος, ἔπειθεν ἀρνεῖσθαι λέγων· αἰδέσθητί
σου τὴν ἡλικίαν, καὶ ἕτερα τούτοις ἀκόλουθα, ὧν[43]
ἔθος αὐτοῖς λέγειν· ὄμοσον τὴν καίσαρος τύχην,
μετανόησον, εἰπόν· αἶρε τοὺς ἀθέους. ὁ δὲ Πολύκαρπος ἐμβριθεῖ τῷ προσώπῳ εἰς πάντα τὸν ὄχλον τὸν ἐν
τῷ σταδίῳ ἀνόμων ἐθνῶν ἐμβλέψας καὶ ἐπισείσας
αὐτοῖς τὴν χεῖρα, στενάξας τε καὶ ἀναβλέψας εἰς τὸν
οὐρανὸν εἶπεν· αἶρε τοὺς ἀθέους. 3. ἐγκειμένου δὲ τοῦ

---

[37] μετὰ πολλῆς c v   [38] ὡς . . . καρούχας: om. a
[39] μὴ: μηδὲ c v

am not about to do what you advise." 3. Having failed to persuade him, they began speaking horrible words and hastily shoved him out, so that when he came down out of the carriage he scraped his shin. But he did not turn around, but quickly walked on in haste as if he had not been hurt. And he was led into the stadium, where there was such an uproar that no one could be heard.

9

But as he entered the stadium a voice came to Polycarp from heaven: "Be strong, Polycarp, and be a man *[Or: be courageous]*."[7] No one saw who had spoken, but those among our people who were there heard the voice. Finally, when he was brought forward, there was a great uproar among those who heard that Polycarp had been arrested. When he was brought forward the proconsul asked if he was Polycarp. When he said he was, the proconsul began trying to persuade him to make a denial, saying, "Have respect for your age," along with other related things they customarily say: "Swear by the Fortune of Caesar, repent, and say 'Away with the atheists.'" But Polycarp looked with a stern face at the entire crowd of lawless Gentiles in the stadium; and gesturing to them with his hand, he sighed, looked up to heaven, and said, "Away with the atheists."

[7] Josh 1:6.

---

40 μετὰ σπουδῆς g Eus.: om. m
41 ἀνδρίζου b h m p Eus: add μετά σου εἰμί c v
42 Πολύκαρπος (add ὁ ἐπίσκοπος c v) g Eus.: om. m
43 ὧν m: ὡς g: ἃ Eus.

ἀνθυπάτου καὶ λέγοντος· ὄμοσον, καὶ ἀπολύω σε,
λοιδόρησον τὸν Χριστόν, ἔφη ὁ Πολύκαρπος· ὀγδοή-
κοντα καὶ ἓξ ἔτη δουλεύω⁴⁴ αὐτῷ, καὶ οὐδέν με ἠδίκη-
σεν.⁴⁵ καὶ πῶς δύναμαι βλασφημῆσαι τὸν βασιλέα
μου τὸν σώσαντά με;

10

Ἐπιμένοντος δὲ πάλιν αὐτοῦ καὶ λέγοντος· ὄμοσον
τὴν καίσαρος τύχην, ἀπεκρίνατο· εἰ κενοδοξεῖς,⁴⁶ ἵνα
ὀμόσω τὴν καίσαρος τύχην, ὡς σὺ λέγεις, προσποιεῖ
δὲ ἀγνοεῖν με, τίς εἰμι, μετὰ παρρησίας ἄκουε· Χριστιανός εἰμι. εἰ δὲ θέλεις τὸν τοῦ Χριστιανισμοῦ
μαθεῖν λόγον, δὸς ἡμέραν καὶ ἄκουσον. 2. ἔφη ὁ
ἀνθύπατος· πεῖσον τὸν δῆμον. ὁ δὲ Πολύκαρπος εἶπεν·
σὲ μὲν καὶ λόγου ἠξίωκα· δεδιδάγμεθα γὰρ ἀρχαῖς
καὶ ἐξουσίαις ὑπὸ τοῦ θεοῦ τεταγμέναις τιμὴν κατὰ τὸ
προσῆκον τὴν μὴ βλάπτουσαν ἡμᾶς ἀπονέμειν· ἐκεί-
νους δὲ οὐχ ἡγοῦμαι ἀξίους τοῦ ἀπολογεῖσθαι αὐτοῖς.

11

Ὁ δὲ ἀνθύπατος εἶπεν· θηρία ἔχω, τούτοις σε παρα-
βαλῶ, ἐὰν μὴ μετανοήσῃς. ὁ δὲ εἶπεν· κάλει,
ἀμετάθετος γὰρ ἡμῖν ἡ ἀπὸ τῶν κρειττόνων ἐπὶ τὰ

---

⁴⁴ δουλεύω m Eus.: ἐχὼ δουλεύων g

3. The proconsul became more insistent and said, "Take the oath and I will release you. Revile Christ." But Polycarp responded, "For eighty-six years I have served him, and he has done me no wrong. How can I blaspheme my king who has saved me?"

10

When the proconsul persisted and said, "Swear by the Fortune of Caesar," Polycarp answered, "If you are so foolish as to think that I will swear by the Fortune of Caesar, as you say, and if you pretend not to know who I am, listen closely: I am a Christian. But if you wish to learn an account of Christianity, appoint a day and listen." 2. The proconsul replied, "Persuade the people." Polycarp said, "I think you deserve an account, for we are taught to render all due honor to rulers and authorities appointed by God,[8] in so far as it does us no harm. But as to those, I do not consider them worthy to hear a reasoned defense."

11

The proconsul said, "I have wild beasts, and I will cast you to them if you do not repent." He replied, "Call them! For it is impossible for us to repent from better to worse; it is

[8] Rom 13:1; 1 Pet 2:13.

---

45 οὐδέν με ἠδίκησεν b h p Eus.: ἐφύλαξέν με m: ἀλλὰ καὶ μᾶλλον διεφύλαξέν με ἀπὸ παντὸς κακοῦ c v: add semperque servatus L

46 εἰ κενοδοξεῖς a Eus.: ἐκεῖνο δόξης m: ἐκεῖνο δόξειν b c v: μή μοι γένοιτο p

χείρω μετάνοια· καλὸν δὲ μετατίθεσθαι ἀπὸ τῶν χαλεπῶν ἐπὶ τὰ δίκαια. 2. ὁ δὲ πάλιν πρὸς αὐτόν· πυρί σε
ποιήσω δαπανηθῆναι, εἰ τῶν θηρίων καταφρονεῖς, ἐὰν
μὴ μετανοήσῃς. ὁ δὲ[47] Πολύκαρπος εἶπεν· πῦρ[48] ἀπει-
λεῖς τὸ πρὸς ὥραν καιόμενον καὶ μετ᾽ ὀλίγον σβεν-
νύμενον· ἀγνοεῖς γὰρ τὸ τῆς μελλούσης κρίσεως καὶ
αἰωνίου κολάσεως τοῖς ἀσεβέσι τηρούμενον πῦρ.
ἀλλὰ τί[49] βραδύνεις;[50] φέρε, ὃ βούλει.

12

Ταῦτα δὲ καὶ ἕτερα πλείονα[51] λέγων θάρσους καὶ
χαρᾶς ἐνεπίμπλατο, καὶ τὸ πρόσωπον αὐτοῦ χάριτος[52]
ἐπληροῦτο ὥστε[53] οὐ μόνον μὴ[54] συμπεσεῖν ταραχθέντα[55] ὑπὸ τῶν λεγομένων πρὸς αὐτόν, ἀλλὰ τοὐναν-
τίον τὸν ἀνθύπατον ἐκστῆναι, πέμψαι τε τὸν ἑαυτοῦ
κήρυκα ἐν μέσῳ τοῦ σταδίου κηρῦξαι τρίς· Πολύκαρπος ὡμολόγησεν ἑαυτὸν Χριστιανὸν εἶναι. 2. τούτου
λεχθέντος ὑπὸ τοῦ κήρυκος, ἅπαν τὸ πλῆθος ἐθνῶν τε
καὶ Ἰουδαίων τῶν τὴν Σμύρναν κατοικούντων ἀκατασ-
χέτῳ θυμῷ καὶ μεγάλῃ φωνῇ ἐπεβόα· οὗτός ἐστιν ὁ
τῆς ἀσεβείας[56] διδάσκαλος, ὁ πατὴρ τῶν Χριστιανῶν,
ὁ τῶν ἡμετέρων θεῶν καθαιρέτης, ὁ πολλοὺς διδάσκων μὴ θύειν μηδὲ προσκυνεῖν τοῖς θεοῖς.[57] ταῦτα
λέγοντες ἐπεβόων καὶ ἠρώτων τὸν Ἀσιάρχην Φίλιπ-
πον, ἵνα ἐπαφῇ τῷ Πολυκάρπῳ λέοντα. ὁ δὲ ἔφη, μὴ

47 ὁ δὲ a b h m: ὁ ἅγιος c v: ὁ δὲ ἅγιος p: om. Eus.

good, though, to change from what is wicked to what is right." 2. Again the proconsul said to him, "If you despise the wild beasts, I will have you consumed by fire, if you do not repent." Polycarp replied, "You threaten with a fire that burns for an hour and after a short while is extinguished; for you do not know about the fire of the coming judgment and eternal torment, reserved for the ungodly. But why are you waiting? Bring on what you wish."

12

While he was saying these and many other things, he was filled with courage and joy, and his face was full of grace, so that not only did he not collapse to the ground from being unnerved at what he heard, but on the contrary, the proconsul was amazed and sent his herald into the center of the stadium to proclaim three times, "Polycarp has confessed himself to be a Christian." 2. When the herald said this, the entire multitude of both Gentiles and Jews who lived in Smyrna cried out with uncontrollable rage and a great voice, "This is the teacher of impiety, the father of the Christians, the destroyer of our own gods, the one who teaches many not to sacrifice or worship the gods." Saying these things, they began calling out to Philip, the Asiarch, asking him to release a lion on Polycarp. But he said that he

---

48 πῦρ μοι m   49 τί: μὴ c v
50 βραδύνῃς c h v   51 πλείονα: om. m
52 χάριτος θείας c v   53 ὥστε: ὥσπερ c h v
54 μὴ om. m   55 ταραχθέντα b m Eus.: -θέντος a c h p v
56 ἀσεβείας g: Ἀσίας m Eus. L
57 τοῖς θεοῖς g: om. m Eus.

εἶναι ἐξὸν αὐτῷ, ἐπειδὴ πεπληρώκει τὰ κυνηγέσια. 3.
τότε ἔδοξεν αὐτοῖς ὁμοθυμαδὸν ἐπιβοῆσαι, ὥστε τὸν
Πολύκαρπον ζῶντα κατακαῦσαι.[58] ἔδει γὰρ τὸ τῆς
φανερωθείσης[59] ἐπὶ τοῦ προσκεφαλαίου ὀπτασίας
πληρωθῆναι, ὅτε ἰδὼν αὐτὸ καιόμενον προσευχόμενος
εἶπεν ἐπιστραφεὶς τοῖς σὺν αὐτῷ πιστοῆς προφητικ ς·
δεῆ με ζῶντα κατακαυθῶναι.[60]

13

Ταῦτα οὖν μετὰ τοσούτου τάχους ἐγένετο, θᾶττον ἢ
ἐλέγετο,[61] τῶν ὄχλων παραχρῆμα συναγόντων ἔκ τε
τῶν ἐργαστηρίων καὶ βαλανείων[62] ξύλα καὶ φρύγανα,[63] μάλιστα Ἰουδαίων προθύμως, ὡς ἔθος αὐτοῖς,
εἰς ταῦτα ὑπουργούντων. 2. ὅτε δὲ ἡ πυρκαϊὰ[64] ἡτοι-
μάσθη, ἀποθέμενος ἑαυτῷ πάντα τὰ ἱμάτια καὶ λύσας
τὴν ζώνην ἐπειρᾶτο καὶ ὑπολύειν ἑαυτόν, μὴ πρότερον
τοῦτο ποιῶν διὰ τὸ ἀεὶ ἕκαστον τῶν πιστῶν
σπουδάζειν, ὅστις τάχιον τοῦ χρωτὸς αὐτοῦ ἅψηται·
παντὶ γὰρ καλῷ[65] ἀγαθῆς ἕνεκεν πολιτείας καὶ πρὸ
τῆς μαρτυρίας ἐκεκόσμητο. 3. εὐθέως οὖν αὐτῷ
περιετίθετο τὰ πρὸς τὴν πυρὰν ἡρμοσμένα ὄργανα.
μελλόντων δὲ αὐτῶν καὶ προσηλοῦν,[66] εἶπεν· ἄφετέ με
οὕτως· ὁ γὰρ δοὺς ὑπομεῖναι τὸ πῦρ δώσει καὶ χωρὶς

---

[58] κατακαῦσαν Eus. L (exureret): καύσαι m: κατακαυθῆναι
g   [59] φανερωθείσης g: add αὐτῷ m Eus.
[60] κατακαυθῆναι a b c h p: κανθῆναι v: καῆναι m Eus.

384

could not do so, since he had already concluded the animal hunts. 3. Then they decided to call out in unison for him to burn Polycarp alive. For the vision that had been revealed about the pillow had to be fulfilled; for he had seen it burning while he prayed. And when he turned he said prophetically to the faithful who were with him, "I must be burned alive."

13

These things then happened with incredible speed, quicker than can be described. The crowds immediately gathered together wood and kindling from the workplaces and the baths, with the Jews proving especially eager to assist, as is their custom. 2. When the pyre was prepared, Polycarp laid aside all his garments and loosened his belt. He was also trying to undo his sandals, even though he was not accustomed to do so, since each of the faithful was always eager to do it, to see who could touch his skin most quickly. For he was adorned with every good thing because of his exemplary way of life, even before he bore his testimony unto death. 3. Immediately the instruments prepared for the pyre were placed around him. When they were about to nail him, he said, "Leave me as I am; for the one who enables me to endure the fire will also enable me

---

61 ἢ ἐλέγετο m Eus.: τοῦ λεχθῆναι g

62 καὶ βαλανείων g Eus. (L): om. m

63 καὶ φρύγανα om. m   64 πυρκαϊὰ g: πυρὰ m Eus.

65 παντὶ γὰρ καλῷ b: ἐν παντὶ γὰρ Eus.: πράξεις γὰρ καλὰς c h p v: πάσης γὰρ m: πράτει ᾧ καλὼ (?) γὰρ a

66 προσηλοῦν: add αὐτὸν Eus.: add ἐν τῷ ξύλῳ c v

τῆς ὑμετέρας ἐκ τῶν ἥλων[67] ἀσφαλείας ἄσκυλτον[68] ἐπιμεῖναι τῇ πυρᾷ.

14

Οἱ δὲ οὐ καθήλωσαν μέν, προσέδησαν δὲ αὐτόν. ὁ δὲ ὀπίσω τὰς χεῖρας ποιήσας καὶ προσδεθείς, ὥσπερ κριὸς ἐπίσημος ἐκ μεγάλου ποιμνίου εἰς προσφοράν, ὁλοκαύτωμα δεκτὸν τῷ θεῷ ἡτοιμασμένον, ἀναβλέψας εἰς τὸν οὐρανὸν εἶπεν· Κύριε ὁ θεὸς ὁ παντοκράτωρ, ὁ τοῦ ἀγαπητοῦ καὶ εὐλογητοῦ παιδός σου Ἰησοῦ Χριστοῦ πατήρ, δι᾽ οὗ τὴν περὶ σοῦ ἐπίγνωσιν εἰλή-φαμεν, ὁ θεὸς ἀγγέλων καὶ δυνάμεων καὶ πάσης τῆς κτίσεως παντός τε τοῦ γένους τῶν δικαίων, οἳ ζῶσιν ἐνώπιόν σου· 2. εὐλογῶ σε, ὅτι ἠξίωσάς με τῆς ἡμέρας καὶ ὥρας ταύτης, τοῦ λαβεῖν με[69] μέρος ἐν ἀριθμῷ τῶν μαρτύρων ἐν τῷ ποτηρίῳ τοῦ Χριστοῦ σου εἰς ἀνάστασιν ζωῆς αἰωνίου ψυχῆς τε καὶ σώματος ἐν ἀφθαρσίᾳ πνεύματος ἁγίου· ἐν οἷς προσδεχθείην ἐνώπιόν σου σήμερον ἐν θυσίᾳ πίονι καὶ προσδεκτῇ, καθὼς προητοίμασας καὶ προεφανέρωσας καὶ ἐπλή-ρωσας, ὁ ἀψευδὴς καὶ ἀληθινὸς θεός. 3. διὰ τοῦτο καὶ περὶ πάντων σὲ αἰνῶ, σὲ εὐλογῶ, σὲ δοξάζω διὰ τοῦ αἰωνίου καὶ ἐπουρανίου ἀρχιερέως Ἰησοῦ Χριστοῦ, ἀγαπητοῦ σου παιδός, δι᾽ οὗ σοὶ σὺν αὐτῷ[70] καὶ

to remain in the pyre without moving, even without the security of your nails."

14

So they did not nail him, but they tied him. And when he placed his hands behind his back and was tied, he was like an exceptional ram taken from a great flock for a sacrifice, prepared as a whole burnt offering that is acceptable to God. Looking up into heaven he said, "Lord God Almighty, Father of your beloved and blessed child Jesus Christ, through whom we have received knowledge of you, the God of angels, of powers, and of all creation, and of every race of the upright who live before you, 2. I bless you for making me worthy of this day and hour, that I may receive a share among the number of the martyrs in the cup of your Christ, unto the resurrection of eternal life in both soul and body in the immortality of the Holy Spirit. Among them may I be received before you today as a sacrifice that is rich and acceptable, just as you prepared and revealed in advance and now fulfilled—the true God who does not lie. 3. For this reason and for all things I praise you, I bless you, I glorify you through the eternal and heavenly high priest Jesus Christ, your beloved child, through whom be glory to

---

67 ἐκ τῶν ἥλων: om. m
68 ἄσκυλτον m: ἀσκύλτως Eus.: ἀσάλευτον g
69 με b h p v: om. a c m Eus.
70 δι᾽ οὗ σοὶ σὺν αὐτῷ m Eus. (L): μεθ᾽ οὗ σοὶ g

πνεύματι ἁγίῳ δόξα⁷¹ καὶ νῦν⁷² καὶ εἰς τοὺς μέλλοντας
αἰῶνας.⁷³ ἀμήν.

15

Ἀναπέμψαντος δὲ αὐτοῦ τὸ ἀμὴν καὶ πληρώσαντος
τὴν εὐχήν, οἱ τοῦ πυρὸς ἄνθρωποι⁷⁴ ἐξῆψαν τὸ πῦρ.
μεγάλης δὲ ἐκλαμψάσης φλογός, θαῦμα⁷⁵ εἴδομεν, οἷς
ἰδεῖν ἐδόθη· οἳ καὶ ἐτηρήθημεν εἰς τὸ ἀναγγεῖλαι τοῖς
λοιποῖς τὰ γενόμενα. 2. τὸ γὰρ πῦρ καμάρας εἶδος
ποιῆσαν, ὥσπερ ὀθόνη πλοίου ὑπὸ πνεύματος πλη-
ρουμένη, κύκλῳ περιετείχισεν τὸ σῶμα τοῦ μάρτυρος·
καὶ ἦν μέσον οὐχ ὡς σὰρξ καιομένη, ἀλλ᾽ ὡς ἄρτος
ὀπτώμενος ἢ ὡς χρυσὸς καὶ ἄργυρος ἐν καμίνῳ πυ-
ρούμενος· καὶ γὰρ εὐωδίας τοσαύτης ἀντελαβόμεθα,
ὡς λιβανωτοῦ πνέοντος⁷⁶ ἢ ἄλλου τινὸς τῶν τιμίων
ἀρωμάτων.

16

Πέρας γοῦν ἰδόντες οἱ ἄνομοι μὴ δυνάμενον αὐτοῦ τὸ
σῶμα ὑπὸ τοῦ πυρὸς δαπανηθῆναι, ἐκέλευσαν προσ-
ελθόντα αὐτῷ κομφέκτορα παραβῦσαι ξιφίδιον. καὶ
τούτου ποιήσαντος, ἐξῆλθεν περιστερὰ καὶ⁷⁷ πλῆθος
αἵματος, ὥστε κατασβέσαι τὸ πῦρ καὶ θαυμάσαι
πάντα⁷⁸ τὸν ὄχλον, εἰ τοσαύτη τις διαφορὰ μεταξὺ

---

⁷¹ δόξα m (add κράτος) Eus.: ἡ δόξα g

you, with him and the Holy Spirit, both now and for the ages to come. Amen."

15

When he sent up the "Amen" and finished the prayer, the men in charge of the fire touched it off. And as a great flame blazoned forth we beheld a marvel—we to whom it was granted to see, who have also been preserved to report the events to the others. 2. For the fire, taking on the appearance of a vaulted room, like a boat's sail filled with the wind, formed a wall around the martyr's body. And he was in the center, not like burning flesh but like baking bread or like gold and silver being refined in a furnace. And we perceived a particularly sweet aroma, like wafting incense or some other precious perfume.

16

Finally, when the lawless ones saw that his body could not be consumed by the fire, they ordered an executioner to go up and stab him with a dagger. When he did so, a dove came forth, along with such a quantity of blood that it extinguished the fire, striking the entire crowd with amazement that there could be so much difference between the

---

72 νῦν: add καὶ ἀεὶ m (L)   73 μέλλοντας αἰῶνας a b c h v Eus.: αἰῶνας τῶν αἰώνων m p L

74 ἄνθρωποι (ἄνδρες h) g Eus.: ὑπουργοὶ m

75 θαῦμα m Eus. (L): add μέγα g

76 πνέοντος: om. m   77 περιστερὰ καὶ G (L): om. Eus.

78 πάντα: om. m

τῶν τε ἀπίστων καὶ τῶν ἐκλεκτῶν·[79] 2. ὧν εἷς καὶ οὗτος γεγόνει ὁ[80] θαυμασιώτατος[81] Πολύκαρπος, ἐν τοῖς καθ᾽ ἡμᾶς χρόνοις διδάσκαλος ἀποστολικὸς καὶ προφητικὸς γενόμενος ἐπίσκοπός τε[82] τῆς ἐν Σμύρνῃ καθολικῆς[83] ἐκκλησίας. πᾶν γὰρ ῥῆμα, ὃ ἀφῆκεν ἐκ τοῦ στόματος αὐτοῦ, καὶ ἐτελειώθη καὶ τελειωθήσεται.

17

Ὁ δὲ ἀντίζηλος[84] καὶ βάσκανος[85] πονηρός,[86] ὁ[87] ἀντικείμενος τῷ γένει τῶν δικαίων, ἰδὼν τό τε μέγεθος αὐτοῦ τῆς μαρτυρίας καὶ τὴν ἀπ᾽ ἀρχῆς ἀνεπίληπτον πολιτείαν, ἐστεφανωμένον τε τὸν τῆς ἀφθαρσίας στέφανον καὶ βραβεῖον ἀναντίρρητον ἀπενηνεγμένον, ἐπετήδευσεν, ὡς μηδὲ τὸ σωμάτιον[88] αὐτοῦ ὑφ᾽ ἡμῶν ληφθῆναι, καίπερ πολλῶν ἐπιθυμούντων τοῦτο ποιῆσαι καὶ κοινωνῆσαι τῷ ἁγίῳ αὐτοῦ σαρκίῳ. 2. ὑπέβαλεν γοῦν Νικήτην τὸν τοῦ Ἡρώδου πατέρα, ἀδελφὸν δὲ Ἄλκης, ἐντυχεῖν τῷ ἄρχοντι, ὥστε μὴ δοῦναι αὐτοῦ τὸ σῶμα· μή, φησίν, ἀφέντες τὸν ἐσταυρωμένον τοῦτον ἄρξωνται σέβεσθαι· καὶ ταῦτα[89] ὑποβαλλόντων καὶ ἐνισχυόντων τῶν[90] Ἰουδαίων, οἳ καὶ ἐτήρησαν, μελλόντων ἡμῶν ἐκ τοῦ πυρὸς αὐτὸν λαμβάνειν, ἀγνοοῦντες, ὅτι οὔτε τὸν Χριστόν ποτε καταλιπεῖν

[79] ἀπίστων καὶ τῶν ἐκλεκτῶν: πιστῶν καὶ τῶν ἀπίστων c v
[80] ὁ μακάριος καὶ m
[81] θαυμασιώτατος m Eus. L: add μάρτυς g

unbelievers and the elect. 2. One of the latter was this most astounding Polycarp, who in our time was an apostolic and prophetic teacher and bishop of the universal church in Smyrna. For every word that came forth from his mouth was fulfilled and will be fulfilled.

17

But the jealous and envious Evil One, the enemy of the race of the upright, having seen the greatness of Polycarp's death as a martyr and the irreproachable way of life that he had from the beginning—and that he had received the crown of immortality and was awarded with the incontestible prize—made certain that his poor body was not taken away by us, even though many were desiring to do so and to have a share in [Or: to commune with; or: to have fellowship with] his holy flesh. 2. So he incited Nicetas, the father of Herod and brother of Alce, to petition the magistrate not to hand over his body, "Lest," he said, "they desert the one who was crucified and begin to worship this one." The Jews instigated and strongly urged these things, and kept watch when we were about to take him from the fire. For they did not realize that we are never able to abandon

---

82 τε a b p: om. h m Eus.

83 καθολικῆς a b h p Eus.: ἁγίας m L

84 ἀντίζηλος a b c h v Eus.: ἀντίδικος p: ἀντικείμενος m

85 βάσκανος b (p ?) Eus.: add καὶ a c h m v

86 πονηρὸς δαίμων c v   87 ὁ a b h p Eus.: add καὶ m: add πάντοτε c v   88 σωμάτιον m Eus. L: λείψανον g

89 ταῦτα m (L): add εἶπον Eus.: add εἰπὼν g: add εἰπὲν a

90 τῶν a h p v (Eus.): om. b c m

δυνησόμεθα, τὸν ὑπὲρ τῆς τοῦ παντὸς[91] κόσμου τῶν σωζομένων[92] σωτηρίας παθόντα, ἄμωμον ὑπὲρ ἁμαρτωλῶν, οὔτε ἕτερόν τινα σέβεσθαι. 3. τοῦτον μὲν γὰρ υἱὸν ὄντα τοῦ θεοῦ προσκυνοῦμεν, τοὺς δὲ μάρτυρας ὡς μαθητὰς καὶ μιμητὰς τοῦ κυρίου ἀγαπῶμεν ἀξίως ἕνεκα εὐνοίας ἀνυπερβλήτου τῆς εἰς τὸν ἴδιον βασιλέα καὶ διδάσκαλον· ὧν γένοιτο καὶ ἡμᾶς κοινωνούς[93] τε καὶ συμμαθητὰς γενέσθαι.

18

Ἰδὼν οὖν ὁ κεντυρίων τὴν τῶν Ἰουδαίων γενομένην[94] φιλονεικίαν, θεὶς αὐτὸν ἐν μέσῳ, ὡς ἔθος αὐτοῖς,[95] ἔκαυσεν. 2. οὕτως τε ἡμεῖς ὕστερον ἀνελόμενοι τὰ τιμιώτερα λίθων πολυτελῶν καὶ δοκιμώτερα ὑπὲρ χρυσίον ὀστᾶ αὐτοῦ ἀπεθέμεθα, ὅπου καὶ ἀκόλουθον ἦν. 3. ἔνθα ὡς δυνατὸν ἡμῖν συναγομένοις ἐν ἀγαλλιάσει καὶ χαρᾷ παρέξει ὁ κύριος ἐπιτελεῖν τὴν τοῦ μαρτυρίου αὐτοῦ ἡμέραν γενέθλιον, εἴς τε τὴν τῶν προηθληκότων[96] μνήμην καὶ τῶν μελλόντων ἄσκησίν τε καὶ ἑτοιμασίαν.

19

Τοιαῦτα τὰ κατὰ τὸν μακάριον Πολύκαρπον, ὃς σὺν τοῖς ἀπὸ Φιλαδελφίας δωδέκατος ἐν Σμύρνῃ μαρτυρή-

[91] παντὸς: om. m   [92] τῶν σωζομένων: om. m

Christ, who suffered for the salvation of the entire world of
those who are being saved, the one who was blameless for
sinners; nor are we able to worship any other. 3. For we
worship this one who is the Son of God, but we love the
martyrs as disciples and imitators of the Lord. And they are
worthy, because of their unsurpassable affection for their
own king and teacher. May we also become partners and
fellow disciples with them!

18

When the centurion saw the contentiousness caused by
the Jews, he placed Polycarp's body in the center and
burned it, as is their custom. 2. And so, afterwards, we removed his bones, which were more valuable than expen-
sive gems and more precious than gold, and put them in a
suitable place. 3. There, whenever we can gather together
in joy and happiness, the Lord will allow us to commemorate the birthday of his martyrdom, both in memory of
those who have already engaged in the struggle and as a
training and preparation for those who are about to do so.

19

Such are the matters pertaining to the blessed Polycarp,
who along with those from Philadelphia was the twelfth

---

93 κοινωνοὺς a b h m L: συγκοινωνοὺς p Eus.

94 Ἰουδαίων γενομένην a b h p Eus.: λεγομένων Ἰουδαίων
m (v?): λεγομένων c   95 ὡς ἔθος αὐτοῖς m Eus.: τοῦ πυρὸς
g: om. L   96 τῶν προηθληκότων a m p Eus.: τῶν ἠθληκότων
(b): αὐτοῦ c h v

σας, μόνος ὑπὸ πάντων⁹⁷ μνημονεύεται, ὥστε καὶ ὑπὸ
τῶν ἐθνῶν ἐν παντὶ τόπῳ λαλεῖσθαι· οὐ μόνον διδάσκαλος γενόμενος ἐπίσημος, ἀλλὰ καὶ μάρτυς
ἔξοχος,⁹⁸ οὗ τὸ μαρτύριον πάντες ἐπιθυμοῦσιν μιμεῖ-
σθαι κατὰ τὸ εὐαγγέλιον Χριστοῦ γενόμενον. 2. διὰ
τῆς ὑπομονῆς καταγωνισάμενος τὸν ἄδικον ἄρχοντα
καὶ οὕτως τὸν τῆς ἀφθαρσίας στέφανον ἀπολαβών,
σὺν τοῖς ἀποστόλοις καὶ πᾶσιν δικαίοις ἀγαλλιώμενος δοξάζει τὸν θεὸν καὶ⁹⁹ πατέρα¹⁰⁰ καὶ εὐλογεῖ τὸν
κύριον ἡμῶν Ἰησοῦν Χριστόν, τὸν σωτῆρα τῶν ψυχῶν
ἡμῶν καὶ κυβερνήτην τῶν σωμάτων ἡμῶν καὶ ποιμένα
τῆς κατὰ τὴν οἰκουμένην καθολικῆς¹⁰¹ ἐκκλησίας.¹⁰²

20

Ὑμεῖς μὲν οὖν ἠξιώσατε διὰ πλειόνων δηλωθῆναι
ὑμῖν τὰ γενόμενα, ἡμεῖς δὲ κατὰ τὸ παρὸν ἐπὶ κεφα-
λαίῳ μεμηνύκαμεν διὰ τοῦ ἀδελφοῦ ἡμῶν Μαρκίω-
νος.¹⁰³ μαθόντες οὖν ταῦτα καὶ τοῖς ἐπέκεινα ἀδελφοῖς
τὴν ἐπιστολὴν διαπέμψασθε, ἵνα καὶ ἐκεῖνοι δοξάζω-
σιν τὸν κύριον τὸν ἐκλογὰς ποιοῦντα ἀπὸ τῶν ἰδίων
δούλων. 2. τῷ δὲ δυναμένῳ πάντας ἡμᾶς εἰσαγαγεῖν
ἐν τῇ αὐτοῦ χάριτι καὶ δωρεᾷ εἰς τὴν αἰώνιον¹⁰⁴ αὐτοῦ
βασιλείαν, διὰ τοῦ παιδὸς αὐτοῦ, τοῦ μονογενοῦς
Ἰησοῦ Χριστοῦ, ᾧ ἡ¹⁰⁵ δόξα, τιμή, κράτος, μεγαλωσύνη εἰς τοὺς αἰῶνας. προσαγορεύετε πάντας τοὺς

---

⁹⁷ πάντων G: add μᾶλλον Eus. (L)

martyr in Smyrna; but he alone is remembered by all, discussed even by the outsiders in every place. For he was not only an exceptional teacher but also a superb martyr. Everyone longs to imitate his martyrdom, since it occurred in conformity with the gospel of Christ. 2. Through endurance he overcame the unjust ruler and thus received the crown of immortality. And now he rejoices together with the apostles and all those who are upright, and he glorifies God the Father and blesses our Lord Jesus Christ, the savior of our souls, pilot of our bodies, and shepherd of the universal church throughout the world.

20

You had asked for a lengthier explanation of what took place, but for the present we have mentioned only the principal points through our brother Marcion. When you have learned these things, send our letter to the brothers who are further afield, that they may also glorify the Lord who selects his chosen ones from among his own slaves. 2. And now to the one who is able to lead us all by his grace and gift into his eternal kingdom, through his child, the unique one, Jesus Christ, be the glory, honor, power, and greatness forever. Greet all the saints. Those who are with

98 ἐξοχώτατος a c h v   99 τὸν θεὸν καὶ: θεὸν m
100 πατέρα g: add παντακράτορα m L
101 καθολικῆς g L: ἁγίας m   102 ἐκκλησίας: add καὶ τὸ πανάγιον καὶ ζωοποιὸν πνεῦμα c v (L)
103 Μαρκίωνος m: Μαρκιανοῦ L: Μάρκου a b h p
104 αἰώνιον a b h p: ἐπουράνιον m
105 ᾧ ἡ a b h p (L): om. m

ἁγίους. ὑμᾶς οἱ σὺν ἡμῖν προσαγορεύουσιν καὶ[106] Εὐάρεστος, ὁ γράψας,[107] πανοικεί.

21

μαρτυρεῖ δὲ ὁ μακάριος Πολύκαρπος μηνὸς Ξανθικοῦ δευτέρᾳ ἱσταμένου, πρὸ ἑπτὰ καλανδῶν Μαρτίων, σαββάτῳ μεγάλῳ, ὥρᾳ ὀγδόῃ.[108] συνελήφθη δὲ ὑπὸ Ἡρώδου ἐπὶ ἀρχιερέως Φιλίππου Τραλλιανοῦ, ἀνθυπατεύοντος Στατίου Κοδράτου, βασιλεύοντος δὲ εἰς τοὺς αἰῶνας[109] Ἰησοῦ Χριστοῦ. ᾧ ἡ δόξα, τιμή, μεγαλωσύνη, θρόνος αἰώνιος ἀπὸ γενεᾶς εἰς γενεάν. ἀμήν.[110]

22

ἐρρῶσθαι ὑμᾶς εὐχόμεθα, ἀδελφοί, στοιχοῦντας τῷ κατὰ τὸ εὐαγγέλιον λόγῳ Ἰησοῦ Χριστοῦ, μεθ' οὗ[111] δόξα τῷ θεῷ καὶ πατρὶ καὶ ἁγίῳ πνεύματι[112] ἐπὶ σωτηρίᾳ τῇ τῶν ἁγίων ἐκλεκτῶν, καθὼς ἐμαρτύρησεν ὁ μακάριος Πολύκαρπος, οὗ γένοιτο ἐν τῇ βασιλείᾳ Ἰησοῦ Χριστοῦ πρὸς τὰ ἴχνη εὑρεθῆναι ἡμᾶς.[113] 2. ταῦτα μετεγράψατο μὲν Γάϊος ἐκ τῶν Εἰρηναίου, μαθητοῦ τοῦ Πολυκάρπου, ὃς καὶ συνεπολιτεύσατο τῷ Εἰρηναίῳ. ἐγὼ δὲ Σωκράτης ἐν Κορίνθῳ ἐκ τῶν Γαΐου

---

[106] καὶ αὐτὸς m
[107] γράψας a b h p L: add τὴν ἐπιστολὴν m

us greet you, as does Evaristus, the one who is writing the letter, with his entire household.

21

But the blessed Polycarp bore his witness unto death on the second day of the new month of Xanthikos, February 23, on a great Sabbath, at 2:00 in the afternoon. But he was arrested by Herod while Philip of Tralles was high priest, Statius Quadratus was proconsul, and Jesus Christ was ruling as king forever. To him be the glory, honor, greatness, and eternal throne, from one generation to the next. Amen.

22

We bid you farewell, brothers, you who conduct yourselves in the word of Jesus Christ according to the gospel; with him be glory to God, both Father and Holy Spirit [*Or: God, and the Father, and the Holy Spirit*], for the salvation of his holy chosen ones, just as the blessed Polycarp bore witness unto death. May we be found to have followed in his footsteps in the kingdom of Jesus Christ! 2. Gaius transcribed these things from the papers of Irenaeus, a disciple of Polycarp; he also lived in the same city as Irenaeus. And I, Socrates, have written these things in Corinth from the

---

108 ὀγδόη a b h p L: ἐνάτη m
109 αἰῶνας a b h p: add τοῦ κυρίου ἡμῶν m L
110 ᾧ . . . ἀμήν a b h L: om. m p   111 οὗ πᾶσα p
112 καὶ πατρὶ . . . πνεύματι a b h: om. p
113 ἐρρῶσθαι . . . ἡμᾶς: om. m L

ἀντιγράφων ἔγραψα. ἡ χάρις μετὰ πάντων. 3. ἐγὼ δὲ
πάλιν Πιόνιος ἐκ τοῦ προγεγραμμένου ἔγραψα ἀναζη-
τήσας αὐτά, κατὰ ἀποκάλυψιν φανερώσαντός μοι τοῦ
μακαρίου Πολυκάρπου, καθὼς δηλώσω ἐν τῷ καθεξῆς,
συναγαγὼν αὐτὰ ἤδη σχεδὸν ἐκ τοῦ χρόνου κεκμηκότα, ἵνα κἀμὲ συναγάγῃ ὁ κύριος Ἰησοῦς Χριστὸς
μετὰ τῶν ἐκλεκτῶν αὐτοῦ εἰς τὴν οὐράνιον βασιλείαν
αὐτοῦ, ᾧ ἡ δόξα σὺν τῷ πατρὶ καὶ[114] ἁγίῳ πνεύματι εἰς
τοὺς αἰῶνας τῶν αἰώνων. ἀμήν.

Alternate Epilogue From the Moscow Codex

Ταῦτα μετεγράψατο μὲν Γάϊος ἐκ τῶν Εἰρηναίου συγγραμμάτων, ὃς καὶ συνεπολιτεύσατο τῷ Εἰρηναίῳ,
μαθητῇ γεγονότι τοῦ ἁγίου Πολυκάρπου. 2. οὗτος γὰρ
ὁ Εἰρηναῖος, κατὰ τὸν καιρὸν τοῦ μαρτυρίου τοῦ
ἐπισκόπου Πολυκάρπου γενόμενος ἐν Ῥώμῃ, πολλοὺς
ἐδίδαξεν· οὗ καὶ πολλὰ αὐτοῦ συγγράμματα κάλ-
λιστα καὶ ὀρθότατα φέρεται, ἐν οἷς μέμνηται Πολυκάρπου, ὅτι παρ᾽ αὐτοῦ ἔμαθεν· ἱκανῶς τε πᾶσαν
αἵρεσιν ἤλεγξεν καὶ τὸν ἐκκλησιαστικὸν κανόνα καὶ
καθολικόν, ὡς παρέλαβεν παρὰ τοῦ ἁγίου, καὶ παρέδωκεν. 3. λέγει δὲ καὶ τοῦτο· ὅτι συναντήσαντός ποτε
τῷ ἁγίῳ Πολυκάρπῳ Μαρκίωνος, ἀφ᾽ οὗ οἱ λεγόμενοι
Μαρκιωνισταί, καὶ εἰπόντος· ἐπιγίνωσκε ἡμᾶς, Πολύκαρπε, εἶπεν αὐτὸς τῷ Μαρκίωνι· ἐπιγινώσκω, ἐπιγινώσκω τὸν πρωτότοκον τοῦ σατανᾶ. 4. καὶ τοῦτο δὲ
φέρεται ἐν τοῖς τοῦ Εἰρηναίου συγγράμμασιν, ὅτι ᾗ

copies made by Gaius. May grace be with everyone. 3. And I, Pionius, then sought out these things and produced a copy from the one mentioned above, in accordance with a revelation of the blessed Polycarp, who showed it to me, as I will explain in what follows. And I gathered these papers together when they were nearly worn out by age, so that the Lord Jesus Christ may gather me together with his chosen ones into his heavenly kingdom. To him be the glory with the Father and the Holy Spirit forever and ever. Amen.

Another Epilogue, From the Moscow Manuscript

Gaius transcribed these things from the writings of Irenaeus; he also lived in the same city with Irenaeus, a disciple of the holy Polycarp. 2. For this Irenaeus was in Rome when the bishop Polycarp was martyred, and he taught many people. And many of his writings—which are excellent and supremely true—are in circulation; in them he remembers Polycarp, because he studied under him. He powerfully refuted every heresy and passed on the ecclesiastical and universal rule of faith, as he received it from the holy one. 3. He also says that Marcion, from whom come those who are called Marcionites, once met the holy Polycarp and said, "You need to recognize us, Polycarp." But he then replied to Marcion, "I do recognize you—I recognize the firstborn of Satan!" 4. This also is found in the writings of Irenaeus, that on the day and hour

---

114 καὶ b p: add τῷ h

ἡμέρᾳ καὶ ὥρᾳ ἐν Σμύρνῃ ἐμαρτύρησεν ὁ Πολύκαρπος, ἤκουσεν φωνὴν ἐν τῇ Ῥωμαίων πόλει ὑπάρχων ὁ
Εἰρηναῖος ὡς σάλπιγγος λεγούσης· Πολύκαρπος
ἐμαρτύρησεν. 5. ἐκ τούτων[115] οὖν, ὡς προλέλεκται, τῶν
τοῦ Εἰρηναίου συγγραμμάτων Γάϊος μετεγράψατο, ἐκ
δὲ τῶν Γαΐου ἀντιγράφων Ἰσοκράτης ἐν Κορίνθῳ.
ἐγὼ δὲ πάλιν Πιόνιος ἐκ τῶν Ἰσοκράτους ἀντιγράφων
ἔγραψα κατὰ ἀποκάλυψιν τοῦ ἁγίου Πολυκάρπου
ζητήσας αὐτά, συναγαγὼν αὐτὰ ἤδη σχεδὸν ἐκ τοῦ
χρόνου κεκμηκότα, ἵνα κἀμὲ συναγάγῃ ὁ κύριος Ἰησοῦς Χριστὸς μετὰ τῶν ἐκλεκτῶν αὐτοῦ εἰς τὴν
ἐπουράνιον αὐτοῦ βασιλείαν· ᾧ ἡ δόξα σὺν τῷ πατρὶ
καὶ τῷ υἱῷ καὶ τῷ ἁγίῳ πνεύματι εἰς τοὺς αἰῶνας τῶν
αἰώνων. ἀμήν.

[115] τούτων cj. Bihlmeyer: τούτου m

that Polycarp was martyred in Smyrna, Irenaeus, who was in the city of the Romans, heard a voice like a trumpet saying, "Polycarp has been martyred." 5. And so, as was indicated before, Gaius made a transcription from the writings of Irenaeus, as Isocrates did, in Corinth, from the copies of Gaius. And then I, Pionius, wrote a copy from those of Isocrates, in accordance with a revelation of the holy Polycarp, after seeking out these writings and gathering them together when they were nearly worn out by age, so that the Lord Jesus Christ may gather me together with his chosen ones into his heavenly kingdom. To him be the glory, with the Father and the Son and the Holy Spirit, forever and ever. Amen.

DIDACHE

THE TEACHING OF THE
TWELVE APOSTLES

INTRODUCTION

Few manuscript discoveries of modern times have created the stir caused by the discovery and publication of the *Didache* in the late nineteenth century. Found by Philotheos Bryennios in 1873 in the Library of the Holy Sepulchre in Constantinople (as part of the manuscript Hierosolymitanus, which also contains the texts of 1 and 2 Clement, Barnabas, and the long recension of Ignatius), and published by him ten years later, the *Didache* was immediately seen to be one of most important literary remains of early Christianity outside of the New Testament. For here was not only a very early presentation of the ethical teachings known as the "two paths" (or the "two ways"), familiar already from the Epistle of Barnabas and later texts, but also the earliest surviving descriptive account of the Christian rituals of baptism and eucharist, along with instructions involving itinerant Christian apostles and prophets in an age before the church hierarchy of bishop, presbyters, and deacons was firmly in place. Some scholars immediately recognized the antiquity of the account, dating it to the beginning of the second century or the end of the first—that is, even before some of the books of the New Testament were written. Almost everyone realized that here at last was a book that had achieved near canonical status in some early Christian circles, known by title from discussions of the church Fathers but for the most part lost to history some time after the fourth century.

Overview

The *Didache* is given two titles in the only complete manuscript: "The Teaching (Greek: Διδαχή) of the Twelve Apostles," and, immediately following, "The Teaching of the Lord Through the Twelve Apostles to the Gentiles." Neither title claims that the book was actually written by the apostles, simply that it conveys their teachings; it is, therefore, anonymous rather than pseudonymous. The book as a whole is usually considered a "church manual" or a "church order," the first of its kind to survive.

The *Didache* begins with a set of ethical instructions known as the "two paths, one of life and one of death" (1.1). The path that leads to life involves following the commandments of God, principally the commandment to love God and one's neighbor, and to adhere to the "Golden Rule" (1.2). The first four chapters of the book explicate these commandments, first in words that reflect the teachings of Jesus (without naming him), especially as found in the Sermon on the Mount (ch. 1), then in a series of positive and negative ethical injunctions (chs. 2–4). The path that leads to death involves contrary sorts of behavior, as delineated in chapter 5.

After a transitional chapter, the author shifts to discuss church ritual, explaining how to baptize (ch. 7), fast (8.1), pray (8.2), and celebrate the communal thanksgiving meal or eucharist (chs. 9–10; giving the appropriate eucharistic prayers).

Attention then shifts in chapter 11 to the question of

how to deal with itinerant Christian teachers, apostles, and, especially, prophets, indicating their special status before God but warning of possible abuses. Following then some further instructions for communal worship (ch. 14) and life (ch. 15), including the need to "elect . . . bishops and deacons," the discussion moves to a concluding apocalyptic scenario, which indicates what will happen in the final days when havoc breaks out on earth before the final coming of the Lord "on the clouds of the sky." The text breaks off abruptly at this point. Possibly its original ending was lost.

Integrity

The *Didache* obviously contains several discrete discussions: the two paths, the "church order" (which may comprise two distinct units, one on liturgical practices and the other on the treatment of itinerant "apostles and prophets"), and the apocalyptic discourse. Moreover, there is no necessary connection between them, except that provided perhaps by an editor, for example, the indication in 7.1 that the teaching of the two paths was to be given prior to the performance of baptism. For these reasons, scholars have long maintained that the document is in fact a composite piece rather than a literary unity. If this is correct, then the different portions of the text may well have been composed in different times and places, only to be assembled together at a secondary level at a later time. When and where each of the portions derived, and when and where they were finally assembled, and then possibly subjected to further editorial revision, are a matter of ongoing debate.

When the *Didache* was first published in 1883, its opening description of the two paths was recognized as closely parallel to the already well known Epistle of Barnabas, chapters 18–20 (see Introduction there). The question immediately raised was whether Barnabas had borrowed its teaching of the two paths from the *Didache*, or the *Didache* borrowed from Barnabas. It was soon recognized, however, that the matter was not so simple, as comparable descriptions of the two paths could be found in other early Christian writings, including the *Teaching of the Apostles* (= *Doctrina Apostolorum*), the *Apostolic Church Order*, and the Life of Shenute. Comparable teachings were eventually found in non-Christian Jewish texts, especially in the *Manual of Discipline* from the Dead Sea Scrolls. This wide range of texts utilizing a teaching of the two paths let to the general consensus that both the *Didache* and Barnabas had drawn their teaching from an independent source, now lost. Given the absence of distinctively Christian language in the teaching of the two paths and its clear parallels now in the *Manual of Discipline*, it is generally thought that the document underlying all of these documents was originally Jewish.

Once that was established, however, one still had to deal with the circumstance that the first chapter of the *Didache*—the beginning of the explication of the path of life—appears to summarize key teachings found in Matthew's Sermon on the Mount. Most scholars have considered this section, then, to be a later addition to the two-paths teaching, interpolated into it either by the Didachist (i.e., the one who compiled the document out of previous sources) or by the author of the source he used. Hence this section 1.3b–2.1 is often called the "Gospel Section."

The so-called "Church Order" (chs. 7–15) may have derived from another source (or two), which provided instruction concerning the most important Christian rituals
and practices (baptism, fasting, prayer, eucharist) and concerning the activities—evidently common to this and surrounding communities—of itinerant Christian apostles,
teachers, and prophets. The situation presupposed in
these chapters appears to be quite ancient in that the
churches are not ruled by a single bishop or a presbytery,
and outsiders coming in to a community are assumed to
have considerable authority and sway. The churches being
addressed, that is to say, are only beginning to establish
their own internal structures: here they are told to elect
the right kind of men as their bishops (plural) and deacons
(15.1).

Moreover, the communities appear to have close and
immediate connections with non-Christian Jews. This is
seen above all in (a) the anti-Jewish polemic—in 8.1 Jews
(known to fast on Mondays and Thursdays) are simply
called "hypocrites"—and the emphasis that Christians
need to fast and pray differently from them (8.1–2); (b) the
christological imagery of the eucharistic prayers, which
speak, for example, of Jesus as "the vine of David," and uti-
lize Jewish or Jewish-Christian prayer forms such as "Hosanna to the God of David," and "Maranatha" (9.2; 10.6);
and (c) the insistence that true prophets are to be the community's "high priests" and thus provided for by tithes that
Jews would have given to support the priests serving in the
Temple (ch. 13).

The concluding chapter appears to combine features of
the apocalyptic discourses of Jesus as found in Matthew
and Luke. But here, as in the earlier description of the two

paths, it is not clear if the author, whether the Didachist or his source, is relying on written texts or on oral traditions rooted in the sayings of Jesus. In any event, it appears that the abrupt ending, "Then the world will see the Lord coming on the clouds of the sky," was not the way the document originally concluded. It is worth noting that the scribe of Codex Hierosolymitanus, our only complete text of the *Didache*, uncharacteristically left the final portion of the page blank after these words, without the punctuation he normally used to indicate the ending of a book. He, at least, appears to have thought that there was more to come, even though the text he was copying must have broken off at this point.

There are other portions of the text that suggest its composite character. One of its most striking passages is found in two of the surviving witnesses (the Coptic fragment and the *Apostolic Constitutions*; see below). Here, at the end of the eucharistic prayers over the cup of wine and bread are instructions concerning a third prayer, to be spoken over the ointment used for ceremonial anointing (or possibly over incense burned during the ceremony; see Gero): "But concerning the matter of the ointment, give thanks as follows, saying, 'We give you thanks, O Father, for the ointment you have made known to us through Jesus your child. To you be the glory forever. Amen'" (10.7).

Numerous explanations have been put forth to account for the composite character of the text, for example, that the *Didache* underwent a number of revisions at different times at the hands of the same, or perhaps different, redactors. Possibly, however, it is simplest to think that the Didachist himself, who was responsible for the final edition of the text, worked with earlier sources (the two paths, the church order, the apocalyptic discourse), putting them together, providing transitions (e.g., 2.1; 7.1), and adding materials (e.g., the "Gospel Section") as he saw fit (Niederwimmer).

Date and Location

These various sources then could have been produced at different times. The teaching of the two paths may have been taken over from a Jewish (or Jewish-Christian) source written as early as the mid-first century; the church order seems to presuppose a situation prior to the second century, before internal church structures were widely in place; the apocalyptic discourse could have been composed almost any time during the first two centuries. As to the date of the Didachist himself, opinions again vary, but most would put the time of his composition sometime around the year 100, possibly a decade or so later.

With respect to the place of composition, many scholars prefer to think of Syria, where, for example, the reference to wheat growing on hillsides (9.4) would make sense (unlike Egypt) and where the close interactions of Jews and Christians presupposed by parts of the text can be documented. But Jews and Christians (and Jewish Christians) were in close contact in numerous places. And the early circulation of the text in Egypt (possibly quoted in Clement of Alexandria; mentioned by Athanasius as read in the churches; cited by Didymus the Blind, possibly as Scripture; preserved in a papyrus in Oxyrhynchus) along with the liturgical use of the term "fragment" (9.3), otherwise known from Egyptian liturgy, have suggested to some that Egypt may have been its place of origin. Others have

411

pointed out that some of the sources may have derived from one location or another (Syria or Egypt), but that the final composition may have been put together elsewhere. At the end of the day, it is probably impossible to say where the document was produced.

Manuscripts

The manuscript tradition of the *Didache* is unusually complicated. The Codex Hierosolymitanus (dated 1056) remains the only surviving complete text, although as indicated, it may break off before the original ending. In addition there is a Greek papyrus of 1.3c–4a and 2.7b–3.2a, which comes from a miniature codex of the fourth century which may have served as an amulet, discovered at Oxyrhynchus (Egypt). There is also a fifth-century Coptic fragment of 10.3b–12.2a, which some scholars suspect represents a scribe practicing his copying skills on a spare sheet of papyrus (see especially F. S. Jones and P. Mirecki in Jefford). Moreover, virtually the entire text of the *Didache*, with modifications and interpretive comments, is reproduced in Greek (as came to be recognized after Bryennios's discovery) in the *Apostolic Constitutions* (book 7), a fourth-century church order. There are also traces of a somewhat paraphrastic Ethiopic translation of *Didache* 11.3–13.7 and 8.1–2, preserved as part of the Ethiopian church order. These, then, are the major witnesses to the text.

In the early twentieth century a Georgian copy of the *Didache* turned up, which was then itself copied and carefully collated against the Greek, before being lost. It now appears, however, that the Georgian was actually a modern

translation of the *Didache*, not an independent witness to
its text.

At one time it was thought that portions of the *Didache*
could be found in (a) the Latin "Doctrina Apostolorum,"
which was then touted as a Latin "version," (b) the Greek
"Apostolic Church Order," (c) its "Epitome," and (d) several later sources. It appears, however, that as is the case
with the Epistle of Barnabas, these documents did not uti-
lize the *Didache* per se, but had independent access to the
"teaching of the two paths," and so are witnesses to the ongoing survival of this teaching, rather than direct witnesses
to the *Didache* itself (see esp. Niederwimmer). They can
only be used indirectly, then, as evidence of the wording of
the two paths teaching taken over by the *Didache*.

As indicated, the *editio princeps* was published by
Philotheos Bryennios in 1883, based entirely on Codex
Hierosolymitanus. A photographic facsimile edition of the
manuscript was published by J. Rendel Harris in 1887.

Abbreviations

H	Codex Hierosolymitanus (1056 CE; complete)
P	Oxyrhynchus Papyrus 1782 (4th c.; 1.3c–1.4a; 2.7b–3.2a)
Cop	Coptic version (5th c.; 10.3b–12.2a)
Eth	Ethiopic version (preserved in the Ethiopic church order; 8.1–2; 11.3–13.7)
Const	Apostolic Constitutions, Book 7 (4th c.; complete, with some modifications)
Doct	Doctrina Apostolorum ("Teaching of the Apos-tles")

413

Apos   Apostolic Church Order
Barn   Epistle of Barnabas

SELECT BIBLIOGRAPHY

Aldridge, Robert E. "The Lost Ending of the Didache." VC 53 (1999) 1–15.

Audet, Jean-Paul. *La Didachè*. Ébib. Paris: Gabalda, 1958.

Draper, Jonathan A. *The Didache in Modern Research*. Leiden: Brill, 1996.

Gero, Stephen. "So-called Ointment Prayer in the Coptic Version of the Didache: A Re-evaluation." *HTR* 70 (1977) 67–84.

Giet, Stanislas. *L'énigme de la Didachè*. Paris: Ophrys, 1970.

Harris, J. Rendell. *The Teaching of the Apostles.* London: Clay and Sons, 1887.

Jefford, Clayton N., ed. *The Didache in Context: Essays on its Text, History, and Transmission*. Leiden: Brill, 1995.

Kraft, Robert. *Barnabas and the Didache*. Vol. 3 of *The Apostolic Fathers: A New Translation and Commentary,* ed. R. M. Grant. New York: Thomas Nelson, 1965.

Layton, Bentley. "Sources, Date and Transmission of Didache 1:3b-2:1." *HTR* 61 (1968) 343–83.

Niederwimmer, Kurt. *The Didache: A Commentary.* Tr. Linda Maloney. Hermeneia; Minneapolis: Fortress, 1998 (German original, 1989; 2nd ed. 1993).

Peterson, Erik. "Über einige Probleme der Didache-Überlieferung." In *Frühkirche, Judentum, und Gnosis*, ed. E. Peterson. Rome: Herder, 1959; 146–82.

Rordorf, Willy, and Andre Tuilier. *La Doctrine des douze*

apôtres (Didachè). SC 248. Paris: Cerf, 1978; 2nd ed. 1998.

Schöllgen, Georg. "Die Didache als Kirchenordnung: Zur Frage des Abfassungszweckes und seinen Konsequensen für die Interpretation." *JAC* 29 (1986) 5–26.

Vokes, Frederick Ercolo. "Life and Order in an Early Church: the Didache." *ANRW* II.27.1 (1993) 209–33.

ΔΙΔΑΧΗ ΤΩΝ ΔΩΔΕΚΑ
ΑΠΟΣΤΟΛΩΝ

Διδαχὴ κυρίου διὰ τῶν δώδεκα ἀποστόλων τοῖς ἔθνεσιν.

1

Ὁδοὶ δύο εἰσί, μία τῆς ζωῆς καὶ μία τοῦ θανάτου, διαφορὰ δὲ πολλὴ μεταξὺ τῶν δύο ὁδῶν.

2. Ἡ μὲν οὖν ὁδὸς τῆς ζωῆς ἐστιν αὕτη· πρῶτον ἀγαπήσεις τὸν θεὸν τὸν ποιήσαντά σε, δεύτερον τὸν πλησίον σου ὡς σεαυτόν· πάντα δὲ ὅσα ἐὰν θελήσῃς μὴ γίνεσθαί σοι, καὶ σὺ ἄλλῳ μὴ ποίει.

3. Τούτων δὲ τῶν λόγων ἡ διδαχή ἐστιν αὕτη· εὐλογεῖτε τοὺς καταρωμένους ὑμῖν καὶ προσεύχεσθε ὑπὲρ τῶν ἐχθρῶν ὑμῶν, νηστεύετε δὲ ὑπὲρ τῶν διωκόντων ὑμᾶς· ποία γὰρ χάρις, ἐὰν ἀγαπᾶτε τοὺς ἀγαπῶντας ὑμᾶς; οὐχὶ καὶ τὰ ἔθνη τοῦτο[1] ποιοῦσιν; ὑμεῖς δὲ φιλεῖτε[2] τοὺς μισοῦντας ὑμᾶς, καὶ οὐχ ἕξετε

---

[1] τοῦτο P Const: τὸ αὐτὸ H
[2] φιλεῖτε P Const: ἀγαπᾶτε H

THE TEACHING OF THE
TWELVE APOSTLES

The teaching of the Lord through the twelve apostles to the Gentiles [Or: nations].

1

There are two paths, one of life and one of death, and the difference between the two paths is great.

2. This then is the path of life. First, love the God who made you, and second, your neighbor as yourself.[1] And whatever you do not want to happen to you, do not do to another.[2]

3. This is the teaching relating to these matters: Bless those who curse you, pray for your enemies, and fast for those who persecute you. For why is it so great to love those who love you? Do the Gentiles not do this as well? But you should love those who hate you[3]—then you will

---

[1] Matt 22:37–39; Mark 12:30–31; Luke 10:27; Deut 6:5; Lev 19:18.

[2] Cf. Matt 7:12; Luke 6:31.

[3] Cf. Matt 5:44, 46–47; Luke 6:28, 32–33, 35.

ἐχθρόν.[3] 4. ἀπέχου τῶν σαρκικῶν[4] ἐπιθυμιῶν. ἐάν τίς
σοι δῷ ῥάπισμα εἰς τὴν δεξιὰν σιαγόνα, στρέψον
αὐτῷ καὶ τὴν ἄλλην, καὶ ἔσῃ τέλειος· ἐὰν ἀγγαρεύσῃ
σέ τις μίλιον ἕν, ὕπαγε μετ᾽ αὐτοῦ δύο· ἐὰν ἄρῃ τις
τὸ ἱμάτιόν σου, δὸς αὐτῷ καὶ τὸν χιτῶνα· ἐὰν λάβῃ
τις ἀπὸ σοῦ τὸ σόν, μὴ ἀπαίτει· οὐδὲ γὰρ δύνασαι. 5. παντὶ τῷ αἰτοῦντί σε δίδου καὶ μὴ ἀπαίτει·
πᾶσι γὰρ θέλει δίδοσθαι ὁ πατὴρ ἐκ τῶν ἰδίων
χαρισμάτων. μακάριος ὁ διδοὺς κατὰ τὴν ἐντολήν·
ἀθῷος γάρ ἐστιν. οὐαὶ τῷ λαμβάνοντι· εἰ μὲν γὰρ
χρείαν ἔχων λαμβάνει τις, ἀθῷος ἔσται· ὁ δὲ μὴ
χρείαν ἔχων δώσει δίκην, ἱνατί ἔλαβε καὶ εἰς τί· ἐν
συνοχῇ δὲ γενόμενος ἐξετασθήσεται περὶ ὧν ἔπραξε,
καὶ οὐκ ἐξελεύσεται ἐκεῖθεν, μέχρις οὗ ἀποδῷ τὸν
ἔσχατον κοδράντην. 6. ἀλλὰ καὶ περὶ τούτου δὲ
εἴρηται· ἱδρωσάτω ἡ ἐλεημοσύνη σου εἰς τὰς χεῖράς
σου, μέχρις ἂν γνῷς, τίνι δῷς.

2

Δευτέρα δὲ ἐντολὴ τῆς διδαχῆς· 2. οὐ φονεύσεις, οὐ
μοιχεύσεις, οὐ παιδοφθορήσεις, οὐ πορνεύσεις, οὐ
κλέψεις, οὐ μαγεύσεις, οὐ φαρμακεύσεις, οὐ φονεύσεις
τέκνον ἐν φθορᾷ οὐδὲ γεννηθὲν[5] ἀποκτενεῖς. 3. οὐκ

[3] ἐχθρόν: add ἄκουε τί σε δεῖ ποιοῦντα σῶσαι σοῦ τὸ
πνεῦμα πρῶτον πάντων P   [4] σαρκικῶν P: add καὶ σωμα-
τικῶν H: add καὶ κοσμικῶν Const
[5] γεννηθὲν Const, cf. Barn Apos Doct: γεννηθέντα H

418

have no enemy. 4. Abstain from fleshly passions.[4] If anyone slaps your right cheek, turn the other to him as well,[5] and you will be perfect.[6] If anyone compels you to go one mile, go with him two. If anyone takes your cloak, give him your shirt as well. If anyone seizes what is yours, do not ask for it back,[7] for you will not be able to get it. 5. Give to everyone who asks, and do not ask for anything back.[8] For the Father wants everyone to be given something from the gracious gifts he himself provides. How fortunate is the one who gives according to the commandment, for he is without fault. Woe to the one who receives. For if anyone receives because he is in need, he is without fault. But the one who receives without a need will have to testify why he received what he did, and for what purpose. And he will be thrown in prison and interrogated about what he did; and he will not get out until he pays back every last cent.[9] 6. For it has also been said concerning this: "Let your gift to charity sweat in your hands until you know to whom to give it."[10]

2

And now the second commandment of the teaching. 2. Do not murder, do not commit adultery,[11] do not engage in pederasty, do not engage in sexual immorality. Do not steal, do not practice magic, do not use enchanted potions, do not abort a fetus or kill a child that is born. 3. Do not de-

[4] 1 Pet 2:11. [5] Matt 5:39.
[6] Matt 5:48. [7] Matt 4:41, 40; Luke 6:29–30.
[8] Luke 6:30. [9] Cf. Matt 5:26; Luke 12:59.
[10] Source unknown. [11] The following passage elaborates Exod 20:13–17; cf. Matt 19:18; 5:33.

ἐπιθυμήσεις τὰ τοῦ πλησίον, οὐκ ἐπιορκήσεις, οὐ
ψευδομαρτυρήσεις, οὐ κακολογήσεις, οὐ μνησικακή-
σεις. 4. οὐκ ἔσῃ διγνώμων οὐδὲ δίγλωσσος· παγὶς
γὰρ θανάτου ἡ διγλωσσία. 5. οὐκ ἔσται ὁ λόγος σου
κενὸς οὐδὲ ψευδής.[6] 6. οὐκ ἔσῃ πλεονέκτης οὐδὲ ἅρπαξ
οὐδὲ ὑποκριτὴς οὐδὲ κακοήθης οὐδὲ ὑπερήφανος. οὐ
λήψῃ βουλὴν πονηρὰν κατὰ τοῦ πλησίον σου. 7. οὐ
μισήσεις πάντα ἄνθρωπον, ἀλλὰ οὓς μὲν ἐλέγξεις,
περὶ ὧν δὲ προσεύξῃ, οὓς δὲ ἀγαπήσεις ὑπὲρ τὴν
ψυχήν σου.

3

Τέκνον μου, φεῦγε ἀπὸ παντὸς[7] πονηροῦ καὶ ἀπὸ
παντὸς[8] ὁμοίου αὐτοῦ. 2. μὴ γίνου ὀργίλος, ὁδηγεῖ
γὰρ ἡ ὀργὴ πρὸς τὸν φόνον, μηδὲ ζηλωτὴς μηδὲ
ἐριστικὸς μηδὲ θυμικός· ἐκ γὰρ τούτων ἁπάντων φόνοι
γεννῶνται. 3. τέκνον μου, μὴ γίνου ἐπιθυμητής, ὁδηγεῖ γὰρ ἡ ἐπιθυμία πρὸς τὴν πορνείαν, μηδὲ αἰσχρο-
λόγος μηδὲ ὑψηλόφθαλμος· ἐκ γὰρ τούτων ἁπάντων
μοιχεῖαι γεννῶνται. 4. τέκνον μου, μὴ γίνου οἰωνο-
σκόπος, ἐπειδὴ ὁδηγεῖ εἰς τὴν εἰδωλολατρίαν, μηδὲ
ἐπαοιδὸς μηδὲ μαθηματικὸς μηδὲ περικαθαίρων, μηδὲ
θέλε αὐτὰ βλέπειν μηδὲ ἀκούειν·[9] ἐκ γὰρ τούτων
ἁπάντων εἰδωλολατρία γεννᾶται. 5. τέκνον μου, μὴ

[6] κενὸς οὐδὲ ψευδής (Const, cf. Doct): ψευδῆς οὐ κενὸς
ἀλλὰ μεμεστωμένος πράξει H

sire what belongs to your neighbor, do not commit perjury, do not give false testimony, do not speak insults, do not bear grudges. 4. Do not be of two minds or speak from both sides of your mouth, for speaking from both sides of your mouth is a deadly trap. 5. Your word must not be empty or false. 6. Do not be greedy, rapacious, hypocritical, spiteful, or haughty. Do not entertain a wicked plot against your neighbor. 7. Do not hate anyone—but reprove some, pray for others, and love still others more than yourself.

3

My child, flee from all evil and everything like it. 2. Do not be prone to anger, for anger leads to murder; nor be zealous, contentious, or irascible. For from all these are born acts of murder. 3. My child, do not be filled with passion, for passion leads to sexual immorality; nor be foul-mouthed or lecherous. For from all these are born acts of adultery. 4. My child, do not practice divination[12] since this leads to idolatry; nor use incantations or astrology or rites of purification, nor even wish to see or hear these things. For from all these is born idolatry. 5. My child, do not be a

12 I.e., through the flight of birds.

---

7 παντὸς πράγματος P
8 ἀπὸ παντὸς om. P
9 μηδὲ ἀκούειν Georgian, cf. Apos Doct: om. H

γίνου ψεύστης, ἐπειδὴ ὁδηγεῖ τὸ ψεῦσμα εἰς τὴν κλο-
πήν, μηδὲ φιλάργυρος μηδὲ κενόδοξος· ἐκ γὰρ τούτων
ἁπάντων κλοπαὶ γεννῶνται. 6. τέκνον μου, μὴ γίνου
γόγγυσος, ἐπειδὴ ὁδηγεῖ εἰς τὴν βλασφημίαν, μηδὲ
αὐθάδης μηδὲ πονηρόφρων· ἐκ γὰρ τούτων ἁπάντων
βλασφημίαι γεννῶνται. 7. ἴσθι δὲ πραΰς, ἐπεὶ οἱ
πραεῖς κληρονομήσουσι τὴν γῆν. 8. γίνου μακρό-
θυμος καὶ ἐλεήμων καὶ ἄκακος καὶ ἡσύχιος καὶ
ἀγαθὸς καὶ τρέμων τοὺς λόγους,[10] οὓς ἤκουσας. 9. οὐχ
ὑψώσεις σεαυτὸν οὐδὲ δώσεις τῇ ψυχῇ σου θράσος. οὐ
κολληθήσεται ἡ ψυχή σου μετὰ ὑψηλῶν, ἀλλὰ μετὰ
δικαίων καὶ ταπεινῶν ἀναστραφήσῃ. 10. τὰ συμβαί-
νοντά σοι ἐνεργήματα ὡς ἀγαθὰ προσδέξῃ, εἰδώς, ὅτι
ἄτερ θεοῦ οὐδὲν γίνεται.

4

Τέκνον μου, τοῦ λαλοῦντός σοι τὸν λόγον τοῦ θεοῦ
μνησθήσῃ νυκτὸς καὶ ἡμέρας· τιμήσεις δὲ αὐτὸν ὡς
κύριον. ὅθεν γὰρ ἡ κυριότης λαλεῖται, ἐκεῖ κύριός
ἐστιν. 2. ἐκζητήσεις δὲ καθ᾽ ἡμέραν τὰ πρόσωπα τῶν
ἁγίων, ἵνα ἐπαναπαῇς τοῖς λόγοις αὐτῶν. 3. οὐ ποιήσεις[11] σχίσμα,[12] εἰρηνεύσεις δὲ μαχομένους· κρινεῖς
δικαίως, οὐ λήψῃ πρόσωπον ἐλέγξαι ἐπὶ παραπτώμασιν. 4. οὐ διψυχήσεις, πότερον ἔσται ἢ οὔ.
5. Μὴ γίνου πρὸς μὲν τὸ λαβεῖν ἐκτείνων τὰς

[10] λόγους Const Doct, cf. Doct: add διὰ παντός H

liar, since lying leads to robbery; nor be fond of money or vain. For from all these are born acts of robbery. 6. My child, do not be a complainer, since this leads to blasphemy; nor be insolent or evil-minded. For from all these are born blasphemies. 7. But be meek, since the meek will inherit the earth.[13] 8. Be patient, merciful, innocent, gentle, and good, trembling at the words you have heard. 9. Do not exalt yourself or become impertinent. You should not join forces with the high and mighty, but should associate with the upright and humble. 10. Welcome whatever happens to you as good, knowing that nothing occurs apart from God.

4

My child, night and day remember the one who speaks the word of God to you; honor him as the Lord. For where his lordship is discussed, there the Lord himself is. 2. Every day seek out the company of the saints, that you may find comfort in their words. 3. Do not create a schism, but bring peace to those who are at odds. Give a fair judgment; do not show favoritism when you reproach others for their unlawful acts. 4. Do not be of two minds, whether this should happen or not.

5. Do not be one who reaches out your hands to receive

13 Matt 5:5; Ps 37:11.

---

11 ποιήσεις Const Doct, cf. Barn Apos: ποθήσεις H
12 σχίσμα H, cf. Barn: σχίσματα Const Doct, cf. Apos

χεῖρας, πρὸς δὲ τὸ δοῦναι συσπῶν. 6. ἐὰν ἔχῃς διὰ
τῶν χειρῶν σου, δὸς εἰς λύτρωσιν ἁμαρτιῶν σου. 7. οὐ
διστάσεις δοῦναι οὐδὲ διδοὺς γογγύσεις· γνώσῃ γάρ,
τίς ἐστιν ὁ τοῦ μισθοῦ καλὸς ἀνταποδότης. 8. οὐκ
ἀποστραφήσῃ[13] ἐνδεόμενον, συγκοινωνήσεις δὲ πάντα τῷ ἀδελφῷ σου καὶ οὐκ ἐρεῖς ἴδια εἶναι· εἰ γὰρ ἐν
τῷ ἀθανάτῳ κοινωνοί ἐστε, πόσῳ μᾶλλον ἐν τοῖς
θνητοῖς;

9. Οὐκ ἀρεῖς τὴν χεῖρά σου ἀπὸ τοῦ υἱοῦ σου ἢ ἀπὸ
τῆς θυγατρός σου, ἀλλὰ ἀπὸ νεότητος διδάξεις[14] τὸν
φόβον τοῦ θεοῦ. 10. οὐκ ἐπιτάξεις δούλῳ σου ἢ
παιδίσκῃ, τοῖς ἐπὶ τὸν αὐτὸν θεὸν ἐλπίζουσιν, ἐν
πικρίᾳ σου, μήποτε οὐ μὴ φοβηθήσονται τὸν ἐπ'
ἀμφοτέροις θεόν· οὐ γὰρ ἔρχεται κατὰ πρόσωπον
καλέσαι, ἀλλ' ἐφ' οὓς τὸ πνεῦμα ἡτοίμασεν. 11. ὑμεῖς
δὲ οἱ[15] δοῦλοι ὑποταγήσεσθε τοῖς κυρίοις ὑμῶν[16] ὡς
τύπῳ θεοῦ ἐν αἰσχύνῃ καὶ φόβῳ.

12. Μισήσεις πᾶσαν ὑπόκρισιν καὶ πᾶν ὃ μὴ
ἀρεστὸν τῷ κυρίῳ.[17] 13. οὐ μὴ ἐγκαταλίπῃς ἐντολὰς
κυρίου, φυλάξεις δὲ ἃ παρέλαβες, μήτε προστιθεὶς
μήτε ἀφαιρῶν. 14. ἐν ἐκκλησίᾳ ἐξομολογήσῃ τὰ
παραπτώματά σου, καὶ οὐ προσελεύσῃ ἐπὶ προσευχήν σου ἐν συνειδήσει πονηρᾷ. αὕτη ἐστὶν ἡ ὁδὸς τῆς
ζωῆς.

[13] ἀποστραφήσῃ Const, cf. Apos: add τὸν H
[14] διδάξεις H, cf. Barn: add αὐτοὺς Doct Const
[15] οἱ Const: om. H

but draws them back from giving. 6. If you acquire something with your hands, give it as a ransom for your sins. 7. Do not doubt whether to give, nor grumble while giving. For you should recognize the good paymaster of the reward. 8. Do not shun a person in need, but share all things with your brother and do not say that anything is your own.[14] For if you are partners in what is immortal, how much more in what is mortal?

9. Do not remove your hand from [Or: Do not refrain from disciplining; or: Do not shirk your responsibility towards] your son or daughter, but from their youth teach them the reverential fear of God. 10. Do not give orders to your male slave or female servant—who hope in the same God—out of bitterness, lest they stop fearing the God who is over you both. For he does not come to call those of high status, but those whom the Spirit has prepared. 11. And you who are slaves must be subject to your masters as to a replica of God, with respect and referential fear.

12. Hate all hypocrisy and everything that is not pleasing to the Lord. 13. Do not abandon the commandments of the Lord, but guard what you have received, neither adding to them nor taking away.[15] 14. Confess your unlawful acts in church, and do not come to your prayer with an evil conscience. This is the path of life.

[14] Acts 4:32.
[15] Deut 4:2; 12:32.

---

[16] ὑμῶν Doct Const: ἡμῶν H
[17] κυρίῳ H: add οὐ ποιήσεις Doct, cf. Const Barn

425

5

Ἡ δὲ τοῦ θανάτου ὁδός ἐστιν αὕτη· πρῶτον πάντων
πονηρά ἐστι καὶ κατάρας μεστή· φόνοι, μοιχεῖαι,
ἐπιθυμίαι, πορνεῖαι, κλοπαί, εἰδωλολατρίαι, μαγεῖαι,
φαρμακίαι, ἁρπαγαί, ψευδομαρτυρίαι, ὑποκρίσεις,
διπλοκαρδία, δόλος, ὑπερηφανία, κακία, αὐθάδεια,
πλεονεξία, αἰσχρολογία, ζηλοτυπία, θρασύτης, ὕψος,
ἀλαζονεία, ἀφοβία.[18] 2. διῶκται ἀγαθῶν, μισοῦντες
ἀλήθειαν, ἀγαπῶντες ψεῦδος, οὐ γινώσκοντες μισθὸν
δικαιοσύνης, οὐ κολλώμενοι ἀγαθῷ οὐδὲ κρίσει
δικαίᾳ, ἀγρυπνοῦντες οὐκ εἰς τὸ ἀγαθόν, ἀλλ᾽ εἰς τὸ
πονηρόν· ὧν μακρὰν πραΰτης καὶ ὑπομονή, μάταια
ἀγαπῶντες, διώκοντες ἀνταπόδομα, οὐκ ἐλεοῦντες
πτωχόν, οὐ πονοῦντες ἐπὶ καταπονουμένῳ, οὐ γινώσκοντες τὸν ποιήσαντα αὐτούς, φονεῖς τέκνων,
φθορεῖς πλάσματος θεοῦ, ἀποστρεφόμενοι τὸν
ἐνδεόμενον, καταπονοῦντες τὸν θλιβόμενον, πλουσίων
παράκλητοι, πενήτων ἄνομοι κριταί, πανθαμάρτητοι·
ῥυσθείητε, τέκνα, ἀπὸ τούτων ἁπάντων.

6

Ὅρα, μή τις σε πλανήσῃ ἀπὸ ταύτης τῆς ὁδοῦ τῆς
διδαχῆς, ἐπεὶ παρεκτὸς θεοῦ σε διδάσκει. 2. εἰ μὲν γὰρ
δύνασαι βαστάσαι ὅλον τὸν ζυγὸν τοῦ κυρίου, τέλειος
ἔσῃ· εἰ δ᾽ οὐ δύνασαι, ὃ δύνῃ, τοῦτο ποίει. 3. περὶ δὲ
τῆς βρώσεως, ὃ δύνασαι βάστασον· ἀπὸ δὲ τοῦ εἰδω-
λοθύτου λίαν πρόσεχε· λατρεία γάρ ἐστι θεῶν νεκρῶν.

5

And the path of death is this. First of all it is evil and
filled with a curse: murders, adulteries, passions, sexual
immoralities, robberies, idolatries, feats of magic, sorcer-
ies, rapacious acts, false testimonies, hypocrisies, split
affection, deceit, arrogance, malice, insolence, greed, ob-
scenity, jealousy, impertinence, pride, haughtiness, irrev-
erence. 2. It is filled with persecutors of the good, haters of
the truth, lovers of the lie, who do not know the reward of
righteousness, nor cling to the good nor to a fair judgment,
who are alert not to do good but to do evil; from whom
meekness and patience are far removed. For they love
what is vain and pursue a reward, showing no mercy to the
poor nor toiling for the oppressed nor knowing the one
who made them; murderers of children and corruptors
of what God has fashioned, who turn their backs on the
needy, oppress the afflicted, and support the wealthy. They
are lawless judges of the impoverished, altogether sinful.
Be delivered, children, from all such people.

6

Take care that no one lead you astray from the path of this
teaching, since that one teaches you apart from God. 2 For
if you can bear the entire yoke of the Lord, you will be perfect; but if you cannot, do as much as you can. 3. And concerning food, bear what you can. But especially abstain
from food sacrificed to idols; for this is a ministry to dead
gods.

---

18 ἀφοβία Const Doct*, cf. Barn: add θεοῦ Doctᶜ: om. H

7

Περὶ δὲ τοῦ βαπτίσματος, οὕτω βαπτίσατε· ταῦτα πάντα προειπόντες, βαπτίσατε εἰς τὸ ὄνομα τοῦ πατρὸς καὶ τοῦ υἱοῦ καὶ τοῦ ἁγίου πνεύματος ἐν ὕδατι ζῶντι. 2. ἐὰν δὲ μὴ ἔχῃς ὕδωρ ζῶν, εἰς ἄλλο ὕδωρ βάπτισον· εἰ δ' οὐ δύνασαι ἐν ψυχρῷ, ἐν θερμῷ. 3. ἐὰν δὲ ἀμφότερα μὴ ἔχῃς, ἔκχεον εἰς τὴν κεφαλὴν τρὶς ὕδωρ εἰς ὄνομα πατρὸς καὶ υἱοῦ καὶ ἁγίου πνεύματος. 4. πρὸ δὲ τοῦ βαπτίσματος προνηστευσάτω[19] ὁ βαπτίζων καὶ ὁ βαπτιζόμενος καὶ εἴ τινες ἄλλοι δύνανται· κελεύεις δὲ νηστεῦσαι τὸν βαπτιζόμενον πρὸ μιᾶς ἢ δύο.

8

Αἱ δὲ νηστεῖαι ὑμῶν μὴ ἔστωσαν μετὰ τῶν ὑποκριτῶν. νηστεύουσι γὰρ δευτέρᾳ σαββάτων καὶ πέμπτῃ· ὑμεῖς δὲ νηστεύσατε τετράδα καὶ παρασκευῇ. 2. μηδὲ προσεύχεσθε ὡς οἱ ὑποκριταί, ἀλλ' ὡς ἐκέλευσεν ὁ κύριος ἐν τῷ εὐαγγελίῳ αὐτοῦ, οὕτω προσεύχεσθε· πάτερ ἡμῶν ὁ ἐν τῷ οὐρανῷ, ἁγιασθήτω τὸ ὄνομά σου, ἐλθέτω ἡ βασιλεία σου, γενηθήτω τὸ θέλημά σου ὡς ἐν οὐρανῷ καὶ ἐπὶ γῆς· τὸν ἄρτον ἡμῶν τὸν ἐπιούσιον δὸς ἡμῖν σήμερον, καὶ ἄφες ἡμῖν τὴν ὀφειλὴν ἡμῶν, ὡς καὶ ἡμεῖς ἀφίεμεν τοῖς ὀφειλέταις ἡμῶν, καὶ μὴ εἰσενέγκῃς ἡμᾶς εἰς πειρασμόν, ἀλλὰ ῥῦσαι ἡμᾶς ἀπὸ τοῦ πονηροῦ· ὅτι σοῦ ἐστιν ἡ δύναμις

7

But with respect to baptism, baptize as follows. Having said all these things in advance, baptize in the name of the Father and of the Son and of the Holy Spirit,[16] in running water. 2. But if you do not have running water, baptize in some other water. And if you cannot baptize in cold water, use warm. 3. But if you have neither, pour water on the head three times in the name of Father and Son and Holy Spirit. 4. But both the one baptizing and the one being baptized should fast before the baptism, along with some others if they can. But command the one being baptized to fast one or two days in advance.

8

And do not keep your fasts with the hypocrites.[17] For they fast on Monday and Thursday; but you should fast on Wednesday and Friday. 2. Nor should you pray like the hypocrites,[18] but as the Lord commanded in his gospel, you should pray as follows: "Our Father in heaven, may your name be kept holy, may your kingdom come, may your will be done on earth as in heaven. Give us today our daily bread *[Or: the bread that we need; or: our bread for tomorrow]*. And forgive us our debt, as we forgive our debtors. And do not bring us into temptation but deliver us from the evil one *[Or: from evil]*. For the power and

16 Matt 28:19. 17 Cf. Matt 6:16.
18 Cf. Matt 6:5.

---

19 προνηστευσάτω H: νηστευσάτω Const

καὶ ἡ δόξα εἰς τοὺς αἰῶνας. 3. τρὶς τῆς ἡμέρας οὕτω προσεύχεσθε.

9

Περὶ δὲ τῆς εὐχαριστίας, οὕτως εὐχαριστήσατε· 2. πρῶτον περὶ τοῦ ποτηρίου· εὐχαριστοῦμέν σοι, πάτερ ἡμῶν, ὑπὲρ τῆς ἁγίας ἀμπέλου Δαυὶδ τοῦ παιδός σου, ἧς ἐγνώρισας ἡμῖν διὰ Ἰησοῦ τοῦ παιδός σου· σοὶ ἡ δόξα εἰς τοὺς αἰῶνας. 3. περὶ δὲ τοῦ κλάσματος· εὐχαριστοῦμέν σοι, πάτερ ἡμῶν, ὑπὲρ τῆς ζωῆς καὶ γνώσεως,[20] ἧς ἐγνώρισας ἡμῖν διὰ Ἰησοῦ τοῦ παιδός σου· σοὶ ἡ δόξα εἰς τοὺς αἰῶνας. 4. ὥσπερ ἦν τοῦτο τὸ[21] κλάσμα διεσκορπισμένον ἐπάνω τῶν ὀρέων καὶ συναχθὲν ἐγένετο ἕν, οὕτω συναχθήτω σου ἡ ἐκκλησία ἀπὸ τῶν περάτων τῆς γῆς εἰς τὴν σὴν βασιλείαν· ὅτι σοῦ ἐστιν ἡ δόξα καὶ ἡ δύναμις διὰ Ἰησοῦ Χριστοῦ εἰς τοὺς αἰῶνας. 5. μηδεὶς δὲ φαγέτω μηδὲ πιέτω ἀπὸ τῆς εὐχαριστίας ὑμῶν, ἀλλ᾽ οἱ βαπτισθέντες εἰς ὄνομα κυρίου· καὶ γὰρ περὶ τούτου εἴρηκεν ὁ κύριος· μὴ δῶτε τὸ ἅγιον τοῖς κυσί.

10

Μετὰ δὲ τὸ ἐμπλησθῆναι οὕτως εὐχαριστήσατε· 2. εὐχαριστοῦμέν σοι, πάτερ ἅγιε, ὑπὲρ τοῦ ἁγίου

---

[20] καὶ γνώσεως H Cop: om. Const

the glory are yours forever."[19] 3. Pray like this three times a day.

9

And with respect to the thanksgiving meal *[Literally: eucharist]*, you shall give thanks as follows. 2. First, with respect to the cup: "We give you thanks, our Father, for the holy vine of David, your child, which you made known to us through Jesus your child. To you be the glory forever." 3. And with respect to the fragment of bread: "We give you thanks, our Father, for the life and knowledge that you made known to us through Jesus your child. To you be the glory forever. 4. As this fragment of bread was scattered upon the mountains and was gathered to become one, so may your church be gathered together from the ends of the earth into your kingdom. For the glory and the power are yours through Jesus Christ forever." 5. But let no one eat or drink from your thanksgiving meal unless they have been baptized in the name of the Lord. For also the Lord has said about this, "Do not give what is holy to the dogs."[20]

10

And when you have had enough to eat, you should give thanks as follows: 2. "We give you thanks, holy Father, for

[19] Matt 6:9–13.
[20] Matt 7:6.

---

[21] τὸ cj. Gebhardt: om. H

ὀνόματός σου, οὗ κατεσκήνωσας ἐν ταῖς καρδίαις
ἡμῶν, καὶ ὑπὲρ τῆς γνώσεως καὶ πίστεως καὶ ἀθανασίας, ἧς ἐγνώρισας ἡμῖν διὰ Ἰησοῦ τοῦ παιδός
σου· σοὶ ἡ δόξα εἰς τοὺς αἰῶνας. 3. σύ, δέσποτα
παντοκράτορ, ἔκτισας τὰ πάντα ἕνεκεν τοῦ ὀνόματός
σου, τροφήν τε καὶ ποτὸν ἔδωκας τοῖς ἀνθρώποις εἰς
ἀπόλαυσιν, ἵνα σοι εὐχαριστήσωσιν,[22] ἡμῖν δὲ
ἐχαρίσω πνευματικὴν τροφὴν καὶ ποτὸν καὶ ζωὴν
αἰώνιον διὰ[23] τοῦ παιδός σου. 4. πρὸ[24] πάντων
εὐχαριστοῦμέν σοι, ὅτι δυνατὸς εἶ· σοὶ[25] ἡ δόξα εἰς
τοὺς αἰῶνας. 5. μνήσθητι, κύριε, τῆς ἐκκλησίας σου
τοῦ ῥύσασθαι αὐτὴν ἀπὸ παντὸς πονηροῦ καὶ τελει-
ῶσαι αὐτὴν ἐν τῇ ἀγάπῃ σου, καὶ σύναξον αὐτὴν ἀπὸ
τῶν τεσσάρων ἀνέμων,[26] εἰς τὴν σὴν βασιλείαν, ἣν
ἡτοίμασας αὐτῇ· ὅτι σοῦ ἐστιν ἡ δύναμις καὶ ἡ δόξα
εἰς τοὺς αἰῶνας. 6. ἐλθέτω χάρις καὶ παρελθέτω ὁ
κόσμος οὗτος. Ὡσαννὰ τῷ θεῷ[27] Δαυίδ. εἴ τις ἅγιός
ἐστιν, ἐρχέσθω· εἴ τις οὐκ ἔστι, μετανοείτω· μαρὰν
ἀθά· ἀμήν. 7. τοῖς δὲ προφήταις ἐπιτρέπετε εὐχαριστεῖν, ὅσα θέλουσιν.[28]

22 ἵνα σοι εὐχαριστήσωσιν Η: om. Cop Const
23 διὰ Η Const: add Ἰησοῦς Cop
24 πρὸ Η Const: περὶ Cop
25 σοὶ Cop: σὺ Η: σύ· σοὶ cj. Harnack
26 ἀνέμων Cop Const: add τὴν ἁγιασθεῖσαν Η
27 θεῷ Η: υἱῷ Const: οἴκῳ Cop
28 θέλουσιν Η: add περὶ δὲ τοῦ λόγου τοῦ μύρου οὕτως
εὐχαριστήσατε λέγοντες· εὐχαριστοῦμέν σοι, πάτερ, ὑπὲρ

your holy name which you have made reside in our hearts, and for the knowledge, faith, and immortality that you made known to us through Jesus your child. To you be the glory forever. 3. You, O Master Almighty, created all things for the sake of your name, and gave both food and drink to humans for their refreshment, that they might give you thanks. And you graciously provided us with spiritual food and drink, and eternal life through your child. 4. Above all we thank you because you are powerful. To you be the glory forever. 5. Remember your church, O Lord; save it from all evil, and perfect it in your love. And gather it from the four winds into your kingdom, which you prepared for it. For yours is the power and the glory forever. 6. May grace come and this world pass away. Hosanna to the God of David. If anyone is holy, let him come; if any one is not, let him repent. Maranatha![21] Amen." 7. But permit the prophets to give thanks *[Or: hold the eucharist]* as often as they wish.[22]

---

[21] Cf. 1 Cor 16:22.

[22] Two important witnesses add a verse (with variations): "But concerning the matter of the ointment, give thanks, saying, 'We give you thanks, O Father, for the ointment you have made known to us through Jesus your child. To you be the glory forever, Amen.'"

τοῦ μύρου οὗ ἐγνώρισας ἡμῖν διὰ Ἰησοῦ τοῦ παιδός σου· σοὶ ἡ δόξα εἰς τοὺς αἰῶνας· ἀμήν. Cop Const

11

Ὃς ἂν οὖν ἐλθὼν διδάξῃ ὑμᾶς ταῦτα πάντα τὰ προ-
ειρημένα, δέξασθε αὐτόν· 2. ἐὰν δὲ αὐτὸς ὁ διδάσκων
στραφεὶς διδάσκῃ ἄλλην διδαχὴν εἰς τὸ καταλῦσαι,
μὴ αὐτοῦ ἀκούσητε· εἰς δὲ τὸ προσθεῖναι δικαιοσύνην
καὶ γνῶσιν κυρίου, δέξασθε αὐτὸν ὡς κύριον.

3. Περὶ δὲ τῶν ἀποστόλων καὶ προφητῶν, κατὰ τὸ
δόγμα τοῦ εὐαγγελίου οὕτω ποιήσατε. 4. πᾶς δὲ ἀπόστολος ἐρχόμενος πρὸς ὑμᾶς δεχθήτω ὡς κύριος·[29]
5. οὐ μενεῖ δὲ εἰ μὴ[30] ἡμέραν μίαν· ἐὰν δὲ ᾖ χρεία, καὶ
τὴν ἄλλην· τρεῖς δὲ ἐὰν μείνῃ, ψευδοπροφήτης ἐστίν.
6. ἐξερχόμενος δὲ ὁ ἀπόστολος μηδὲν λαμβανέτω εἰ
μὴ ἄρτον, ἕως οὗ αὐλισθῇ· ἐὰν δὲ ἀργύριον αἰτῇ,
ψευδοπροφήτης ἐστί.

7. Καὶ πάντα προφήτην λαλοῦντα ἐν πνεύματι οὐ
πειράσετε οὐδὲ διακρινεῖτε· πᾶσα γὰρ ἁμαρτία
ἀφεθήσεται, αὕτη δὲ ἡ ἁμαρτία οὐκ ἀφεθήσεται. 8. οὐ
πᾶς δὲ ὁ λαλῶν ἐν πνεύματι προφήτης ἐστίν, ἀλλ᾽ ἐὰν
ἔχῃ τοὺς τρόπους κυρίου. ἀπὸ οὖν τῶν τρόπων
γνωσθήσεται ὁ ψευδοφροφήτης καὶ ὁ προφήτης.
9. καὶ πᾶς προφήτης ὁρίζων τράπεζαν ἐν πνεύματι, οὐ
φάγεται ἀπ᾽ αὐτῆς, εἰ δὲ μήγε ψευδοπροφήτης ἐστί.
10. πᾶς δὲ προφήτης διδάσκων τὴν ἀλήθειαν, εἰ ἃ
διδάσκει οὐ ποιεῖ, ψευδοπροφήτης ἐστί. 11. πᾶς δὲ
προφήτης δεδοκιμασμένος, ἀληθινός, ποιῶν εἰς

[29] δεχθήτω ὡς κύριος: om. Cop Eth
[30] εἰ μὴ Eth: om. H

11

And so, welcome anyone who comes and teaches you everything mentioned above. 2. But if the teacher should himself turn away and teach something different, undermining these things, do not listen to him. But if his teaching brings righteousness and the knowledge of the Lord, then welcome him as the Lord.

3. But act towards the apostles and prophets as the gospel decrees. 4. Let every apostle who comes to you be welcomed as the Lord. 5. But he should not remain more than a day.[23] If he must, he may stay one more. But if he stays three days, he is a false prophet. 6. When an apostle leaves he should take nothing except bread, until he arrives at his night's lodging. If he asks for money, he is a false prophet.

7. Do not test or condemn a prophet speaking in the Spirit. For every sin will be forgiven, but not this sin.[24] 8. Not everyone who speaks in the Spirit is a prophet, but only one who conducts himself like the Lord. Thus the false prophet and the prophet will both be known by their conduct. 9. No prophet who orders a meal[25] in the Spirit eats of it; if he does, he is a false prophet. 10. Every prophet who teaches the truth but does not do what he himself teaches is a false prophet. 11. You are not to condemn any prophet who has been approved and is true, and

[23] "More than" is not found in the Greek, but the context and 12:2 justify the emendation, which is supported by the Ethiopic version.

[24] Cf. Matt 12:31.

[25] This may refer to a meal for the needy.

μυστήριον κοσμικὸν ἐκκλησίας, μὴ διδάσκων δὲ
ποιεῖν, ὅσα αὐτὸς ποιεῖ, οὐ κριθήσεται ἐφ' ὑμῶν· μετὰ
θεοῦ γὰρ ἔχει τὴν κρίσιν· ὡσαύτως γὰρ ἐποίησαν καὶ
οἱ ἀρχαῖοι προφῆται. 12. ὃς δ' ἂν εἴπῃ ἐν πνεύματι·
δός μοι ἀργύρια ἢ ἕτερά τινα, οὐκ ἀκούσεσθε αὐτοῦ·
ἐὰν δὲ περὶ ἄλλων ὑστερούντων εἴπῃ δοῦναι, μηδεὶς
αὐτὸν κρινέτω.

12

Πᾶς δὲ ὁ ἐρχόμενος ἐν ὀνόματι κυρίου δεχθήτω·
ἔπειτα δὲ δοκιμάσαντες αὐτὸν γνώσεσθε, σύνεσιν γὰρ
ἔχετε[31] δεξιὰν καὶ ἀριστεράν. 2. εἰ μὲν παρόδιός ἐστι
ὁ ἐρχόμενος, βοηθεῖτε αὐτῷ, ὅσον δύνασθε· οὐ μενεῖ
δὲ πρὸς ὑμᾶς εἰ μὴ δύο ἢ τρεῖς ἡμέρας, ἐὰν ᾖ ἀνάγκη.
3. εἰ δὲ θέλει πρὸς ὑμᾶς καθῆσθαι, τεχνίτης ὤν,
ἐργαζέσθω καὶ φαγέτω. 4. εἰ δὲ οὐκ ἔχει τέχνην, κατὰ
τὴν σύνεσιν ὑμῶν προνοήσατε, πῶς μὴ ἀργὸς μεθ'
ὑμῶν ζήσεται Χριστιανός. 5. εἰ δ' οὐ θέλει οὕτω
ποιεῖν, χριστέμπορός ἐστι· προσέχετε ἀπὸ τῶν
τοιούτων.

13

Πᾶς δὲ προφήτης ἀληθινός, θέλων καθῆσθαι πρὸς
ὑμᾶς, ἄξιός ἐστι τῆς τροφῆς αὐτοῦ. 2. ὡσαύτως
διδάσκαλος ἀληθινός ἐστιν ἄξιος καὶ αὐτὸς ὥσπερ ὁ

who acts on behalf of the earthly mystery of the church, even if he does not teach others to do what he himself does, since he has his judgment with God. For even the ancient prophets behaved in this way. 12. Do not listen to anyone who says in the Spirit, "Give me money" (or something else). But if he tells you to give to others who are in need, let no one judge him.

12

Everyone who comes in the name of the Lord should be welcomed. Then, when you exercise your critical judgment, you will know him; for you understand what is true and what is false. 2. If the one who comes is simply passing through, help him as much as you can. He should not stay with you more than two or three days, if need be. 3. If he wants to remain with you, and is a tradesman, let him work and eat. 4. If he does not have a trade, use your foresight to determine how he as a Christian may live among you without being idle *[Or: through your understanding you should know in advance that no idle Christian is to live among you]*. 5. If he does not want to behave like this, he is a Christmonger. Avoid such people.

13

Every true prophet who wants to settle down with you deserves his food. 2. So too a true teacher, like the worker,

---

31 ἔχετε Cop Const Eth: ἔξετε (H)

ἐργάτης τῆς τροφῆς αὐτοῦ. 3. πᾶσαν οὖν ἀπαρχὴν
γεννημάτων ληνοῦ καὶ ἅλωνος, βοῶν τε καὶ προβάτων
λαβὼν δώσεις τὴν ἀπαρχὴν τοῖς προφήταις· αὐτοὶ
γάρ εἰσιν οἱ ἀρχιερεῖς ὑμῶν. 4. ἐὰν δὲ μὴ ἔχητε
προφήτην, δότε τοῖς πτωχοῖς. 5. ἐὰν σιτίαν ποιῇς, τὴν
ἀπαρχὴν λαβὼν δὸς κατὰ τὴν ἐντολήν. 6. ὡσαύτως
κεράμιον οἴνου ἢ ἐλαίου ἀνοίξας, τὴν ἀπαρχὴν λαβὼν
δὸς τοῖς προφήταις. 7. ἀργυρίου δὲ καὶ ἱματισμοῦ καὶ
παντὸς κτήματος λαβὼν τὴν ἀπαρχὴν ὡς ἄν σοι
δόξῃ, δὸς κατὰ τὴν ἐντολήν.

14

Κατὰ κυριακὴν δὲ κυρίου συναχθέντες κλάσατε ἄρτον
καὶ εὐχαριστήσατε, προεξομολογησάμενοι[32] τὰ παραπτώματα ὑμῶν, ὅπως καθαρὰ ἡ θυσία ὑμῶν ᾖ. 2. πᾶς
δὲ ἔχων τὴν ἀμφιβολίαν μετὰ τοῦ ἑταίρου αὐτοῦ μὴ
συνελθέτω ὑμῖν, ἕως οὗ διαλλαγῶσιν, ἵνα μὴ κοινωθῇ
ἡ θυσία ὑμῶν. 3. αὕτη γάρ ἐστιν ἡ ῥηθεῖσα ὑπὸ
κυρίου· ἐν παντὶ τόπῳ καὶ χρόνῳ προσφέρειν μοι
θυσίαν καθαράν· ὅτι βασιλεὺς μέγας εἰμί, λέγει κύριος, καὶ τὸ ὄνομά μου θαυμαστὸν ἐν τοῖς ἔθνεσι.

---

[32] προεξομολογησάμενοι cj. Gebhardt: προσεξομολογη-
σάμενοι H

deserves his food.[26] 3. Therefore you shall take every first portion of the produce from the wine vat and the threshing floor, and the first portion of both cattle and sheep, and give it to the prophets. For they are your high priests. 4. If you do not have a prophet, then give it to the poor. 5. If you make bread, take the first portion and give it according to the commandment. 6. So too if you open a jar of wine or oil, take the first portion of it and give it to the prophets. 7. And take the first portion of your money, clothing, and everything you own, as it seems good to you, and give it according to the commandment.

14

On the Lord's own day, when you gather together, break bread and give thanks *[Or: celebrate the eucharist]* after you have confessed your unlawful deeds, that your sacrifice may be pure. 2. Let no one quarreling with his neighbor join you until they are reconciled, that your sacrifice may not be defiled.[27] 3. For this is the sacrifice mentioned by the Lord: "In every place and time, bring me a pure sacrifice. For I am a great King, says the Lord, and my name is considered marvelous among the Gentiles."[28]

[26] Matt 10:10.
[27] Cf. Matt 5:23–24.
[28] Mal 1:11, 14.

15

Χειροτονήσατε οὖν ἑαυτοῖς ἐπισκόπους καὶ διακόνους ἀξίους τοῦ κυρίου, ἄνδρας πραεῖς καὶ ἀφιλαργύρους καὶ ἀληθεῖς καὶ δεδοκιμασμένους· ὑμῖν γὰρ λειτουργοῦσι καὶ αὐτοὶ τὴν λειτουργίαν τῶν προφητῶν καὶ διδασκάλων. 2. μὴ οὖν ὑπερίδητε αὐτούς· αὐτοὶ γάρ εἰσιν οἱ τετιμημένοι ὑμῶν μετὰ τῶν προφητῶν καὶ διδασκάλων. 3. ἐλέγχετε δὲ ἀλλήλους μὴ ἐν ὀργῇ, ἀλλ᾽ ἐν εἰρήνῃ ὡς ἔχετε ἐν τῷ εὐαγγελίῳ· καὶ παντὶ ἀστοχοῦντι κατὰ τοῦ ἑτέρου μηδεὶς λαλείτω μηδὲ παρ᾽ ὑμῶν ἀκουέτω, ἕως οὗ μετανοήσῃ. 4. τὰς δὲ εὐχὰς ὑμῶν καὶ τὰς ἐλεημοσύνας καὶ πάσας τὰς πράξεις οὕτως ποιήσατε, ὡς ἔχετε ἐν τῷ εὐαγγελίῳ τοῦ κυρίου ἡμῶν.

16

Γρηγορεῖτε ὑπὲρ τῆς ζωῆς ὑμῶν· οἱ λύχνοι ὑμῶν μὴ σβεσθήτωσαν, καὶ αἱ ὀσφύες ὑμῶν μὴ ἐκλυέσθωσαν, ἀλλὰ γίνεσθε ἕτοιμοι· οὐ γὰρ οἴδατε τὴν ὥραν, ἐν ᾗ ὁ κύριος ἡμῶν ἔρχεται. 2. πυκνῶς δὲ συναχθήσεσθε ζητοῦντες τὰ ἀνήκοντα ταῖς ψυχαῖς ὑμῶν· οὐ γὰρ ὠφελήσει ὑμᾶς ὁ πᾶς χρόνος τῆς πίστεως ὑμῶν, ἐὰν μὴ ἐν τῷ ἐσχάτῳ καιρῷ τελειωθῆτε. 3. ἐν γὰρ ταῖς ἐσχάταις ἡμέραις πληθυνθήσονται οἱ ψευδοπροφῆται καὶ οἱ φθορεῖς, καὶ στραφήσονται τὰ πρόβατα εἰς λύκους, καὶ ἡ ἀγάπη στραφήσεται εἰς μῖσος· 4. αὐξα-

15

And so, elect for yourselves bishops and deacons who are worthy of the Lord, gentle men who are not fond of money, who are true and approved. For these also conduct the ministry of the prophets and teachers among you. 2. And so, do not disregard them. For these are the ones who have found honor among you, along with the prophets and teachers. 3. Do not reprimand one another in anger, but in peace, as you have learned from the gospel. Let no one speak with a person who has committed a sin against his neighbor, nor let him hear anything from you, until he repents. 4. But say your prayers, give to charity, and engage in all your activities as you have learned in the gospel of our Lord.

16

Be watchful for your life. Do not let your lamps be extinguished or your robes be loosed; but be prepared. For you do not know the hour when our Lord is coming.[29] 2. Gather together frequently, seeking what is appropriate for your souls. For the entire time of your faith will be of no use to you if you are not found perfect at the final moment. 3. For in the final days the false prophets and corruptors of the faith will be multiplied. The sheep will be turned into wolves, and love into hatred. 4. For when lawlessness in-

[29] Cf. Matt 24:42; Luke 12:40; cf. Mark 13:35,37.

νούσης γὰρ τῆς ἀνομίας μισήσουσιν ἀλλήλους καὶ
διώξουσι καὶ παραδώσουσι, καὶ τότε φανήσεται ὁ
κοσμοπλανὴς ὡς υἱὸς θεοῦ καὶ ποιήσει σημεῖα καὶ
τέρατα, καὶ ἡ γῆ παραδοθήσεται εἰς χεῖρας αὐτοῦ, καὶ
ποιήσει ἀθέμιτα, ἃ οὐδέποτε γέγονεν ἐξ αἰῶνος.
5. τότε ἥξει ἡ κτίσις³³ τῶν ἀνθρώπων εἰς τὴν πύρωσιν
τῆς δοκιμασίας, καὶ σκανδαλισθήσονται πολλοὶ καὶ
ἀπολοῦνται, οἱ δὲ ὑπομείναντες ἐν τῇ πίστει αὐτῶν
σωθήσονται ὑπ᾽ αὐτοῦ τοῦ καταθέματος. 6. καὶ τότε
φανήσεται τὰ σημεῖα τῆς ἀληθείας· πρῶτον σημεῖον
ἐκπετάσεως ἐν οὐρανῷ, εἶτα σημεῖον φωνῆς σάλπιγγος, καὶ τὸ τρίτον ἀνάστασις νεκρῶν· 7. οὐ πάντων δέ,
ἀλλ᾽ ὡς ἐρρέθη· ἥξει ὁ κύριος καὶ πάντες οἱ ἅγιοι μετ᾽
αὐτοῦ. 8 τότε ὄψεται ὁ κόσμος τὸν κύριον ἐρχόμενον
ἐπάνω τῶν νεφελῶν τοῦ οὐρανοῦ . . .

³³ κτίσις H: κρίσις cj. Hilgenfeld: πίστις cj. Harris

creases they will hate, persecute, and betray one another.[30] Then the world-deceiver will be manifest as a son of God. He will perform signs and wonders,[31] and the earth will be delivered over into his hands. He will perform lawless deeds, unlike anything done from eternity. 5. Then all human creation will come to the fire of testing, and many will fall away and perish, but those who endure in their faith will be saved[32] by the curse itself.[33] 6. Then the signs of truth will be manifest:[34] first a sign of a rip *[Or: of a stretching]* in the sky, then a sign of the sound of a trumpet,[35] and third a resurrection of the dead. 7. But not of all the dead. For as it has been said, "The Lord will come and all of his holy ones with him."[36] 8. Then the world will see the Lord coming on the clouds of the sky . . .[37]

[30] Cf. Matt 24:10–12.
[31] Cf. Mark 13:22.
[32] Cf. Matt 24:10, 13.
[33] The meaning is obscure.
[34] Cf. Matt 24:30.
[35] Cf. Matt 24:31; 1 Cor 15:52; 1 Thess 4:16.
[36] Zech. 14:5; 1 Thess 3:13.
[37] Cf. Matt 24:30.

Composed in ZephGreek and ZephText by
Technologies 'N Typography, Merrimac, Massachusetts.
Printed on acid-free paper and bound by
Edwards Brothers, Ann Arbor, Michigan